The Origins of Fascism in Italy

Gaetano Salvemini

*Edited and with an Introduction
by Roberto Vivarelli*

Harper & Row, Publishers
New York Evanston San Francisco London

THE ORIGINS OF FASCISM IN ITALY

Editorial matter, introduction, and notes
copyright © 1973 by Roberto Vivarelli.

Copyright © 1973 by Paolo Sylos Labini, Chairman of the Committee for the Reprint of the Works of Gaetano Salvemini. All rights reserved. Printed in the United States of America. No part of this book may be used or reproduced in any manner without written permission except in the case of brief quotations embodied in critical articles and reviews. For information address Harper & Row, Publishers, Inc., 10 East 53d Street, New York, N.Y. 10022. Published simultaneously in Canada by Fitzhenry & Whiteside Limited, Toronto.

LIBRARY OF CONGRESS CATALOG CARD NUMBER: 78–181836

STANDARD BOOK NUMBER: 06–136068–6

Designed by Ann Scrimgeour

Contents

Introduction

Written in 1942 and based on one of the lecture courses that Gaetano Salvemini gave at Harvard University, this work was never published during the author's life. A mimeographed copy of it, however (with the somewhat misleading title *Italy between the First and Second World Wars 1919–1939*), was left in Widener Library, and Salvemini had with him a second copy, bearing a few hand corrections, which was later used for the Italian translation published posthumously in 1961.[1] But the original text, in a perhaps not flawless and yet quite lively English which Salvemini (like many other European scholars who moved to America when already aged) managed to write not without some effort, has remained unknown to the public until the present edition. The reasons why, in spite of its finished form, Salvemini never had it published, are not completely clear. Presumably it was a question of circumstances. First, he was taken by the more urgent task, which he achieved in 1943 with Giorgio La Piana—his intimate friend and collaborator during all these years[2]—of discussing the political future of Italy with the aim of showing, through the lesson of history, that any political solution limited to the dispatch of Mussolini could not render justice to the Italian people. In order to remove Fascism

---

[1] G. Salvemini, *"Lezioni di Harvard": L'Italia dal 1919 al 1929*, in *Scritti sul fascismo*, Vol. 1, ed. R. Vivarelli (Milan: Feltrinelli, 1961).
[2] G. Salvemini and G. La Piana, *What to do with Italy* (New York: Duell Sloan and Pearce; London: Gollancz, 1943).

from Italy and restore a democratic regime, it was necessary to strike at the forces that made the victory of Fascism possible. Then, the war coming to an end, Salvemini may have felt the need of a fresh approach to his subject and further investigations in new sources, now that it was possible again for him to go back to Italy. The desire to rewrite his books, put them in a better form, add some new documentation, revise some of his previous judgments, remained very strong in Salvemini until his death. And yet this is not a work written in a hurried way, but rather the conclusive result of a long period of research and reflection upon the subject.

Born in 1873, Salvemini was sixty-nine in 1942 and at the fullness of his intellectual capacity. Between the end of the last century and the first quarter of the new, he had been one of the leading Italian historians. But, in addition to his academic achievements, he had been very active in politics, mostly as a political writer and commentator, a strong supporter of social reforms, first—until 1911—as a member of the Socialist party, then as editor of his own weekly magazine, L'Unità, one of the most significant papers in the political culture of Liberal Italy. In 1914–15 he had been a fervent supporter of Italy's intervention in the First World War against the Central Empires, in the hope that a new international order, which would put an end to all war, could originate from the victory of the Entente. At the end of the war, as a follower of the democratic principles which for a while found their leadership in President Wilson, he immediately clashed with the Italian Nationalistic forces that would eventually merge with the Fascist movement. Salvemini was elected to Parliament in 1919 as an independent and kept his seat until the elections of 1921, in which he did not take part. At the end of 1920, L'Unità came to an end. In those two years he fought passionately against the foreign policy supported by the Nationalists. Indeed, before Salvemini could possibly become an anti-Fascist, Fascists were, from the very beginning, strongly anti-Salvemini, and, when eventually Mussolini came into power, Salvemini's place in the ranks of the opposition was already well established. As the dictatorship started turning the screw to suffocate any dissenting voice, Salvemini's life in Italy became harder and harder. In June 1925, involved with a group of young friends and pupils in the publication of the first clandestine anti-Fascist paper Non Mollare, he was arrested and, though acquitted in July for insufficient evidence, his position was now untenable and even his life was in danger. On August 16, 1925, with the help of some younger friends (among them Federico Chabod, who was later to become a well-known historian), Salvemini succeeded in illegally crossing the French border and expatriated. In November 1925, he resigned from his chair of modern history at the University of Florence. "The Fascist dictatorship," we read in his resignation letter, "has totally suppressed in our country the state of liberty without which the teaching of history at a university level, as I see it, is deprived of any dignity, since it must cease to be the instrument of a free civil education and accept, instead, to be reduced either to a servile adulation of the party in power, or to a mere exercise of erudition alien to the moral conscience of the teacher as well as to that of the students."[3]

Salvemini's exile lasted more than twenty years, during which he spent some of his best energies in debunking the official lies of the Fascist propaganda and exposing to an international public the real nature of Mussolini's dictatorship and its brutality. Of this intense activity the most significant documents are three books which still remain milestones in the literature on Italian Fascism: *The Fascist Dictatorship in Italy* (New York: Henry Holt and Company, 1927; and, in a new enlarged edition, London: Jonathan Cape, 1928), *Mussolini Diplomate* (Paris: Grasset, 1932), and *Under the Axe of Fascism* (New York: Viking Press; London: Gollancz, 1936). Meanwhile, in 1934, Salvemini had been offered a permanent position at Harvard University, where he was to remain until his retirement and his return to Italy in 1948. At Harvard he resumed his position as a teacher, and, as a teacher who presents his facts in an orderly way and upon them develops his sober reflections, Salvemini composed in 1942 his final work on Italian Fascism.

At that time the state of research concerning Italian Fascism was indeed not very advanced. In Italy there certainly was a large bulk of Fascist literature, but, with the possible exception of a short work by Gioacchino Volpe *(Storia del movimento fascista),* generally this literature had nothing to do with critical scholarship. Outside Italy many books had been published which should be placed under the heading of "current affairs," but, apart from a few exceptions (like the work by Herman Finer), even when they did not repeat Fascist propaganda clichés, they had quite a journalistic

---

[3] G. Salvemini, *Memorie di un fuoruscito,* ed. G. Arfé (Milan: Feltrinelli, 1960), p. 32.

tone. The only work of outstanding value and scientific merit was one by
Angelo Tasca (under the pen name of A. Rossi), *La naissance du fascisme*,
published in 1938.[4] This work very convincingly dispelled the legend that,
at the end of 1920, Italy was threatened by a Bolshevik revolution from
whose coils Fascism claimed to have saved the country. In so doing, Tasca
had rightly restated one of the central points in Salvemini's work of 1928,
where, among other things, Salvemini already disproved the thesis that by
assuming power Mussolini saved the Italian economy from bankrupcy and
restored the state budget. Eventually both Tasca and Salvemini came to
the conclusion that Fascism in Italy was the result of a political crisis rather
than an economic one. But while Tasca, who had been a Communist up
to 1929 and politically very active in the years after the First World War,
was mainly interested in showing how the mistakes of the Socialist party
were largely responsible for the political crisis which brought Fascism to
power, Salvemini had taken upon himself the task of indicating the connivance of the Liberal state as the key to the Fascist success. Now, in his work
of 1942, this thesis finds a broader illustration and a further development.

It may be worth noticing that, quite in contrast with some of his harshest
and most famous denunciations which, as a contemporary, Salvemini had
launched many years before, the judgment he now passed on Giolitti's work
preceding the war was quite moderate both in form and in substance.
Reviewing the course of Italian history prior to 1914, he did not attenuate
Giolitti's responsibility, through the persistent and systematic manipula-
tion of three subsequent elections, in demolishing the prestige of Parliament, thus enlarging the already existing gap between country and government. But, already introducing a note he will stress two years later in a
famous preface to a study of the so-called Giolittian era,[5] Salvemini openly
admitted that until 1914 the Italian regime was a democracy in the making
and that such a process had not been interrupted by the man who held
power almost continously between 1904 and 1914: Giovanni Giolitti. The
problem that remained to be tackled, therefore, was to see why and how
such a progressive process had been stopped and reversed. Notwithstanding
his past position as a supporter of Italy's intervention in the First World
War, this time Salvemini, accepting Tasca's judgment, did not hesitate to

---

[4] Paris: Gallimard, 1938; English translation, *The Rise of Italian Fascism, 1918–1922*
(London: Methuen, 1938).
[5] A.W. Salomone, *Italy in the Giolittian Era: Italian Democracy in the Making, 1900–1914*,
introductory essay by G. Salvemini (Philadelphia: University of Pennsylvania Press, 1945).

relate the events of May 1915 to the March on Rome and branded as a *coup d' état* the decision imposed upon Parliament to go to war. But the responsibility for this drastic setback is put by Salvemini on the whole "Liberal party," in such a way as to leave the door open to a later resumption of some of his old charges against Giolitti.

In Salvemini's consideration of the origins of Italian Fascism, the inclusion of the period prior to 1919 was a novelty. However, even in this work, the attention does remain focused on the years following the war, about which Salvemini had every reason to confirm some of his previously stated points. Already in his work of 1928, Salvemini had stressed how, even in the years 1919–20—the so-called red biennium—the real danger to the stability of the Liberal state consisted in the various plots of a Nationalistic reaction backed by the army, rather than in a Bolshevik revolution. This thesis was here confirmed and more precisely illustrated. Indeed, one of Salvemini's most important original contributions to the problem of Italian Fascism was the attention he gave to the army and the role it played in granting Mussolini's victory. The second point that was restated concerns the responsibility of the Crown and the king's acquiescence, particularly at the time of the Matteotti affair, in letting Mussolini recover his strength, get rid of his opponents, and eventually establish a real dictatorship. The third point concerns the connivance of the Liberal state—the government, the police, the bench (in addition to the army, of course)—in supporting or condoning the criminal activities of the Fascist movement in 1920–22. Salvemini's charges in this direction, which, though open to revision in several details, nonetheless remain generally indisputable even today, repeat almost verbatim what he had already written in 1928.

Another point was taken up again, but for a further and very substantial elaboration: this is the point concerning the "parliamentary paralysis." Such an expression, already coined by Salvemini in his work of 1928, had been used to describe the difficulty in forming a majority in the Chamber after the 1919 elections and, therefore, to explain the instability of any cabinet during those crucial years. The immediate reason for this dangerous disfunction was self-evident: the new Chamber being divided into three sections (156 Socialists, 100 "Populists," and a body of 250 deputies split into many political groups), no single section had a majority. But while in 1928 Salvemini had not paid any particular attention to the new Catholic party and its special role as an essential element of any parliamentary coalition, here he goes into a very extensive analysis of the character of this party (which he calls "Populist") and the part it played. Through such an investigation, which points out the lack of autonomy of the new Populist party whose political action was always open to ecclesiastical interference, Salvemini strikes at the Catholic Church. It was the Catholic Church, Salvemini says, that, in preventing any attempt to form an anti-Fascist coalition before October 1922, made inevitable the choice of Mussolini as prime minister; it was the Catholic Church that, by forcing Don Sturzo to resign his office in 1923, broke the resistance of the Populists and paved the way to Mussolini's parliamentary victory of April 1924. The pro-Fascist attitude of the Church will be crowned by the Conciliation of 1929, with which, rather significantly, Salvemini ends his story.

Of course, like most works of history, this one reflects the existing political situation. In considering "what to do with Italy" after the end of the war and Mussolini's collapse (which at that time one could already take for granted), Salvemini's concern was how to prevent the establishment of a fascism without Mussolini. This might have happened had the king been able to separate the Crown from the Fascists, which is what he tried to do in the summer of 1943, rallying around himself all the conservative forces of the country. Such a political operation could count—Salvemini feared —on Churchill's support, while it was not clear what attitude the American government would have taken. In the light of this problem, which was always present in the mind of Salvemini when writing these pages, we can better understand the particular emphasis he puts in this work upon the responsibility of the Crown and the Church for supporting Mussolini's regime. It was Salvemini's firm conviction that the new Italy should have done away with the House of Savoy and that the new Italian government should have abolished the Concordat. Yet the general picture provided in this work has safely passed the test of time.

Today, with the archives open and many new sources available, we know much more of what actually happened in that period. In fact, in the last twenty-five years, there have been a large number of studies, many based on fresh research, so that our canvas now can be substantially enriched. We also tend to consider that a political crisis of such importance must be more closely related to the changing patterns of the whole society, and therefore we try to give due regard to economic and institutional structures as well as intellectual mood. Furthermore, our general point of view has now changed, and we tend to relate the origins of Fascism to more general questions in connection both with the previous course of Italian history and with some trends in the history of Europe. Nevertheless this work by Salvemini is far from being superseded. The problem of the origins of Fascism, for which Italy provides the first and perhaps the most typical example, is attracting more and more attention. For the knowledge of this problem, Salvemini's work, together with Tasca's, still remains the best general introduction.

Roberto Vivarelli

Select Bibliography
(Since 1945)
GENERAL

P. Alatri, *Le origini del fascismo*, 2d ed. (Rome: Editori Riuniti, 1961).

I. Bonomi, *La politica italiana dopo Vittorio Veneto* (Turin: Einaudi, 1953).

F. Catalano, *L'Italia dalla dittatura alla democrazia (1919–1948)* (Milan: Lerici, 1965).

F. Chabod, *A History of Italian Fascism*, trans. from Italian by M. Grindrod (London: Weidenfeld & Nicolson, 1963).

F. Gaeta, *Nazionalismo italiano* (Naples: Edizioni Scientifiche, 1965).

P. Nenni, *Storia di quattro anni (1919–1922)* (Rome: Einaudi, 1946).

R. Paris, *Histoire du fascisme en Italie: I. Des origines à la prise du pouvoir* (Paris: Maspero, 1962).

G. Procacci, "Appunti in tema di crisi dello Stato liberale e di origini del fascismo," *Studi Storici* 6 (1965).

L. Salvatorelli and G. Mira, *Storia d'Italia nel periodo fascista* (Turin: Einaudi, 1956).

G. Salvemini, "Fu l'Italia prefascista una democrazia?" *Il Ponte*, January–March 1952.

E. Santarelli, *Storia del movimento e del regime fascista*, 2 vols. (Rome: Editori Riuniti, 1967).

C. Seton-Watson, *Italy from Liberalism to Fascism, 1870–1925* (London: Methuen, 1967).

C. Sforza, *L'Italia dal 1914 al 1944 quale io la vidi* (Milan: Mondadori, 1946).

A. Tasca, *Nascita e avvento del Fascismo*, new ed. (Florence: La Nuova Italia, 1950).

N. Valeri, *Da Giolitti a Mussolini. Momenti della crisi del liberalismo* (Florence: Parenti, 1956).

R. Vivarelli, *Il dopoguerra in Italia e l'avvento del fascismo (1918–1922)*, Vol. 1: *Dalla fine della guerra all'impresa di Fiume* (Naples: Istituto Italiano per gli Studi Storici, 1967).

R. Vivarelli, "Italy 1919-21: The Current State of Research," *Journal of Contemporary History* 3 (1968).

FIRST WORLD WAR

V. De Caprariis, "Partiti politici ed opinione pubblica durante la Grande Guerra", *Atti del XLI congresso di storia del Risorgimento italiano (Trento, 9–13 ottobre 1963)* (Rome: Istituto per la Storia del Risorgimento Italiano, 1965).

P. Melograni, *Storia politica della Grande Guerra, 1915–1918* (Bari: Laterza, 1969).

P. Pieri, *L'Italia nella Prima Guerra Mondiale (1915–1918)* (Turin: Einaudi, 1965).

B. Vigezzi, *Da Giolitti a Salandra* (Florence: Vallecchi, 1969).

B. Vigezzi, *L'Italia di fronte alla Prima Guerra Mondiale*, vol. 1: *L'Italia neutrale* (Milan-Naples: Ricciardi, 1966).

R.A. Webster, "From Insurrection to Intervention: The Italian Crisis of 1914," *Italian Quarterly* 5–6 (1961–62).

FOREIGN POLICY

P. Alatri, *Nitti D'Annunzio e la questione adriatica* (Milan: Feltrinelli, 1959).

A. Cassels, *Mussolini's Early Diplomacy* (Princeton: Princeton University, 1970).

E. Di Nolfo, *Mussolini e la politica estera italiana, 1919–1933* (Padua: Cedam, 1960).

H.S. Hughes, "The Early Diplomacy of Italian Fascism, 1922–1932," in Craig and Gilbert, eds., *The Diplomats 1919–1939* (Princeton: Princeton University, 1953).

I.J. Lederer, *Yugoslavia at the Paris Peace Conference* (New Haven and London: Yale University, 1963).

G. Rumi, *Alle origini della politica estera fascista (1918–1923)* (Bari: Laterza, 1968).

D.I. Rusinow, *Italy's Austrian Heritage, 1919–1946* (Oxford: Oxford University, 1969).

M. Toscano, *Storia diplomatica della questione dell'Alto Adige* (Bari: Laterza, 1967).

ECONOMY AND BIG BUSINESS

M. Abrate, *La lotta sindacale nella industrializzazione in Italia 1906–1926* (Turin: L'Impresa, 1967).

A. Caracciolo, "La grande industria nella prima guerra mondiale," in Caracciolo, ed., *La formazione dell'Italia industriale*, 2d ed. (Bari: Laterza, 1969).

V. Castronovo, *Giovanni Agnelli* (Turin: U.T.E.T., 1971).

F. Catalano, *Potere economico e fascismo. La crisi del dopoguerra 1919–1921* (Milan: Lerici, 1964).

P. Grifone, *Il capitale finanziario in Italia* (Rome: Einaudi, 1945); 2d ed., with an introduction by V. Foa (Turin: Einaudi, 1971).

P. Melograni, *Gli Industriali e Mussolini. Rapporti tra Confindustria e fascismo dal 1919 al 1929* (Milan: Longanesi, 1972).

E. Rossi, *Padroni del vapore e fascismo*, 2d ed. (Bari: Laterza, 1966).

R. Sarti, *Fascism and the Industrial Leadership in Italy, 1919–1940. A Study in the Expansion of Private Power under Fascism* (Berkeley: University of California Press, 1971).

MUSSOLINI AND THE FASCIST MOVEMENT

V. Castronovo, *La stampa italiana dall'Unità al Fascismo* (Bari: Laterza, 1970).

R. De Felice, *Mussolini il rivoluzionario 1883–1920* (Turin: Einaudi, 1965).

R. De Felice, *Mussolini il fascista. I: La conquista del potere 1921–1925* (Turin: Einaudi, 1966).

I. Kirkpatrick, *Mussolini: A Study in Power* (New York: Hawthorn, 1964).

G. Rumi, "Mussolini e il 'programma' di San Sepolcro," *Il Movimento di Liberazione in Italia*, April–June 1963.

N. Valeri, *D'Annunzio davanti al Fascismo* (Florence: Le Monnier, 1963).

R. Vivarelli, "Benito Mussolini dal Socialismo al Fascismo," *Rivista Storica Italiana* 79 (1967).

CATHOLICS

G. De Rosa, *Storia del movimento cattolico in Italia: Il Partito Popolare Italiano* (Bari: Laterza, 1966).

F.L. Ferrari, *L'Azione Cattolica e il "Regime"* (Florence: Parenti, 1957).

E. Pratt Howard, *Il Partito Popolare Italiano* (Florence: La Nuova Italia, 1957).

R.A. Webster, *The Cross and the Fasces: Christian Democracy and Fascism in Italy* (Stanford: Stanford University, 1960).

SOCIALISTS

G. Arfé, *Storia del Socialismo italiano (1892–1926)* (Turin: Einaudi, 1965).

G. Berti, "Appunti e ricordi 1919–1926," *Annali Istituto Giangiacomo Feltrinelli* 8 (1966).

J.M. Cammett, *Antonio Gramsci and the Origins of Italian Communism* (Stanford: Stanford University, 1967).

P. Spriano, *Storia del Partito comunista italiano. I: Da Bordiga a Gramsci* (Turin: Einaudi, 1967).

A. Tasca, *I primi dieci anni del PCI* (Bari: Laterza, 1971).

THE OCCUPATION OF THE FACTORIES

G. Bosio, *La grande paura. Settembre 1920: L'occupazione delle fabbriche nei verbali inediti delle riunioni degli Stati generali del movimento operaio* (Rome: Samonà e Savelli, 1970).

1920. La grande speranza: L'occupazione delle fabbriche in Italia, special number of *Il Ponte*, October 1970.

P. Spriano, *L'occupazione delle fabbriche. Settembre 1920* (Turin: Einaudi, 1964).

C. Vallauri, *Giolitti e l'occupazione delle fabbriche* (Milan: Giuffrè, 1971).

GIOLITTI, BONOMI, FACTA

G. De Rosa, *Giolitti e il Fascismo in alcune sue lettere inedite* (Rome: Edizioni di Storia e Letteratura, 1957).

E. Ferraris, *La marcia su Roma veduta dal Viminale* (Rome: Leonardo, 1946).

A. Repaci, *La marcia su Roma mito e realtà*, 2 vols. (Rome: Canesi, 1963).

D. Veneruso, *La vigilia del Fascismo: Il primo ministero Facta nella crisi dello Stato liberale in Italia* (Bologna: Il Mulino, 1968).

R. Vivarelli, "Bonomi e il Fascismo in alcuni documenti inediti," *Rivista Storica Italiana* 72 (1960).

THE ARMY AND THE JUDICIARY

M. Michaelis, "Il generale Pugliese e la difesa di Roma," *La Rassegna Mensile di Israel*, 28 (1962).

G. Neppi Modona, *Sciopero, potere politico e magistratura 1870–1922* (Bari: Laterza, 1969).

E. Pugliese, *Io difendo l'Esercito* (Naples: Rispoli, 1946).

G. Rochat, *L'esercito italiano da Vittorio Veneto a Mussolini (1919–1925)* (Bari: Laterza, 1967).

FASCISM AFTER THE MARCH ON ROME

A. Aquarone, *L'organizzazione dello Stato totalitario* (Turin: Einaudi, 1965).

R. De Felice, "I fatti di Torino del dicembre 1922," *Studi Storici* 4 (1963).

R. De Felice, *Mussolini il fascista. II: L'organizzazione dello Stato fascista 1925–1929* (Turin: Einaudi, 1968).

M. Del Giudice, *Cronistoria del processo Matteotti. Note e ricordi* (Palermo: Lo Monaco, 1954).

A. Lyttelton, "Fascism in Italy: The Second Wave," *Journal of Contemporary History* 1 (1966).

G. Rossini, ed., *Il delitto Matteotti tra il Viminale e l'Aventino: Dagli atti del processo De Bono davanti all'Alta Corte di Giustizia* (Bologna: Il Mulino, 1966).

G. Salvemini, "Nuova luce sull'affare Matteotti," *Il Ponte,* November 1955.

E.R. Tannenbaum, *The Fascist Experience. Italian Society and Culture 1922–1945* (New York: Basic Books, Inc., 1972).

THE CHURCH

A.C. Jemolo, *Chiesa e Stato in Italia negli ultimi cento anni* (Turin: Einaudi, 1949).

F. Margiotta Broglio, *Italia e Santa Sede dalla Grande Guerra alla Conciliazione* (Bari: Laterza, 1966).

E. Rossi, *Il manganello e l'aspersorio* (Florence: Parenti, 1958).

G. Salvemini, *Stato e Chiesa in Italia,* ed. E. Conti (Milan: Feltrinelli, 1969).

P. Scoppola, *La Chiesa e il fascismo. Documenti e interpretazioni* (Bari: Laterza, 1971).

LOCAL STUDIES

E. Apih, *Italia fascismo e antifascismo nella Venezia Giulia* (Bari: Laterza, 1966).

L. Arbizzani, "L'avvento del fascismo nel Bolognese," *Movimento Operaio e Socialista* 10 (1964).

A. Bernieri, "Il fascismo a Carrara tra il 1919 e il 1931," *Movimento Operaio e Socialista* 10 (1964).

G. Bianco and G. Perillo, *I partiti operai in Liguria nel primo dopoguerra* (Genoa: Istituto Storico della Resistenza in Liguria, 1965).

R. Cantagalli, *Storia del fascismo fiorentino 1919–1925* (Florence: Vallecchi, 1972).

A. Cervetto, "Dopoguerra rosso e avvento del fascismo a Savona," *Rivista Storica del Socialismo,* October–December 1958.

R. Colapietra, *Napoli tra dopoguerra e fascismo* (Milan: Feltrinelli, 1962).

S. Colarizi, *Dopoguerra e fascismo in Puglia* (Bari: Laterza, 1971).

G. Faina, *Lotte di classe in Liguria dal 1919 al 1922* (Genoa: Istituto Storico della Resistenza in Liguria, 1965).

G. Miccichè, "La Sicilia dall'occupazione delle terre al fascismo: 1919–1922," *Movimento Operaio e Socialista* 16 (1970).

R. Muratore, "Il dopoguerra rosso e le origini del fascismo nel Novarese," *Rivista Storica del Socialismo,* July–December 1959.

C. Ronchi Bettarini, "Note sui rapporti tra fascismo 'cittadino' e fascismo 'agrario' in Toscana," *La Toscana nell'Italia unita: aspetti e momenti di storia toscana 1861–1945* (Florence: Unione Regionale delle Province Toscane, 1962).

S. Sechi, *Dopoguerra e fascismo in Sardegna. Il movimento autonomistico nella crisi dello Stato liberale (1918–1926)* (Turin: Fondazione Luigi Einaudi, 1969).

C. Silvestri, *Dalla redenzione al fascismo: Trieste 1918–1922* (Udine: Del Bianco, 1959).

C. Silvestri, M. Fabbro, S. Spadaro, "Le origini del movimento fascista," Istituto di Storia Medioevale e Moderna della Facoltà di Lettere e Filosofia dell'Università di Trieste, *Fascismo, Guerra, Resistenza: Lotte politiche e sociali nel Friuli-Venezia Giulia 1918–1945* (Trieste: Libreria Internazionale "Italo Svevo," 1969).

M. Vaini, *Le origini del fascismo a Mantova (1914–1922)* (Rome: Editori Riuniti, 1961).

1

Italy
from 1871 to 1919

Of the three European countries now under dictatorial rule, Russia, Italy and Germany, Italy alone had formerly a democratic form of government. In Tsarist Russia as well as in Imperial Germany, before the World War, all sovereign powers were either directly or indirectly in the hands of the Crown, of the military caste, and of the civil bureaucracy. In both Russia and Germany, the establishment of republican governments followed a military collapse. The new democratic institutions had no tradition behind them. They were the product of military defeat. The Russian democratic regime did not even have time to emerge from chaos and create its own organs. What collapsed under the communist onslaught was not a democracy but the attempt to create one out of the ruins of the Tsarist regime. The dictatorship of the Communist party, however far-reaching and radical it may be as a social and economic experiment, has been up to the present another form of absolutism in the place of tsarism. In Germany, the defeat that caused the removal of the Hohenzollern and of the other princely dynasties shook but did not destroy the power of the military caste; this soon reorganized itself. The old bureaucracy remained unaffected. The Weimar Republic did not even dare to suppress the privileges and confiscate the property of the princely houses, Junkers, and military leaders who had been responsible for the defeat. It came into existence primarily to appease the victors. The military caste permitted it to live as long as the international situation made its maintenance a necessity. They discarded

1

it as soon as the grip of the victors over Germany, in the form of military occupation and financial reparations, was released. What collapsed before the attack of the Nazis was not an established democracy but merely a democracy of sufferance.

Where we find actual collapse of democratic institutions is Italy. In this country, political liberty had been achieved through a half-century of sufferings and struggles (1820–70), and in 1922, when the collapse occurred, the free regime had behind itself another half-century of life. During this half-century, the Italian ruling classes were confronted with the task of building up an administrative and economic system capable of holding together. This was a more formidable problem in Italy than it had been in the United States of America after the [American] Revolution. Both in America and in Italy, the fond hopes of immediate prosperity—to come as if by magic once independence from the foreigner had been achieved —met with disappointment during the first period of readjustment. But unlike America, Italy consisted of sections, each one of which had for thirteen centuries lived under different sovereigns and different systems of government. Local discordant traditions and prejudices had to be unlearned. The civil service, the system of taxation, the army and navy, and public education all needed to be either reorganized or created. The country had no coal and only scant deposits of iron, the two essential raw materials of nineteenth century industry. Railways were thirty years behind those of central and western Europe; the mountainous structure of the land made them costly to construct and to maintain. There were no industries to speak of. Agriculture in northern Italy was, on the whole, not behind that of the neighboring countries. But in southern Italy spring and summer rain is scarce. All the rivers of southern Italy taken together do not carry as much water as the single river Adda, one of the numerous tributaries of the Po in northern Italy. Irrigation is thus not available, and agriculture is heavily handicapped by drought. In the barren mountains which cover a quarter of the country and practically the whole of southern Italy, the rain on the deforested slopes causes formidable landslides which destroy the farms in the valleys and create marshes which breed malaria mosquitoes.

The conditions of the rural populations were everywhere abominable. Pellagra ravaged them in the north, malaria in the south. In the city of Naples, at that time the most populous of Italy, the cemetery destined for the poor classes consisted of 365 tombs, one for each day of the year. The dead—on an average 200 a day—were carried to the cemetery like the rubbish of the city, on carts, and were dumped pellmell in the tomb devoted to that day, after which it was shut until its turn came again the next year.[1] There were provinces—that of Potenza, for example—in which cemeteries were practically unknown. The dead of the lower classes were carried to the church on stretchers, uncovered or covered with a mere sheet, and dumped unceremoniously into the common grave which was dug under the floor of the church and poisoned the air with decay. In some cities, the poor were thrown into natural whirlpools, the bottoms of which were unknown, or else they were abandoned among the nettles of so-called cemeteries, which were the gathering places of semistarved dogs. The dogs would go scavenging after them, dragging bones and half-gnawed skulls into the roads.[2]

The hostility of the Papacy, brigandage, a very high percentage of illiteracy in the masses, a large public debt inherited from the former local states and in part due to the wars of independence, and the work of unification made the task of the new regime almost desperate.

After a decade (1860–70) of painful readjustment, the economic development of Italy up to the War of 1914–15 falls roughly into three periods: first, fifteen years of progress, steady though slow (1871–85); then fifteen years of depression (1886–99); and finally, fifteen years of growing prosperity until the outbreak of the war.

In 1860, Italy possessed barely 1,100 miles of railway, of which only sixty-two were in the south; in 1914, 11,200 miles. In 1862, Italy possessed 10,000 tons of steam shipping; in 1914, 933,000 tons. In 1881, Italy imported 2 million tons of coal; in 1913, nearly 11 million. In 1860, Italy did not use electricity; in 1882, the first plants were installed; in the fiscal year 1913–14, Italy consumed 23 billion kilowatt hours.[3] In 1881, Italy's imports amounted to 1.2 billion lire (43.7 lire per head of the population) and her exports to 1.1 billion (41.1 lire per head); in 1913 her imports totaled 3.6 billion (102.9 lire per head) and her exports 2.5 billion (70.9 lire per head).[4] The difference of 1 billion lire between imports and exports was more than compensated by the so-called invisible exports—that is to say, tourist traffic, remittances from emigrants, and freights of the merchant

---

[1] R. Fucini, *Napoli a occhio nudo* (Firenze: Le Monnier, 1878), pp. 98–101.
[2] E. Pani Rossi, *La Basilicata* (Verona: Civelli, 1868), pp. 252–55.
[3] The Italian fiscal year begins July 1 and ends June 30 of the following year.
[4] One dollar corresponded to about five Italian lire.

marine.[5] In 1881, savings bank deposits totaled 781 million lire (27.65 per head); in 1913, 4.7 billion (132.31 per head). In 1860, the government of the newly united Italy could rely upon a revenue of no more than 500 million lire. In the first fifteen years of the new regime (1861–75), expenditure greatly exceeded revenue. In 1866, revenue totaled 600 million and expenditure 1.2 billion. In 1875, revenue began to exceed the expenditure, and up till 1885 the budget showed a surplus. From 1886 to 1897, deficits reappeared; but from 1898 to 1911, the budgets showed considerable surpluses. The war for the conquest of Libya (1912) caused deficits in the budgets of 1912–14; but economic and financial conditions were sound, and, but for the War of 1914–18, the Libyan crisis would soon have been safely weathered. A consolidated debt bond with a face value of 100 lire could be bought for 40 lire in 1866; between 1899 and 1911, Italian state securities stood above par; in 1906, 4 percent consols to the value of 12 billion lire were redeemed and a new issue successfully floated at 3.5 percent. The bonds dating from the old regime (2,000 million) and those issued in the first decade of the new regime (6,000 million) were nearly all held by foreign (particularly French) investors; they were little by little acquired by Italian investors, and in 1907, not more than 650 million were still foreign-owned. The Libyan war only caused consols to drop to 98.59.

The population increased from 27 million in 1870 to 35.5 million in 1914. This increase was due not only to the high birth rate, but also to a lower death rate resulting from progress in sanitation and in the standard of living. The latter fact can be proved by the consumption of wheat. The wheat produced in the country rose from a yearly average of 3.6 million tons in the last ten years of the nineteenth century to 5 million tons in the five years preceding the War of 1914–15. At the same time, imports of wheat increased from a yearly average of 6.6 million tons in the last five years of the nineteenth century to a yearly average of 13.5 million tons in the five years preceding the war. The consumption of wheat rose by four-fifths, while the population only increased by one-eighth.

In 1860, 78 percent of the population over six years of age was illiterate; by 1911, the percentage dropped to 38 percent. Illiteracy had practically disappeared among the rising generation of northern Italy and had been

[5] B. Stringher, "Sur la balance des paiements entre l'Italie et l'etranger," *Bulletin de l'Institut International de Statistique*, Vol. 19; P. Jannaccone, *La bilancia del dare e dell'avere internazionale con particolare riguardo all'Italia* (Milan: Treves, 1927), pp. 90 ff., 100–04.

sharply reduced among the youth of southern Italy. Of the young people who attained their twentieth year in 1927, and therefore had gone to school before or during the war, 87 percent knew how to read and write.[6]

The intellectual progress which took place among the upper and middle classes during the half-century from 1871 to 1920 can be measured by a single fact: from 1875 to 1888, an *Enciclopedia Italiana* was published in which nine-tenths of the items were but a lamentable rehash of *Larousse* and of the *Encyclopedia Britannica*. This was the best Italian intelligentsia could do at that time. In 1921, a new Italian encyclopedia was planned; in 1922 it was announced to the public, and in 1929 its first five volumes appeared. It is, without any shadow of doubt, superior to all similar works published since the beginning of this century in all countries. It is a monument to the two generations of men who from 1870 to 1920 reconstructed the Italian culture. Signor Volpe, official historian of the Fascist dictatorship, writes:

> There were in Italy ferments of activity, forces of renovation and urge for constructive work. Twenty years had not gone by between the transfer of the capital to Rome (1871) when the wonderful energies, the hard work, the capacity for renovation shown by the Italian people, and its response to the stimuli of the surrounding world, gave results visible to all careful observers. Political unity and the action of the government urged, helped and transformed all these energies into real values.[7]

The reader will find in the pages of this historian a summary account of the achievements of the free regime: the balancing of the budget, construc-

---

[6] *Annuario Statistico Italiano: 1931*, p. 79.

[7] G. Volpe, *L'Italia in cammino: L'ultimo cinquantennio* (Milan: Treves, 1927), p. 59. This book is to be read together with B. Croce, *A History of Italy from 1871 to 1915* (Oxford: Clarendon Press, 1929), which gives the liberal version. A good outline of the subject was given in 1908 by an American historian who had a wide knowledge of the Italian background: W.R. Thayer, "Thirty Years of Italian Progress," in *Italica: Studies in Italian Life and Letters* (Boston: Houghton Mifflin and Co., 1908). For a more detailed account of all phases of Italian history from 1871 to 1910, see the three volume work published by the Accademia dei Lincei, *Cinquant'anni di storia italiana* (Milan: Hoepli, 1911). A collection of excellent yearbooks from 1910 to 1922 was published by R. Bachi, *L'Italia economica* (Turin: Roux e Viarengo, and later Città di Castello: S. Lapi). A first-rate account of Italy's economic history from 1871 on is E. Corbino, *Annali dell'economia italiana*, 5 vols. (Città di Castello: Tip. Leonardo da Vinci, 1931–38). A shorter but equally excellent outline has been given by V. Porri, *L'evoluzione economica italiana nell'ultimo cinquantennio* (Rome: Stab. Tip. Colombo, 1926).

tion of roads and railways, reclamation of lands, creation of industries and expansion of commerce, establishment of public schools and scientific institutions, provisions for the care of the historical and artistic treasures of Italy, social legislation for the protection of labor and for the welfare of the working classes.

As happened in all other countries, the process of industrialization and the improvement of agriculture gave rise in Italy to the formation of a Socialist party and the organization of workers. Socialism contributed no little to the intellectual and moral uplift and to the political education of the working classes. The awakening and organization of labor—notwithstanding the occasional disorders, strikes, riots, and conflicts that marked, in Italy as elsewhere, the rise of socialism—strongly contributed to national unification.[8]

It would be easy to reproach pre-Fascist politicians with all kinds of mistakes and misdeeds, ill-advised undertakings, unused opportunities, waste, and extravagance. Not all the problems that confronted the country were solved. Not always were the solutions adopted the best nor the methods employed the most efficient. Could all problems have been solved in so short a time? Has there ever been in history any country which solved all its problems in half a century and without blunders? If one judges the handiwork of the pre-Fascist politicians by the standard of some flawless ideal—the method of the political reformer—there is no politician who would not be sent to hell. But if one adopts the method of the historian —that is, if one compares, as far as Italy is concerned, the starting point in 1871 with the point of arrival, the First World War, the poverty of national resources with the wealth of other countries—one can not fail to conclude that no country in Europe had made such strides in such short time.

In 1920, an Italian statistician reduced into numerical indices the economical movement of Italy, France, Austria, Germany, and England from 1886–90 to 1906–10, taking as his base of comparison the years 1901–05 to which he assigned the number 1,000. He found that in 1886–90, Italy stood at 771 points from the index number 1,000 of 1901–05; France, 711; Germany, 615; Great Britain, 776. Such figures mean that,

---

[8] In E. Ludwig, *Talks with Mussolini* (Boston: Little, Brown and Co., 1933), p. 83, Mussolini says: "However it may have been in other lands, here in Italy, Socialism was a unifying factor. All Italian historians have recognized this. The Socialists of Italy were advocates of one idea and of one nation."

given the starting point, the progress made in the fifteen years from 1886 to 1901 had been the greatest in England and in Italy and smallest in Germany—where, however, a marvelous forward push had taken place between 1871 and 1885. In the five years between 1906 and 1910, the progress was represented by the following numbers: Italy, 1296; France, 1205; Germany, 1192; Great Britain, 1055. In other words, it was greatest in Italy.[9]

The outcome of the economic, intellectual, and political development of the half-century may be measured by a single fact: in the war against Austria in 1866, a few years after Italy emerged from absolutist stagnation, a small skirmish, in which the Italian army lost no more than 800 men, sufficed to create such confusion, and to bewilder the military chiefs to such an extent, that no further initiative was possible. During the World War, the Italian people had more than 500,000 men killed in battle, another 500,000 maimed, and 1,000,000 dead from epidemics, but they stood their ground, and in the autumn of 1918 they witnessed the collapse of the Austrian army and the Austrian Empire.

AUTHOR'S NOTES TO CHAPTER 1

Whoever approaches the history of Italy from 1870 to 1922 without a sharp critical sense runs the risk of being sidetracked by two causes of error.

First of all, Italian political literature of that period was drenched with a flood of bitter criticism about everything and everybody. The conservatives, who had been in power until 1876 and after that were no longer able to have their own way, criticized the cabinets which were not conservative enough. The republicans, the socialists, and the anarchists criticized them because they did not allow them to stage a revolution. Those who desired an honest and efficient administration and more rapid social progress criticized them because they were not honest enough or because they were downright dishonest, not efficient enough, and not progressive enough. Everyone, even the politicians who were in power, was disheartened by the big gap which divided the mediocre life of every day from the alluring expectations which had been conceived during the struggles and the sufferings of the Risorgimento. Then, after 1922, the Fascists overturned the

[9] G. Mortara, *Lezioni di statistica economica e demografica* (Roma: Athenaeum, 1920), pp. 261–62.

procedure. Everything that was or was not being done in Italy under Mussolini's dictatorship became a monument of wisdom, of efficiency, of success.

The result of all this is that the historian is faced with a mass of pessimistic literature which sprang up spontaneously in Italy in the period before 1922, and with an equally large mass of adulatory literature which was promoted by the Fascist government in the period after 1922. Under these two circumstances, he easily concludes, in agreement with Fascist propaganda, that "nothing was done" in Italy before Mussolini began to work miracles.

Typical specimens of such Fascist historiography are to be found in L. Villari, *The Awakening of Italy: the Fascist Regeneration* (London: Methuen and Co., 1924), pp. 1–8; *Italy* (New York: C. Scribner's Sons, 1929), pp. 79–134; and the articles on Italy in the *Encyclopedia Britannica*, 14th ed., under "Italy," (pp. 806–17). The Fascist version has been meekly swallowed up by most English-speaking "experts" in Italian history. Among these the most lamentable are H. W. Schneider (*Making the Fascist State* [New York: Oxford University Press, 1928], pp. 1–15, and *The Fascist Government of Italy* [New York: D. Van Nostrand, 1926], pp. 22–25); H. Goad (*The Making of the Corporate State* [London: Christopher, 1932], pp. 27–38); and G. B. McClellan (*Modern Italy*, [Princeton, N.J.: Princeton University Press, 1933], pp. 135–200). One does not understand how such a Mt. Everest of ignorance, stupidity, and dishonesty as was the last writer could have been entrusted by Princeton University with the task of teaching Italian history.

In 1901, two well-equipped and honest British historians, Bolton King and Thomas Okey, published a book, *Italy To-Day*. They wrote under the impact of the severe economic crisis and misgovernment under which the country had been laboring during the closing years of the nineteenth century, and they presented a pessimistic picture. But they also realized that "underneath the slough of misgovernment and corruption, and political apathy, there is a rejuvenated nation, instinct with the qualities that make a great people" (Preface, p.vi). In 1910, Okey, then Regius Professor of Italian at Oxford, contributed a chapter on contemporary Italy to the *Cambridge Modern History* and took notice of the progress made during the last ten years, though still in a rather pessimistic mood. Signor Villari, in the *Fortnightly Review* of November 15, 1912, strongly blamed Okey's unwarranted pessimism:

The average foreigner knows nothing about the Italy that works and produces, and his ideas on the Kingdom may be summed up in half a dozen stock aphorisms: Italy is the poorest country in the world; the mass of people are beggars; and they are all incredibly lazy; beggars and thieves abound; the Government is utterly corrupted; and politicians and employees have no other thought than of enriching themselves at the expense of the public. . . . Sentimental radicals . . . see only a struggle between rich and oppressed victims below. This is the attitude often taken up by the English democrats; we have a characteristic example of it in the writings of Mr. Thomas Okey, whose chapter on Italy in the Twelfth Volume of the *Cambridge Modern History* gives a most distorted and libelous view of Italian affairs.

After Mussolini's advent, Okey told me that he had been struck by the fact that there were unexpectedly large sales of *Italy To-Day*. On seeking the reason for the renewed demand, he found that Fascist propaganda agents in England and America recommended the book to those desirous of forming an idea of pre-Fascist Italy. In his *Fascist Experiment,* Villari wrote:

When people, especially foreign observers, talk about Mussolini's alleged destruction of "constitutional liberty" in Italy, they seem entirely oblivious of what had happened before. Two English writers, Messrs. Bolton King and Thomas Okey, in a volume *Italy To-Day,* published in 1901, in Chapter I, give a picture of what Italy was under the so-called liberal Governments (p. 89).

It was like advising people to read a book on the Southern states after the Civil War if they wanted to form an idea of the history of the United States during the nineteenth century.

Mr. C.E. McGuire (*Italy's International Economic Position* [New York: Macmillan, 1926], has never heard of the period of Italian financial prosperity between 1900 and 1914, and therefore states (pp. 52–71) that the whole history of Italy from 1860 to 1925 was a series of deficits, and that only with the coming of Fascism did the Italian budget show a surplus. We shall see that no Fascist surplus ever existed.

After Mussolini, in December 1928, announced his determination to reclaim all the uncultivated lands in Italy, it became the custom to speak of land reclamation in Italy as if it had been invented by Mussolini. For instance, Villari (*Italy*, pp. 13, 263, 264) gives no other information about what had been accomplished in this field before 1922 except that the efforts aimed at draining marshes and improving agriculture were brought to nothing by the parliamentary intrigues and by the lack of cooperation with private initiatives on the part of the government and of the local bodies: "During *and after the war* (italics ours), when the antimalarial measures were relaxed and reclamation work was suspended, there was a recrudescence of malaria even in Venetia" (p. 11).

The truth is that from 1882 to 1915, 332,000 hectars (1 hectar = 2.47 acres) of former swamp land were completely reclaimed and put under cultivation; 416,000 hectars had already been reclaimed but were still intermingled with lands on which the work had progressed but had not yet been finished; and work had begun on 444,000 hectars. From 1900 to 1914, the government spent 390 million gold lire for land reclamation, and it was estimated that 353 million gold lire would be needed to finish the work already started.[10]

The war slowed down this as all other works which were not immediately urgent. But as soon as the war was over, the work was actively taken up again. On October 17, 1919, the American commercial attaché in Rome wrote in the *Commerce Reports:* "Every effort is being made by the government not only to compel the cultivation of the largest area available, but also to encourage the use of modern intensive methods of farming." In the four years from July 1, 1918, to June 30, 1922, 664 million lire were spent for this purpose.[11]

The reclamation works were the pride of the Italian agriculturalists. In the province of Ferrara, from 1862 to 1912, the land cultivated increased from 100 to 200,000 hectars, and the production of grain soared from 500,000 to 1.2 million quintals.[12] The reclamation of the island of Ariano (12,000 hectars), finished in 1906, only cost the State 2,829,722 lire, and in 1922 the State took in for taxes, duties, customs, and other additional taxes a sum five times greater. The inhabitants of the section increased from 15,538 in 1901 to 25,572 in 1921; heads of cattle rose from 3,695 in

---

[10] Camera dei deputati, Sessione 1913–15, Doc. xxxiv, 20 luglio 1915, *Terza relazione sulle bonifiche*, pp. 22–69, 101–16; V. Peglion, *Le bonifiche in Italia* (Bologna: Zanichelli, 1924), p.8.

[11] *Il bilancio dello Stato dal 1913–14 al 1929–30* (Roma: Istituto Poligrafico dello Stato, 1931), p. 370.

[12] Peglion, *Le bonifiche in Italia*, p. 5.

1902 to 8,557 in 1921; production was valued in 1924 at a value seven times greater than the production before the reclamation.[13] In the plain of Catania, the estate "Costantina," which before the war was a meadow of three hundred hectars, in 1923 was covered with one hundred thousand trees, 300,000 vines, and many other highly productive crops, and it had a value fifteen times greater than that of ten years before.[14] In December 1922, the two British commercial attachés at Rome wrote as follows:

> An area exceeding a total of 500,000 acres (this figure is less than the real figure of 332,000 hectars) of what have become some of the richest lands in northern Italy, has already been reclaimed and brought under cultivation by work extending over 40 years. The most important pumping station yet erected in connection with the many land reclamation schemes, that of the Ongaro Inferiore, was inaugurated during the summer of 1922. It is designed to drain a large area in lower Venetia, and its completion marks a notable step forward in the work of converting malarious marsh lands into fertile agricultural country. As the law also empowered the State to assist local irrigation consortia by meeting one-third of the expense of irrigation works of national importance, place has been made by the foremost Italian irrigation expert for the irrigation of some 500,000 acres of the Padan Valley. Added to this, many other irrigation schemes are planned or are in process of completion, in connection with large water-power stations, like those on the Sila Plateau in Calabria and on the Alto Belice in Sicily.[15]

In April 1923, a group of Dutch agriculturalists visiting the reclamations of Ferrara and Chioggia were full of admiration to discover an "Italian Holland."[16] That Holland had not risen from the sea in one night. It had cost a half-century of hard work.

---

[13] Peglion, *Le bonifiche in Italia*, pp.6–7; S. Trentin, *Per un nuovo orientamento della legislazione in materia di bonifiche* (Venezia: Tipografia della "Cooperativa Casa del Popolo," 1919), p.13.

[14] A. De Stefani, *L'azione dello Stato italiano per le opere pubbliche (1862-1924)* (Rome: Libreria dello Stato, 1925), p. 131. For the reclamations of Ca Lino between the Adige and the Brenta, of the gardens of Chioggia, of the dunes of Cavazuccherina, and of the swamps in the province of Brescia—all works which were finished in 1922—and for the works begun in the so-called Sienese crete and in the so-called calanchi of Emilia, consult Peglion, *Le bonifiche in Italia*, pp. 18, 19, 34, 38, 90, 91.

[15] J.H. Henderson and H.C.Z. Carpenter, *Report on the Commercial Industrial and Economic situation in Italy, December 1922* (Department of Overseas Trade, 1923), p. 54.

[16] F. Virgilii, *L'Italia agricola odierna* (Milano: Hoepli, 1930), p. 200.

Of course it would have been possible to do more and better. No work in this world is so rapid and so perfect that it could not be improved upon, and no work is so slow and so poorly done that it could not be done more slowly and poorly. But no well-informed and honest man has the right to make out that before the coming of Mussolini, nothing had been done in Italy in this field of land reclamation.

It is true that during the war of 1915–18, the breakdown of land reclamations in Venetia and the life in the muddy trenches and the malarial zones of Macedonia and Albania brought about a violent recrudescence of malaria. But at the close of the war, the struggle against malaria was vigorously resumed and the situation rapidly improved. The malaria deaths which had jumped from 0.6 per 10,000 inhabitants in 1914 to 1.8 by 1919, dropped to 1.1 by 1922.[17]

The case of Mr. Villari is that of a propaganda agent who willfully tries to mislead his readers. But even students of unimpeachable moral integrity have not escaped Fascist pitfalls.

Let us take as an example the case of a diligent, fair-minded and exceptionally well-gifted Australian woman, Margot Hentze, who in 1939 published a book, *Pre-Fascist Italy: The Rise and Fall of the Parliamentary Regime* (London: George Allen and Unwin Ltd.), the fruit of honest, if not fortunate, research. Hentze admits that the material progress of the country was "phenomenal" and "prodigious," but nobody advised her to make a methodical study of the progress which was a part of the history of Italy from 1871 to 1915. Vice versa, she consistently echoed the affirmation that since 1870 the nation had felt something like a process of spiritual starvation—starvation, not in artistic production, but in means of self-expression and in general use of creative power; instead of finding "her political vocation, Italy seemed to have embarked on a course carrying her further and further away from it." (p. 137). If Hentze had made use of these meaningless words "starvation," "means of self-expression," and "political vocation" to describe the lamentations that many Italians were accustomed to raise to the skies, she would have given an exact picture of that aimless discontent that was the disease of the Italian spirit in the period which she studied and which was one of the sources of the Fascist movement. But she made those words her own, and thus wrote pages entirely lacking in common sense.

[17] *Annuario Statistico Italiano: 1919*, and following years.

Hentze admits that Italy was a poor country, but she joins with the Fascists in reproving the Italian politicians for not following a foreign policy of expansion at a time when other countries were following imperialistic policies (pp. 149–51). But could a poor country adopt an imperialistic policy without breaking its neck? Where has Italy been led by Mussolini's imperialism? Hentze would have shown greater wisdom if she had not blamed those Italian politicians who followed a prudent and modest foreign policy, and if she had not joined the Fascists in praising precisely that Francesco Crispi who led Italy, in 1896, to the colonial disaster of the battle of Adowa, except realizing in a moment of good sense that the period of Crispi had been "disastrous" (p. 231).

Hentze does not allow herself any statement withoug quoting her good authorities. The only thing is that she continually chooses her authorities with the same criterion as one who, wishing to write the history of the Roosevelt administration, used only the evidence furnished by Mr. Hoover, or one who, wishing to write the history of the Harding, Coolidge, and Hoover administrations, used only the speeches made by the Democratic candidates in the presidential elections from 1920 to 1928.

The defeat of Caporetto during the World War often is called up by Italian Fascists and non-Italian innocents when they have to show that Italy was in a state of administrative and military inefficiency before Mussolini came in and put her "on the map."

During the World War, there were many other defeats besides that of Caporetto. In August 1914, the French and English armies suffered a terrible rout in what is generally known as the "Battle of the Frontiers." They had to abandon a tenth of French territory, not to speak of Belgium. The Germans penetrated to within thirty miles from Paris. A hundred French generals were dismissed as incapable. That disaster occurred in the first weeks of the war, in spite of the fact that the French were fighting a defensive war on their own soil. The French army turned the tables at the Marne, but even then the Germans remained on French soil for four years. The World War was for the Austrian army a series of Caporettos during the first six months of its operation. The Russians, after May 1915, did nothing but go from one Caporetto to another. A few months before Caporetto, the French army disintegrated almost from top to bottom as a consequence of the butchery brought down upon them by General Nivelle in April 1917. From the end of May to June 15, there were mutinies in seventy-five regiments of infantry, twenty-three battalions of "chasseurs," and twelve regiments of artillery.[18] If the Germans had had a better information service, and had attacked at that moment, they would have inflicted upon the French army a defeat which perhaps would have been irreparable.

The Italians had been in the war for two and one-half years before they were routed in an offensive war on enemy soil. In May and June 1917, an attempt at breaking the Austrian lines had cost 132,000 casualties, and in August and September, another attempt had cost 148,000 casualties.[19] The French army, in April 1917, had had no more than 112,000 casualties. The French soldiers had mutinied for much less than the Italians, had they rebelled. Historians and military critics agree that the responsibility for the defeat was to be allotted to the army chiefs, and that the disbandment of the soldiers developed *in the rear* after the Austrians had broken the front and penetrated deeply into the Italian lines where no preparations for further defence had been made.[20] The French rout in 1940 has been but a Caporetto on a more gigantic scale. However, in Italy, in 1917, as soon as a suitable line of defense, the Piave river, was at hand, and before they received any help whatsoever from France or England, the Italian army stopped the Austrian advance.

This is what a distinguished English historian and statesman, Lord Tweedsmuir, who died in 1940 as governor of Canada and wrote under the pen name of John Buchan, has to say in his *History of the Great War* (4: 55 ff.) about the aftermaths of Caporetto in Italy:

> The spirit of the nation rose gallantly to the call of danger
> . . . . All—almost all—sections of the nation faced the crisis
> with splendid fortitude. Party quarrels were forgotten, there
> was little recrimination for past blunders, and the resolution
> of a united Italy was braced to meet the storm. Only a few
> extremists, to whom the disaster was not unwelcome, stood
> aloof. . . . If ever panic was to be forgiven it was on those
> nightmare miles where troops were set a task too high for
> human valor. But to its eternal glory the Third Army did not

[18] M. Berger et P. Allard, *Les secrets de la censure pendant la guerre* (Paris: Editions des Portiques, 1932), p. 181, n.1.
[19] L. Cadorna, *La guerra alla fronte italiana* (Milano: Treves, 1921), p. 97.
[20] See N. Papafava, *Badoglio a Caporetto* (Torino: P. Gobetti, 1923); G. Volpe, *Ottobre 1917: dall'Isonzo al Piave* (Milan: Libreria d'Italia, 1930); E. Caviglia, *La dodicesima battaglia: Caporetto* (Verona: A. Mondadori, 1934); R. Bencivenga, *La sorpresa strategica di Caporetto* (Rome: Tip. della Madre di Dio, 1932); and P. Pieri, "La crisi dell'ottobre-novembre 1917," *Nuova Rivista Storica*, March-June 1935, pp. 224–54.

fail. The Third Army's retreat was one of those performances we call inexplicable. It made an Italian stand possible and deprived the enemy of the crowning triumph which he almost held in his hands. . . . The greatest glory of all was won by the Cavalry . . . who again and again charged the enemy and sacrificed themselves with cheerfulness that the retreat might win half an hour's respite. The stand must be on the Piave. . . . While the Duke of Aosta was struggling westward, De Robilant had fallen back from Cadore and was moving with all haste towards the middle Piave. By the 10th of November Cadorna (chief of the Italian army) was everywhere back on the Piave, and the retreat ended. It had been conducted wholly by Italian troops, and the credit was Italy's alone. . . . The Allied reinforcements could not come into line at once, though the certainty of them simplified the problem and eased the mind of Italy as to her reserves, and *the defense of the Piave for some weeks must be maintained by her alone.* . . . On the whole front the most crucial point was the mass of Monte Grappa. If it were carried, the enemy could debouch from the Brenta Valley and turn the flank of the Piave defense. . . . To hold it, boys of seventeen and eighteen were brought up from the deposits and the garrisons often after only a month's training. In the moment of their country's agony they flung themselves into the desperate breach. . . . The rest of November saw a desperate struggle especially in the Monte Grappa quarter. Blow after blow was delivered, blows which were gallantly parried, though the weary Italian armies had slowly to give ground . . . . *It was not till December 4th* that Plumer (chief of the British) and Fayolle (chief of the French) permitted De Robilant to concentrate on the Grappa. . . . The retreat of the Piave welded Italy into closer union and roused that ancient untamable spirit which was one of her legacies from Rome.

In March 1918, the English and French again suffered a terrible defeat in the battle of the Chemin des Dames and had to retreat for about thirty miles. Vice versa, in June 1918, the Italians won the great battle of the Piave, the first victory of the anti-German Entente after a long drawn out succession of disasters. The battle of the Piave had the same strategical and historical importance during the last year of the war as the battle of the Marne had had during the first year. That defeat sounded the last hour of the Austro-Hungarian Empire.

Yet the only battles which people remember when they think of the First World War are the battle of the Marne, which was won by the French, and the battle of Caporetto, which was lost by the Italians. Why?

1 The leaders of all other armies accepted their failures in dignified silence, whereas the commander-in-chief of the Italian army, Cadorna (who, with Capello and Badoglio, was one of the three army chiefs responsible for the disaster), in an official communiqué which was broadcast all over the world leveled against his own soldiers the charge of cowardice and treachery. He should have been court-martialed, not for losing the battle, but for calumniating his own men in order to exculpate himself. The Fascist government has, instead, erected a mausoleum to him.

2 Italian war aims regarding Dalmatia, the Near East, and colonial territories in Africa were in contrast with those of the British and French governments and their Yugoslav and Greek vassals. As a consequence, not only the German and Austrian propaganda machines, but also those of Italy's great and small allies, were anxious to discredit the Italian war effort and thus make out that there was no ground for her "outmoded imperialistic ambitions." The Caporetto defeat was just what they needed, and thus Caporetto became a kind of obligatory motif in all their music.

3 The governments of the other countries made as little fuss as possible about their own military misfortunes. For example, the English government, after the terrifying disasters of Passchendaele (August–September 1917) and Cambrai (November 1917) (on which one can read D. Lloyd George, *War Memoirs*), conducted an inquiry, the results of which were published in not more than twenty-two lines of the *London Times* on January 16, 1918. The House of Commons took good care not to make any fuss, and thus everything was hushed up. In Italy, after Caporetto, a great commission of inquiry was created to trace the responsibility for the disaster. The commission worked for eighteen months and, in the summer of 1919, put out a huge report

in three big folio volumes. The newspapers seized upon that report and discussed it for weeks, exchanging accusations and counteraccusations. Then the Chamber of Deputies started to discuss, and discussed it from September 6 to 10. In this way, even those who would have forgotten Caporetto were forced to think about it again and again, the only result being an enormous loss of time and breath in a discussion which no longer had any practical effect.

4   In all other countries, military "experts" and official historians have taken good care to gloss over as much as they could the misfortunes of their own armies, or extenuate them when they could not wholly ignore them. About the moral disintegration which, in the summer of 1917, threatened the French army, even today we have only very summary information. In a book of 694 big pages, H. Bidou (*Histoire de la Grande Guerre* [Paris: Gallimard, 1936]), is careful enough to devote no more than six pages to Nivelle's failure and no more than one page and fifteen lines to the following mutinies. In Italy, after the defeat of Caporetto, bitter controversy arose about those responsible for it. The Socialists, the Catholics, Pope Benedict XV, and those "liberal" politicians who, together with the Socialists and the Catholics, had not favored the continuation of war, were charged with the disaster. No doubt the discouragement which had laid its hold upon the soldiers after three years of war and the Russian collapse contributed to moral disintegration among the Italian forces after the military breakdown had become clear, and the recriminations of Socialists, Catholics, and antiwar "liberals" had their share in creating a low morale. "Defeatist" groups were at work in Italy as well as in all belligerent countries. Then, during the whole of these last twenty years, the Fascists and their associates in Italy and abroad have rehashed Caporetto day in and day out as one of the most striking crimes committed by Italian politicians before the Fascists rescued Italy from such a mire. They assiduously ignore the Catholics and Pope Benedict XV (upon whom, after Caporetto, Mussolini heaped the most

violent insults), and they focus their charges upon the "liberals" and Socialists who deliberately undermined the morale of the soldiers (Villari, *Awakening of Italy,* pp. 24–43; Goad, *The Making of the Corporate State,* p. 39). They overlook the fact that the three army chiefs responsible for the Caporetto disaster were not members of a democratic Italian parliament. In all countries, even in parliamentary countries, the choice of the army chiefs is outside the control of parliament. It is made by a small number of people, most of whom are other military chiefs. In democratic countries, the citizens and their representatives can only demand and obtain the dismissal of the army chiefs after they have blundered.

2

The
Postwar Crisis

The World War of 1914–18 dislocated the economic life of Italy no less than that of all other countries, belligerent and neutral.[1] Branches of production, which before the war had been rudimentary, swelled to enormous proportions, while branches previously flourishing dried up. Others were deformed in order to be adapted to war requirements. When the war was over, peace industries had to be substituted for those of the war period. Many mushrooming concerns had to be deflated or actually done away with. The whole commercial system had to be rebuilt. New sources of raw material and new markets had to be secured, in competition with the industries and trade of other nations, which were provided with larger means and engaged in a lively struggle for the control of markets and products.

The railways and rolling stock had been subjected to exceptional wear and tear. One of the greatest obstacles to the resumption of industrial activities and the normal functioning of the railways was the dearth of coal, imported, as it was, mostly from England. In 1919, it cost at times as much

---

[1] The economic history of Italy during the war and the post war years, 1914–22, may be drawn from: the invaluable reports sent out during these years by the commercial attachés of the American Embassy in Rome and published by the Bureau of Foreign and Domestic Commerce of the Department of Commerce, U.S.A.; R. Bachi, *L'Italia economica, 1915–1922;* G. Mortara, *Prospettive economiche:* 1921, 1922 and 1923; L. Einaudi's article in the *Encyclopedia Britannica,* 1926, pp. 573ff.; and *La condotta economica e gli effetti sociali della guerra italiana,* (Bari, Laterza, 1933), especially chapters 4 and 5.

as $56 a ton, and often there was none to be had, on account of the strikes of the English miners, dockers, and longshoremen.

During the war the agricultural classes—old men, women, and children —by dint of strenuous labor had succeeded in maintaining production at a level not much lower than that of the prewar period, but the soil had become exhausted. Large numbers of cattle had been slaughtered without replacement. Wood had been substituted for coal in industry, and forests had been cut down for this reason and for military requirements. The territories along the former Austro-Hungarian frontier, which had been the field of military operations, were ruined: 163,000 private houses, 435 town halls, 255 hospitals, 1,156 schools, 1,000 churches, and 1,222 cemeteries had been destroyed or damaged; eighty works of marsh reclamation affecting an area of about 300,000 acres had collapsed; 216 miles of roads had broken down; 450,000 heads of cattle had disappeared. When the war was over, fertilizers, machinery, and means of transport were difficult to obtain.

During the war, imports exceeded exports by a yearly average of $1.1 billion, and the invisible exports ceased almost completely. This deficit in the balance of trade had to be met by foreign loans. It was also by means of loans from the Allied governments that the Italian lira had been kept up during the war and in the first postwar months. In the second half of 1919, the Italian government had to fall back on its own resources. It had to meet the extraordinary war liabilities that were maturing and that from July 1918 to July 1922 amounted to four billion dollars. Such a sum of money, tremendous for a country like Italy, could not be raised entirely through taxation, though taxes were ruthlessly augmented. The treasury had to increase the national debt and to inflate the currency. The circulation and the public debt increased as shown in the following table:[1]

	Circulation (millions)	Internal Debt (millions)
1914, June 30,	2,764	15,765 gold lire
1918, June 30,	12,183	48,402 paper lire
1919, June 30,	14,803	60,213 ″ ″
1920, June 30,	20,355	74,496 ″ ″
1921, June 30,	20,704	86,482 ″ ″
1922, June 30,	20,371	92,856 ″ ″

[1] Banca Commerciale Italiana, *Movimento economico dell'Italia: Quadri statistici per gli anni 1921–1925*, Vol. 15 (Milano, 1927), pp. 91 ff; *Il Bilancio dello Stato dal 1913–14 al 1929–30 e la finanza fascista a tutto l'anno VIII* (Roma: Istituto Poligrafico della Stato, 1931), pp. 228–30.

Such methods were inevitable, and all belligerent governments did the same. But they were unsound. Inflation of currency always brings about depreciation of currency. In July 1914, when paper currency amounted to 2,764 million lire, the rate of exchange to the dollar stood at 5.17 lire. By June 1919, the lira went down to 8.05 to the dollar; in December 1919, to 13.07; in June 1920, to 16.89; in December 1920, to 28.57.[2] Depreciation of currency brought about soaring prices. Taking as 100 the Italian average prices in 1913, the index number during 1919 and 1920 ran as follows: June, 1919, 451; December 1919, 576; June, 1920, 795; December 1920, 825. There was a real economic upheaval.

Workers in town and country, unable to live on their old wages (whose purchasing power was falling rapidly), demanded higher wages. When their demands were rejected or answered too slowly, they struck. Officials of the central government and of the municipalities and those workers who were engaged in public services followed the example of the workers in private concerns.

Into the midst of this economic upheaval crept the propagandists of anarchism and bolshevism, preaching strikes, local and general, the occupation of factories and of the land, sabotage and obstructionism, hoping thus to pave the way for social revolution. Not only economic strikes but also "solidarity" and political strikes were frequent. Many of them were on the most trivial pretext and exasperating, especially those which occurred in the essential services such as the railways, streetcars, postal and telegraph facilities, and the light and food supplies of the large towns.[3]

These causes of unrest were common to all countries and could not be avoided. Peace, hard work, patience, and time were the only remedies for such diseases. In Italy another terrible moral crisis intermingled itself with them and practically brought the country to the verge of disintegration.

In the Treaty of London (April 26, 1915), by which Italy had pledged herself to intervene in the war against Germany and Austria, the Italian foreign minister, Sonnino, had been promised in return by the cabinets of the anti-German Entente that, in the event of victory, Italy would get: (1) Italian-speaking Trentino; (2) German-speaking South Tyrol; (3) the cities of Gorizia and Trieste and western Istria, which were inhabited by an

---

[2] Mortara, *Prospettive economiche 1922*, p. 374.
[3] A fair-minded résumé of the causes for the general unrest is given by Mortara, *Prospettive economiche 1923*, pp. 421–22. See also E. A. Mowrer, *Immortal Italy* (New York: D. Appleton and Co., 1922), pp. 317–29. The book of this intelligent and honest American eyewitness is one of the most valuable sources of information.

Italian majority; (4) the hinterlands of Gorizia, Trieste, and eastern Istria, which was inhabited by a compact Slav population; (5) most of Dalmatia and of the Dalmatian islands, which were inhabited by an overwhelming Slav majority; (6) a free hand in Albania and in those Greek islands near Asia Minor which are called the Dodecanese and which the Italian government had wrested in 1912 from the Turks; and (7) territorial acquisitions proportionate to the conquests England and France would make at the expense of Turkey in the Near East and at the expense of Germany in Africa. During the war, the Italian foreign office and the general staffs of the Italian army and navy organized a systematic propaganda to convince the Italian people that all these territorial acquisitions were indispensable to the welfare and the prestige of the nation.

When the war was over, the Italian negotiators at the peace conference obtained without difficulty what they expected under headings 1, 2, and 3. But the war had brought about, together with the dismemberment of the Austro-Hungarian Empire, the rise of Yugoslavia (United Kingdom of the Serbs, Croatians, and Slovenes). Sonnino, at the peace conference, had to dispute the Italo-Slavic and Slavic territories assigned to Italy by the Treaty of London (headings 4 and 5), not with the Hapsburgs, who had vanished from the scene, but with the representatives of the newborn Yugoslav government.

The problem of Fiume came to increase Italian difficulties. This city was inhabited by an Italian majority. It had always enjoyed within the Austro-Hungarian Empire the status of a free city, analogous to that of Hamburg in Germany. Sonnino, in the Treaty of London, had pledged that the Italian government should leave Fiume to Croatia. The Italian majority of the city might have consented to remain as a free city in a plurinational Austro-Hungarian-Croat state, if Austria-Hungary had not been dismembered. Now they rebelled at the idea of being deprived of their traditional immunities and left to the mercy of the Croats. All Italians, regardless of political creed, were determined to support the Italians of Fiume on this point. Even those who were persuaded that a friendly compromise should be worked out between Italians and Yugoslavs joined the ranks of the protesters and demanded that the city retain at least its traditional autonomy under the protectorate of Italy. The matter was of no great importance in itself. No vital Italian or Yugoslav interests were involved. As an American journalist put it, the Italians were screaming for an orange, forgetful that gold mines were available elsewhere.

There was but one way to solve this problem: not to exact strict respect for the Treaty of London but to use it as a basis for negotiations in order to reach a better settlement. The British and French foreign offices, who were pledged by the terms of the Treaty of London to assign Dalmatia to Italy, now wished to assign it to Yugoslavia; vice versa, Italy was pledged by the same treaty to assign Fiume to Croatia, but all Italians were averse to yielding it to Yugoslavia. The Italian negotiators should have consented to the revision of the Treaty of London, giving up Dalmatia on the condition they received Fiume. Such a settlement of the problem was finally agreed upon by Italy and Yugoslavia between 1920 and 1924, without Yugoslavia's going to rack and ruin or Italy's becoming more powerful or happier on account of Fiume.

Sonnino and Prime Minister Orlando did everything they could to make the problem important and insoluble during the peace negotiations. Sonnino, as foreign minister, went on demanding Dalmatia, which had been assigned to Italy by the Treaty of London, while Orlando, as prime minister, appealing to the principle of nationality on behalf of all Italians, demanded, in addition, the city of Fiume. The Italian negotiators invoked the right of nationality in Fiume and ignored it in Dalmatia, invoked the Treaty of London in Dalmatia and ignored it in Fiume.

These tactics were the more preposterous in that Sonnino and Orlando in the peace conference had to square accounts not only with the English and French diplomats, who were bound by the Treaty of London, but also with President Wilson, who had not subscribed to that treaty and had no obligation toward Italy. He was ready to assign to her the Trentino, South Tyrol, Gorizia, Trieste, and western Istria, but did not admit her claims to Dalmatia, Fiume, eastern Istria, or most of the hinterlands of Gorizia and Trieste.

As soon as they encountered Wilson's opposition, Sonnino and Orlando unloosed against him in the Italian press a campaign of recriminations, threats, and insults which had the effect of stiffening his resistance to the point of absurdity.

In the miserable rift which ensued between Sonnino, who was demanding the pound of flesh promised him, and Wilson, who had not signed that treaty and was not pledged to enforce it, Lloyd George and Clemenceau could evade the promises made in the Treaty of London. Wilson's opposition had not been contemplated when the Treaty of London was made. Such opposition was the business of the Italians and not of the British or

French. They assumed the innocent attitude of disinterested spectators. Thus, the problem of the hinterlands of Gorizia and Trieste, of eastern Istria, Fiume, Dalmatia, and Albania remained in the air. While Italian politicians, journalists, and professors raged over Fiume and Sonnino and Orlando were battling with Wilson, Lloyd George and Clemenceau swallowed up 282,000 square miles and 140,000 square miles (respectively) of the German colonies in Africa and divided among themselves all the territories in the Near East not inhabited by Turkish populations. The city of Smyrna and its district, which had been promised to Sonnino during the war (Treaty of St. Jean de Maurienne, 1917), were turned over to the Greeks. The territorial compensations which Italy should have received in the Near East and in Africa were left for future negotiations. One of the compensations that Sonnino had hoped to wrest from Clemenceau and Lloyd George during the peace negotiations was some kind of a free hand in Ethiopia. London and Paris firmly refused. The simple-hearted British and the chivalrous French diplomats exploited to the full the fact that they no longer needed Italian cannon fodder to go on fighting. The promises which they had made in order to drag Italy into the war and hold her bound until Germany was defeated could be disregarded with impunity. They did not stop to think that behind Sonnino and Orlando stood a nation whose sacrifices in the war deserved better consideration.

This diplomatic defeat had far-reaching effects. In 1914, Italy had not been attacked on her own soil, like Belgium and France, nor had she been suddenly pitchforked into war without time for reflection, like Germany, Austria-Hungary, England, or Russia. For nine months, from August 1914 to May 1915, the question of whether Italy should or should not intervene in the war had been argued threadbare. A country which argues for nine months about a question of war or peace is bound to split up into conflicting factions. This happened in the United States in 1939–41. It happened in Italy in 1914–15. All Italian parties split up into "interventionists" and "neutralists." The division lasted throughout the war.

When the war was over and freedom of speech and of the press was restored, the controversy, which during the war had been stifled, broke out with violence. Now that the failure of the Italian negotiators in the peace conference had become evident, those politicians and newspapers who in 1915 had opposed Italy's entrance into the war could boast that *they* had been right in trying to spare the Italian people a war from which it could reap no profits. *They* had foreseen the "treachery" of the "perfidious" allies. It had been for *this* reason that they had opposed Italy's entrance into the war on the side of those allies. All those who had been in favor of the war were held responsible for the diplomatic "disaster" in which the country had been involved. The time had come when they must render account for their crime. And behold, as if all this were not enough, the very politicians who had dragged Italy into the conflict, the newspapers that had fanned the flames of war, were now singing to the people in every key that the blood of 500,000 dead and 500,000 disabled men had been shed in vain since the "perfidious allies" had not given them Dalmatia, Asia Minor, Ethiopia, and what not. The people had been promised that this was to be the last war, the war to end all wars, and that peace was to be assured to their children and their children's children. And now, after three and one-half years of appalling toil, they were told that they had "won the war but lost the peace," that their victory had been "mutilated" by America, England, and France, and that they must prepare to take revenge for the futility of that war.

The French government, too, did not succeed in obtaining all that it wanted at the peace conference: it secured neither the detachment from Germany of the left bank of the Rhine nor the annexation of the Saar, nor the dismemberment of Germany. Notwithstanding this, the French people did not pass through a crisis of desperation and exasperation like that which made so many Italians lose their heads completely. Poincaré, Clemenceau, and Foch did not go to their people clamoring that France had been robbed of her victory, that France was ruined, that France had to prepare to make war on her allies in order to seize what these allies had refused her. What would have happened in France if nearly all the newspapers, deputies, and ministers who were responsible for the war, or who had deplored the war, had started a campaign of wild recrimination like that which in Italy was indulged in by Orlando, Sonnino, the general staffs of the army and navy, newspapers, and politicians? Would the French soldiers have returned contentedly to their homes, or would they have slain the ministers, deputies, and journalists who had brought about the war and who now announced that the "vital interests" of the nation had gone to rack and ruin because of it? The Italian people, even under such insane treatment, did not massacre those responsible for the war, whatever their creed or party, as they would have deserved. Instead they fell into a state of morbid irritation.

Whoever wishes to understand the unrest of the postwar years in Italy must keep in mind not only the physical exhaustion produced by three and one-half years of suffering, but also and above all the poisonous defeatist propaganda to which the Italian people were subjected in 1919. The history of Italy and of its social unrest and political disturbances in the postwar period appears in its true light only when it is set against the psychological background of "mutilated victory."

In his *Goliath*, Borgese has described with a master hand the disease which gnawed the souls of the Italian intelligentsia from 1870 to the World War. This was the Roman-imperial cancer: the memory of and nostalgia for the grandeur of the Roman Empire, coupled with a restless urge for impossible achievements, engendering disappointment, bitterness, and self-vilification. Italy was crushed by her past. Americans have no past. They live in the future. This is their greatest asset and luck. A certain amount of intelligent self-criticism is a useful corrective to silly national self-satisfaction: it has been aptly described as that "divine discontent" which leads men to greater and greater improvements. But absurd expectations and ceaseless self-debasement are poisonous drugs which create persecution-mania and make for blunders. Instead of comparing their present with their immediate past and realizing the strides their people were making through silent and heroic labor, the Italian intelligentsia contrasted present conditions with the memories of past greatness or with the dreams of impossible primacies. The consequence was that no measure of progress could satisfy them. They had words only to lament the mediocrity, the incapacity, the dishonesty, and the failures of their politicians.

Never was this Italian disease as widespread and violent as in the years following the First World War: "An unprecedented miracle of psychopathic alchemy had been performed. Italy, or at least the intellectual and political élite to which an evil destiny had entrusted Italy, had transubstantiated a victory into a disaster. . . . The nation, masochism-stricken, exulted in frustration."[4] The Italians, alone among the victorious people, were affected by a specific ailment of their own. Pride of victory that brings self-confidence was superseded by the gloomy pessimism of defeat.

[4] G. A. Borgese, *Goliath: The March of Fascism* (New York: The Viking Press, 1937), p. 149.

3

Italy's Recovery

Until the summer of 1920, there were moments in which it could be feared that a political catastrophe could not be avoided. Yet the fatal crisis never came. There was never any economic breakdown. On the contrary, as soon as the war was over, a process of recovery began to take place and, notwithstanding difficulties of all kinds, was quick and steady. Let us choose a few indications from among thousands.

In a country such as Italy, which does not possess coal mines, imports of coal are an indication of economic activity. When they increase, economic activities are on the upgrade; when they decrease, this means that there is a depression. In 1913, on the eve of the World War, Italy imported 11.8 million tons of coal. During the war, imports went down to 5.8 million tons. By 1922, coal imports reached 9.6 million tons. At the same time the consumption of electric power was steadily going up.

Another characteristic index of economic activity is the movement of goods on the railways. In 1913, Italian railways carried 37.4 million tons. By 1918, there was a drop to 28.9 million tons. In 1922, the railways carried 36.2 million tons—that is to say, they had regained all the ground lost during the war.[1] At the same time, the number of trucks

[1] *Annuario Statistico Italiano: 1919-1921*, p. 507.

and lorries was rapidly increasing. About one billion lire a year were spent in repairing the railway lines and adding new rolling stock all over the country.

The number of limited companies, which in 1918 was 3,463 with a capital of 7,257 million lire, rose in 1919 to 4,520 with a capital of 13,014 million lire; to 5,541 with a capital of 17,784 million in 1920; to 6,191 with a capital of 20,350 million lire in 1921; and to 6,850 with a capital of 21,395 million lire in 1922.

The amounts deposited in the postal and other savings institutions rose from 7,906 million lire in 1918 to 10,643 million lire in 1919, to 13,213 million in 1920, to 15,576 million in 1921, and to 17,250 million in 1922.

December 1919 and January 1920 were among the most agitated moments of that disturbed period: strikes on the railways and in the postal services, in private industry and in agriculture, and numerous street riots which provoked general strikes in protest. Yet a national loan floated in January 1920 brought in eighteen billion lire—a sum far in excess of any national loan which had been floated before or was floated afterwards. Political events often stand to the economic life of a nation as the waves on the surface stand to the depths of the sea: whilst the former are lashed by the winds, the latter remain unmoved.

During 1920, the year of the greatest disturbances, unemployment was insignificant. The great strikes of that year were made possible by the scarcity of labor, while the inflation was raising the cost of living and driving the workers to demand higher wages. "The peasants and workers," wrote an economist in 1921, "have never enjoyed such well-being and comfort as during these years."[2] This well-being was not due to high wages: in 1921, wages of industrial workers had a purchasing power scarcely ten per cent higher than those of 1913. But in 1919 and 1920, every member of the working-class family—man, woman, or boy—was gainfully employed.

After December 1920, a slow process of deflation began, and the value of the lira improved in consequence. The following table gives, month by month, the currency and the rate of exchange for 1920-22:[3]

[2] M. Pantaleoni, *Bolscevismo Italiano* (Bari Laterza, 1922), p. xvii.
[3] Banca Commerciale Italiana, *Movimento economico dell' Italia: quadri statistici per gli anni 1921-1925* (Milano, 1927), vol. XV, pp. 94–95, 130–31.

Months	1920		1921		1922	
	Circula-tion (million lire)	Rate of exchange of dollar	Circula-tion (million lire)	Rate of exchange of dollar	Circula tion (million lire)	Rate of exchange of dollar
1	18,167	13.98	21,808	28.25	21,300	22.94
2	17,979	18.21	21,472	27.34	20,802	20.45
3	18,465	19.03	21,309	26.04	20,657	19.55
4	18,963	22.94	20,823	21.65	20,257	18.68
5	19,397	19.86	20,575	18.73	19,866	19.04
6	20,355	16.89	20,704	19.84	20,371	20.07
7	20,441	17.28	20,485	21.90	20,545	21.96
8	20,500	20.54	20,387	23.51	20,293	22.28
9	21,458	22.89	20,702	23.54	20,537	23.41
10	21,846	25.67	20,846	25.33	20,761	23.97
11	22,022	27.55	20,468	24.29	20,513	22.09
12	22,277	28.57	21,755	22.69	20,559	19.88

The general upward trend, despite seasonal oscillations, is undeniable.[4] In December 1923, Mortara wrote:

> The end of 1920 marks a decisive turn in the recent history of our country: inflation was stopped, the balance of our international payments gradually restored and bolshevism shown to be powerless. As a result, the economic life of the country resumed a more even rhythm. As the principal feature of the two years 1919–20 was the instability of the purchasing power of money, so its stability is the principal feature of the two years 1921–22.[5]

Government taxation and local ratings were radically reformed, and taxpayers were ruthlessly squeezed. Revenue in the national budget rose from 9,175 million lire in 1918–19 to 15,207 million lire in 1919–20, to 18,820 million lire in 1920–21, and 19,790 million lire in 1921–22.

The liabilities connected with the World War, which were then maturing, were punctually met. They amounted to 25.5 billion lire in 1918–19, 12.4 billion lire in 1919–20, 22.3 billion lire in 1920–21, 18.2 billion lire

[4] Mortara, *Prospettive Economiche 1923*, p. xviii: "The steadiness of the dollar exchange from the second half of 1920 onwards bears out this decided improvement in our international situation."

[5] Mortara, *Prospettive Economiche 1923*, p. 377; *Prospettive Economiche 1924*, p. 407.

in 1921–22, and fell to 4.8 billion lire in 1922–23. The heaviest strain was felt in the four years immediately after the war.[6] In December 1921, Professor Mortara, one of Italy's leading economic experts, predicted that by 1924 the deficit in the budget might disappear.[7]

In the dispatches sent from Italy to Washington during those years by the American commercial attachés and printed in *Commerce Reports*, there is never the slightest indication of any state of economic breakdown. On the contrary, all information leads to the inference that the country was in a state of intense economic activity and revivescence: "Many American firms are extending their business connections in Italy" (October 16, 1919). The Italians who had emigrated to America were so little frightened by "bolshevism" that they were returning to Italy with their pockets full of money: "The wealth brought back by these people forms at present a large source of income in southern Italy" (August 14 and October 10, 1919). "Textile industries have reached a point where they are able not only to supply the ordinary needs of Italy, but to produce a surplus for export" (August 22, 1919). "The year 1919 was an extremely prosperous one . . . a period of unusual activity which has since continued" (July 22, 1920). Nor were tourists being scared away: "The volume of tourist traffic is now steadly increasing, and the big hotels report a fair amount of business" (October 22, 1920). The Italians were even indulging in the luxury of organizing an international art exposition at Venice (April 15, 1920):

> The Italian people have given tangible evidence of their faith in the ultimate ability of their government to support the financial burden it has been called upon to assume as a direct result of the war. The increase of over 35 percent in the deposits in the Italian savings banks from December 1913 to October 1919. . . . demonstrates very clearly that the Italian people are ready to confide their savings to the government. Another indication of the same attitude is given by the prices of the securities comprising the consolidated 5 percent loan issued in 1917 at 86.50 lire. These securities have been consistently selling above the price of issue and at the present time are quoted at 87 lire, in spite of the fact that the campaign for the new 5 percent loan is being carried on with the utmost vigor. In 1866, after the

[6] *Il Bilancio dello Stato dal 1913–14 al 1929–30* (Roma: Istituto Poligrafico dello Stato, 1931), p. 225.
[7] Mortara, *Prospettive Economiche 1922*, p. xx.

wars of Italian independence, the 5 percent bonds issued at that time fell to about 41 (February 20, 1920).

Almost without exception Italian industries have been and are extremely active; whenever possible electric power has been utilized; the use of fuel oil is steadily increasing; an exceptional demand for agricultural implements exists; automobile manufacturers are swamped with orders; the increase in the demand for manufactured silk products has been very marked, so much so that silk manufacturers are declining to accept any new orders for delivery before 1921; this may be accounted for by the greater purchasing power which has been acquired by certain classes of the population who are spending their increased earnings freely on articles of personal adornment; exports of silk textiles have practically ceased; moreover, silk textiles are being imported from Switzerland and are selling freely in spite of high prices; during the past six months the Italian banks report a volume of business considerably greater than in their period of greatest activity during the war; both the savings deposits and the deposits on current accounts have increased rapidly; the security market has been active, and prices have been well sustained (April 27, 1920).

According to the figures published by the ministry of the treasury, ordinary deposits increased from 1,491,170,560 lire on June 30, 1914 to 3,567,426,189 lire on June 30, 1919, and savings deposits from 6,000,548,747 lire to 13,586,086,947 lire. The money deposited in the banks would not have been so utilized if the depositors had had debts on which they were obliged to pay interest, for necessarily such interest would be greater than that received on their bank deposits. The pawnshops are practically bare. . . . For several years there have been very few business failures in Italy and none of importance (July 30, 1920).

The amount of net investments in banking enterprises is (during the first six months of 1920) far greater than that in any of the other industries and reaches a figure never even approached by any other up to now. The investments in textile industries have in the first six months of 1920 reached a figure almost ten times greater than that for the corresponding period of 1919 (February 10, 1921).

From 1919 to 1922, in the frontier provinces devastated by the war, private houses, churches, hospitals, schools, roads, canals, bridges, aqueducts, and railroad lines were rebuilt or repaired, and agricultural implements and livestock were replaced, at an aggregate outlay of over eight billion lire.[8] Italian aviators, flying airplanes built in Italy, won the Schneider Cup in the international contests of 1920 and 1922. In 1920 the municipality of Milan appointed Toscanini as head of the Scala Theater, which had, during those years, the most glorious successions of performances in its history. The *Enciclopedia Italiana* was planned in 1920–21. At the end of 1920, symptoms of the industrial and commercial crisis, which was already evident in the world markets, began to appear also in Italy. Riccardo Bachi wrote:

> The crisis was evident in the world-markets during the second half of 1920, and now warns us of difficult times and severe economic stress ahead. It made itself just felt in the past spring (1920) in Japan, whence it spread step by step over the entire world. The immediate future promises great economic hardships.[9]

Fortunately, the crops of 1921 were good and offset the industrial drawback. Italian economic life, at the end of 1921, showed all the symptoms of convalescence. Giorgio Mortara wrote in December, 1921:

> Italy has decidedly improved her condition in the course of 1921. It would be too much to say that she lies on a bed of roses. Nevertheless, remembering the difficulties overcome yesterday, we can consider without undue fears the difficulties of today. Agricultural industry, the base of our economic life, seems to be distinctly on the way to recover normal conditions; the deep depression consequent on the war has passed away. Not less reassuring, perhaps even more so, is the situation of cattle breeding. The mineral industries suffer the foreign and domestic depression—some of their branches, however, are active. The textile industries, which, taken as a whole, are among the most important and vital of the transforming industries of Italy, support better the slackened demand: active in finding new outlets, and quick to adapt production to the tastes of the markets, they passed without excessive expansion through the war period, and in the same way, without undue restriction, they traverse these years of laborious readjustment. The food industries are also

[8] A. Serpieri, *La guerra e le classi rurali italiane* (Bari: Laterza, 1930), pp. 235–239.
[9] R. Bachi, *L'Italia Economica nell'anno 1919*, pp. xii, 193, 224.

firm: many of them find in the home markets a wide field
for the absorption of their products. The electrical industry
is expanding: the production of power is inferior to the
demand. Under the impulse of necessity, plants for the
exploitation of Italy's building industry, and that of building
materials, are still vegetating feebly, the difficulties which
paralyzed them during the past years being not yet overcome, although there is some improvement. Some branches
of mechanical industry are still active, either by their own
vitality like the motor car industry, or thanks to government
orders like those which provide railway material. The industries which languish most are those which, born and developed during the war, had a fictitious appearance of prosperity: with a return to less abnormal conditions, organs which
once were useful and necessary become parasitical and
superfluous, or out of proportion to needs: the eliminations
and restrictions which take place today were inevitable from
the day of the armistice. On the whole, the depression of the
industries which transform raw materials appears serious and
widespread even in Italy, but is far from reaching the intensity which has been the lot of the big industrial countries,
such as the United States and the United Kingdom. The
working of the railways has distinctly improved. The mercantile fleet has increased. In the ports, things, without
being altogether satisfactory, are improving. The uneasiness
in several home industries has occasioned widespread unemployment. Against these depressing phenomena may be set
the comforting fact of the greater steadiness and efficiency
of labor. A good source of hope for the economic future of
Italy is to be found in the progress of foreign trade. In 1921
the excess of imports over exports diminished from ten to
twelve billion to five to six billion. The expenditure of tourists in Italy has increased sufficiently to compensate for the
reduction which has occurred in the remissions of the emigrants. Our foreign debt has perhaps increased in 1921, but
certainly in a much smaller degree than in 1920. The year
1922 promises well as regards foreign exchanges. It will
perhaps be necessary, during the first months of the year, to
increase to some extent the import of coal, to make up for
the dearth of hydroelectric power; but the prosperity of the
agriculture and cattle breeding in 1921 makes large imports
of corn and of other foodstuffs unnecessary. The exports of
fruit and vegetables, in spite of many market difficulties,
reach a sufficiently high figure. The influx of tourists does
not seem to abate—indeed it seems to increase. (Mortara,
Prospettive economiche 1922, pp. xv-xx).

The year 1922 began under less propitious auspices: the failure of the great metallurgical firm of Ansaldo Brothers and of one of the four big Italian banks, the Banca Italiana di Sconto, caused great loss of people's savings. Furthermore, a long drought in the fall of 1921 and insufficient rain in the winter of 1922 failed to replenish the reservoirs of the electric plants, which in the summer of 1922 were unable to meet all the demands of industry. The crops, too, were exceptionally poor in 1922. The government met the crisis in electricity by importing power from Switzerland.[10] By October the American commercial reports read as follows:

> The outstanding feature of the Italian economic situation in the past month of September is the improved outlook in the textile, metallurgical, and automobile industries. Money and credit are easier. The prices of the securities on the exchange are again rising. During the last six months the general trend has been upward.

At the end of 1922, the economic situation of the country, according to Mortara, was as follows:

> The economic activity of the country has strengthened steadily during the course of this year. The people work with greater faith in the future, and with greater steadiness and regularity. Agriculturalists, in spite of the poverty of the harvest, have succeeded in keeping supplied certain notable channels of export, and have reopened others. Stock-breeders, in spite of the drought, have remained in a reasonably good position. The electric industry has been restored to vigor. The industries concerned with the manufacture of raw materials, and agricultural and pastoral products continue to pick up. The state of the cotton industry can fairly be called good, that of silk and wool satisfactory, and that of the minor textile industries hopeful. The iron industry, however, is still depressed. In the mechanical industries some branches are flourishing; others vegetate, others threaten to disappear altogether. Among chemical industries there is a necessary movement on foot to eliminate those to which Italy does not offer a propitious home: others are returning to their early vigor. The lowering of the price of building materials has assisted the revival of the building

---

[10] Bachi, L'Italia economica nell'anno 1921, pp. 221, 305.

industry. Railway transport is being slowly reorganized: complaints against delays and irregularity of delivery are growing less. The improved conditions of the ports is easing sea-transport, which had greatly suffered from their disordered state. For two years now Italy has done without the help of foreign capital, on which she still relied in 1919 and 1920. The increase of paper money is already stopped (Mortara, *Prospettive economiche 1923*, pp. xvi–vii).

Riccardo Bachi wrote, at the end of 1922: "The machinery of Italian economics showed itself on the whole far more solid and consistent than might have been expected. At a year's distance from the acutest point of the crisis, a hint of blue appears in the sky and gives hope of better things" (Bachi, *L'Italia economica nell'anno 1921*, pp. vi–vii).

Italian recovery during those years seems almost miraculous. To explain it, one must take note of three facts:

(a) The World War, while dislocating the economic machinery of the country, left it strengthened in many ways. Several industries enlarged their plants and adopted more efficient methods to supply products which could not be imported from abroad. A law which exempted war profits from surtax if invested in extension of factories or improvement of machinery led all firms to lay down large amounts of capital on better equipment.[11] As soon as the war was over, emigrants' remittances, the tourist traffic, and the earnings of the mercantile marine started again to flow. In 1921 and 1922, the Italian government no longer resorted to foreign loans, though the excess of imports over exports amounted to eight billion lire yearly. This shows that the balance of international payments was restored by 1922.[12]

(b) The 610.8 million pounds sterling borrowed during the war from England and the 1,648 million dollars borrowed from the United States were received in goods. Of these only a portion consisted of arms, ammunition, food, and clothes for soldiers, which vanished into thin air. A large

---

[11] L. Einaudi, *La guerra e il sistema tributario italiano* (Bari: Laterza, 1928), pp. 148 ff.

[12] Mortara, *Prospettive Economiche 1923*, p. xvii: "Our emigrants' remittances and tourists' expenditure have almost certainly been sufficient to compensate the deficit in the balance of trade. In the last two years, Italy has made herself independent of foreign credit, which was still necessary in 1919 and 1920." Count Volpi, minister for the treasury in Mussolini's cabinet, wrote in *Rassegna Italiana*, Dec. 1925, p. 786: "Already in 1921 and 1922 our balance of international payment was quite different from that of 1919 and 1920. It revealed a certain improvement in the economic situation of our country, showing, after the crisis of the war and of the immediate postwar period, the gradual resumption of work and of international trade."

share consisted of raw materials, machinery, and implements for industry and agriculture. At the end of the war, machinery and implements still were available, and vast quantities of imported supplies were accumulated in government storehouses. The government sold them to the public at much lower cost than their value, yet it derived from them more than three billion lire.[13] On the other hand, until the end of 1925, no payment was made on account of foreign debt, and in 1925, when the moment came to foot the bills, the reparations received from Germany served to pay the installments due to England and America. If the external debt should ever have been paid off, it would have wrecked the whole economic structure of the country. But since it never was met, war loans, to a large extent, contributed to invigorate the Italian economic structure. The war cost the Italian *government* no more than the internal debt, while it cost the Italian *people* the internal wealth destroyed during the war *minus* that share of the imported wealth which had not been destroyed. The war brought about vast displacements of wealth from individuals to individuals, but it did not diminish the wealth of the country as a whole.

Not even the government debt was as disastrous as it might appear at first sight. The ninety-three billion lire, with which that debt was represented at the end of 1922, were paper and not gold lire. At the rate of the exchange prevailing in 1922, ninety-three billion lire were worth around four billion gold dollars. The national debt of Italy in 1914 amounted to three billion gold dollars. This means that the War of 1914–18 cost the Italian government no more than one billion gold dollars. The unification of Italy had brought about, from 1859 to 1870, an increase in national debt of 1.2 billion gold dollars. In 1922, the thirty-nine million Italians were in a position to withstand the strain of one billion gold dollars much better than the twenty-seven million of 1871.

(c) Last but not least, there was always the labor of the Italian people, ready to do their part. No wonder, therefore, if as soon as the war was over, a process of recovery took place.

The revival became apparent so soon that in 1920, one of the most important banking firms, Credito Italiano, noted "the growth of older industries, vast new installations, a more rational system of work and a great transformation of technical methods." "The economic structure of the

[13] A. De Stefani, *Documenti sulla condizione finanziaria ed economica dell 'Italia* (Rome: Libreria dello Stato, 1923), p. 337; *Il Bilancio dello Stato dal 1913–14 al 1929–30,* pp. 606, 611.

country has notably improved during these last years. Industries have become more varied, so that the cycle of production in which, before, gaps were discernible, is today more complete."[14]

Other observers write:

> The war stimulated nearly every branch of industry, and the introduction of the shift system led to the expansion of plant and to new kinds of manufacture in which by-products, formerly neglected, could be utilized. The extraction of iron ore, pig iron production and steel showed great increases. In addition to arms and munitions the requirements of the army included a vast number of commodities ranging from cloth to canvas, from shoes to motor-cars, from rubber to paper and from chemicals to naval dockyards.[15]

> During the war the creation of new power stations, the extension of those already in existence, and the greatly increased demand for current production produced a rapid development in the production and consumption of electrical energy, which was obtained almost exclusively from water-power, especially during the last two years of the war.[16]

> The Italian wool industry, about 1913, commanded 800 thousand spinning-wheels, 16 thousand mechanical looms and about 20 thousand hand looms. There were installed, at the end of 1918, about 1,035 thousand spinning-wheels and 17 thousand mechanical looms. During the war years, a part of the greater demand for manufactured woolen goods was supplied by the importation of finished clothes, but by far the greater part of it was met by the vastly developed internal production.[17]

> Our fleet has been almost entirely renewed. In 1914 less than a quarter of the total tonnage was composed of ships less than ten years old: today the proportion is nearly one half. Ships more than twenty years old formed then two-fiths of the total tonnage: today they form little more than one-fifth. The number of ships of 501 to 4,000 tons' freight

[14] Credito Italiano, L'Italie économique: son évolution progressive au cours des vingt-cinq dernières années et sa situation actuelle, 1895–1920 (Milan, 1920), pp. 104, 108.

[15] L. Einaudi, "Italy," Encyclopedia Britannica, 1926, p. 574.

[16] Mortara, Prospettive economiche 1923, p. 278.

[17] Mortara, Prospettive economiche 1922, pp. 163–65. Cf. Einaudi, "Italy," Encyclopedia Britannica, 1926, p. 574: "Washing and combing are no longer done almost entirely abroad, thanks to the improvements in machinery and equipment which have been made since 1915, especially in Piedmont and the Vicentino."

> capacity has fallen from 321 in December 1914 to 287 in
> October 1921; but the number of those 4,001 to 8,000 tons'
> freight capacity has risen from 202 to 251, and of those of
> more than 8,000 tons' freight capacity from 13 to 122. This
> last class formed one-twentieth of the entire tonnage on the
> eve of the war: today it forms six-twentieths."[18]

We do not mean that Italy enjoyed prosperity and happiness during those years. Italy was a patient recovering from a terrible illness—the illness of the World War. She underwent a severe crisis, but it was a crisis of readjustment and not one of disorganization.

It is true that at the peace conference the Italian delegates piled blunder upon blunder. But, after all, neither their blunders nor the bad faith of Lloyd George and Clemenceau, nor the lack of understanding on Wilson's part, actually inflicted any mortal wound upon the essential interests of the Italian nation.

As a result of the war, the Austro-Hungarian Empire had been dismembered. No longer was Italy threatened upon her eastern frontier and in the Adriatic by a hostile power controlling fifty-one million subjects. Italy's neighbors on the East were now the Republic of Austria and newly created Yugoslavia. The former had no more than ten million inhabitants and was disarmed and neutralized. The latter had a population of twelve million and was more interested in cultivating Italian friendship against the German-Hungarian-Bulgarian danger than in alienating Italy by a preconceived policy of hostility. If one compares the postwar situation of France with that of Italy, one must conclude that Italy's success in the World War had outranked that of France. By eliminating the Austro-Hungarian Empire from the map of Europe, Italy had, in fact, essentially solved the problem of her security toward Central Europe. France, on the contrary, was still confronted with the compact mass of Germany: the problem of her security had remained unsolved. As Germany reorganized, the value of Italian friendship could not but increase in the eyes of France, Germany, and the Danubian countries. Italy, which seventy years before had been a mere "geographic expression," had now become, not only in words but in actual fact, one of the great European powers.

[18] Mortara, *Prospettive economiche 1922*, pp. 330–31. Cf. Einaudi, "Italy": "The losses from submarines and mines were more than replaced by the shipping taken over in Trieste and Istria, and the ships as a whole are faster and more modern than before the war."

The failure to annex Dalmatia to Italy was not a thing to be regretted. Dalmatia would not have increased either Italy's wealth or her security. It is a poor and rocky country peopled by more than 500,000 wildly nationalist Slavs. There was an Italian majority only in the city of Zara; outside Zara, not more than 20,000 Italians were scattered amidst a Slavic sea. Racial minorities unwillingly annexed can scarcely constitute a gain for any country. Had she conquered Dalmatia, Italy would have had to maintain a considerable part of her army there on a permanent war footing in order to hold down the Slav population. In the event of another European war involving Italy, she would have been forced to immobilize in that province important military forces to protect its 350-mile frontier against an attack from the Slavonic hinterland. Such an army of occupation could be used to greater advantage in the protection of more vital Italian frontiers—those toward France or Central Europe. Dalmatia would not have given Italy mastery of the Adriatic. Mastery of the sea is assured by the most powerful mobile naval forces if they can rely on a single well-organized naval base. Numerous naval bases are of no avail. They neither move nor fight. The experience of the War of 1915–18 has shown that the magnificent naval bases of the eastern Adriatic, though controlled by the Austrian navy, did not permit the Austrians to undertake any important naval action, because they had weaker naval forces than the Entente. Even after the annexation of Dalmatia by Italy, there would have remained on the eastern coasts of the Adriatic and beyond Italian control the naval base of Cattaro. In a sea as small as the Adriatic, Cattaro alone—provided it were buttressed by a powerful fleet of its own—would have sufficed to hold the Italian fleet at bay unless Italy had occupied the whole of the eastern coast as far as the Albanian frontier. This would have obliged the Italian army to protect a treacherous line extending over even more than 350 miles. Moreover, a vast merchant marine would have been needed to transport from Italy to Dalmatia the supplies indispensable to the army stationed in this barren and hostile country while a strong navy should have protected the lines of communication between that army and its bases in Italy. These forces would have had to be deflected from Italy's lifelines in the Tyrrhenian and Ionian Seas to the Adriatic. In short, even from the strategic standpoint (one might say especially from the strategic standpoint), the conquest of Dalmatia would have been a gross blunder.

It is also true that at the peace conference Clemenceau, Lloyd George, and Wilson snatched Smyrna away from Orlando and Sonnino and turned it over to Greece. But if ever a bad turn resolved itself into a piece of good luck, it was this. The English and French diplomats had assigned to themselves all the territories in the Near East occupied by non-Turkish populations, to whom they presented themselves as their liberators from the Turkish yoke, while they had reserved for Italy the choice morsel of Smyrna and its environs in the very heart of Turkish strength. Italy would have had to sustain a long and arduous war against the Turks on their national soil. By drawing the Turkish forces against itself in a long and difficult war, the Italian army in Asia Minor would have assumed at its own risk, and at the expense of the Italian people, the burden of guaranteeing the security of the French and English "mandates" in the Near East. The Greeks would have been wiser to refuse to step into the shoes of the Italians and to ask the French and British to keep the gift of Smyrna for themselves. They would have avoided the disaster of 1922. The sad fate of the Greeks made all sensible Italians thank God for having endowed Lloyd George, Clemenceau, and Wilson with nasty dispositions.

Finally, it is true that when the former German colonial possessions in Africa were divided among the victors, the Italian diplomats were excluded from sharing in the spoils and did not succeed in obtaining the right to expand toward Ethiopia. Colonies are symbols of superiority, and every country that wants to be regarded as powerful must possess some, just as every millionaire must own a Rolls Royce and deck his wife or his mistress with jewels. Moreover, colonial possessions appeal irresistibly to the imagination of a people like the Italians, crowded in a land insufficient to their needs. There can be no doubt that by their short-sighted policy the former allies sowed seeds of ill-will which had to bear fruit. Even those Italians who had been most critical of Sonnino's blunders and considered his territorial claims as useless were disgusted with the bad faith of the English and French negotiators.

But when all this has been said, the fact remains that the failure to obtain a free hand against Ethiopia was not a real loss for Italy. Whoever has even a rudimentary knowledge of the climatic conditions of that country knows that it is unfit for the absorption of white labor, and consequently could be of no help to Italy in the solution of her problem of surplus population. Had the Italian government obtained a free hand in Ethiopia in 1919 from France and Britain, the senseless war that broke out in 1935 would have broken out several years earlier. Instead of wasting time and effort demanding African colonies, the Italian negotiators should have worked to obtain emigration treaties, free access to raw materials, and a fair settlement of the war debts.

The problem which Sonnino and Orlando had tangled or ignored during the peace conference began to be disentangled as soon as they went out of office (July 1919).

In September 1919, Prime Minister Nitti concluded with the Paris cabinet a labor treaty which guaranteed to Italian immigrants in France treatment analogous to that received by French workers. This treaty was far more valuable for the Italian people than any colonial conquest in Africa. Italian immigration into France assumed greater importance than before, and France became the largest outlet for Italian labor after the United States, Canada, and Australia closed their doors.

As regards the colonial compensations that the French government owed for the German colonies it had obtained in Africa, it offered no more than a few wretched tracts of desert land south of the Tunisian territory and to the east of the Fezzan, including the caravan road from Ghadames to Ghat. The Italian negotiators asked for more deserts toward Lake Tchad. But Italy's actual control in Tripolitania did not extend at that time much beyond the coastline. The Italians, for the time being, accepted the rectification of the frontier as offered by France but declared that these dry bones were not sufficient. The dispute was left open.

At this same time—September 1919—the British government agreed to turn over to Italy the oasis of Djaraboub in Cyrenaica and Djubaland on the shores of the Indian Ocean. In April 1920, the boundaries of the last territory were more definitely fixed by the Milner-Scialoia accord. After making these promises, the English government postponed the actual transfer under the pretext that all questions submitted to the peace conference must be settled beforehand and that among these questions there was the final disposal of the Greek islands of the Dodecanese which Italy had held since the Italo-Turkish War of 1911-12. As for the oasis of Djaraboub, Italy was in no position to take it over because at that time her control in Cyrenaica did not extend beyond the coastline. Moreover, Djaraboub was claimed by Egypt as part of its territory, and in 1922 London agreed to the independence of Egypt. Thus the Italians had to discuss the question of Djaraboub no longer with England but with Egypt. And, of course, unless they had found it to their advantage to bring pressure upon Egypt, the London cabinet would have religiously respected Egyptian "self-determination."

In the summer of 1920, Italy managed to extricate herself from a predicament which, at that moment, might have had serious consequences in her internal politics. Italy had established a sort of protectorate over Albania during the war. Many men and much money would have been needed to make this protectorate effective over the unruly mountain tribes. When a revolt broke out in June 1920, the government decided to dispatch troops. A regiment bound for Albania mutinied at Ancona. The government had the sense to understand that it was impossible to embark upon a new war —even though it was only a "colonial" war—before the blood of the World War had grown cold. This was a demonstration of what might have happened if conquests had been undertaken at that time in Asia Minor or in Ethiopia. On August 3, 1920, in an accord at Tirana with the Albanian chieftains, it recognized the government which had been formed at Lushna. The accord was followed (September 2, 1920) by the withdrawal of the Italian troops from Albanian territory. On December 17, 1920, Albania was admitted to the League of Nations. But Italy retained possession of the island of Saseno at the entrance of the bay of Vallona in order to deprive this bay of all military value: it could not serve as a base of operations either for Italy or against her. Furthermore, in 1921, the Great Powers agreed that "the violation of the frontier and any attempt against the independence of Albania would constitute a danger to the security of Italy." In case this danger should manifest itself, the restoration of the frontiers would be entrusted to Italy. This was a disguised "free hand" left to the Italian government toward Albania. The League of Nations should never have allowed one of its members to be dealt with as a sphere of influence of another member. It should have refused to register that agreement. It did not. It "capitulated" to wrongdoers.

The most acute problem of foreign policy, that of Italo-Yugoslav relations, was given a sensible solution by Foreign Minister Sforza through the Treaty of Rapallo (November 1920). By this treaty, the Belgrade government agreed that Italy should annex the cities of Gorizia and Trieste, their hinterland as far as the Yugoslav frontier of 1940, and the whole of Istria as far as the doors of Fiume. The Rome government left to Yugoslavia all of Dalmatia except the city of Zara, which was annexed to Italy. Fiume remained an autonomous city-state, and a joint corporation of Fiumans, Italians, and Yugoslavs was to be set up for the management of its maritime interests. In December, this treaty was approved by an overwhelming majority in the Chamber of Deputies and in the Senate. D'Annunzio, in

Fiume, protested that he would die rather than surrender. When he realized that the government meant business, he declared that Italy "was not worthy that he should die for her" and vanished. No serious disturbance occurred in Italy on his account.

In January 1921, a "Pact of Guarantee" was signed in which Yugoslavia, Czechoslovakia, Rumania, and Italy agreed never to allow the restoration of the Hapsburgs either in Austria or in Hungary. The way was being opened for the Italian government to serve as mediator between the governments which had fallen heir to the Austro-Hungarian Empire and those of Austria, Hungary, and Bulgaria, in order to correct, little by little, the too-drastic provisions of the Treaty of Trianon. Italy was thus in a position to wield valuable moral and political influence in the Balkan peninsula and in the Danube basin without being suspected of "Machiavellianism" or "imperialism."

As regards Italian territorial ambitions in Asia Minor, Sforza was the first among the Western statesmen to recognize that Turkey was no longer prewar Turkey, forced to scatter her forces to keep in subjection Christian populations in the Balkan peninsula and Arab peoples in the Near East. She had acquired solid national compactness and was henceforth to be reckoned with. Sforza therefore relinquished all territorial claims in Asia Minor, obtained from the Turks a most favorable commercial treaty, and left the English, the French, and the Greeks to fight it out with the Turks. The other colonial questions were dropped for the time being. As long as the country had not overcome the postwar crisis it should not scatter its forces in de luxe oversea adventures.

Despite the Treaty of Rapallo, the status of Fiume remained unsettled. As soon as the city was abandoned to itself during the first half of 1921, it became the scene of violent struggles, not only between Italians and Slavs, but between the Italians who accepted the status of a free city and those who wanted outright annexation to Italy. In the summer of 1921, the Italian government sent troops to occupy the city. The government of Belgrade did not protest. Thus, although the status of the city remained unsettled, the problem had lost the artificial and absurd animus that had characterized it in 1919 and 1920.

Since the Italian government showed itself ready to identify the interests of its country with those of peace, it obtained without difficulty naval parity with France for dreadnoughts at the Washington Conference in 1921. When the first international conference was called in April 1922, at which the representatives of the Entente and those of Russia and Germany were to meet, the Italian city of Genoa was chosen as the seat of the conference. More than any other country, Italy had wiped out the rancors of war. She seemed the most appropriate "hostess" for both victors and vanquished.

In postwar Europe, Italy adjoined on the continent France and Switzerland, which had no demands to make of her, a neutralized Austria, and a friendly and allied Yugoslavia. In the Mediterranean, neither France nor England was interested in troubling her, provided that she did not make trouble. She was not engaged, like France and England, in costly conflicts in the Near East. She had abstained from all intervention in Russia on the side of the White generals.

Italy had emerged from the First World War with her vital organs tired but unimpaired. If in her economic structure she was a sick person who was rapidly recovering from a serious but not mortal disease, in her international position she was like Molière's imaginary invalid: she was unhappy about sicknesses she did not have. She needed only a rest cure.

Instead of getting a rest cure, she got a treatment of Fascist strychnine which brought about twenty years of convulsions.

AUTHOR'S NOTE TO CHAPTER 3.

To credit the Fascist regime with "bringing order out of the chaos," all the journalists affiliated with Fascist propaganda have described the postwar crisis in the most appalling colors. A book soon embodied the Fascist version, Signor Villari's *Awakening of Italy*. Signor Villari did not need to worry about, or waste time on, conscientious and tiresome research and documentation. He only needed as rapidly as possible to put on the market a book which might become a handy source of information for whoever wanted to form an idea of Italian affairs, and *Awakening of Italy*, published at the beginning of 1924, met such a need and constituted what might be called the Fascist "Vulgate." Then the publishers of the *Encyclopedia Britannica* put their concern at Mussolini's service, and Signor Villari rehashed his "Vulgate" in the 1926 supplement (II, 558–571) and in the 1929 and 1938 editions of the Encyclopedia. Thus the Fascist version reached an immense public in all countries and become daily bread of any college professor who wanted, without any headaches, to become an "expert" in Italian recent history. One who wanted to collect all the misstatements which have been circulated about the history of Italy from 1919 on would be like one who wanted to empty the ocean with a spoon. We will limit ourselves to gathering a few flowers here and there to enable the readers to guess at the immense whole from some of its parts.

It has been repeated again and again that Mussolini, in October 1922, found a deficit of fifteen billion lire in the budget and that he brought it down to three billion during the first fiscal year of his own administration. To be sure, if we compare the deficits of the years 1919–22 with that of the first Fascist budget[19] we cannot but be struck by the contrast:

	DEFICIT		
1918–19	23,345	million	lire
1919–20	11,494	"	"
1920–21	20,955	"	"
1921–22	17,169	"	"
"March on Rome"			
1922–23	3,260	"	"

These figures, however, do not tell the whole story. The deficit which the dictatorship had to meet in its first fiscal year (1922–23) was not the deficit its predecessors had had to meet from July 1, 1921, to June 30, 1922. There may be a heavy deficit in a given fiscal year, while at the same time measures are taken which will in the following year result in a surplus. What an incoming cabinet inherits from its predecessor is not the deficit of the preceding fiscal year, but the revenue and expenditure of the current year. The enormous deficits in the years immediately following the war were due to the liquidation of the exceptional expenses connected with the war. In May 1923, Signor De Stefani, minister in Mussolini's cabinet from October 1922 to July 1925, pointed out this fact in the following words:

> The budget deficits of the last few years do not result solely from the discrepancy between current revenue and current expenditure, but from the fact that the deficits are swelled by many exceptional items dependent on the war. These instead of being acknowledged in the budgets of their own years weighed down the balance sheet of succeeding years. If the revenue and expenditure of 1921 are purged of all these items, the normal budget closes with a considerably smaller deficit. Also for 1922, the normal deficit is diminished to no small extent if the war claims are deducted.

[19] F. A. Repaci, *La finanza italiana nel ventennio 1913–1932* (Torino: G. Einaudi, 1934), p. 68.

Signor De Stefani took good care not to give definite figures.[20] If we search them out in the official documents in which they are buried, we find the following figures:[21]

	DEFICITS		EXCEPTIONAL EXPENDITURE DEPENDENT ON THE WAR	
1918–19	23,345	million lire	25,683	million lire
1919–20	11,494	" "	12,424	" "
1920–21	20,955	" "	22,329	" "
1921–22	17,169	" "	18,264	" "
"March on Rome 1922–23	3,260	" "	4,837	" "

This table shows that the deficits resulted solely from the exceptional war claims. The heaviest strain was felt in the four years immediately after the war. When in 1922–23 the strain relaxed, the deficit likewise fell.

It would be labor lost to look for a fair statement of these facts in the panegyrics of Fascist finance with which "propaganda" has inundated the world.

In May 1923, Signor De Stefani, while admitting that the deficit inherited by the new regime was "considerably smaller" than the figures shown in the budgets of 1920–21 and 1921–22, asserted:

> In the period immediately preceding the March on Rome, the feeling that the deficit was a permanent evil was general among the members of the government. The official documents of the time reflect their anxiety at the seriousness of

[20] De Stefani, *Documenti*, pp. 169–71. The Fascist deputy Signor Olivetti also admitted in 1925 that if one deducts from the budgets of 1921 and 1922 the liquidated war claims and the cost of the industrial undertakings entered into during the war for food, supplies, transport, etc. (which costs were wound up during these two years), the deficit for 1921 would be "notably less," and that for 1922 "also very much decreased" *(Relazione della Giunta del bilancio per gli esercizi dal 1912–13 al 1923–24* [Rome, 1925], p. 23. He also took good care not to give actual figures. Count Volpi, too, in his speech of December 9, 1926, referring to the decrease in war liabilities, did not quote definite figures. See also G. Matteotti, *Reliquie* (Milan: Corbaccio, 1924), pp. 120, 142, 174, 196, 205.

[21] The figures given here correspond neither to those given by G. Paratore (*Alcune note di politica monetaria* [Rome: Modernissima, 1925], pp. 49–54; and "La situazione economica e finanziaria Italiana," *Rassegna internazionale*, 1925, series 2, fasc. 4–6) nor to those given by the Banca Commerciale Italiana (*Movimento economico dell'Italia*, p. 160), nor to those given in the *Rendiconto Generale per l'esercizio 1925–26* (nota preliminare, pp. 104, 107, 112). My figures are drawn from the official Fascist publication *Il bilancio dello Stato dal 1913–14 al 1929–30*, and from Repaci, *La finanza italiana nel ventennio 1913–32*. All data, however, whichever their source, lead to the same conclusion.

the situation and their feeling that the forces of recuperation were inadequate. These forces were created by the humble *(sic)* volunteers of the New State.[22]

The "official documents" quoted in proof of this statement were the report of the parliamentary subcommittee on the budget estimates for 1923 (presented to the Chamber on June 28, 1922) and the survey of the financial situation made to the Chamber in July 1922 by Signor Peano, then minister of the treasury.

If one looks at these two documents, one finds in them no traces of despair, no "feeling that the forces of recuperation were inadequate," though there was no concealment as to the difficulties still remaining.

Here are some opinions of cabinet ministers and financial experts in the years preceding the "March on Rome." Signor Meda, then minister of the treasury, said in the Chamber on December 19, 1920:

> We are determined to surmount our difficulties and are convinced that it is not only necessary but also possible to do so. It is possible because our financial situation arises from exceptional conditions, not peculiar to Italy but shared by the whole world, and which cannot fail to improve in the not too distant future. The budget of 1921 points to an improvement on its predecessor and that of 1922 marks a first step in the decline of the deficit. Let there be no false hopes, but also no dejection in our souls and in our efforts.

In the Chamber on July 26, 1921, Signor De Nava, the successor of Signor Meda in the treasury, said:

> If we compare the deficit of 1921 with the more formidable ones of the preceding years, the situation, which was in all respects alarming, seems improving. But the figure in itself, and the crisis through which our industries and commerce are passing, show us that the hour of difficulty is not yet behind us, and that for several years to come we must fear a deficit, which will have to be met by incurring debts.

On December 8, 1921, he estimated that in the budget of 1923, the deficit would be reduced to no more than three thousand million. And so

---

[22] Speech of May 13, 1923: *L'opera finanziaria del Governo Fascista*, Rome, 1923, p. 17.

it turned out. On July 12, 1922, the eve of the "March on Rome," Signor Peano, the successor of Signor De Nava, rectifying in the Chamber his predecessor's figures, estimated for the following fiscal year a deficit of 3,998 million. He added:

> The most important financial circles in the world are not pessimistic about our financial and economic situation. This is proved by the fact that offers of loans have been repeatedly made to us by important English and American bankers. The government has not found it necessary to accept these offers, so as not to burden the international balance of our payments with new debts and because we think *aes alienum aeterna servitus.*

The "members of government" whom Signor De Stefani in May 1923 endowed with a pusillanimity designed to contrast unfavorably with Fascist heroism, reappeared three years later dressed up as "parliamentary experts" in Signor Villari's *Fascist Experiment:* "The parliamentary experts were convinced that the deficit was destined to reappear permanently in successive budgets, as there seemed to be no way of eliminating it."

How "amazing and dramatic" the financial situation was on the eve of the "March on Rome" is shown by concrete figures given by Count Volpi in a speech to the Senate on December 9, 1926: "The revolution of October 1922 inherited from the preceding governments a budget, which, in the June of that year, showed a deficit of 15,760 million."

No information about the exceptional expenses dependent on the war is to be found in C. E. McGuire's *Italy's International Economic Position.* No wonder, therefore, that he came to the conclusion that "to the Fascist administration is due full credit for this decisive improvement" in Italian finances (p.85).

In 1927, the "parliamentary experts" who had been invented by Signor Villari, in the hands of Mr. T.W. Lamont, partner of the Morgan Bank, became "one of the leaders of the party in power": "One of the leaders of the party in power declared at that time that a budget deficit was inevitable for an indefinite number of years."[23]

The case of Lamont deserves peculiar attention, owing to the authority

---

[23] *Survey Graphic,* New York, March 1927, p. 724.

of the man as a partner in one of the greatest banks of the world. In April 1925, he made the following correct statement:

> Immediately after the signature of the Peace Treaty, Italy undertook with great courage the rehabilitation of her national finances. The system of the country was reorganized in accordance with postwar needs and, without counting upon doubtful reparation payments, the Italian Finance Ministry set about covering all the current expenditures of the government by means of current revenue. As the result of this policy, Italian budgetary deficits were reduced from nearly fifteen billion lire in 1919 to about three billion lire in 1922.[24]

In 1927 he gave a quite different version:

> When the present regime (the Fascist regime) came into power towards the end of 1922, Italy seemed to be tottering on the brink below which lay communism and Bolshevism. ... The finances of the central government were unsound; government debt was piling up. ... Budgetary deficits had reached an alarming size though the previous governments had already effected a large reduction in the deficit. In the fiscal year 1920–21, two years before the present government came in, the deficit had been over seventeen billion lire. Through strict control of expenditure and by a courageous tax program this situation was brought under control. The deficit in 1922–23, the year of the advent to office of the present government, was reduced to about three billion lire.[25]

Thus Lamont ignored the claims dependent on the War of 1914–18 which had to be paid off, and he pronounced that previous to the March on Rome the public debt "was piling up" owing to the fact that Italian finances "were unsound."

In 1927 Lion wrote:

> The budget deficit of about 160 million lire in the fiscal year 1914 had grown to almost 23 billion in 1918–19. So ominous

[24] *Trade Bulletin of the Italy-America Society,* April 1925, pp.1–2.
[25] *Survey Graphic,* March 1927, pp. 723–24.

> were the prospects that De Nava, minister of the treasury,
> announced a *further* deficit of about 5 billion in the state
> budget, on July 26, 1921. The ominous gaps that previous
> administrations had made in the sides of the ship of finance
> were due to Bolshevist pressure intent on the destruction of
> capital.[26]

She was the first to discover that the deficit in the budget of 1918–19
had almost amounted to twenty-three billion and that "Bolshevist pressure" had made itself felt on the Italian government in that fiscal year when
a conservative cabinet was in power.

From Lamont's article, the "leader of the party" passed in 1928 into the
memoirs of Mussolini:

> Let us turn to the amazing and dramatic financial situation.
> A leader of the Liberal party in Parliament, Peano, six
> months before the March on Rome, had defined the deficit
> of our budget by a figure of more than six billions! The
> financial situation was then, according even to the declara-
> tion of our opponents, desperately serious. I know what a
> difficult inheritance I had received. It had come down to me
> as a legacy from the errors and weaknesses of those who had
> preceded me.[27]

The *London Times* of December 23, 1927, admitted that the effort to
wipe out the deficit resulting from the war had already been carried on with
remarkable success before the Fascists came into power:

> *As soon as the war was over,* the Italian government set
> about the difficult task of setting its house in order, and by
> the time Signor Mussolini came into power, the actual ex-
> cess of current expenditure over revenue had been reduced
> to a *comparatively small* sum. With admirable courage, Si-

---

[26] "The Economic Life of Fascist Italy," *Dublin Review,* October 1927, pp. 279–81.
[27] B. Mussolini, *My Autobiography* (New York: Charles Scribner's Sons, 1928), pp. 240–41.
This book was put on the market in England and in America in a folder on which the
facsimile of the autographic declaration of Mussolini was printed, stating that it was his
only authentic autobiography. A few years later, Mussolini himself stated that his "authentic" autobiography was a fraud, concocted with his consent by his brother Arnaldo
and former United States Ambassador Child (Mussolini, *Vita di Arnaldo* Rome; 1933,
pp. 124–25). The *duce's* brother was responsible for its lies and the former ambassador
for its stupidities. From now on we shall cite this book as Mussolini's *Pseudo-Autobiography.*

gnor De Stefani and his successor, Count Volpi, *continued to carry out the policy of their predecessors in office* and obtained a real balance which has been steadily maintained.

Thus the *Times*, in commending the courage of those who "continued" the work, said nothing of the courage of those who had reduced the deficit to a "comparatively small sum." The Italian press went a further step. Its report of the article ran: "The *Times* outlines the history of Italian financial restoration; above all the balancing of the budget, *initiated* with admirable courage by Signor De Stefani, and carried on by his successor Volpi" (*Corriere della Sera*, December 23, 1927).

If the financial history has been manhandled without pity, despite the fact that all in all it can be reconstructed from data easy to gather and check, one can guess what has been done with the economic history, which is much more complex and more difficult to interpret. Along our way we will come across the most gross and unscrupulous misstatements which have accumulated on this subject. Here it suffices us to give a few examples.

1 Count Volpi, while reviewing in the *Rassegna Italiana* (December 1925, pp. 786–87) the record of Italy, enveloped the monetary events of 1919–22 in the following smoke-screen: "The lira underwent violent agitations and this state of things lasted until the end of 1922. In the first half of 1922 the exchanges, compared with the first half of 1921, showed improvement. But they began to worsen again in the second half up until November." C.E. McGuire (*Italy's International Economic Position* [New York: Macmillan, 1926], p. 187), simply echoed Count Volpi: "After falling precipitately in 1919–20, the lira oscillated nervously until the winter of 1921–22."

2 McGuire (*Italy's International Economic Position*, pp. 39, 303–05), while admitting that in 1922 Italy's foreign debt did not increase, maintained that in 1921 she contracted foreign debts to the amount of about 3,800 thousand lire, but gives not the slightest proof of this. He simply asserts that the deficit in the trade balance of 1921 was only partly compensated by invisible exports and concludes that to pay the debt of 1921 she must have resorted to no less than

3.800 thousand lire of foreign loans. Thus he satisfies his will to believe that the economic convalescence of Italy began only when Mussolini came to power.

Even the credit for the *Enciclopedia Italiana* has been stolen from the pre-Fascist regime and attributed to Mussolini. In the *New York Times* of August 18 and 27, 1939, it was hailed as "the most monumental literary and scientific product of the Fascist regime." To be sure, its thirty-six volumes were published from 1929 to 1939 under Mussolini. But they were not written by infants who had been born and educated after 1922 under the influence of Mussolini. The encyclopedia was the work of Italian scholars who had been educated during the previous half-century in the schools of the free Italian regime. The Fascist environment made itself felt in the encyclopedia only in some fields, like contemporary history, political sciences, history of religion, history of the Catholic Church, and in all these cases it exerted a degrading influence.

From 1919 to 1921, the United States had among its commercial attachés in Italy a certain Mr. A.P. Dennis, who sent to Washington many reports that were published in the *Commercial Reports*. In none of these reports was Italy described as a country plunged in economic chaos and misery. The same Mr. Dennis, in August 1929, described the condition of Italy from 1919 to 1922 in the following terms:

> One's general impression of the black years of 1919, 1920 and 1921 were slackness—endless, tantalizing, heartbreaking slackness. Tens of thousands of soldiers still in uniform turned their hands to no useful account. Five husky laborers were employed by the state railways to do the work of two men. The country swarmed with beggars. Chaos, disorder, poverty reigned supreme. Lack of coal, lack of bread, worst of all lack of discipline. . . . Every man exercised not only the God-given liberty to talk but the license to act. One strike after another disheartened and demoralized the business enterprises of the country.[28]

Was Mr. Dennis lying in the period from 1919 to 1921, or in 1929?

In April 1927, Dr. Nicholas Murray Butler, president of Columbia University, described in the following terms the abyss out of which Mus-

[28] *World's Work*, August 1929.

solini had pulled Italy: "Six million Italians were one day without water to drink or with which to cleanse themselves. The railways had broken down, the postal service was wrecked, the roads were in disrepair; brigandage, anarchy, and crime were rampant everywhere."[29]

George Bernard Shaw, writing in the *Manchester Guardian* (October 28, 1927), stated bluntly that Italy during those years was not provided with "her daily material needs" and that Mussolini, as soon as he came into power (October 1922) brought "order out of chaos and compelled Italy to work and no longer to starve." Shaw did not need to give any evidence to substantiate his statement. He believes that "all truths ancient and modern are divinely inspired" and that he himself is one of the instruments of revelation. To be sure, he adds modestly, "I know by observation and introspection that the instrument on which the inspiring force plays, may be a very faulty one and may end by making the most ridiculous nonsense of his message." And he remarks, also with good reason, "I am often appalled at the avidity and credulity with which new ideas are snatched at and adopted without a scrap of sound evidence. People will believe anything that amuses them, gratifies them, or promises them some sort of profit."[30] There could be no better illustration of the truth of these remarks than his own statements about conditions in Italy before the March on Rome, if instead of "ideas" we substitute "facts"—a substitution which makes still more appalling the credulity of those who state them without a scrap of sound evidence.

Since one of the facts most consistently employed by those who describe Italy as starving from 1919 to 1922 is the great number of strikes, it would be well to bear in mind that strikes were common in all countries during the postwar years. In France, the railwaymen and the postal employees did not even wait for the end of the war before striking, whereas in Italy the railway and postal employees waited until 1920 to strike. In Italy, demobilization gave occasion to none of those seditious movements which broke out in the British army soon after the armistice, nor was there ever, as there was in England in September 1919, a general railway strike, which paralyzed the whole economic life of the country for nine days. In Belgium during 1919 and 1920, there were so many strikes that the *Revue du Travail*, an official publication of the government, had to devote twenty-

---

[29] N.M. Butler, *Looking Forward* (New York: Charles Scribner's Sons, 1932), p. 191.
[30] G.B. Shaw, *The Adventures of the Black Girl in Her Search of God* (London: Constable, 1932), p.59.

one columns of the index in its volume for 1920 to the enumeration of the strikes of the two preceding years. In the United States there were 2,665 strikes, with 4,160,000 strikers during 1919. A police strike, such as occurred in Boston, never took place in Italy.

4

Italian Backwardness
and "Volksgeist"

It would seem that the Italians should have felt no need of discarding free institutions just at the moment they should have been proud of the results they had achieved under them. What was to be expected was rather a step forward toward more advanced forms of democracy. How then did it happen that just at this moment they made room for a dictatorship?

If we agreed with the Marxists of the strict observance, there would be no ground for discussing such a matter. Political democracy, according to their view, is not "true, substantial" democracy, because the institutions of political or "formal" democracy become "truly" democratic only when they are supplemented with those of economic democracy. Soviet Russia alone is a "true" democracy, despite the fact that she has discarded the institutions of political democracy and owing to the fact that she professes to possess the institutions of economic democracy. As a consequence, Hitler and Roosevelt, Churchill and Mussolini, all past, present, and future rulers of peoples are or will be dictators unless they adopt communistic doctrine and practices. As a consequence, there was no breakdown of democratic institutions in Italy since there were no democratic institutions there. As a consequence there is no problem to be solved.

We do not wish to quarrel about words. But we do not wish to have our ideas mixed up by arbitrary use of words. The word "democracy" always has meant a political constitution which grants all citizens, without discrimination of social class, religious creed, race, or political affiliation, all

55

the personal rights (habeas corpus, freedom of thought, freedom of worship, the right to follow one's calling, etc.) and all the political rights (freedom of speech, of the press, of association, of assembly, of representation in local and national government, etc.). According to the traditional meaning of the word, a political constitution *is* democratic even if the lower classes are unable to take advantage of their political rights and privileges to strip the upper classes of their political and economic power, and so to pass from political to economic democracy. And according to the traditional meaning of the word, a dictatorial or totalitarian constitution is one which has discarded the personal and political rights of the subject. If one wants to break away from the traditional meaning of words and term as dictatorship what traditionally is termed political democracy, and so put into one single box Roosevelt and Hitler, Churchill and Mussolini, one does not understand anything any longer in human affairs unless one starts again putting into two different boxes dictatorship No. 1, let us say the United States, which has political but not economic democracy, and dictatorship No. 2, Nazi Germany, which has neither economic nor political democracy. Thus as regards Italy, the problem is whether her pre-Fascist regime is to be put under dictatorship No. 1 or dictatorship No. 2. We go on terming as democracy what the Marxists of the strict observance should term dictatorship No. 1. And that is all.

Signor Ferrero is of the opinion that Italy did not have a democracy but a political system intermediate between the old absolutistic governments and the democracies of France and Switzerland:

> Although Parliament performed various functions, all of great importance, it was nevertheless not a governing organ. It controlled the ministry to a certain extent; it was the mouthpiece, if not of the whole people, of numerous and widespread sections of opinion and of great interests; it served the statesmen as a kind of gymnasium in which to train themselves for the ministry. But the actual direction of public affairs lay elsewhere and descended from above, where was concealed what might be called "the oligarchy of the elders"—a little group of high officials and influential parliamentarians, all grown old. In order to be one of this group—and I begin to see that this perhaps was not a bad thing—it was necessary to have grey hair. This little group of oldish men was supported not only by Parliament, which always oscillated a little with each wave of public opinion,

but also, and more especially, by the two most solid organs of the state—the monarchy and the bureaucracy. It was this group which, invisible to outside observers, ruled the country and decided all matters of capital importance. They seemed to be controlled by Parliament and sought to act in accord with it so as to give it a share of their own responsibility, but when the occasion arose they knew how to thwart it and to bend it to their own will.

In short, the Italian political regime was a "paternal democracy," in which "thirty million individuals were governed by thirty individuals for the benefit of three hundred thousand families."[1]

This theory also would lead us to the conclusion that no democracy broke down in Italy, and that therefore there is no matter to worry about.

Ferrero's picture of pre-Fascist Italy is correct. His mistake springs from the fact that he assumes that in France (in 1925, when he was writing) or in Switzerland, or in any other countries for which he was willing to admit the existence of democratic institutions, things were taking place in an essentially different way from that of pre-Fascist Italy.

As a matter of fact, the French national elections of 1936 were carried on with the slogan: "Fight against the two hundred families" that were said to control the economic, financial, and political structure of the country. According to the opinion of G.K. Chesterton and many other observers, England is ruled by her weekend aristocracy. In 1938, many people in England complained that England's foreign policy was determined by a small circle of pro-German magnates, the "Cliveden set," so named after Lady Astor's country home where the leaders of the Conservative party gathered during their weekends to play charades. A book published in 1939 (Simon Haxey, *Tory M.P.* [London, Gollancz, 1939]) has collected convincing evidence to show that the M.P.s of the Tory party belong to a network of capitalist interests which have nothing to do with the masses of the British people; another book published in 1941 (H.E. Dale, *The Higher Civil Service of Great Britain* [Oxford University Press]) shows that no more than 600 men direct the 120,000 civil servants of Great Britain and act as a bridge between the administrative machine and the cabinet ministers, at the back of whom are the Tory M.P.s. Thus no more than 1,000 men actually rule Great Britain. A description of the American

---

[1] G. Ferrero, *La Democrazia Italiana* (Milano: Edizioni della Rassegna Internazionale, 1925), pp. 12–13, 16.

democracy given in 1938 was strikingly similar to that which Ferrero gave in 1925 of pre-Fascist Italy:

> The United States is owned and dominated by a hierarchy of sixty of the richest families, buttressed by no more than ninety families of lesser wealth. Outside this plutocratic circle there are perhaps three hundred and fifty other families, less defined in development and in wealth, but accounting for most of the incomes of $100,000 or more that do not accrue to members of the inner circle. These families are the living center of the modern industrial oligarchy which dominates the United States, functioning discreetly under a *de jure* democratic form of government behind which a *de facto* government, absolutist and plutocratic in its lineaments, has gradually taken form since the Civil War. This *de facto* government is actually the government of the United States—informal, invisible, shadowy. It is the government of money in a dollar democracy.[2]

There must be much of the truth in this picture since other writers have arrived at the same conclusions[3] and since, according to Secretary Ickes, America is witnessing a struggle to the finish between plutocracy and democracy, which will last "until America's sixty families or America's 120 million people win" (Address of December 30, 1937).

In no democratic regime is the government run by the whole or even by the majority of the population. It is conducted by that party which for the time being is upheld by the votes of the majority of the electorate, and this majority is not the majority of the whole population but only of that section of the population which is interested in politics to the extent of voting in elections. All parties are organized minorities which try to gain the support of the majority of the electorate, and this majority of the electorate in its turn is but a minority of the entire population. Again, within the minority in power there are more or less clandestine coteries who pull the strings behind the scenes. In totalitarian regimes things are not different. Yet a difference, and an essential one, does exist between an oligarchic or totalitarian regime and a democratic regime. Under an oligarchic or totalitarian regime, political rights (freedom of speech, of the

---

[2] F. Lundberg, *America's Sixty Families* (New York: The Vanguard Press, 1937), p.3.
[3] H. Agar and A. Tate, *Who owns America?* (Boston-New York: Houghton Mifflin Co., 1936); and A. Rochester, *Rulers of America* (New York: International Publishers, 1936).

press, of association and assembly) are legally the privileges of one minority which possesses a monopoly of power *by its own right.* A democratic constitution grants the same political rights to all citizens without distinction of class, religion, race, or political affiliation. Consequently, a democracy is a regime of free competition among free minorities, even in those countries where the masses are politically minded and organized. But this is no reason for regarding a democratic regime as identical with an oligarchic or a totalitarian regime. Under a democratic regime the electorate can dismiss the party in power and through the use of this political right they can make their impact felt upon the decisions of the ruling minority. Under an oligarchic or totalitarian regime that section of the population which is not enfranchised, or the whole population, do not have this power.

The free regime was created in Italy between 1848 and 1870 by an oligarchy of the upper classes. During the fifty years which followed the Risorgimento, the lower classes gradually raised themselves to a higher economic, intellectual, and moral level. As a consequence they demanded and got an ever-increasing share of economic and political influence. Ferrero himself writes that at the beginning of the present century "those thirty individuals and those three hundred thousand families" saw the middle and lower classes slowly awakening and beginning to exercise their own sovereignty:

> This awakening caused disturbance in the public mind, weakened the ruling oligarchy and led to the establishment of universal suffrage. . . . The war worked a revolution, because, by shaking up the middle and lower classes, it hastened their emancipation through universal suffrage. In the elections of 1919 and of 1921, those thirty individuals and those three hundred thousand families saw for the first time—and their blood froze in their veins—millions of electors voting according to their own conviction or caprice. This emancipation through universal suffrage was a fruit which sooner or later was bound to ripen.[4]

To be sure, there were weak spots in Italian political structure, and they have to be taken into account if the breakdown of democratic institutions in Italy has to be explained. As we shall see, the working of Parliament had become more and more unsatisfactory. But Parliament is but one of the

[4] Ferrero, *La Democrazia in Italia*, pp. 17, 21–22.

institutions of democracy. During the half-century of free regime, liberty of the press, of speech, and of association had taught large sections of the electorate to rise above personal interests and local prejudices. The people were taking an ever-increasing interest in public life. The widest newspaper circulation in 1880 had been only 25,000 copies a day; in 1914 it was 600,000. Between 1860 and 1880 not more than 250,000 voters went to the polls. In the parliamentary elections of 1913, five million voters went to the polls. In southern Italy elections were vitiated by pressure and violence on the part of the government, but public life was honest and decent in northern Italy.

In Italy during the World War there were never any cases of savage persecution against the adversaries of the war as such, as occurred in America. There were no suppressions of newspapers, condemnations to thirty years' imprisonment for the crime of pacifism, dismissal of teachers, embargo on the teaching of German, and other forms of imperfect liberal training. The writer of the present book during those years openly criticized the foreign policy of the government and stubbornly opposed the plan to annex Dalmatia to Italy, and there never was the least idea that he could have been dismissed from his post as a university teacher. If this is not democracy—imperfect democracy, to be sure, democracy in the making—nobody will ever know what democracy really is.

To be sure, universal suffrage, the characteristic feature of a democratic constitution, was enacted in Italy only in 1912. Until 1881 the franchise had been granted only to those males who were twenty-five years of age or over, who paid at least forty lire (eight dollars) a year in direct taxes, and who could read and write. In that year, the enfranchised numbered 622,000 —that is, 2.2 percent of the population; under a system of universal male suffrage, about 30 percent of the population would have had a right to vote. In 1882 the franchise was extended to those males who were at least twenty-one years of age and could read and write, regardless of whether they paid any direct taxes; but if the citizen was not registered among the taxpayers he had to prove that he had at least attended the third grade in a municipal school. Thus 2,112,000 (7.39 percent of the population) were registered, and between 1882 and 1912 the number increased to 3,329,000 or 9.28 percent of the population. In 1912, a fresh electoral reform took place which extended the franchise to all males who were either more than thirty years of age or had served in the army or navy, regardless of whether they could read and write. It was felt that experience of life is more important than a knowledge of reading and writing. Millions of peasants were still illiterate, yet they had been to America and had returned home with their savings and with a greater experience of life than, for example, a young gentleman who read French novels and had never yet faced in his life a greater practical difficulty than that of arranging his necktie in front of his mirror. Thus the electorate jumped to 8,672,000, or 24.2 percent of the population. But if universal suffrage was slow in coming, the other institutions of political democracy were half a century old.

Even fairminded observers have accepted and spread the opinion that the Italians were not interested in using their political rights, and they give as evidence of their indifference the low percentage of Italian voters on election day.[5] And it is a fact that the citizens who went to the polls in Italy on election day fluctuated betwen 55 and 60 percent of the eligible voters.[6] The significance of this fact appears when one bears in mind that:

1 There exists no people under the sun who possess such a perfect education that everybody, none excepted, goes to the polls on election day. In the United States, in the 1932 presidential election, only 40 million voters cast their ballots, namely 57 percent; in 1936, 45.8 million, or 62 percent; and in 1940, 49.6 million, or 65 percent.

2 In the United States, the citizen registers during the electioneering campaign in the place where he resides, under the heat of political controversy. In Italy the citizen was registered by the town clerk in the place where he was born, and had to cast his ballot there, unless during the month of December he foresaw an oncoming electioneering campaign and sent in an application to the clerk to have his registration transferred to his present residence. Thus many civil servants, businessmen, and workers who were not in their birthplaces on election day would have had to make long and costly trips to cast their ballots. This led to many

---

[5] B. King and T. Okey, *Italy To-day* (London: Nisbet & Co., 1901), pp. vi, 14–15; H. Finer, *Mussolini's Italy* (London: Gollanz, 1935), pp. 65–66; M. Hentze, *Pre-Fascist Italy* (London: Allen & Unwin Ltd., 1939), pp. 40–41.

[6] Signor Bruno Roselli, speaking before the New York Foreign Policy Association on January 22, 1927 (*Italy under Fascism*, p.10), said: "Sixty percent of possible voters never were willing to avail themselves of the privilege which was given them." He gave sixty percent as the number, not of those who went, but of those who did not go to the polls.

abstentions. Again, those who were serving their three years of compulsory military service could not vote and were given as absentees in statistics. When the first election by universal male suffrage took place in 1913, many millions of workers were earning their livelihood as emigrants in Austria, Germany, Switzerland, France, the Mediterranean basin, North and South America. Thus in 1913 no more than 60.4 percent and in 1919 56.6 percent, of the registered voters went to the polls. If one bears in mind these circumstances, one has to conclude that the percentage of Italian voters compares not unfavorably with that in England, which, as a rule, is around 78–80 percent.

In 1903, in the weekly *Minerva*, a political writer, Federico Garlanda, made the following remarks:

All citizens among us discuss politics. Every respectable Italian spends one or two hours a day at a cafe discussing politics until he is out of breath. One supports the left, another supports the right. One talks republicanism, another socialism. But if you ask each one of those spirited debaters—Please, which is your party?—you may be sure that 99 times out of 100 the answer will be: I belong to no party.

Discussing politics too much is perhaps not an indication of wisdom. But it certainly is not an indication of indifference. Vice versa, belonging to no party might be regarded as wisdom. The only thing one cannot truthfully say is that the Italians were indifferent to politics.

During the years of the civil war and terror, 1921–26, the anti-Fascists in Italy lost 4,000 men and women in their stubborn resistance to the Fascist onslaught. This is hardly evidence that they were not interested in upholding their political liberties. When the premises of a paper were burned down by the Fascists, its readers were quick to send subscriptions so that the premises could soon be reestablished. This hardly shows that they were not interested in upholding the freedom of the press. To be sure, the masses of the Italian people had not reached the same level of political maturity that could be observed in Switzerland, Belgium, Holland, the Scandinavian countries, England, and even France. But no people has ever found a perfect democratic education ready-made in its cradle. England and France were politically backward before they became what they were at the beginning of the present century. In the time of the Duke of Wellington, the English parliamentary system was still an awkward compound of incoherent privileges and corrupt practices. If backwardness is the explanation of Fascism, England in 1832 should have given birth to a Fascist dictatorship and not to the Reform Act. From 1871 to 1877, there was always a danger in France that the democratic republic would collapse and that the country would revert to some form of absolutism. Why, instead of falling back toward a despotic regime, did France pass to a democratic regime? And why, in 1940, did that democratic regime disastrously collapse? Was France more backward in 1940 than in 1877? If backwardness were the explanation of Fascism, Italy should have developed Fascism when she was more backward than in 1922. She should not even have tried free institutions, but have remained somnolent and prostrate under her old despotic governments. In any case, why did she put an end to her free institutions, not in 1880, let us say, but forty years later? The Fascist movement did not originate in southern Italy, the most backward part of the country, but in northern Italy, which had reached a level of civilization not very far from that of the central European countries. Backward southern Italy succumbed to Fascism only after north Italian Fascism had come into power.

Before 1933, an explanation of Italy's "backwardness" and unfitness for democracy was seen by some persons in the fact that Italy was a Roman Catholic country. A Roman Catholic mentality is regarded in Protestant countries as a "backward" mentality. However, after the Weimar Republic broke down in Germany, in 1933, it was impossible to ignore the fact that Germany was more than half Protestant and that the German Protestants did not make a better showing in fighting Nazism than the Catholics. Nobody could have said that Germany was a "backward" country. When Hitler came into power, an American review expressed confidence that the German labor movement was too solidly founded to be shattered by government brutality or swerved from its course by nationalist intoxication: "Hitler will not be able to ride roughshod over Social Democrats, Communists, and trade-unions as did Benito Mussolini in the less industrially developed Italy."[7] Experience showed that German trade unions were "coordinated"

---

[7] *The New Republic*, March 15, 1933.

with less resistance than Italian trade unions in a less industrially developed country. The Italians stubbornly withstood the Fascist onslaught for four full years after Mussolini had come into power. And so far as the nationalist intoxication is concerned, German trade unions in the Saar, the most industrialized region in the world, gave 92 percent of their votes to Hitler in the plebiscite of 1934—a free plebiscite. We do not recall these facts in order to show that Germany was more "backward" than Italy. We want only to make clear that the victory of Fascism or Nazism cannot be explained by "backwardness" in either Italy or Germany.

After conquering Italy and Germany, Fascism made its appearance in France, Belgium, England, the United States, and Canada—countries which nobody dares to brand as "backward," and in 1940 a Fascist dictatorship, the Vichy regime, arose in France. (We leave out of consideration Austria, Poland, Yugoslavia, Rumania, Greece, Hungary, and other countries, which were blessed with more or less coherent forms of dictatorship, since they were regarded as "backward" and therefore would have little bearing upon the present discussion.) After these experiences, few Americans, Englishmen, and Frenchmen repeat any longer today what was a common slogan a few years ago: "It can't happen here," "*Chez nous ça ne peut pas arriver.*" Almost extinguished is the race of those just men who believed that they were under the particular protection of the Almighty, that the Fascist hailstorm would lay waste only their neighbor's field, and that Nazi typhoid fever would strike only the house opposite theirs. Whether we like it or not, Fascism is not a peculiar feature of "backward" countries but is a universal phenomenon, the explanation of which is to be sought elsewhere than in "backwardness."

An Englishman of high intelligence, and a great authority on the history of the Italian Risorgimento, has remarked that the Italian cities of the Middle Ages were not acquainted with representative government, and has found in this fact the key to understanding why Italy went Fascist:

> The city governed the surrounding district despotically. It was itself governed by its direct democracy, or by its own oligarchy, or by its own dictator. When it changed its government, it did so not by a general election, but by a row in the piazza. The citizens gathered together and clubbed some unpopular person, or pulled down his house. . . . And so, in the autumn of 1922, while we were putting a conservative government in power by holding a general election, the

> Italians achieved a similar object by a series of rows in the piazza all over Italy, culminating in a grand national "row in the piazza"—Signor Mussolini's march on Rome. . . . People sometimes ask me, why could the Italians have not effected the change of government that they desired by means of a general election? . . . I reply by pointing the inquirer to their social and political history, which had unfitted them for expressing themselves by means of a general election. It is really very difficult for thirty or forty millions of people to get the government they desire by means of a general election, unless they are to the manner born. We have this obscure inherited instinct. The Italians have it not. . . . How then do the Italians naturally express their wishes? I have already told you—through a concourse of citizens in each city. When the soul, the mind, or the passions of the Italian people require to have vent, they find it in a row in the piazza.[8]

All this is lively and well written. But it overlooks a great deal of pertinent fact.

In 1183, thirty-two years before the birth of Magna Charta, the Italians wrested from Emperor Frederick Barbarossa the Treaty of Constance, which granted self-government to all the cities of northern Italy, whereas the English Magna Charta contained the rights and privileges of only a handful of feudal barons. What was the English "obscure instinct" doing in 1183? Why did it awaken only in 1215? During the thirteenth century, while England's "instinct" was taking its first, insecure steps toward the representation of the merchants in Parliament, the lower middle classes in northern and central Italy were trying to gain control of their city governments and abolished serfdom among the peasantry.

They did not succeed in establishing a parliamentary regime. There were many "rows in the piazza" everywhere. But were the Wars of the Roses, perchance, fought on the moon and not in the streets of England? Italian social struggles led to despotic institutions. Tyrants arose everywhere in Italy. But was Henry VIII a constitutional king before whom Italian tyrants had any reason to feel humble? Was the revolution of 1648 anything else but a "grand row" in the streets of England? And was the revolution of 1688 brought about by a parliamentary election?

---

[8] G.M. Trevelyan, *The Historical Causes of the Present State of Affairs in Italy.* Sydney Ball memorial lecture delivered before the University of Oxford, October 31, 1923 (London: H. Milford, 1923), pp. 7–9.

English "obscure instinct" worked rather badly even as far as later times are concerned. Any high school boy would flunk if he did not have at his fingers' ends the fact that in England only in 1807 was the slave trade legally forbidden, and slavery was not abolished in the British colonies until 1833; that the trade union right was granted to laborers only in 1824 and Catholics were emancipated only in that same year; that during the first three decades of the nineteenth century the municipal corporations, thanks to a voting system even more absurd than that prevailing in parliamentary elections, were controlled by petty, ignorant, inefficient, and often dishonest oligarchies; that the Reform of 1832 granted the franchise to no more than half of the middle classes; that even after 1832 the English elections continued for many years to be characterized by bribery and other manifold forms of corruption; that only after 1839 did the pressgang fall into disuse; that in 1844 the home secretary still searched private correspondence and there does not yet exist a law forbidding such practices; that only in the second half of the nineteenth century did the freedom of the press become secure; that only in 1853 were the newspaper duties repealed, which made newspapers costly and consequently less accessible to the lower classes; that the Jews obtained the right to sit in either House only in 1866; that only in 1867 were the rest of the middle classes and the city laborers enfranchised; that the field laborers had to wait until 1885 to be enfranchised; that until 1872 the vote was public so that the tenant farmers had to vote according to the dictates of their landlords; that only in 1918 was the plural vote, which gave a substantial advantage to property, abolished; that among the working classes as late as in 1841, not one boy out of ten and not one grown person in fifty could read and write; that only in 1833 did Parliament grant 20,000 pounds sterling to help the local bodies in the construction of elementary school buildings, only in 1856 was a ministry of education established, and only in 1870 did popular education begin to become organized in a well-knit system. One does not know whether by parliamentary "obscure instinct" one has to explain the fact that in 1914 an unlawful army of "volunteers" sprang up in northern Ireland among Englishmen with the avowed program of opposing Home Rule by force if Parliament enacted it, and that the leaders of the British Conservative party approved of such an antiparliamentary threat. When, in 1920, the British government sent the "Black and Tans" to teach the Irishmen how to behave, were they—the British government and not the Irish—prompted by that parliamentary "obscure instinct," the monopoly on which has been vested by the

Almighty in the English? It does not seem that the "Black and Tans" gave evidence of their parliamentary "obscure instinct" in the drawing rooms of their own sweethearts sipping cups of tea rather than by "rows" in the Irish streets. The clashes which broke out in the autumn of 1936 between Fascists and anti-Fascists in Leeds, London, and Liverpool, when many combatants were taken to hospitals, were no more nor less than "rows" in the streets and not contests by ballots.

Bees, ants, and newborn babies instantly perform their instinctive motions which are perfectly adapted to their aims. This has never been the case with English "instinct." The English people has had to win its democratic institutions during centuries of conscious moral and intellectual effort, errors and trials, successes and failures, ups and downs, forward and backward movements, frictions and often tremendous waste.

The German philosophers and historians of the first half of the nineteenth century fancied that each people has been endowed with deepseated instincts of its own which control its development and explain its history. Everybody knew that in the Italy of the Middle Ages the Guelphs and the Ghibellines used to murder each other in the streets, for which reason Romeo and Juliet could not marry and came to a pitiful end. Everybody knew also that in the Renaissance Caesar Borgia and many other tyrants had been in control over the Italian people. The case of England was just the opposite, for everybody knew that she had received Magna Charta in 1215. Thus, Italian "Volksgeist" was tyrannical, while English "Volksgeist" was parliamentarian. Liberal German historians who admired English free institutions announced that the thirst for liberty was an essential feature of Teutonic English instinct. Why the Teutonic liberal "Volksgeist" performs its wonders in a country like England, inhabited by a crossbreed of Celts and Teutons, instead of developing in Germany, where the Teutonic race had remained (so they said) unmixed with its "Volksgeist," nobody ever bothered to explain. Now that Germany has become a totalitarian country, German professors will find out that the pure Aryan "Volksgeist" is not parliamentarian but totalitarian.

The longer the history of a people, the more numerous and manifold are the forms of "Volksgeist" which can be traced in it. Who more faithfully embodied Italian "natural character" or "obscure instinct," Julius Caesar or Romulus Augustus, Saint Francis of Assisi or Casanova, Dante or Machiavelli, Manzoni or D'Annunzio, Toscanini or Mussolini? What is there in common between the instincts of the English in the time of the Saxon kings and the time of David Lloyd George? The English national character, when Henry VIII married six wives one after the other, was not the same as that which forced Edward VIII to abdicate because he wanted to marry a lady who already had had no more than two husbands. If there were a breakdown of democracy in the United States, it would be easy to find proofs of North American Fascist "Volksgeist" in the Ku Klux Klan, Huey Long, Major Hague, the Vigilantes, the Black Legion, the company unions, Father Coughlin, the Roman Catholic bishop of Brooklyn, New York, the lynching of Negroes, etc.

We are far from disputing the fact that at given moments each group of mankind presents given features of its own, not only physical but also psychological. What we do dispute is that an historical development can be explained by "instinct" or "Volksgeist" of "national character." Any lazy mind, as soon as there is somewhere a hole in our knowledge of causes, can stop that hole by one of these words. We must not delude ourselves into believing that we have solved an historical problem when we have cloaked up our ignorance by a tautological fallacy, not seldom springing from nationalistic self-complacency.

If one wants to understand why democratic institutions collapsed in Italy or in France and are in jeopardy everywhere, one has to set aside a priori schemes and empty slogans and must ascertain why and how the Fascist movement arose in a given country, what social groups contributed to it, why and how the struggle between Fascists and anti-Fascists developed, and why and how the Fascists overcame their foes.

We propose such a work for Italy. Here is a problem that deserves a close scrutiny. An inquiry into the origins and development of what was the first outbreak of Fascism in Europe is essential to an understanding of this portent not only in Italy but in all other countries.

5

The
Political Setup in 1914

To understand Italian events in the years when the breakdown of democratic institutions took place, it is necessary to form an idea of which political groups held the ground before the war and had to face the war and the postwar crisis.

In 1914, there was in the Chamber of Deputies a government majority of about 370 out of 508 representatives; outside that majority there were 17 "Republicans," 28 "Reformist Socialists," 50 "Official Socialists," 6 "Nationalists," and about 30 "Conservatives."

The republican tradition of the Risorgimento was still alive in some constituencies, especially in central Italy, and it produced the Republican representatives. But none of them were prepared to spill a single drop of blood to bring about any republic.

The "Reformist" Socialists corresponded to those who, in France, were headed by Jaurès, who in England formed the bulk of the Labour party, and who in Germany were termed "Revisionists." They advocated a gradual, peaceful process of social transformation and, when useful, compromises with the "bourgeois" democratic parties. Their leader was Leonida Bissolati.

The "Official" Socialists consisted of a right and a left wing. To the right wing belonged the most influential chiefs of the trade unionist movement and almost all the fifty deputies, whose leader was Filippo Turati. They were no less "reformist" than those of whom we have spoken just now, but they were not prepared to break away from their old party, in which, since 1912, the left wing had gotten the upper hand. They professed to bow to the will of the majority in the party, hoping that they would change their minds and adopt again the reformist point of view.

The left wing termed themselves "revolutionary" Socialists. They were waiting for the "great day" on which the "proletariat" would make a clear sweep of "capitalism." As a consequence they rejected any compromise with the "bourgeois" parties. They corresponded to the Independent Labour party of Britain or to the majority of the German Sozial-Demokraten, who clung to the Marxian doctrine as expounded by Kautsky.

Benito Mussolini was the leader of the Revolutionary Socialists. He had become chief editor of the *Avanti* in 1912. He was even more to the left than the Italian Socialist left itself. He was in Italy what Lenin was at that time in Switzerland among the Russian emigrees, Hervé in France, and Karl Liebknecht in Germany. Rather than a Socialist, he was an Anarchist.

In July 1910, an Anarchist threw a bomb at the public of the Colon Theater in Buenos Ayres. Mussolini wrote in the weekly *Lotta di Classe (Class War)*, of which he was editor, under the date of July 9, 1910:

> I admit without discussion that in normal times bombs do not belong to socialist methods. But, when a government—be it Republican, Imperial or Bourbon—gags you and puts you beyond the pale of humanity, then one cannot condemn violence in reply to violence, even if it makes some innocent victims.

In the number of July 16, 1910, he insisted:

> In the Colon Theater, on that famous gala evening, all those present represented government reaction. Why call the bomb-thrower a coward simply for disappearing into the crowd? Did not even Felice Orsini attempt to hide? And did not the Russian terrorists, when their *coup* had been carried out, try to avoid arrest? Are they heroic madmen who carry out individual action? They are heroes nearly always, but scarcely ever insane. Was Angiolillo a madman? Was Bresci a madman? Or Sofia Perowskaja? No! Their behaviour drew words of admiration even from bourgeois journalists of high intelligence. In judging these men and their acts, we must

not place ourselves on the mental plane of the bourgeois and the police. It is not we socialists who must cast a stone. Let us acknowledge instead that individual acts have also their value and sometimes are the first signals of profound social transformations.

Angiolillo was the Anarchist who, in 1897, killed the Spanish minister Canovas del Castillo, and Bresci was the Anarchist who killed King Humbert in July 1900.

After the assassination of the Russian minister Stolypin, Mussolini wrote in the *Lotta di Classe* of September 23, 1911:

A just Nemesis struck him down. He was an oblique, sinister and bloodthirsty individual. He deserved his fate. The Russia of the proletarians is now exultant, and waits for dynamite to shatter the bones of the Little Father with the blood-stained hands. The tragic end of the minister of Nicholas II is perhaps the beginning of a new period of revolutionary action. We hope so. In the meantime, all honor to the avenger who has fulfilled the sacred rite.

In March 1912, the Anarchist Alba attempted to shoot the present king of Italy, wounding instead a *cuirassier* in the royal retinue. A group of Reformist Socialist deputies led by Bissolati went to congratulate the king on his escape. At the national Socialist congress in the following July, Mussolini censured them severely and had them expelled from the party. He said:

On March 14 a mason fired his revolver at Victor of Savoy. There were clear precedents for this—that of Bresci and that of Elizabeth of Austria. It might have been hoped that nowadays no Workers' Organization would hang out flags on such an occasion. Clever people should not have let themselves be influenced by sentiment. An attempt on life is an accident which happens to kings just as falling off a bridge is an accident which happens to masons. If we are to shed tears, let us shed them for the masons. Instead of which we had an acrobatic performance. . . . Bissolati went to congratulate the king.[1]

[1] Speech pronounced by Mussolini at the sitting of July 13, 1912, and published in his weekly *Lotta di Classe,* July 13, 1912.

In a speech at Milan on July 22, 1913, he stated: "This proletariat needs a bath in blood." On June 12, 1914, after a week of serious disorder in central Italy, he wrote in the daily *Avanti* of which he was then the chief editor: "We register these events with a little of that justifiable joy which an artist feels when he contemplates his creation. If the Italian proletariat is in the act of acquiring a new mentality, freer and wilder than of old, this is due to our newspaper."

He had and still preserves the marks of an intellectual development that had taken place in disorderly manner amid the turbulent vicissitudes of an impecunious youth, through the hasty readings of newspapers and pamphlets of propaganda, under the goal of having to solve from day to day, no matter where, how, when, not the problem of intellectual growth, but that of material existence. But in stirring up strikes, promoting street demonstrations, and addressing revolutionary mass meeting, he had learned how to arouse and calm at will the emotions of mobs. His philosophic and political conceptions might be reduced to one word: "violence." Through all his inconsistencies, he has remained faithful to that philosophy. Movement, action, audacity, "living dangerously"—these have always been and still are his methods and his slogans.

In June 1914, a Reformist Socialist and future prime minister, Signor Bonomi, painted the following picture of Mussolini:

> For this fierce son of Romagna, the proletariat of Italy is still a sentimental young boy, who goes into tantrums, but who gives in finally when he is spanked. Therefore, one must treat him with a currycomb and drive him forward with kicks. A bleeding is necessary to recreate the blood of the people of Italy. Let the "historic day" come, therefore, the day of battle when the proletariat will find the consciousness of its material force behind the barricades and in the fighting through the streets. Nothing matters now except to win. What matters is to triumph over timidity, fear and prudence which impede and arrest the revolutionary push forward of the proletariat.[2]

The Nationalist party had been formed in 1910 by a group of writers and politicians coming from the intellectual lower middle classes: Luigi Feder-

---

[2] I. Bonomi, *Dieci Anni di Politica Italiana* (Milano: Società Editrice Unitas, 1924), pp. 17–18.

zoni, Alfredo Rocco, Enrico Corradini, Roberto Forges-Davanzati, Francesco Coppola, Maurizio Maraviglia, Paolo Orano, all of whom were destined to become high personnages in the Fascist regime. While Corradini had started in 1896 as an out-and-out Conservative and imperialist, most of the others had entered public life a little later, between 1900 and 1905, as followers of the French Revolutionary Syndicalist Georges Sorel. The proletariat must organize themselves in their trade unions (in French *syndicats*) outside the political and administrative machine created by the "bourgeoisie"; they must entrench themselves in their own organizations as in fortresses from which to wage their class war: the trade unions must act as the cornerstones of the new "syndicalist" society in opposition to the old democratic and parliamentary structure, so as to be able to do away with it on the day of social revolution and enact the dictatorship of the proletariat; the proletariat must emancipate itself from electoral delusions, parliamentary compromise, evolutionist and legal tactics, and the Reformist Socialist leaders.[3]

Their gospel did not find much attention among the trade unions or in the Socialist party. They soon got tired of preaching to deaf ears and jumped from syndicalism to nationalism, even in this following the example of their master, Georges Sorel, who, between 1907 and 1910, turned to the nationalists and monarchists of the *Action Française*. Their new doctrine was but an Italian version of the Prussian state-worship—a "state" deified as the absolute entity before which individual rights count for nothing. To be fair to them, one has to point out that they had never read either Hegel or Treitschke. The Prussian doctrine had come to them through French channels. Their immediate masters were the French Nationalists Barrès, Daudet, and Maurras. The French Nationalists were advocating an antiparliamentary monarchical restoration. They neither believed nor practiced the Catholic religion. But they regarded the organization of the Catholic Church as a great international force and advocated an alliance between state and Church not only to put up a common front against socialism, but also to enhance the influence of France all over the world. The Italian Nationalists did not need any monarchical restoration, but they also advocated the alliance between state and Church against socialism and in competition with the French Nationalists. The French Republic had broken with the Church and had given up the place of the elder daughter

[3] G. Guy-Grand, *La Philosophie Syndicaliste* (Paris: Grasset, 1911); L.L. Lorwin, "Syndicalism," in *Encyclopedia of the Social Sciences*, 14: 496–99.

of the Church which France had once filled. It was for Italy to take that place and, backed by the Catholic Church, to extend her influence throughout the world. An addition (which was peculiarly Italian) to the French system was the discovery that there are in this world "capitalist" and "proletarian" nations, that between "proletarian" nations and "capitalistic" nations there exists an eternal strife similar to the "class struggle" that divides capitalists and proletarians in industrial societies. Italy was a poor and prolific—that is, a "proletarian"—nation. The strife of proletarian Italy against the capitalist nations should supersede the struggle among classes within the nation. If she wished to survive, Italy had to string together all her strength, marshal her "human material" with an iron hand, arm herself to the utmost, and at the right moment attack some capitalist nation weakened by opulence and strip it of its colonies, its mines, its oil wells. They spoke with great emphasis of "Greater Italy" and of the Roman eagles flying again over the whole Mediterranean basin and beyond the Alps. They announced that no human force could ever thwart the imperial destiny of Italy. They urged the creating of a war spirit in the young Italian generation. They insisted upon immediate action, no matter how and where, with a heroic nonchalance of dangers. Into this system of thoughts and emotions the poet D'Annunzio injected a stream of morbid sensuality.

The Nationalists were, first of all, anti-Socialists, for the Socialists were pacifist, internationalist, and hostile to military expenditure and warlike adventure. They were also against parliamentary institutions, for they had no hope of carrying out their plans in a country which was anything but warlike and with a parliament which could not defy the sentiments of the country. When they shifted from the extreme revolutionary left to the extreme conservative right, the only thing they had to do was to attack democracy from the right with the same weapons they had learned to wield when attacking it from the left.

If the Fascist movement has a coherent doctrine, it is due to the fact that the Fascists took over wholesale the Nationalist doctrine. Mussolini himself, during the very first years of his political career, shared the whole of the Syndicalist doctrine. He only was slower in evolving from syndicalism to fascism. While Federzoni, Maraviglia, Forges-Davanzati took the jump much earlier and in 1910 joined Corradini in forming the Nationalist party, Mussolini did not break away from the Socialist party before the autumn of 1914, and only in 1921 did he openly pass over to the Nationalist side of the trench.

The Nationalists found favor among the officers of the army and navy and the leaders of the Foreign Office. They advocated economic self-sufficiency, to be achieved through high tariff duties, as the indispensable means to prepare for war. Therefore they were supported financially by the big industrialists, who, thanks to high protective tariffs and contracts with the government, were thriving at the expense of the consumers and the taxpayers.

The influence of the Nationalist party in the country was wider and deeper than its parliamentary representation would show. Most of its leaders were men of exceptional political shrewdness and endowed with the fire of youth. They all were penniless, but they were backed financially by wealthy people, and therefore they could devote the whole of their time to political activities. Last but not least, the Italian upper, middle, and intellectual classes were all imbibed with a "nationalistic" state of mind. Streams of "nationalistic" thoughts and emotions were to be found even among the Republicans of the extreme left. Let us remember that that mentality which we today call "nationalistic" or "imperialistic" was a peculiar appanage not of the conservative but of the democratic parties in continental Europe during the first half of the nineteenth century, and that only during the second half of the century and during the present century did it become incorporated with the doctrines of the conservative parties. Therefore the appeals of the out-and-out Nationalist politicians evoked wider response than might have been believed by people who stopped at the surface of Italian political life. Journalists more or less closely connected with the Nationalist movement were to be found on the staffs of the most important daily papers, like the *Corriere della Sera* of Milan, the *Stampa* of Turin, the *Giornale d'Italia* of Rome.

The thirty Conservatives who formed an opposition group at the right of the Chamber, and who were led by Antonio Salandra and Sidney Sonnino, at the bottom of their hearts were out and out nationalists, regarded the Nationalist party as the spearhead of what should have been a consistently Conservative party. In 1920 they officially merged with the Nationalist party.

Among the 370 deputies who formed the government coalition there were twenty-nine Catholic deputies. The strength of the Catholics in the country was greater than one might surmise from the number of their representatives. It was estimated that in the national election of 1913, no less than two hundred deputies had begged for and received the support of the Catholics and had pledged themselves with the bishops not to vote for any law which might be regarded as obnoxious to the Vatican.

The Republicans, Socialists, Nationalists, and Catholics had national organizations, which centralized directorates and programs officially agreed upon by national conventions. All the other deputies who formed the bulk of the government coalition were lacking a national organization. They depended on local organizations in their constituencies. In their ranks there was a "more conservative right" and a "more democratic left."

The politicians of the "more conservative right" termed themselves "Liberals." But the term "liberal" in Italy no longer possessed the anticlerical significance which it had had in the first half of the nineteenth century on the European continent, nor was it synonymous with "democratic" as in England. The Italian "Liberal" of the first decade of the twentieth century was a politician whose predecessors, half a century ago, had been "Liberal" and had fought against the privileges of the Catholic clergy; but now they had become good "Conservatives" who refrained from controversies and activities which might create friction with the Catholics. Their "liberalism" consisted in advocating religious liberty for the Catholic Church against whoever would have liked to start another anticlerical fight.

The politicians of the "more democratic left" were used to term themselves "Democrats," but their democracy was content with the *status quo.* They were suspicious of the attempts which the Conservatives might make to curtail those political liberties that had already been attained. They were suspicious of the Catholic clergy, and if any clerical danger had materialized, they would not have opposed an anticlerical tide with the same eagerness as the "Liberals." And they were no less suspicious of the Socialists. Their democracy was no longer "progressive." It had become static.

There were among them seventy "Radicals" who professed to be the heirs of those Radicals who, during the nineteenth century, had advocated more profound political and social reforms than the "Liberals" had been prepared to enact. And to be sure, a few of them were "Radicals" in dead earnest and, like the English Radicals, advocated free trade, decentralization, retrenchment of expenditure, and a policy of international understanding. But they were badly looked upon by their colleagues. The latter had grown wise. They were as much "radical" as the "Liberals" were liberal. They kept their label more for the sake of a tradition which still remained alive in large sections of the electorate, than as a result of real disagreement with the "more democratic" but static left. In actual fact, they were but a section of the government coalition, and lent a certain number of their men to all cabinets. The French "Radicals" of the 1910–40 years were no more "radicals" than the Italian ones.

There were no clearcut lines of division between right and left, but many shades of thought or lack of thought went from the out-and-out Conservatives favorable to an open alliance with the Catholics, to the out-and-out anticlericals for whom an alliance with the Catholics was anathema, without counting those who did not care either about clericalism or anticlericalism and only were concerned with being reelected by constituencies in which the majority of the electorate did not wish to hear either clerical or anticlerical quarrels.

The dominant figure in Italian political life was Giovanni Giolitti. He came from the "more democratic" left wing of the government coalition. He had been minister of the treasury in 1887–89 and prime minister in 1892–94. He was home secretary from 1901 to 1903, and again prime minister almost without interruption from 1904 to 1914. He had been the first Italian statesman to regard trade unions as lawful associations, to admit the strike as a right of the workers instead of as a crime of class war, and to maintain that in labor disputes the government must remain neutral. He was a sensible administrator of public finances: no increase in public debt, no increase in expenditure without a corresponding increase in revenue. And, as we have seen, under his rule, until the Italo-Turkish war of 1911–12 came to upset (though not deeply) the Italian finances, the budget always showed substantial surplus.

The dream of his life was to include all Reformist Socialists—that is to say, not only Bissolati, but also Turati and their followers—in his government coalition, leaving the revolutionaries in the lurch. But at bottom he was a constant Conservative who wanted to buy the Reformist support with the minimum of concessions. He thought the Reformists ought to be satisfied with the political liberties he granted to trade unions and opposition parties and with the rise in the standard of living of the working classes which was taking place during those years.

He inherited from his predecessors the habit of "managing" the elections, but adapted it to the new conditions of the electorate. In the national elections of 1900, forty Socialists had been returned, nearly all in the north. Giolitti realized that in northern Italy, especially in the towns, owing to greater and greater education, the government could no longer "manage" the elections without arousing too great scandals. It was better to leave electors free to vote as they liked. But in the south, which returned about 200 deputies out of the total of 508, it was still possible to "manage" elections. Giolitti's method, therefore, was to leave the elections free in the north and to "manage" them in the south.

What did he do by way of "managing" elections?

Each one of the ninety-three provinces into which Italy was divided had an executive head, the "prefect," who, unlike the American state governor, was not elected by the citizens but was the appointee of the home secretary. To the home secretary he was responsible for the administration of his province. The town councils and mayors were elected by the citizens, but the prefect was entitled to dismiss any mayors and disband town councils, appointing "commissioners" in their stead, any time he deemed that they had misbehaved. This was the worst spot in the political constitution of Italy. The prefect was always in a position to bring pressure upon the mayors and councilors, especially in the backward sections of the country, and against eventual injustice there was no redress. The mayors and town councillors who used their influence in favor of the government candidate during an electioneering campaign remained in office, even if they were the worst public rascals. Those who supported opposition candidates were replaced by government commissioners, even if they were the best available administrators. This method, unscrupulously applied, sufficed to put at the service of the prefect most mayors in the constituency which was to be conquered or kept safe for a government candidate.

Where the electorate was refractory to government pressure and returned mayors or town councilors or deputies who refused to bow, Giolitti had recourse to other means of warfare. When a local municipal election or a national election was to be carried out, the police, in league with government supporters, enrolled the scum of the people and, when necessary, also the underworld of the neighboring districts. In the last weeks before the polls, the opponents were threatened, bludgeoned, besieged in their homes; their canvassers were debarred from addressing meetings, or even thrown into prison until the elections were over; electors suspected of upholding the opposition were refused polling cards; voters favoring government candidates received not only their own polling cards but also those of opponents, emigrants, and deceased electors, and were allowed to vote three, five, ten, twenty times. The government candidates were always the winners. Any southern deputy who tried to disobey Giolitti was sure to be defeated at the next election. Those who were faithful to him were sure of reelection.

Such methods did not need to be applied in all constituencies. They were necessary only where there was danger that an opposition candidate might be elected. Even in such constituencies, there was no need of subduing all opponents. It was enough to concentrate the warfare on no more than a few towns in the constituency, so as to get as many votes as necessary for victory and no more. If, let us say, 4 towns of a constituency were expected to give 1,000 votes to the government and 1,500 to the opposition, the prefect took care of no more than one town so as to steal no more than 500 votes from the opposition and add no more than 500 to those of his protegé. All the other towns were allowed to vote freely, on the condition that no trick on the part of the opposition occurred there.

If the party which had been suffocated appealed to the Chamber, the parliamentary committee on elections, consisting in its huge majority of government followers, did not lack ways and means of delaying investigation. The case was brought before the Chamber one, two, or three years after the election had been fought, when spirits had cooled off and nobody was any longer interested in prehistorical events. As a rule the report rejected charges of corrupt practices. Someone from the extreme left raised his protest. The cabinet solemnly announced that it would take no part in discussing the case, leaving the Chamber to decide freely, and a huge majority upheld the committee on elections. Sometimes the scandal had been so clamorous, and the crimes for which the government followers and the policemen were responsible so evident, that courts had to intervene and pass sentences. But sooner or later an opportune amnesty wiped out all such sentences, and next time the story started again.

Giolitti was not the first home secretary to "manage" elections. But none had ever "managed," one after another, three national elections (1904, 1909, 1913), and he surpassed all in clarity of purpose and methodical lack of scruples.

Thus he got from the south about 150 faithful followers, who owed to him their seats and would be unseated if they became restive. Backed by this solid block, Giolitti could command his terms either to the "more conservative" or to the "more democratic" deputies who came from northern and central Italy. When either of the two groups became noisy and difficult to get along with, he threatened to subject the offending group to reprisals and grant the other group his favor. Thus he checkmated the one against the other, and nobody dared to leave the government fold.

His eloquence was plain, concise, averse to rhetorical fireworks, enlivened from time to time by a humorous but discrete sally, ready to quibble rather than to use sound arguments, intent on soothing passions rather than on exciting them. A humorous theatrical review which had a great success in 1913 showed clericals and anticlericals, monarchists and republicans, conservatives and socialists, each one dressed in his own colors, quarreling, shouting, threatening each other. Giolitti appeared on the stage. Instantly everything quieted down, and everybody reappeared dressed in the same grey clothes.

Giolitti knew that he could not remain in power forever—if for no other reason, because from time to time he had to take some rest. When he thought that the hour for a useful eclipse had struck, he would pull a never-failing trick from his hat. He invented any pretext whatsoever to resign, refusing to succeed himself although it was evident that he had at his beck and call the majority of the deputies, and he advised the king to summon as prime minister one of the leaders of the Conservative opposition. The Chamber never failed to give a vote of confidence to the new cabinet. But after a few months, restlessness set in, the interim cabinet was forced to resign, and Giolitti triumphantly came back, in perfect health and more powerful than ever.

Universal suffrage was enacted in Italy as a result of one of Giolitti's parliamentary tricks. It had always been part and parcel of the program of democratic parties in Italy since the time of Mazzini's apostolate. An energetic campaign for universal suffrage was being conducted by the Socialist parties in Belgium and in Germany during the first decade of the current century. Universal suffrage had been enacted in Austria in 1908. But Giolitti had always been averse to any change in the electoral system of 1882. In 1911, however, he was planning the conquest of Libya. To overcome, or at least weaken, Socialist opposition, he brought in a bill extending the franchise to all males of thirty years and to all those who had served in the army, whether or not they paid direct taxes or could read or write. The Reformist Socialists, led by Bissolati, joined the government coalition in supporting the reform. The party remained in the opposition and expelled Bissolati and his followers. Most Socialist deputies, though at bottom reformists, did not dare to break away from the party. Thus Giolitti failed in his endeavor to bag Turati together with Bissolati. But when, in the autumn of 1911, war broke out, the Socialist party was paralyzed by the split and was unable to raise any efficient opposition. By an act of parliamentary strategy, the country passed from a regime in which the middle and lower classes of the towns were predominant to a regime in which numerically the rural population prevailed.

Giolitti was an exceptionally well gifted parliamentarian. He grasped with extreme shrewdness and lightening rapidity the slightest currents of opinion within the five hundred men who formed the Chamber. But he had little sensitivity for what was going on in the country at large. Here dissatisfaction with the "management" of elections was steadily growing, not only among opponents, but even among non-party citizens. He enacted universal suffrage without realizing its potentialities and deluding himself into the belief that he would control the new electorate as well as the old one. He had not realized that the peasantry of southern Italy was no longer the supine mass of twenty years earlier. When, in 1913, in the constituencies he had to "manage" he was confronted no more with 2 or 3,000 voters, but with 10,000 and more voters, he was forced to increase the dose of violence in strategical points to insure success. He won another of his usual overwhelming victories. But the scandals of southern Italy provoked bitter indignation everywhere.

During the nineteenth century, parliamentary institutions had been attacked in Italy by the remnants of the old absolutist and clerical regimes and by the anarchists of the Bakunin school. Neither of them could do any harm. From Conservatives to Socialists, none could conceive of political life without parliamentary institutions. The national election of 1900 was fought by Democrats, Radicals, Republicans, and Socialists to uphold against the Conservatives the rights and privileges of Parliament. The Conservatives were defeated. During the first decade of the present century, fresh and more dangerous antiparliamentarian currents—the Nationalists from the right and the Revolutionary Socialists from the left—began to batter the institution of Parliament. Just at this moment, Giolitti, during a period of ten years, bored at the institutions from within, unwittingly adding water to the antiparliamentary mills of the Nationalists and the Revolutionary Socialists.

The other institutions of democracy—freedom of speech, freedom of the press, freedom of political association and trade-unionism, elective local government, and parliamentary elections—were working fairly well in the North. But what was the use of elections, even if based on universal suffrage, if they were bound to bring forth only an overwhelming majority of "yes men"? What was the use of a Chamber of representatives which represented only the will of that one man who had been responsible for the election of its majority? While political education was progressing rapidly not only in the North but also in the South, while clearly differentiated parties with permanent organizations were emerging from the amorphous mass, the parliamentary majority, instead of adapting itself to the new conditions, retaliated by locking themselves into a well-knit gang which by hook or by crook kept themselves on their feet. On the eve of the War of 1914–18, Giolitti, as the leader of that gang, was the most powerful man in Parliament but the most unpopular man in the country.

This situation has to be borne in mind if one wants to understand the bad showing Giolitti and his parliamentary majority made when, in May 1915, they were confronted with the issue of peace or war.

AUTHOR'S NOTES TO CHAPTER 5

In his *Memorie della mia vita* (Milano: Treves, 1922; English translation, *Memoirs of my life*, 1923), Giolitti tells us that in 1892, when he was prime minister for the first time, the national elections gave him a "notable majority," but several of the defeated candidates "raised a devilish fuss" as if it were his duty to "support them" (1:68). As a matter of fact, in 1892 no one pretended that he should "support" his opponents. The charge was to the effect that he had "fought by violent and crooked means." His words afford an example of the quibbles he used in Parliament to steer the discussions off the track. That "devilish fuss" was so well founded that nineteen elections were annulled, since he had not had time to perfect his method as he could in the first decade of the twentieth century. From his *Memorie* (1:122–23) we also learn that in 1895 his successor and personal enemy, Crispi, tried to prevent his election without success. But we do not find one single mention of the accusations raised against him on account of the municipal and national elections from 1902 to 1913. Croce, an admirer of Giolitti, also ignores this point in his *History of Italy*.

S. Cilibrizzi (*Storia parlamentare politica e diplomatica d'Italia* [Milano: Soc. Ed. Dante Alighieri, 1923–1940], 5 vols.), gives full particulars of the elections of 1892 (2:458-59, 492), says nothing about the elections of 1904, refers only to the "innumerable governmental acts of pressure and violence" during the elections of 1909 (3:369), and gives an exact idea of the elections of 1913, in which, as he says, "Giolitti, already an expert in the art of manipulating elections, reached the peak of his ability"(4:292). The electoral methods of Giolitti were repeatedly described by G. Salvemini in the fortnightly review *Critica Sociale* (December 16, 1902, and October 15, 1908); and in some books and memoirs: *Il Ministro della Mala Vita* (Firenze: La Voce, 1910); *La elezione di Molfetta* (Firenze: A cura dell'Unità, 1914); *La elezione di Molfetta: i documenti pansiniani* (Firenze: A cura dell'Unità, 1914); *La elezione di Bitonto* (Firenze, L'Unità, 1914). On this last election, a group of other testimonials was collected in a booklet which is also entitled *La elezione di Bitonto* (Firenze: L'Unità, 1914).

King and Okey (*Italy To-Day*, pp.16,122), in describing the Italian situation about 1900, deplore the interference of the prefects with the elections and the use they made of underworld elements as weapons for victory. This fact has also been observed by Finer (p.80). But a systematic study on this phenomenon is lacking.

In our opinion such an investigation would lead to the conclusion that, prior to the electoral reform of 1882, the elections in Italy were usually conducted with methods no worse than those which were in use in other European countries in which the parliamentary regime worked in a satisfactory way. When a constituency in Italy numbered on an average about one thousand registered voters, of whom not even six hundred went to the polls, a candidate insured victory merely by scraping together a few hundred votes, and the home secretary, to displace as many votes as needed to carry the day, had only to make known to the "notables" of the constituency which candidate had been adopted by the government. Everything passed off amicably, without any fuss. This, however, did not preclude the fact that in many constituencies the electors elected opposition deputies. In the national election of 1867, the party in power barely escaped defeat. The electoral reform of 1882, by increasing the number of voters in each constituency to an average of about forty-eight hundred, made the work of the home secretary more difficult when he wanted to bring pressure upon such a body of voters. It happened more frequently that he had to threaten to depose mayors and dissolve municipal councils and threaten or enact acts of violence and bribery. This made the scandal more obvious. Giolitti, in the national election of 1892 and in the elections of 1904 and 1909, brought to perfection the methods of his predecessors. When universal male suffrage was enacted in 1913, and a constituency counted seventeen thousand registered voters, Giolitti had to handle an average of ten thousand voters in each constituency willing to go to the polls, and to subdue them he had to raise more clamorous scandals.

Parliamentary life was considered unhealthy in Italy by all independent and honest observers. And such it was indeed. As a general rule, the root of the evil was attributed to the fact that there did not exist in Italy the two-party system of the Anglo-Saxon countries. We doubt very much the correctness of this diagnosis.

The British House of Commons, during the nineteenth century, every time the Irish MPs split from the Liberal party, had to work, not under a two-, but under a three-party system. When, at the end of the nineteenth century, the Labour party came into being, there arose a four-party system, and the twentieth century never knew again any two-party system. When the Irish Free State was created and the Irish MPs vanished from the House of Commons, the four-party system became again a three-party system, but it became a five-party system when the Independent Labour party and the Communists formed parties of their own. In the United States the administration is steadily confronted with a Democratic and a Republican party, which both split into a majority and minority. Not a two-party, but a four-party system prevails in this country under the traditional two-fold terminology. The two-party system never worked in France, in Germany, or in Austria. In Belgium it broke down when the Socialist party came into being in competition with Catholics and Liberals.

The groups which form modern society are so numerous and fluctuating that it is difficult for them to range themselves under no more than two headings. What matters for the healthy working of a parliamentary regime is not the existence of no more than two parties, but the existence of a majority party which governs and of an opposition which supervises the activities of the party in power. The fact that the opposition consists of one party alone, or of different parties, does not prevent by itself the satisfactory working of the system. In Italy, from 1903 to 1914, there was a coalition which supported the cabinets, and outside that coalition there were opposition groups which supervised the activities of the cabinets. The British House of Commons since 1931 has consisted of a huge Conservative party and an opposition of Liberals and Labourites, without counting the few Independent Labourites and a Communist deputy.

Also the prejudice that in Italy there did not exist parties as well-defined as those which were to be found in Great Britain should be accepted with many qualifications for the fifteen years which preceded the War of 1914–18. There was at that time in Italy a Socialist party, a Catholic party, and a Nationalist party. They were minority parties, but they were parties. And the majority that supported Giolitti was also a party. It was made up, to be sure, of heterogeneous groups. But in what country has there ever existed a homogeneous parliamentary majority? The so-called Conservative majority which has governed England since 1931 consists of heterogeneous groups which run from the most stubborn diehards to MPs who would be more at home in the Labour party. The two parties which contest the predominance in the United States are nothing but two mosaics of local heterogeneous groups which are in a continual state of fluctuation. Not even the totalitarian regimes are supported by homogeneous forces, and in them compromises between conflicting interests are a daily necessity. The only thing is that compromises can be kept more secret than in free regimes. As a consequence, in free regimes the danger of scandals makes more difficult—if not impossible—the worst forms of give and take.

In other words, it seems to us that many criticisms of the Italian parliamentary regime, as it worked on the eve of the First World War, come from the fact that that regime did not correspond to the superstition that "social scientists" have built up of the perfect parliamentary regime, placing it in England—where, as a matter of fact, it had never existed in that perfect form.

The disease of the Italian parliamentary regime—a disease whose seriousness must be extenuated—consisted in the falsification that the government made of the will of the electorate every time there was need. Giolitti was not the first in Italy who made himself responsible for these corrupt practices, but Giolitti used them with fewer scruples than any other, and, above all, he was able to make use of them in three successive national elections.

Mussolini's biography before 1913 has been reconstructed by Dr. Gaudens Megaro in a book, *Mussolini in the Making* (Boston: Houghton Mifflin Co., 1938), which is a model of painstaking diligence and critical method. The pages in which Carlo Sforza *Makers of Modern Europe* (London: Elkins, Mathews & Marist, 1930) and Borgese (*Goliath*, pp. 169–225) give a sketch of Mussolini's character should also be read. Megaro's book should be compared with Signora Mr. Sarfatti's *Dux* (American edition, New

York: Frederick A. Stokes Co., 1925; Italian edition, Milano: Mondadori, 1926); Mussolini's *Pseudo-Autobiography;* and I. De Begnac, *Vita di Benito Mussolini dalle origini al 24 maggio 1915,* 3 vols. (Milano: Mondadori, 1936–40). By comparing Megaro's with Signora Sarfatti's book, more than by following any abstract instruction of historical method, one would learn the difference between forgery and truth, propaganda and history.

If one asks Signora Sarfatti what Mussolini's religious opinions were before he became the *duce* of Fascism, one will hear that her hero "seemed in the earliest period of antireligious bent, without ever sinking into the banality of atheism." That is all. But if we read Mr. Megaro's book, we find that Mussolini was a more colorful character than Signora Sarfatti makes out. In 1904, when he was twenty-one years old, he maintained, in the name of reason, science, evolution, and atheistic materialism, that "God does not exist" and that "the morality of Christ leads to brutishness and cowardice and perpetuates misery." In October 1909, in the town of Forlí, the crowd, after listening to an address by Mussolini, smashed the windows of the bishop's palace, set fire to the wooden fence which surrounded a column surmounted by a statue of a Madonna, and destroyed the slabs of marble at the base of the column. In 1910 Mussolini maintained that socialists should "avoid religious marriage, baptism of children, and all other religious ceremonies" and made the discovery that Christ "by making love to Mary Magdalene and to the wife of the good Pontius Pilate" had demonstrated that "it is possible to attain the glory of the heavens through the womb of a woman."

If, in addition to the story of Mussolini's religious beliefs, one seeks from Signora Sarfatti the story of his political beliefs, one will learn that Mussolini from earliest childhood was fascinated by the story of Rome with its myths and legends: "Rome—that was the one word the boy would write continually on the margin of his lesson book, or carve with his penknife upon the benches"; "he sought comfort in his woes in Caesar and Tacitus and the Aeneid." Could a man who in his earliest childhood read Tacitus be aught but a great patriot when grown up? When he was living in Switzerland "the life taught him to love his country with a deeper love." When he went to Trent, an Italian city which was still a part of the Austrian Empire, he found that a group of socialists there "were in sympathy with Austria and took their tune from Vienna." He therefore dissociated himself from them and joined the other group which combined socialistic doctrine with Italian feelings. On account of his nationalistic activities he was put in jail in Trent and expelled from Austria. "It is clear that his stay in the Trentino was decisive in developing the nationalist tendencies which culminated in Fascism."

Very different is the story which Dr. Megaro has reconstructed with the help of documents. In the autumn of 1903, Mussolini, who had lived in Switzerland for a little more than a year as a socialist agitator, returned to his native town for a few weeks; but since the time was approaching when he would have to perform his military service, he repaired to Switzerland again in January 1904. In February he wrote that "there is indeed an infallible means of destroying from its foundations the infamous military constraint: desertion." In April 1904, the Italian military authorities declared him to be a *renitente di leva* (an evader of military service, or, as the French put it, a *refractaire*). In that same month of April 1904, Mussolini was expelled from the Canton of Geneva, but the intervention of the Swiss socialists saved him from being taken to the Italian frontier. He was allowed to remain in Canton Ticino because as an evader of military service in Italy he could not, according to international law, be handed over to his own government.

In December 1904, Mussolini gave up the plan to destroy the infamous military constraint by means of desertion, took advantage of a pardon granted by the Italian government to those who had failed to answer the army summons, came back to Italy, and in 1905 and 1906 served his regular term in the army. After completing his military service, he plunged again into the socialist movement. In 1909 he lived for eight months as a socialist agitator in the city of Trent. "The proletariat," he wrote, "is antipatriotic by definition and by necessity." He upheld the right of the Italians of Trentino to keep their Italian tongue and to get home rule against the pan-Germans of Tyrol. But the socialists and anarchists have always maintained that racial minorities have the right to keep their own language and culture and to enjoy home rule. Mussolini did not advocate the separation of Trentino from Austria and its annexation to Italy. This was an aspiration, though secret and remote, of the Italian socialists of the Trentino, not of Mussolini. Mussolini's chief concern was social revolution. Signora Sarfatti's statement that Mussolini found two groups in Trent, one favorable to Austria and one to Italy, and that he joined the pro-Italian group against the pro-Austrian, is sheer invention. When, in September 1909, the Austrian government ordered Mussolini's expulsion, it did not think of him as a nationalist but as an insolent revolutionary agitator.

A good many "social scientists" have gone in quest of the sources of Mussolini's political thought, as once upon a time explorers set out to discover the sources of the Nile. But they are wholly ignorant of the history of the Italian socialist movement and of Italian political thought, and neglect to take into account chronology in noticing the manifestations of Mussolini's thought. As a consequence, they discover nothing and pile up nonsense.

To the father of Mussolini, first an active anarchist follower of Bakunin and then an active socialist of the first hour, Dr. Megaro has devoted one of the most interesting chapters in his book. Between the writings of the father and those of the son—we mean the writings of the son while he was still an extremist socialist—there is a striking continuity. "Those who mumble about Mussolini's intellectual father," Dr. Megaro aptly writes, "be he Nietzsche or Sorel, would do well to pause and consider the influence of his real father." It is preposterous to trace to Sorel Mussolini's ideas on the necessity of violence. Mussolini was "a revolutionary child of that Romagna which abounded in rebels who almost instinctively understood the need for violence." When Sorel dissociated himself from the revolutionary syndicalist movement and joined the clerical-royalists of the *Action Française*, anticipating a change which Mussolini was to make fourteen years later, Mussolini heaped upon him a Niagara Falls of abuse, of which Dr. Megaro gives some amusing specimens. This is one of the many revelations contained in his book.

Dr. Megaro also reduces to its just proportions—that is, to nothing—the impact which Pareto is said to have made on Mussolini. He proves that it is open to question whether Mussolini ever attended Pareto's lectures at the University of Lausanne, and that if he did attend them, it could only have been for a few weeks in the spring of 1904. Mussolini's notion of a revolutionary minority seizing power and overthrowing the bourgeoisie through violence was no doubt akin to Pareto's doctrine of the "elite." But the proletarian elite, of which impecunious Mussolini considered himself a member, would supersede the bourgeois elite; whereas Pareto, having inherited from one of his uncles a good deal of money, had a deep worship for the profession of investor and was angry against those bourgeois who did not care to protect that profession. Pareto wished the bourgeoisie to put up a ruthless resistance to socialism and to stamp it out. Since neither the bourgeoisie nor the socialists were willing to follow his advice, he grouped them together in the same condemnation. Nor did Mussolini need to know Pareto's writings and lectures in order to cherish a ruthless socialism that should destroy the decaying bourgeoisie. The *Communist Manifesto* sufficed to school him, and the doctrine of the organized minority overthrowing the bourgeoisie by a *coup de main* was among the Socialists as old as Blanqui. The conspiratory tradition was still alive in Romagna when Mussolini was born there and coincided perfectly with Blanqui's doctrines. Mussolini did not owe anything to Pareto. On the other hand, the doctrine of the "elite" under a form which could please the antidemocratic parties was not invented by Pareto. It came to him from Gaetano Mosca, a brilliant scholar who in 1896 had given a systematic elaboration to the doctrine of the organized minorities as "governing classes"—a more apt term than Pareto's "elite." From 1921 onward Pareto saw in the Fascist movement that ruthless bourgeois antisocialist onslaught whose advent he had wished for twenty years before. It was not Pareto who taught Mussolini. It was Mussolini who fulfilled Pareto's wishes.

When Mussolini became *duce* of Fascism, his hagiographers invented for him a family tree going back to the early Middle Ages and an intellectual genealogy in which Sorel, Pareto, Nietzsche, and many other highly placed personages were recruited to prepare the way for the redeemer. William James also got a niche in that pedigree. The intellectual genealogy, no less than the family tree, was false. For instance, Mussolini has never read one page of James. He only knows that James was a "pragmatist," and he thinks that that word means a man who does not care about principles and is only concerned with practical achievements. Therefore he boasts of being a disciple of William James, who would be horrified if he knew of that definition of pragmatism.

The most amazing fraud which has to be credited to Signora Sarfatti is that to the effect that Mussolini was a good patriot even when, during the Italo-Turkish war of 1911–12, as an extremist Socialist, he was spreading antimilitarist ideas and advocating sabotage. When the war seemed imminent in September 1911, Mussolini summoned the Italian "proletariat" to effect the general strike: "Confidently we await events. War is almost always a prelude to revolution." Socialist demonstrations against war assumed violent form in Forlí where Mussolini was publishing the weekly *Lotta di Classe* (Class War). He spoke and wrote during those days extolling the "new revolutionary mentality" which was "smashing to pieces" reformist and pacifist socialism: "We have been the first to familiarize the workers with the weapon of sabotage." "A few more years of good propaganda and this mass will be capable of great acts of heroism" (Megaro, p. 253–55). Mussolini was arrested, tried, and sentenced to a prison term of one year for "inciting to crime." At the trial he maintained that the general strike had not been proposed by him. He was not a workman but a journalist, and he did not intend to exercise any influence on the proletariat. The strike had been "the merit of the Forlí proletariat." In opposing the Libya expedition, he had taken his stand "on love of country," since the conquest of Libya would have been of no use to the Italian people. His sabotage was not that of vandals and hooligans. His sabotage would respect the safety of citizens: "Mussolini's stand at the trial does not reveal to us his patriotism, but rather his facile capacity for wheedling. In the light of his Socialist writings and activities before and after the trial, which make it clear that he wished to be regarded as antipatriotic, the inescapable conclusion is that he was deliberately insincere in the courtroom." His "predominant preoccupation was to be acquitted" (Megaro, pp. 267–68).

After his accession to power, the Forlí trial became an evidence for the fact that Mussolini always had been a patriot. Nay more, Mussolini was credited with a speech which allegedly he had made at the Forlí trial and which is to be found in Signora Sarfatti's *Dux*, (pp. 174–75). First Beltramelli in 1923 gave a faked summary of that speech. Then Bonavita in 1924 gave two different, but both loose and careless, versions of it. Finally Signora Sarfatti concocted a text which embodied fragments taken from Beltramelli's and Bonavita's faked reports, plus certain variations of her own. Needless to say, the Sarfatti text does not correspond at all with the authentic text of Mussolini's speech as given in November 1911 by Mussolini's own paper, *Lotta di Classe* (Megaro, pp. 269–70).

From Mussolini's *Pseudo-Autobiography*, one only gathers that Mussolini, when still a young man, "threw himself head-foremost into politics" —the politics "of those who sought solutions" (p.13); he "took part in political gatherings"; he "made speeches"; "some intemperance" (in his words) made him "undesirable to the Swiss authorities" (p. 14), and other similar empty formulae. Only once are we informed that he was "the mouthpiece of the intransigent revolutionary socialist factions" (p. 18). But never one single word is to be found about the hero's antipatriotic and antimilitaristic opinions and activities.

In the third volume of the work of De Begnac (pp. 168–71), the "inborn patriotism" of Mussolini is put under a spotlight by a flood of meaningless words, in which his antipatriotism and antimilitarism disintegrate until they are no longer recognizable. As regards the trial of Forlí, we are informed that the only accusation which Mussolini "fought with all his heart" was the accusation of antipatriotism. Mussolini had opposed the expedition to Libya because he wanted "to give a soul to his Italy which did not possess one"; "there was an historic mission to fulfill in the peninsula before going to Africa." The reader is not told that in September 1911, the soul of Mussolini's Italy should have been an antipatriotic, antimilitaristic, and sabotaging soul. The reader is not told that the historic mission which, according to Mussolini in September 1911, was still to be fulfilled in Italy was the social revolution along the lines of Hervé and Lenin.

Yet when the smoke screen of official mystification has been dispelled, thanks to Dr. Megaro's unimpeachable research, there emerges an amazing consistency that extends from Mussolini's infancy to his full maturity. The man who seized power in October 1922 is no other than that "restless and pugnacious little rogue" who more than once returned home with his head bleeding from a blow with a stone, stole decoy birds, struck at a companion but instead of hitting him hit a wall, hurt his knuckles and had to bandage his hand, and stabbed with a penknife another companion who had insulted him. Dr. Megaro produces a portrait of Mussolini at the age of fourteen! That youngster with crossed arms, sealed lips, protruding jaws, and defiant eyes is aleady the *duce* of Fascism who would appear before the crowds in Italy and would be the delight of cartoonists outside Italy.

6

The
Coup D'État
of May 1915

Four months after the national elections of November 1913, in March 1914, Giolitti considered that the moment had come for him to concede the premiership for a little while to the "conservative" opposition. His successor was Salandra, who could have mustered no more than the votes of the thirty Conservatives and the six Nationalists had he had to rely on his strength alone. He was expected to make room for Giolitti as soon as the latter had taken enough rest. But an unpredicted event upset all the calculations of the great parliamentarian: the War of 1914–1918.

Salandra, no less than Giolitti, had always been a determined upholder of Italy's alliance with Germany and Austria. But the treaty of the Triple Alliance merely anticipated a defensive war, and had no war of aggression among its aims.[1] In 1902 the Italian government had pledged itself to the French government never to participate in any war of aggression against France, a pledge which was in keeping with the treaty of the Triple Alliance

---

[1] All the texts of the treaties, from the first of 1882 to the last of 1912, are to be found in A. F. Pribram, *The Secret Treaties of Austria-Hungary:1879–1914* (Cambridge University Press, 1920), 2:64–73; 104–14; 150–62; 220–35; 244–59. The treaty was never designed as an unconditional bond linking together the Allied Powers in view of whatever war might arise. It was always a system of obligations in view of certain strictly defined hypotheses. If war broke out without Germany or Austria being attacked but by their own initiative, the Italian government was not bound to come in. This nature of the alliance has escaped all those historians who speak of a "faithless Italy," among whom, strange to say, is found that same Pribram who, for the first time, published the texts of all the treaties.

and was made public without raising objections on the part of the Berlin and Vienna cabinets.[2] Moreover, the partners of the Triple Alliance were pledged not to take any initiative in major international affairs without previously consulting each other. Last but not least, the cabinets of Vienna and Rome were pledged to abstain from any initiative which aimed at upsetting the *status quo* in the Balkan peninsula. If the *status quo* came to break down as a result of unpredictable events, the two cabinets were to consult each other before taking any steps. Their understanding was to be based on the principle that neither of them would attain any territorial or any other advantages beyond the *status quo* without the other being granted equal advantages.[3]

The ultimatum sent by the Vienna cabinet to Serbia in July 1914 had been preceded by no mutual consultation. The war which ensued from that ultimatum was aimed at upsetting the Balkan *status quo*, and it was a war of aggression, not a defensive war. The Italian government would have been entitled to protest that the treaty of alliance had been violated by the Austrian government. They took a different path. They maintained that the treaty did not pledge them to side with the Central Powers in the oncoming nondefensive war, and therefore, on August 2, 1914, when the general European war broke out, they announced that they would remain neutral. At the same time, they insisted that the treaty of alliance pledged the Austrian government to grant Italy equal compensation for any advantages Austria might get in the Balkans as a result of her war.

Upon the announcement of the Austrian ultimatum on Serbia in July 1914, the Nationalist party in Italy declared itself in favor of immediate intervention in the war on the side of the Central Powers. But they found

---

[2] On June 4, 1902, the Italian government declared to the French government that the treaty of the Triple Alliance did not contain any pledge whereby Italy could be obliged to join in an aggressive war against France, and therefore there was in the treaty nothing which could threaten the security or tranquillity of France. By this declaration, the Italian government pledged itself to interpret the Triple Alliance only in one way: as a strictly defensive and peaceful treaty towards France. Foreign Minister Delcassé made public the contents of this declaration on June 28, the new treaty of alliance was signed by the German, the Italian, and the Austrian governments. A treaty, even when signed, is not operative until ratified. The documents of ratification were exchanged on July 8—that is, five days after Delcassé had made public Italy's pledge. Since the documents of ratification were interchanged after Delcassé's public announcement, and since neither the German nor the Austrian government raised any protest or reservation before exchanging ratifications, much less refused to exchange them, it is evident that they acknowledged Italy's entente with France as being in accordance with the Triple Alliance.

[3] This pledge was unconditional—that is, was operative even if a war broke out in which Italy was not pledged to join the Central Powers.

themselves paralyzed by a vast wave of moral repugnance that became apparent in all classes of the Italian population as soon as the brutality of the Austrian ultimatum was made known. Then the government announced that it would remain neutral. Giolitti announced publicly that the declaration of neutrality was legitimate and had his full consent. The neutrality was received with a profound sense of relief by the overwhelming majority of the Italian people and of the politicians. Salandra suddenly became popular. Giolitti could not have overthrown the cabinet at that time without arousing a wave of anger all over the country.

Conflicting currents, however, were circulating under that unanimity. Soon the Italians split up into two groups: those who intended to maintain the neutrality until the end of the war and who, therefore, called themselves "neutralists," and those who demanded the intervention on the side of the anti-Germanic Entente and who called themselves "interventionists."

A certain number of conservatives grouped around the most important Italian newspaper, *Il Corriere della sera*, declared themselves in favor of the intervention against Austria and Germany, owing to the fact that there was no hope of coming to any understanding with Austria about the Balkan problems, and owing to the fact that German victory would bring about the end of Italian national independence in a German-dominated Europe.

The great majority of the deputies, senators, and influential newspapermen took an attitude of cautious waiting. They thought that the Italian government, after declaring neutrality, ought to negotiate with the Central Powers on the ground of compensations. The more territory the government could seize from the negotiations, the better. After such an internal affair among the powers of the Triple Alliance had been settled, then they should wait and see before taking a final decision on their course. This was the opinion of Salandra, and it was also the opinion of Giolitti. Salandra summed up this outlook in a formula which has remained famous: "sacred egoism."

The Nationalists, as soon as the government had declared itself neutral, rid themselves of any enthusiasm for the Triple Alliance and took on an attitude of reserve. But when Austria suffered her first defeats in Galitia and the German advance was halted at the Marne (September 1914), they began to invoke war against Austria and Germany. One of them, the philosopher Giovanni Gentile, has written: "The essential thing was to go to war: with Germany or against Germany."[4] It was they who formulated and carried on during the war a propaganda campaign for the most extreme program of territorial aggrandizement.

They had their bandleader in Gabriele D'Annunzio. This dilettante of sadistic emotions was rapidly growing old, and his art was losing the vigor of youth. His writings in those years make one think of a waiter who dreams of glory, gold, blood, and lust. In this case of moral teratology, the Italian people, with their common sense and inborn humanity, never understood anything. Whoever had to explain to them the necessity for joining the anti-German Entente never utilized the messages which D'Annunzio was spitting out. One had to remind them of their duties of justice toward the Italians subjected to Austria and toward Belgium traitorously invaded, and had to present the war as the only means of gaining for the tormented world a just peace. But the work of these obscure men was never known or appreciated outside Italy. Outside Italy, D'Annunzio was known as the greatest living Italian poet, and he knew how to arouse publicity around himself. No other country had, like Italy, the bad luck of being represented, during and after the war, in the international intellectual arena by a man who had sunk so low on the scale of moral perversity and literary mediocrity.

The Catholics, in the great majority, declared themselves in favor of neutrality. The Austro-Hungarian Empire was the only great power in Europe whose dynasty was faithful to the Catholic Church and in which the Catholic clergy enjoyed a privileged situation. The victory of the anti-Germanic Entente would have resulted in the detachment of vast territories inhabited by Catholic populations, from the Austrian-Hungarian Empire to Russia, Serbia, and Rumania—that is to say, to countries in which the Greek Orthodox religion was the dominant one. During the War of 1914–18, the Vatican always wanted—and hoped up until the last minute —that the Austrian-Hungarian Empire would come through the crisis undiminished. Therefore, the Italian Catholic organizations worked to keep Italy from going beyond the bounds of neutrality—though, as is their custom in all countries, they acted warily, never wholly committing themselves and always keeping one eye open behind them for an eventual retreat. As we know, the Catholic deputies in the Chamber numbered no more than 29 out of 508, but many other deputies—more than 200—had been

---

[4] G. Gentile, *L'essenza del Fascismo*, in the cooperative book *La Civilta Fascista* (Torino: U.T.E.T., 1928), p.98.

elected in November 1913 by the support of Catholic organizations. These, therefore, were more or less under Catholic influence. On the other hand, the Catholics also hoped that Salandra would snatch some substantial territorial compensation from the Austrian government and thus would be bound to keep neutrality. Therefore, they approved any attempt at bargaining about compensations.

A lively interventionist spirit showed itself among the Radicals and the Reformist Socialists. The most authoritative politician of this interventionist left was Leonida Bissolati. When the ultimatum to Serbia was announced, Bissolati affirmed that Italy, under no conditions, should associate herself with the Central Powers. He would have headed a revolutionary movement if the Italian government had not proclaimed neutrality. Consequently, he approved the declaration of neutrality. But hardly was neutrality declared then he asserted that Italy could not keep aloof from a conflict on which depended the destiny of all Europe. He would never have taken the initiative for a war for any reason. But now the war was there, provoked by others. The victory of the Central Powers would put an end to the independence of all the nations which surrounded the Austrian-German block. Italy was threatened no more and no less than all the other European nations by a German victory. On the other hand, the declaration of neutrality had caused a rift between Italy and the Central Powers. It was necessary for Italy to beware of the revenge which her old allies would take against her neutrality. Therefore, she must contribute to the victory of the anti-Germanic Entente. Last but not least, the democratic parties in the countries of the Entente should not allow a free hand to the nationalist and militarist parties to make war and peace. After helping to defeat Germany, they were to resist the imperialist groups at the moment when the peace would be negotiated. The Italian government should intervene in the general war with a program of justice for all peoples. Following this line of action, it would reinforce the democratic and antiimperialistic currents in the countries of the anti-Germanic Entente, and would help prepare for a peace which would not sow the seeds of a new war. Only on this basis could war be accepted, as one accepts strongly a necessary sacrifice. Otherwise, war would be an unpardonable crime.

The ideas of Bissolati had an inbred weakness. Neither in Italy nor outside Italy were the Democratic and Socialist parties prepared to understand them. Democrats and Socialists everywhere split into two currents, both averse to Bissolati's thought. They either remained bound to pacifist or revolutionary slogans and did not take any interest in the issues raised by the war, or they let themselves be carried away by warlike exaltation and became an easy prey of nationalist propaganda. Bissolati found only a few faithful followers, scattered here and there, in all the conservative and democratic groups and among those Christian Democrats upon whom the Vatican had no control, and who had with Bissolati common moral aspirations untouched by dogmatic disagreements.

The deputies of the official Socialist party and the leaders of the trade-unionist movement were pacifists. Pacifism has the one great advantage: a pacifist does not have to study any international problem in all its elements, which are often terribly complex. It is enough for him to nourish in his head and in his heart one sole idea and one sole sentiment: opposition to war. He has taken a vow not to understand anything and does not need to overwork his brains to keep his vow. Socialist deputies and trade union leaders never took any step beyond their pacifist position. They consistently stood for an inert and whimpering neutrality.

The minor leaders in the local political branches of the party resolutely showed their aversion to the Central Powers, but they no less resolutely refused to be drawn into the camp of the anti-Germanic Entente. They stubbornly clung to the Marxian doctrine as it had been reduced to a catechism and impoverished by the German Socialists. The only war to which the proletariat should dedicate itself was the war against capitalistic society. The proletariat ought to leave the capitalists to fight their own war for the defense of their own fatherland, and meanwhile should keep themselves ready to unleash social revolution, profiting from the "crisis of capitalistic society" which Marx had vaticinated and which had finally come to pass.

During the months of July, August, and September 1914, Mussolini was the leader of these men. As long as there was a danger that the government would decide to intervene on the side of the Central Powers, Mussolini threatened revolution. In the summer of 1914, just as in 1911, he maintained, following the Marxist doctrine, that social revolution must break out to prevent war. In order to stir up the proletariat against war, in 1914 he utilized the general feeling of hostility against Austria and Germany, just as in 1911 he had utilized the argument that the conquest of Libya was economically unwise. But the target at which he aimed in 1914, as in 1911, was always capitalistic society, facing its last hour.

After the government had declared neutrality, Mussolini filled the Socialist newspaper for two months with shouts, protests, accusations, threats against the Italian government, against the "German hordes" (August 5, 1914), against British and French imperialism, against Belgium, against all the world. As regards Belgium, he wrote on September 4, 1914:

> They ask us to shed tears over the martyrdom of Belgium. This is but a sentimental comedy staged by France and Belgium. These two merry wives would like to exploit universal credulity. To us, Belgium is a belligerent country, no different from all others. We do not see why we ought to adopt special views in her regard. It is our right and duty to urge the revolt of the working classes against the happenings of today.

On August 13, he wrote:

> War between nations is the most sanguinary form of class cooperation. The bourgeosie is happy, one can prove it by their press, whenever they can crush the proletariat and their independent class action on the altar of the Fatherland. The dominating cry of these days is: "there are no more parties." It proves our contention. In time of war the bourgeosie confronts the proletariat with the tragic dilemma: either insurrection, easily drowned in blood, or cooperation with them in a joint butchery. This second alternative of the dilemma is cloaked under words as fatherland, duty, territorial integrity, etc. Yet the root of the matter does not change for all. Here is the profound reason that makes us hate war.

And on August 16: "We mean to remain faithful to our Socialist and Internationalist doctrine to the very foundation. The storm may attack us but shall not attack our faith." The conclusion was always the same: Italy must not leave neutrality, and if the government tries to pass from neutrality to war, whether it be against the Central Powers or against the Triple Entente, the proletariat must unleash the social revolution.

Soon, however, some flaws began to creep into his antipatriotic utterances. As early as August 5, 1914, he admitted that if the fatherland were the victim of an aggression, the proletariat should fight in self-defense. And again on September 1, he stated that a war "to resist eventual invasion" would be legitimate even for the Revolutionary Socialists. This was the official doctrine of the party as canonized by international congresses, and no Socialist, even of the strictest observance, could object to it. But at the beginning of September, a former anarchist who had joined the Nationalists in 1911 and in 1914 was campaigning for intervention against the Central Powers. Massimo Rocca (pen name, Libero Tancredi), revealed that Mussolini, while advocating absolute neutrality in his paper, favored intervention against the Central Powers in his talks with his friends. Mussolini reacted as was his habit, by pouring a torrent of abuse on the head of Rocca.[5]

On October 8, he wrote: "I am not ashamed to confess that in the course of these two tragic months, my thought has undergone oscillations, uncertainties, fears. Who, among intelligent men, within Italy and without, has not undergone more or less profoundly such internal crises?"

He was right. Many other pacifists, Socialists, and Anarchists, not only in Italy, went through anguishing moral sufferings and came out of them new men. The most famous case is that of the anarchist Kropotkin, a man of exceptional intelligence and culture and of unimpeachable moral integrity, who, in the summer of 1914, joined in England the ranks of those who advocated war against Germany. Even Bissolati, in Italy, had been a pacifist and an antimilitarist.

As far as Mussolini is concerned, the most plausible hypothesis is that when he was suddenly confronted with the unforseen event of the war, he adopted without further ado the attitude which was to be expected of him, given his revolutionary, antipatriotic, antimilitaristic mentality. A journalist must have an opinion ready for any event at the thick of the moment, and he must express his opinion even before having thought of it. After following this first spontaneous impulse, he underwent a period of internal doubt and disquiet of which no one knew anything. Bit by bit he changed his opinion, while in his paper he was going on playing the old music according to the expectations of his public, which would not allow oscillations, uncertainties, or fears in its unconditional aversion to war. The misfortune of Mussolini arose from the fact that his self-asserting and violent nature did not permit him to show to the public the doubts which were creeping into his distraught soul. He went on handling his pen as one uses a dagger,

---

[5] A. Borghi, *Mussolini Red and Black* (New York: Freie Arbeiter Stimme, 1938), pp.66–69. Borghi's book contains a great deal of information drawn from firsthand sources. It is worth reading, notwithstanding the bitterness which casts a cloud of unjust suspicion around the statements of the violent but honest author.

without accepting any contradiction to what he wrote, while in his heart he was not at all sure of what he would think of the next day.

Suddenly, in October 1914, he declared himself in favor of Italy's intervention in the war against Germany and Austria, and he immediately began to treat those Socialists who did not accept his new standpoint as "irresponsible, traitors, deserters" (October 15). As was natural, the whole party, which until that moment had seen in him the upholder of absolute neutrality, revolted against him. He resigned from the editorship of the Socialist daily. In the middle of November, he started a new daily entitled *Il Popolo d'Italia* (*The People of Italy*).

He had always been impecunious. He could not have started his paper through his own financial resources. Thus instantly everybody began to wonder from where the new funds which supported that journalistic adventure were coming. His former comrades were, of course, the most vociferous in asking the question: "Who does pay?" They knew the answer: "the bourgeosie"; Mussolini had sold himself out to the "bourgeosie." Mussolini reacted by branding them as "imbeciles, stupid, deficient." One day he refused to subject himself to "the absurd demand" that he should reveal the inside of his business (*Popolo d'Italia*, November 20, 1914). Another day he was ready "to open up the doors of his house, to throw open his registers, to show his books," but on the one condition that the manager of the Socialist paper would do the same (November 23, 1914). He threatened to reveal facts which his foes would prefer to be kept in the dark. He had known these facts as chief editor of the Socialist paper, but he had been willing to swallow them as long as he was in accord with his "comrades."

On November 18, the Swiss daily *Neue Zürcherzeitung* and the *Wolff Bureau* published a telegram from Milan which said that it seemed that Mussolini "with no personal means," had at his disposal about five hundred thousand lire and "got French notices from Monsieur Cambon," the former French ambassador to Constantinople and Berlin. Mussolini mocked at such a rumor: "Let them talk, though the story is funny. I am at peace in my conscience and nothing else matters" (November 20). "Do they want to pass me off as a man who has sold himself out? Very well, but they must give proof" (November 20). The "insinuation" of the *Wolff Bureau* was "essentially and more than anything else ridiculous" (November 27). When he was asked to explain why he had gone to Geneva a few days before the first issue of his paper came out, he answered: "I will describe my trip to Geneva when I am willing to do so. That trip was well-known and not at all mysterious" (November 27). To be sure, the trip had not been mysterious. But its purpose remained mysterious. This was the crucial point, and about it Mussolini never gave any explanations. Mussolini had to his advantage the fact that Cambon never had had anything to do with him. But there were many other possible channels between Paris and Italy besides Cambon.

On December 1, the correspondent of the *Neue Zürcherzeitung* stated that he had "sincerely" thought that "the funds were coming from the French Socialist party, and that considering Mussolini's political past, this fact would not be at all detrimental to his honor." Mussolini summoned the journalist to show "what proofs and documents he possessed before he wired such a ridiculous story to his paper and to the German press." "French gold has nothing to do with this newspaper. It does not depend on anybody either inside our outside Italy. I have shown my independence and I will show it" (*Popolo d'Italia*, December 1, 1914). Nobody was in a position to publish the receipts of the money which Mussolini was receiving from France. Only he, or those who supplied him or brought the money to him, could give documents and proofs. Evidence came out many years later. Therefore, Mussolini maneuvered on safe ground when challenging his foes to bring forth "proofs and documents."

On the other hand, it would be unfair to maintain that he changed his mind not before, but after, the money had been promised or given him. It is more likely that he first changed his mind as a result of a crisis which he underwent together with many other decent people in Europe, and only after changing his mind was he driven by the demon of self-assertion to want a paper of his own. He set forth to find money, and he took it wherever he could find it. To a certain extent he was not insincere, even when he was stating that his paper did not depend on anybody either in Italy or outside Italy. In his own daily, he was carrying on his own policy, even if he was supported by French money. Thus, he could feel independent, though he might have asked himself what would have happened to his paper if he had changed his mind again, and whether he would have dared to change his mind again if he had known that his paper would die as a consequence of such a fresh change. These, however, are too subtle distinctions. The Fascist penal code, enacted by Mussolini in 1930, does not discriminate between money received before and money received after a conversion. As a consequence, Article 245 punishes, with penal servitude from five to fifteen years, whoever "holds intelligence abroad in order to engage the Italian State to a declaration or preservation of neutrality, or to a declaration of war," and it raises to twenty years the punishment "if the intelligence has for its object propaganda by means of the press."

Thus, the Italian interventionist movement had to endure not only the moral abasement of being represented by D'Annunzio, but also the suspicion of being subsidized by a foreign government. The Austrian and German newspapers took advantage of this fact. Even the German Chancellor, Bethmann Hollweg, in May 1915, asserted that the Italian cabinet ministers had entered the war because they had been bought by French gold, although he knew perfectly well that in Italy there were journalists who had been bought not only by French gold but by German gold as well, that mercenary journalists in Italy could be counted on two hands, and that they were not cabinet ministers. The latter were as honest and decent as he himself, even if they had taken a path which did not please him.

Mussolini's paper bore the caption, "A Socialist Daily." He flaunted himself as the only authentic guardian in Italy of the Revolutionary Socialist doctrine. He was a Revolutionary Socialist who dissented from his former comrades, who shrank from their revolutionary duty. Woe to the king and to the Italian bourgeosie if they held themselves aloof from the war against German imperialism! A republican and social revolution would punish their cowardice. In July, August, and September 1914, the king and the bourgeoisie would have had to face a revolution if they had gone to war. From November 1914 onwards, they were doomed if they did not go to war. At the same time, Mussolini saw in the war against German militarism the most suitable way to bring about the overthrow of capitalistic society: "Today war, tomorrow revolution." Social revolution would be brought about by the defeat of Germany, and this defeat would be the outcome of Italy's entrance into the war. Thus, the king and the bourgeoisie were doomed not only if they did not go, but also if they did go to war.

Mussolini had nothing in common with Bissolati. Bissolati appealed to idealism and common sense. Mussolini preached a vague mixture of revolutionary syndicalism, anarchism working through bombs, romanticism of 1848, and that brand of violent chauvinism which he had witnessed as a boy in the pubs of his native Romagna.

Among the "Radicals," "Republicans," schismatic Socialists, Revolutionary Syndicalists, and Anarchists who made up the motly crowd of the left-wing interventionist movement, most were undisciplined spirits who preached war for the intoxication of the dangerous gesture rather than for the sake of a well-defined goal. Almost all came from that section of the lower middle classes which is called intellectual because it has been educated above its intelligence, and in whose numerical overabundance, famished restlessness, and moral versatility lies the root of the most profound and dangerous diseases of modern society. The myth of the "revolutionary war" flourished in the brains of these contractors of revolution. The Nationalists found among them plenty of fools to inveigle and agents appropriate to inveigle others. Mussolini was their predestined leader. As soon as he started advocating intervention, they instinctively flocked around him.

Mussolini's revolutionary interventionism produced among the conservatives the same effect as a red flag waved in the face of a bull. It acted as a not irrelevant obstacle against intervention among the well-to-do classes. On the other hand, in the Italian Socialist party, many sincere persons were laboring under grievous pangs of conscience, whether they accepted intervention or whether they remained bound to the pacifist or revolutionary doctrines of socialism. Mussolini would have obtained many conversions to his new point of view had he remained in the party and used friendly and brotherly persuasion. But his egotistic and violent nature never knew the ways of persuasion. He gave himself over to denouncing as traitors of the proletariat, cowards, and good-for-nothings those same Socialists who remained faithful to his former teachings. By his savage attacks on his comrades of the eve, he froze them in their neutralist position. Socialists who, converted to intervention, might have brought with them, if not the whole party, at least a large section of it were reduced to helplessness and silence, or they had to leave the party. Mussolini dug between the Democrats who favored intervention and the Socialist party a ditch that could never be filled in. To a certain extent he raised more obstacles against than he gave help to the movement for intervention.

There existed no homogeneity among either the groups which demanded the intervention of Italy in the European war or those who demanded neutrality. All Italian political parties split up and were thrown into confusion. Conservatives, Catholics, and Socialists in their majorities, and a minority of Radicals and some Nationalists, pulled for neutrality. The campaign for intervention was waged by the Reformist Socialists, the Republicans, the majority of Nationalists, the majority of the Radicals, and those minorities who had deserted the parties favoring neutrality. Each of the two groups was a sort of melting pot in which men of divergent origins and beliefs were boiling. Besides interventionists and neutralists, there was the stolid mass of opportunist politicians who were ready to follow Giolitti whichever way he went.

The great majority of the better classes was favorable to the Central Powers, which they regarded as a solid support for social order. The most important banks and the largest industries were favorable to neutrality, not only because of that sympathy toward autocratic regimes which is common to all wealthy people, but also because the businessmen thought that neutrality avoided the risks of war and allowed them to make money at the expense as much of the Central Powers as of the anti-Germanic Entente. The intervention of Italy in the World War took place against the will of almost all the Italian capitalists.

The social groups who favored intervention were to be found especially among the intellectual class. But the latter, also, was profoundly divided. Among the university professors, many kept aloof from any controversy and would not have been distracted from their studies even by a universal flood. The others split up between interventionists and neutralists; among the interventionists, the Nationalists prevailed; among the neutralists, those who accepted neutrality as a passageway toward intervention on the side of the Central Powers were rather numerous. Secondary school teachers were divided among all possible currents, but those who favored intervention prevailed; some were Nationalist, others followers of Mussolini, still others followers of Bissolati. The elementary school teachers were divided in the same way as the secondary school teachers, but among them the neutralist Socialists—either reformist or revolutionary—were in the majority. Among the independent intellectuals, Benedetto Croce was a neutralist with pro-German leanings; D'Annunzio, as we have seen, was an interventionist with Nationalist tendencies; Guglielmo Ferrero was an interventionist with Bissolatian tendencies. The chiefs of the army and the navy were in favor of intervention, and so were most junior officers.

Under these conditions, the masses of the Italian people never understood why there were persons who wanted to go to war or persons who wanted to remain neutral; why there were Nationalist interventionists or Democratic interventionists; why most Democratic interventionists acted as Nationalists while some followed Bissolati; why, among the neutralists, there were Conservatives who remained faithful to Germany, Catholics who remained faithful to Austria, and Socialists who cared nothing for either Germany or Austria; and why there were Socialists who advocated pacifist neutrality and Socialists who clamored for revolutionary neutrality.

The only thing the Italian people could do in such a Tower of Babel was to conclude that intervention in war was no more than the outcome of capricious perversity on the part of politicians. The groups who favored intervention dragged in their wake no more than a small part of the population. The masses of workers in town and country supported either the Socialists or the Catholics and were in favor of neutrality.

Whoever, in the autumn of 1914, had tried to see into the future would have forseen that Italy would remain neutral, since the great majority of deputies and senators, the Socialist party, the Vatican, the Catholic organizations, the better classes, a strong proportion of the middle classes, and the enormous majority of the working classes in town and country were in favor of neutrality. The government of Vienna based its conduct in its relations with the Italian government upon this assumption. It felt safe from the danger of a war on the Italian frontier, and, therefore, it thought that it did not need to make concessions.

While the Italians were splitting up into neutralists and interventionists, Prime Minister Salandra and Foreign Minister Sonnino never cared to bring any order into that spiritual chaos. They belonged to the old Conservative tradition according to which the right to think and to command belonged to a minority of "notables," whereas the "subjects" had to obey and, if necessary, to die without thinking—or, at the most, thinking what the "notables" wanted them to think. Had Salandra and Sonnino lived in France before the revolution of 1848, they would have been staunch supporters of Guizot, and, by their obstinate arrogance, they would have helped Guizot to make the revolution of 1848 inevitable. They went to war without ever dreaming that it would be waged by millions of men who could not be sent to death without telling them why. They never succeeded in grasping the gravity of a crisis which was turning topsy-turvy not only the international balance of power, but the very foundations of the European social order. They negotiated with the governments of Berlin and Vienna as well as with those of the anti-German Entente, as if no Italian people existed. They never gave any definite advice to their friends about what they should do, nor did they try to enlist possible opponents under their banner. The Italian people, in 1915, like the people of North America in 1917, entered the war with no immediate danger facing them. No one can assert that Italy in 1915, or the United States in 1917, fought a defensive war. There was no Pearl Harbor for Italy in 1915. But the American people found in President Wilson a leader who gave the war an idealistic stamp. Salandra and Sonnino were "realists." To the Italian people they flaunted only the banner of "sacred egoism." It was due also to their "realism" if the Italian people decided that the war was a crime brought upon them by the bad will of their government.

It was only in the first days of May 1915 that everyone understood in Italy that the government had allied itself with the Triple Entente against the Central Powers. Giolitti had never been a partisan of absolute neutrality. He had approved the declaration of neutrality of the month of August. He had approved of Sonnino when, in December, he started negotiations with the cabinet of Vienna on the subject of compensations. He publicly expressed the opinion that Italy would be able to get a "good many things" ("parecchio") without resorting to war, but it is impossible to believe that he thought that the Italian government should negotiate with the purpose of keeping peace at any cost and being content with whatever concessions the cabinet of Vienna granted it. On the other hand, he seems never to have realized that starting negotiations meant going to war if negotiations came to nothing. Such was actually the case. In his *Memoirs,* published in 1922, he admits that the concessions offered by the cabinet of Vienna were not satisfactory. Hence the inference that Salandra and Sonnino had no other alternative except war.

In May 1915, Giolitti might differ from Salandra and Sonnino in the choice of the moment for the declaration of war. He might condemn the territorial aims which Salandra and Sonnino had set up. Instead of that, he stood against the cabinet without giving any reason. What would Giolitti have done had he returned to power? Would he have been content with the concessions the government of Vienna was disposed to make and which he himself, in 1922, was to state to be insufficient? Or would he have declared war against the Central Powers no more nor less than Salandra and Sonnino? Most likely he himself did not know what he was going to do. He only wanted to come back to power. Then he would act day by day according to the circumstances.

Three hundred deputies gave themselves over to an extraparliamentary demonstration in favor of Giolitti. They went to leave their calling cards at his home. Salandra handed in his resignation. At this point another unexpected event upset Giolitti's plans again. All the mistrust, all the hostility, all the hatred that had been accumulating against him in the course of the preceding years massed together and burst forth furiously. In the most important cities and especially in Rome, the interventionists started demonstrations in the streets, vituperating against Giolitti and his parliamentary majority, threatening to kill him. Salandra, who was pledged to declare war no later than May 25, had the police quench all manifestations of the neutralists and leave a free hand to the interventionists.

The interventionists were but a minority in the population. But the majority was divided between incoherent groups who were incapable of any common effort. The pacifist Socialists might have exerted a great influence upon the middle classes and acted as a focal point to all the neutralist currents. But in their party they were submerged by a noisy revolutionary majority, who gave to the campaign for neutrality their own stamp. Thus, the upper and middle classes had to choose between a revolt against the government (from which the revolution threatened by the Socialists might result) and war. They decided that war was the lesser evil. The Catholics also feared war less than revolution. On the other hand, that revolutionary proletariat, of which the Marxists of the strict observance pretended to be the representatives, was nonexistent. The great majority of workers and farmers did not want the war, but not even they cared about social revolution. They submitted to war since a powerful administrative organization seized them and threw them into the furnace, but they did not revolt actively. The Socialist party did not even call a general strike.

At that moment, the parliamentary majority was in agreement with the majority of the country which did not want the war. But it dared not resist the threats of the mobs in the streets. Having been manipulated by the government during three successive elections, it had no prestige to resist the government and those extraparliamentary forces which were supporting the government. It could not act as the representative of the country after ten years of taking no pains to represent it.

No political man dared to take the place of Salandra. Giolitti himself, after provoking the crisis, realized that at that moment it was impossible for him to become prime minister. Salandra and Sonnino remained in power. When, on May 20, the cabinet brought before the Chamber the proposal for the declaration of war, no more than seventy-six deputies (of whom forty-one were Socialists) were stubborn enough to vote against it. Four hundred seven deputies voted in favor of it, but no more than one hundred of them manfully accepted war as a necessity which had to be faced with fortitude. All the others basely submitted to the will of the executive power.

In May 1915, for the first time in Italian public life, the "anomaly" of pseudorevolutionary manifestations was seen, favored—nay even prompted —by the men in power to force the hand of Parliament. In May 1915, Salandra and Sonnino and the "interventionist" groups carried out a true and proper *coup d'état* against the parliamentary majority. Italy had a dress rehearsal of the other *coup d'état* which, in October 1922, was to be the March on Rome.

The governments of France and England had entered the war with the unanimous, or almost unanimous, consent of their peoples. Italy never experienced any "union sacrée." The division between "neutralists" and "interventionists" was unavoidable at the end of nine months of discussions about a war which could not be presented to the people as a defensive one. Salandra and Sonnino made things worse by keeping the country for all those months in a feverish and agonizing state of ignorance and uncertainty. Giolitti added to the errors of Salandra and Sonnino the further blunder of refusing his consent to a war which he himself had helped to make inevitable, by approving negotiations with Austria. All these mistakes led to a *coup d'état*, which infected the Italian atmosphere with the poison of civil war.

AUTHOR'S NOTES TO CHAPTER 6

The evidence about the origin of the funds which made it possible for Mussolini to start and carry on his daily paper falls under two headings: (1) evidence coming from French sources, and (2) evidence coming from Italian sources.

Evidence Coming from French Sources

1 In a book of recollections of an Italian diplomat loyal to Mussolini (D. Varé, *Laughing Diplomat* [London: John Murray, 1938], pp.213–14), one reads the following under November 19, 1922:

> Mantoux told me a story he had heard about him [Mussolini] yesterday from Julien Louchaire, once minister for public instruction in Ribot's Cabinet and director of the French Institute in Florence. . . . The following is the story as told by Louchaire to Mantoux:
> In the early months of 1915 Mussolini's newly founded paper, *Il Popolo d'Italia,* was pressing for the abandonment

of Italy's neutrality and preaching the necessity of her entering the war on the side of the Allies. At that time the French government sent a mission to Italy for purposes of propaganda. . . . As the *Popolo d'Italia* was doing already the best possible propaganda for the Allies, the members of the French mission, having heard that the paper needed funds to carry on with, went to the editor-proprietor and offered to contribute. Mussolini accepted the offer, and a sum was handed over to him, in support of his new journalistic venture. I don't remember what the sum was. Shall we say one hundred thousand lire, or perhaps more? These funds were duly used for the purpose for which they had been offered, and no one in France thought any more about the matter. But a year later, long after Italy had entered the war, a cheque for one hundred thousand lire (or whatever the sum was), bearing Mussolini's signature, was returned to the donors with many expressions of gratitude for the "timely loan." Prime Minister Ribot was told and could hardly believe his ears. Whoever *lends* money to a newspaper? In all the history of journalism it has never happened that a sum spontaneously offered for a specific purpose and successfully used for that purpose should be returned to the giver. At that time, Mussolini was unknown outside Italy and had not come into his own. It shows great independence of character not to remain under an obligation to a foreign government or allow it to be said that he was "financed" by foreigners. Mantoux was much impressed by this story as he told it to me.

Monsieur Mantoux, the well-known historian who acted as interpreter at the Peace Conference of 1919, cannot have said that Monsieur Julien Luchaire (not Louchaire) had ever been minister for public instruction in any French cabinet. Luchaire has never been a cabinet minister in France. Most likely Varé did not remember correctly Mantoux's words. In 1914 and 1915, Luchaire was director of the Institut Français in Milan. He may only have acted as an intermediary between the French mission and Mussolini.

As for the returning of the money to the "donors," this fact seems unlikely, at least in 1916. At that time Mussolini was not in a position to dispense, shall we say, with one hundred thousand francs.

Be that as it may, the fact remains that in November 1922, Varé had no reason to invent his talk with Mantoux, nor did Mantoux have any reason to invent the story related to him by Luchaire, nor did Luchaire have any reason to invent the story of the French money accepted by Mussolini in 1915. In November 1922, in view of the occupation of the Ruhr, the French Foreign Office badly needed Mussolini's support against the British Foreign Office. They wanted to please Mussolini. Most likely this explains why, just at that moment, Luchaire credited him with an act of financial heroism, unprecedented and unparalleled among French journalists. Thus, Luchaire's statement about the money accepted by Mussolini in 1915 must be accepted as an evidence given by a witness who was in a position to be well informed and who had no reason to deceive Mantoux.

When this basic fact has been established, other pieces of evidence acquire a significance which otherwise would be ambiguous.

2 In March 1925, in the course of a political trial before the assizes in Paris, the public prosecutor told the jurors not to forget that thanks to Mussolini's "disinterested efforts" Italy had entered the war on the side of France. The counsel for the anti-Fascist side, Maître Torrès, "solemnly" maintained that Mussolini had been moved by the danger of France only when he had pocketed the sums which had been allotted to his purchase. Neither the public prosecutor nor the counsel for the Fascist side dared to dwell on this point any longer. Outside the courtroom, Maître Torrès gave more definite information:

There was a moment quite at the start when the Italian Socialist party was unanimous against the armed intervention of Italy. The French government was concerned, and considered the matter in a cabinet meeting. They examined the question to see if there were not some means of converting some of the Socialists to the cause of war—a financial means. The name of Mussolini was mentioned. The first payment was 15,000 francs monthly. It was Guèsde's secretary, Dumas, who brought him the money. It was then that *Il Popolo d'Italia* was born, immediately interventionist. That is the exact story, which no one will dare to deny for fear of more crushing documentary evidence.[6]

3 On November 9, 1926, the French deputy, M. Renaudel, wrote in the *Quotidien:* "Many of us remember that the first numbers of the *Popolo d'Italia* were published with the aid of French money. Marcel Cachin knew all this, although he doesn't like to have it talked about." Marcel Cachin, in 1926 a Communist deputy, had been a Socialist member of the "Union Sacrée" during the War of 1914–18, and went to Italy several times on semiofficial missions.

4 On January 9, 1928, the French deputy M. Paul Faure wrote on the *Populaire:* "One day, Jules Guèsde, at that time minister of state, confided to me that we had down there a man who was one of us: Mussolini; we had sent him a first payment of 100,000 francs to launch his newspaper. I cannot say exactly who carried the money; but Cachin, if he wishes, can inform the readers of the *Humanité;* he was then in Italy seeing Mussolini for the French government." There is no agreement between the figures given by Maître Torrès and those given by M. Faure; but a lapse of memory on the part of M. Faure after 18 years was possible, whereas Maître Torrès referred to documents. In any case, M. Cachin remained obstinately silent.

Torrès, Renaudel, and Faure all belonged to French antifascist left groups. None of them was a firsthand witness like Luchaire. They were repeating what was common knowledge among the French politicians. If Luchaire's statement had never been made, one might suspect that the French were calumniating Mussolini. The fact, however, remains that Cachin always kept silent, whereas, as a Communist deputy, he would have been glad to be in a position to protest that he had never acted as an intermediary between the French "bourgeois" government and Mussolini.

6 Borghi, *Mussolini Red and Black*, pp. 87–89.

Cachin's silence means more than Torrès,' Renaudel's, and Faure's words.

Evidence Coming from Italian Sources.

1 On May 3, 1919, a weekly of Milan, *L'Italia del Popolo*, stated that Mussolini had "cashed patriotic cheques from the French government" and challenged him to institute a libel suit: "we have the proofs of what we have said and written." Mussolini ignored the challenge. This fact is as significant as Cachin's silence.

2 In 1926, Massimo Rocca, while living as a refugee in Paris, published the following in the issue June 1926 of the magazine *Nuovo Paese:*

> Then (at the beginning of September 1914) Mussolini met Filippo Naldi, the chief editor of the Bologna daily *Resto del Carlino*. He promised to change sides if Naldi would procure him another paper. He got such a promise. Then he wrote in the *Avanti* an article in which he stated that neutrality should not be absolute but a first step to intervention. The other editors of the *Avanti* of course disowned him. Nevertheless he remained chief editor of the Socialist paper for two more weeks. Meanwhile he was preparing with Naldi the financing of the *Popolo d'Italia* through a first French subsidy. He would be the chief editor and the owner of the paper. When he had attained his end, he handed over his resignation as the chief editor of the *Avanti*. . . . Then he went to Geneva to get the first funds.

In 1926, Naldi also was living as an exile in Paris. He did not contradict Rocca's account. But both Rocca and Naldi belonged to the group of disgruntled Fascists who had left Italy in 1924. The magazine *Nuovo Paese* was published with the purpose of blackmailing Mussolini, and sooner or later its editors made peace with him and acted as Fascist spies in France. Naldi, who in 1926 allowed Rocca's version to pass without contradiction, was a disreputable character, always entangled in shady affairs. In November 1914, he had stated that "as far as he knew, no French gold was to be found in Mussolini's paper" (De Begnac, *Vita di Benito Mussolini*, 3: 583). Therefore Rocca's account has to be left out as long as there is no other more reliable evidence to bear it out.

3 In 1928, Mussolini's *Pseudo-Autobiography* (pp.38–39) gave the following terms about the origins of the *Popolo d'Italia:*

I needed a daily paper. . . . When money alone is concerned, I am anything but a wizard. When it is a question of means or capital to start a project, or how to finance a newspaper, I grasp only the most abstract side, the political value, the spiritual essence of the thing. To me, money is detestable. What it may do is sometimes beautiful and sometimes noble.

It is an admission, or at least a half admission.

4 In 1930, Alceste De Ambris, a revolutionary Syndicalist who, in 1914–15, had fought side by side with Mussolini, while living as a refugee in France wrote as follows in his book *Mussolini: la leggenda e l'uomo*, (Marseilles: E.S.I.L.), p. 26:

Most people find Mussolini abominable because he accepted money from the French government to found the *Popolo d'Italia*. But the abominable feature of the fact is not here. If Mussolini had been interventionist from the very beginning, or if he had become an interventionist afterwards without any personal calculations, we would not brand him guilty for accepting afterwards that money. When one follows the road where his conscience guides him, he may also accept the help which is offered to him and enables him better to follow and attain his goal. Mussolini's profound, radical and never to be forgiven immorality lies in the fact that he deviated from, nay took a road going in the opposite direction in order to gain personal advantage.

De Ambris quotes Rocca's account as his authority. Since Rocca's evidence has to be discarded, De Ambris's statement also becomes devoid of authority.

5 In 1938, Roberto Marvasi, another antifascist refugee, in his *Quartetto: Le Roi, Mussolini, le Pape, D'Annunzio* (Salon: Imprimerie Nouvelle), p.15, stated that in March 1915, two friends and cooperators of Mussolini, one of whom was Alceste De Ambris, went to Paris. To them, Luigi Campolonghi, an Italian journalist who was in contact with the French circles and knew much of what was happening behind the scenes, confided that Giuseppe and Ricciotti Garibaldi, two degenerate grandchildren of the hero of the Italian Risorgimento, prominent among the leaders of the Italian movement for intervention against the Central Powers, were in the pay of the French government. De Ambris was able to ascertain that the fact was true in a conversation with one of the two Garibaldi. De Ambris, Campolonghi, and the third friend decided to enter a protest with Minister Guèsde. Guèsde listened to the protest, and when it was over he called in his *chef de cabinet*, Dumas, had a packet of thousand-franc notes brought in, and gave it to De Ambris to carry to Mussolini: "This is," he said, "a personal remittance from the French comrades. You may rest easy." The money was not refused.

The author of the present book, upon reading this account, wrote to Campolonghi to ask whether or not he could confirm it. Campolonghi answered, in a letter dated August 8, 1938, that "the episode related by Marvasi is true." The other friend of Mussolini who had come from Italy, was a Republican, Dino Roberto:

> De Ambris and Roberto were so taken by surprise that they did not have time to decline the office proposed by Guèsde. Perhaps, having discovered the origin of the funds which were nourishing the *Popolo d'Italia*, they should not have cooperated afterwards with that paper. I did not, and refused consistently to publish one single line in it.

Campolonghi did not add in his letter, perhaps because it was obvious, that the fact was kept secret in order not to provoke a scandal which would have discredited the interventionist movement.

In 1938, Roberto had been interned in Italy on a penal island, and De

Ambris was dead. Therefore, there was no way of checking Marvasi and Campolonghi's account by their evidence. There is no reason to suspect that Campolonghi or Marvasi invented the facts. Yet only after De Ambris' death were they made public by Marvasi. Therefore, it would be wise not to rely too heavily on this source, if only for the reason that after so many years it is likely that some details may have become garbled and insecure.

All in all, Mussolini's silence in 1910, Luchaire's account in 1922, Cachin's silence in 1926 and 1928, and Mussolini's brother's (let us say) half-admission in the *Pseudo-Autobiography* give grounds for reaching a secure conclusion, and from this conclusion Torrès,' Renaudel's, and Faure's statements draw full credit.

Mrs. Sarfatti, in writing her *Dux* (p.163), knew that Mussolini was suspected of having received "French gold." But she dismissed any suspicion on the ground that the paper was created on the basis of an agreement with a publicity agency and with four thousand lire loaned on a bill, and that the premises of the daily consisted of two miserable rooms and four chairs. On such basis she had, in 1914, formed her "persuasion as sure as an instinct." (These words do not appear in the American edition, *The Life of Mussolini*, p. 203). She did not realize that four thousand lire would not even have sufficed to buy the paper for the first issue of the newspaper, that a publicity agency does not risk money on a paper which has not yet been put out, and that Mussolini's paper could not have luxurious quarters unless it wanted to increase the number of those who were asking: "Who does pay?" The only pertinent point in Mrs. Sarfatti's "persuasion" comes from the fact that in February 1915, a committee investigating the sources of Mussolini's funds reached the conclusion that Mussolini's paper had been made possible through a contract he had made with a publicity agency, and that when the agency was no longer willing to support the paper, some "relatives and friends," all people favoring Italy's intervention in war, came in (De Begnac, *Vita di Mussolini*, 3:603–09). The committee would have arrived at a different conclusion if it had had at hand the information which came out later from Luchaire's words and Cachin's silence.

De Begnac *(Vita di Benito Mussolini)* has no doubts about the fact that the financial origins of the paper were "of the purest" (3:395), and, while devoting one hundred pages to relate the glories of his hero in the summer and autumn of 1914, he elegantly rids himself of this affair by giving in the appendix the report of the committee of February 1915. The only tactic he could decently follow on this desperate issue was to slip over it in the greatest possible hurry.

To form an idea of the misconceptions which have been concocted and circulated on Mussolini's political career, a few examples may be recorded.

1 When speaking of Mussolini's life before Italy's intervention in the Great War, Signor Villari, in 1924, took good care not to mention that, up to 1914, Mussolini had been a rabid advocate of the theory that the proletariat had no concern in national defense. Signor Villari was content with saying that "from the moment war broke out, Mussolini instinctively understood the necessity for Italian intervention, and never wavered in his conviction" (*The Awakening of Italy*, p.19).

The truth is that Mussolini preached neutrality during August and September 1914. It was not until October 18 that he began to preach intervention.

2 In August 1914, the leader of the Socialists in the Italian-speaking Trentino (annexed to the Austrian Empire) fled to Italy and joined the campaign for Italy's intervention in war against the Central Powers. (When war was declared, he volunteered and in 1916 was captured and hanged by the Austrians.) The Socialist daily *Avanti* (of which Mussolini was the editor-in-chief), in a correspondence from Rome, made fun of a war "the aim of which would be to liberate from Austria a people who absolutely did not wish to be detached from Austria." Battisti sent a letter to Mussolini protesting against such a statement.

Mussolini had worked under Battisti in Trento for some time in 1909 and had remained on friendly terms with him. He could not withhold the publication of his protest and he gave it on September 14. But while Battisti had put his letter under the caption "Do not blaspheme," Mussolini chose the neutral caption "Trentini e Trentino" ("The Trentino and its inhabitants"). Moreover, he deleted from the letter the last sentences, which run:

If Italy can not remember us, so be it. If working for our redemption would result in her ruin, we will continue to endure servitude. All this may be! Forget us if you wish, but do not say that we do not desire to be detached from Austria. It is an offence. It is a blasphemy.

Battisti's letter, so mutilated, was introduced by the following words: "We can not deny hospitality to this letter which a comrade and dear friend from Trento, who is now a fugitive in Italy, has sent us to correct an affirmation contained in one of our correspondences from Rome."[7]

In De Begnac's *Vita di Benito Mussolini* (3:367), one only reads: "The neutralists . . . fought every kind of Irredentism. They even went so far as to say that in Trentino the inhabitants wanted to maintain the Hapsburg dominion." One is not told that the "neutralists" are the Rome correspondent of the *Avanti* and Mussolini himself. Then one finds the final sentences of Battisti's letter without being told that Mussolini had withheld them.

3 In an article, "Mussolini: a patriotic Socialist," published by Umberto Morelli in the *English Review* (February, 1926, p.207), one reads:

In the beginning of the war, all Mussolini's efforts were concentrated against the Nationalists, who were inclined to favor fighting against France, and he paralyzed their machinations; and when he had succeeded in compelling Italy to remain neutral, he immediately began to work for the war of liberation of the two provinces—Trento and Trieste.

The fact is that the Nationalists found no following in Italy when they tried to advocate intervention side by side with the Central Powers. It is throwing dust in people's eyes to credit Mussolini with a decisive influence on the course of events during those days. He was but a small cog in a huge machine.

The Italian government declared its neutrality on August

[7] Cesare Battisti, *Scritti politici* (Firenze: Le Monnier, 1923), p.189.

2, whereas Mussolini went on preaching, not intervention, but neutrality up until October 1914. It is not true, therefore, that "immediately he began to work for the war of liberation of the two provinces Trento and Trieste."

Mussolini and the "Fascists of the First Hour"

Within Italy and without, it was the general opinion that the Italian intervention in the war would shortly bring about the defeat of the Central Powers and the end of the war. Perhaps this would have happened had the Italian and Rumanian armies entered the conflict in the first months of 1915 when the Austrian army was undergoing disasters on the Russian and Serbian fronts. At the beginning of March, the idea that Italy and Rumania should attack Austria just at that moment aroused waves of panic among the men in power in Vienna and in Budapest. At the end of May, when Italy entered the war without any move on the part of Rumania, the Russian armies had already been put out of commission in the so-called battle of Gorlice. As a consequence, the Austrian High Command could now displace large forces from the Russian to both the Italian and Serbian fighting fronts. In addition, the Italian High Command showed a total lack of imagination and skill in all military operations. The war, instead of lasting a few months, dragged on for three and one-half years.

The parliamentary majority, who unwillingly had voted for war in May 1915, remained passive and lethargic during the first months. But as fast as the difficulties multiplied, they took courage and started repeating: "We told you so." At the same time, the Official Socialist deputies became more and more aggressive in their criticism. And there was plenty of reason for criticism in the inept conduct of the war and the clumsy and inefficient working of the civilian administration.

To support the war cabinets against the onslaught from the Socialists, those deputies who had favored intervention or had sincerely accepted it after it had become unavoidable formed themselves into a "Bundle of National Defence" ("Fascio di Difesa Nazionale"), whose members ranged from the Nationalists of the extreme right to the Reformist Socialists of the extreme left. They were no more than 150, pinned against the Official Socialists and their more or less cautious supporters. The House always remained divided among a stubborn minority who favored a war to the finish, another stubborn minority who advocated an immediate end of war by "any peace whatsoever" ("una pace qualunque"), and a distraught majority who did not know whether to wish a victory which would mean their political bankruptcy or a stalemate which would assuage their rancor. They voted against the Official Socialists or deserted the sittings when the Official Socialists demanded the immediate end of the war, but they repeated in the lobbies the well-known refrain: "We told you so."

In the country at large, the longer the war lasted, the heavier became the sacrifices demanded from the soldiers on the fighting front and from the civilian population at home, and the wider and deeper became the discontent. This phenomenon was common in Europe to all belligerent countries. Strikes increased in Germany, Austria, France, and England, as well as in Italy. In Germany, those Socialist deputies who opposed the continuation of the war and had fought for a year against the majority of their colleagues dissociated themselves from them in the spring of 1917 and formed an Independent Socialist party. In Italy there was no need for the Socialist party to split up, because both right Reformist and left Revolutionary wings had been united against intervention and were united against the continuation of the war.

When the war was over and the soldiers began to be demobilized, they returned home embittered by the maltreatment their families had endured in three and one-half years of war. They loathed every kind of brass hat and those politicians who had wanted the war, or had voted for the war in May 1915 and had continued to vote for its continuation even if they had not wanted it.

In the course of the war, the politicians had made extravagant promises of social, economic, and political reforms. A renewal, root and branch, of the whole national life was to testify to the nation's gratitude to those who had shed their blood in her service. On November 20, 1918, that same Salandra, who had led Italy to the declaration of war upon Austria, proclaimed: "The war is a revolution, yes, a very great revolution. Let no one think that after the storm it will be possible to make a peaceful return to the old order. Let no one think that the old habits of leisurely life can be resumed." The same day, Prime Minister Orlando, who had run the government during the last year of war, boasted in a speech to the Chamber of Deputies: "This war is at the same time the greatest political and social revolution in history, surpassing even the French Revolution." Of course neither of them meant by "revolution" an armed revolt from illegal parties against the established government. They only meant a reshaping of the whole social and political structure through basic, but lawful, reforms. But what those revolutionary reforms should be, they never disclosed; and perhaps they themselves never knew. After they had made their "revolutionary" speeches, they promptly proceeded to forget them. The only reforms the soldiers were aware of, when they were demobilized, were a bundle of cloth from which to cut their civilian suits when they were home, a bonus of twenty dollars apiece, and nothing more. But they remembered. The wealthy people ("i signori"), they said, had got the substance of war profits, and the soldiers the shadow of empty promises.

In 1919, there were all the conditions in Italy for a thorough reform of the social and economic structure in the direction of, what we term today, economic democracy. The three and one-half years of war had created in the Italian people a new mentality which not even a half-century of socialist propaganda would have been able to create: an acute intolerance of present conditions, a secure expectation of great changes, and the burning desire to have an active share in the building up of a better world. The idea that the past was dead and would not rise again was accepted even by the Conservatives. Men like Salandra and Orlando felt incapable of stemming the tide. Social and political reforms were lying there at hand for whoever wanted to seize them. It would have been possible to apply them to those industries which during the war had greatly expanded and had made excessive and often dishonest profits, and which now needed to be helped by the government if they were to survive the crisis of transition from war to peace. It would have been possible to transfer the ownership of land from absentee proprietors to those tenants or sharecroppers who cultivated them with their own work and that of their families. It would have been possible to draw up a gigantic plan of public works to repair the destruction of the war, reorganize the railroads, modernize the highway system, resume and extend the work of land reclamation, and rehouse the most distressed sections of the great cities. It would have been possible to enact the eight-hour day of work, old age pensions, insurance against unemployment and illness. It would have been possible to organize a more intensive struggle against illiteracy in southern Italy and a new system of education for the boys and girls of the working classes everywhere. It would have been possible to adopt a foreign policy of good sense which put aside the dreams of Orlando and Sonnino and the Nationalists, sincerely supported President Wilson in withstanding the maneuvers of Lloyd George and Clemenceau at the peace conference, and made possible a radical reduction in military expenses in a pacified world. Any party or any coalition of parties which had adopted a program of this kind would have found no resistance standing in its way.

Italy had been born between 1859 and 1870 under an oligarchical regime. In 1882, it had passed to an electoral regime in which the middle and lower middle classes prevailed. In 1912 she had been endowed with a regime in which, thanks to the almost universal suffrage, the working classes legally predominated. In 1919 the franchise became universal without limitations, because the law of 1912 had granted the franchise to whoever had done military service, and from 1915 to 1918 everyone in Italy had done military service. The universal suffrage in the hands of the working classes could have served as an instrument for immediate far-reaching changes which, hardly five years before, would have been considered in the realms of the impossible. Who could have headed such a "revolutionary" movement—not in the sense of a violent overthrow of the existing regime, but in the sense of its complete remodeling?

At the end of 1918, when victory had crowned the hopes of those political groups who had willed the war and stubbornly supported it to the bitter end, the Nationalists saw no limits to their ambitions. In December 1918, two of them, Signor Rocco and Signor Coppola, in announcing the publication of a new review, *Politica*, defined in the following orgiastic terms the outline of Italy's future foreign policy:

> Everything summons Italy to the fulfillment of her imperial mission: the tradition of Rome, of Venice, of Genoa; the political genius of the race which has always been a master in the art of governing the peoples; her geographical position, which, while connecting her by land with the continent of Europe, permits her to dominate from the centre the whole Mediterranean basin where today pulsates the

heart of three continents. Here is the duty, here is the mission of Italy. As history proves, every time life has returned to this fatal peninsula and a racial and political unity, a strong and organized power, has established itself, the iron necessity of things has drawn Italy beyond her boundaries, towards that sea of three continents and towards the shores that it bathes, to which she is called by a natural vocation, superior to every force and every conflicting will.

The Nationalists worked in accord with Prime Minister Orlando, Foreign Minister Sonnino, and the chiefs of the army and navy.

But as soon as the war was over, the alliance which had arisen during the war between them and Bissolati's followers vanished forever. During the war, Bissolati—a man of fifty-eight but a brilliant mountain climber—had volunteered, had been seriously wounded, had returned after his recovery to the fighting front, and had won two medals for acts of bravery. In June 1916, after Salandra's resignation from the premiership, he had consented to join Sonnino in a Cabinet of National Unity, but he had never subscribed to Sonnino's peace aims. When the war was over, he resumed his liberty of action, and he demanded that the Italian war aims be defined by the entire cabinet before the Italian peace negotiators left for the peace conference. He was averse to the annexation of South Tyrol, inhabited by a German population, and to the annexation of Dalmatia, inhabited by a Slav population. These annexations were unjust and would have made inevitable new wars. He was convinced that the plan of Prime Minister Orlando and Foreign Minister Sonnino—that is, to demand Dalmatia according to the terms of the Pact of London, was absurd; the Italian negotiators must renounce Dalmatia but demand Fiume. Furthermore, a just and enduring peace had been promised to the combatants. The Italian negotiators must join with President Wilson in his fight against Clemenceau and Lloyd George for a peace without unjust hardships against Germany. They ought to have helped Wilson to create the League of Nations, "a superior form of international life," in order to "gain from the war the sacred reward of liberating man from the slavery of war."[1]

Prime Minister Orlando sided with Sonnino. Bissolati resigned from his ministerial office (December 1918) and announced that he would deliver a political address at the Scala Theater of Milan to make known what

---

[1] L. Bissolati, *La politica estera dell' Italia dal 1897 al 1920* (Milano: Treves, 1923), pp.396–98.

Italy's peace aims should be according to his estimation.

When he started his address, a mob, headed by Mussolini, aroused such a tumult in the theater that Bissolati was unable to make himself heard and had to give up.

During the war, Mussolini had joined the army when his class was called up (August 31, 1915). He has published his war diary, which has been translated into English (*My Diary: 1915–17* [Boston: Small, Maynard and Co., 1925]). From this source we learn that he remained under arms from September 1, 1915, to February 23, 1917. During these eighteen months, he spent no more than four months on the fighting front. Of these four months, one and one-half months were spent in a zone "which was the quietest, perhaps, of the entire front" (p.134). In short, he participated in true and proper military operations for not more than two and one-half months without ever taking part in any battle. On February 23, 1917, he was wounded, not in action, but as a consequence of the bursting out of a shell in an Italian mortar. On February 24, 1917, the *Popolo d'Italia* stated that the wounds were not dangerous. When he had recovered from his injuries, he asked and got exemption from further military service, not as being unable to serve, but as being indispensable to the management of the *Popolo d'Italia*.

In 1915, he had been averse to all forms of imperialism and had opposed the plan of annexing Dalmatia to Italy.[2] Now he was in the front rank of those who clamored for Fiume, Dalmatia, Asia Minor, and colonies in Africa, and who prevented Bissolati from addressing the public of the Scala Theater. Borgese, who was present at that meeting, relates that Bissolati, when he recognized Mussolini in the chorus, turned to his friends who were nearest to him and said: "I will not give that man the honor of fighting him" ("Quell'uomo no!").[3]

Side by side with Mussolini's gangsters in the Scala Theater, on that evening of January 1919, were to be found the Futurists. From the article devoted to Futurism in the *Enciclopedia Italiana* (16:227–31), written by Futurist leader F.T. Marinetti himself, we learn that Futurism was "an

---

[2] Mussolini's articles in *Popolo d'Italia*, Jan. 24 and 28 and April 8, 1915, stated that "Italy must reject those programs which are not justified by reasons of justice and liberty and resolve themselves into nationalism and imperialism"; in Dalmatia, Italy ought to be satisfied with protecting the Italians living there "against the attempts at enslaving them through governmental pressure." See also H. Massoul, "Les étapes de la révolution Fasciste," *Mercure de France*, Nov. 1932, pp.513–41.

[3] G.A. Borgese, *Goliath: The March of Fascism* (New York: The Viking Press, 1937); p.143.

artistic-political movement, overpowering, original, quickening, created by F.T. Marinetti at Milan in 1909." The article and political program of the new movement advocated an explosive art and life; the carrying of Italian pride to the point of apoplexy; the abolition of culture and logic, of museums and universities, of the monarchy and the papacy; the worship of modernity; an abstract type of painting that is to represent tones, sounds, odors, weights, and mysterious forces; "heroism and buffoonery in art and in life"; and other humbug of the same kind. Having inherited a good-sized fortune from his father, Marinetti was able to organize a noisy publicity around himself and his movement by means of billboards, leaflets, lectures, dramatic spectacles, and musicals. No one ever took him seriously. People went to Futurist meetings in the theaters only in order to throw tomatoes and other humorous missiles at the actors and musicians. The Futurist school did not produce a single work of art that did not call forth derision. Anything good produced by any member of the school was done after he had ceased to play the clown in Marinetti's train.

During the months of Italy's neutrality in 1914–15, the Futurists clamored for Italy's intervention. They were rabidly anti-Socialist and anti-Catholic, and in addition rabidly anti-German. One of their most glorious exploits during the war was a demonstration they made against Toscanini because Toscanini was playing German music in Italy during an anti-German war. Toscanini threw away the baton and refused to play any kind of music at all. After the war, Marinetti became rabidly "anti-Bolshevist," but his anti-Bolshevism still remained anti-Catholic and ultrarevolutionary. Mussolini never officially joined the Futurists, since they had already their leader in Marinetti and there was no room among them for two leaders. But Futurists and Mussolini's followers always worked hand in glove.

In the campaign of slander against Bissolati, the Nationalists marched side by side with Mussolini and Marinetti, and behind those three vanguard groups stood all those politicians and papers who were supporting Orlando's and Sonnino's policies. There were among them those same men and papers who had followed Giolitti in 1915 and who, for the sake of avoiding Italy's entrance into the war, had been willing to renounce not only Dalmatia and Fiume, but Trieste and Istria as well. Now all of them clamored unanimously not only for Trieste and Istria, but also for Fiume and Dalmatia to its last clump of shrubs. The more territories they demanded, the more successful would be their attack on those responsible for war if they were unable to fulfill all expectations. The Socialists cared little for Dalmatia, Fiume, Asia Minor, or Africa. They made a pretense of Olympian indifference towards the problems that were to be discussed at the peace conference. Only "class-conscious proletariat" was capable of bestowing peace and justice upon the world. They were engrossed with making the proletariat class-conscious.

Thus, no more than a half-dozen dailies all over Italy, foremost among them the great Milan daily *Corriere della Sera*, supported Bissolati. Even two of those politicians who had always been considered intimate friends of Bissolati and who, together with him, had taken part in the Orlando cabinet, deserted him and remained in the cabinet. Bissolati was left with no more than a handful of friends. The Nationalists hated them because they opposed the annexation of Dalmatia. The Socialists and neutralists hated them because they had favored Italy's entrance into the war. Their arguments were unheeded. Orlando and Sonnino now could go to the peace conference with full powers to enforce their demand for the Treaty of London plus Fiume.

After his triumph over Bissolati in January 1919, Mussolini, in March, made himself head of a "fighting fascio" ("Fascio di combattimento") which arose in Milan. The Italian word "fascio" means a "bundle of sticks." In pre-Fascist Italy it was applied to any kind of political group (bundle) or associations. Mussolini's Fascists in March 1919 numbered less than one hundred. In the early days of the movement the word "fascio" was associated only with the idea of "bundle" and not with that of the "fasces" of the Roman lictors. Soon, however, the word "fasci" suggested the device of taking the Roman "fasces" as the symbol of the Fascist movement.

The program of the first Fascist group advocated proclamation of the Italian Republic, universal suffrage for both sexes, decentralization of the executive power, abolition of the Senate and of the political police, abolition of all titles of nobility, abolition of military conscription and of secret diplomacy, confiscation of episcopal revenues, dissolution of joint stock companies and suppression of banks and stock exchanges, a census of personal wealth and confiscation of unproductive capital, the granting of the land to cooperative societies of peasants, and the entrusting of the management of industries and of public services to unions of skilled workers. "All the afterwar platitudes, all the most extreme and absurd expectations of that neurotic period were embodied in the programme of the nascent party."[4]

[4] C. Avarna di Gualtieri, *Il Fascismo* (Torino: Gobetti, 1925), p. 17

Mussolini's motto was: Fight for the revolutionary fruits of a revolutionary war: "The hour of social revolution has once for all arrived. If social revolution has now become possible, the credit for it is not due to the Socialists, who are revolutionists only in words, but to us, the true revolutionists who worked in favor of war, thus paving the way to the revolution."

He opposed the Socialists, not because they were revolutionists, but because they revealed themselves to be unwilling to plan and incapable of carrying out social revolution. He branded the Socialists as "Bolshevists" and called himself an "anti-Bolshevist," but he never cooperated either with the moderate against the extreme Socialists or with the conservative parties against the Socialists. He stood alone in the attitude of the ultrarevolutionary prophet, urging the masses to revolt against everybody and everything and to believe in him alone.

It is useless to try to find any coherence in Mussolini's intellectual hodgepodge during this hysterical period. In 1932, looking back upon the early days of Fascism, he made the following admission. "There was no specific doctrinal plan in my mind at that time. . . . Fascism was not nursed by a doctrine elaborated beforehand at the desk; it was born from the need of action and for action."[5] As an ultrarevolutionist, he reviled all the old constitutional parties; but as a patriot who had wished the war and inveighed more than anyone else against the neutralists, he went hand in hand with the Nationalists, the most conservative group of all. As an ultrarevolutionist and ultranationalist at one and the same time, he impeached the democratic parties and democratic forms of government, but he also demanded a republic with universal suffrage for both sexes, judges elected by the people, decentralization of the executive power, and all kinds of restrictions upon the functions of the state; that is to say, he advocated an ultrademocratic form of government.

Yet beneath that chaotic mixture of fragments drawn from the most

[5] Mussolini, *Fascism; Doctrine and Institutions* (Rome: "Ardita", 1935), p.16. In an appendix to this treatise are collected some extracts from various writings and speeches of Mussolini's, which try to suggest the idea that Mussolini's thought developed with coherence from the first barely sketched outlines in 1919 to that which had become by 1928 his definitive doctrine. By the same method—that is, by suppressing all that one wants to ignore in Mussolini's writings and speeches—one can portray Mussolini as an anarchist or a conservative, as an internationalist or a nationalist, as an atheist or a Father of the Church, as an upholder of birth control or a minister of the breed-more-children religion, as a friend or an enemy of any country, and so on *ad infinitum.* The compiler of the "final edition" of Mussolini's *Scritti e Discorsi* did not content himself with ignoring all those writings and speeches which placed his hero's contradictions and inconsistencies too much in the limelight; he also falsified those texts which he did not exclude from the collection. This fact has been demonstrated by Dr. Megaro in *Political Science Quarterly* (June 1936), and in *The Journal of Modern History* (September 1936).

diverse and contradictory political philosophies, there were some deep-seated, basic emotions which controlled his behavior and gave it a consistent direction. In the first place, he hated the Socialists, whose leader he had been up until the autumn of 1914, and who now threw mud at him as a renegade and traitor and charged him with being an accomplice of the "capitalist class" in the carnage of the World War. Second, he had borrowed from revolutionary syndicalism, anarchism, and Leninist communism a contempt for parliamentary institutions and the cult of violence as a political weapon. Third, he had borrowed from the Nationalists their appeal to patriotic exaltation. Such were in 1919, and still are in 1924, the basic springs of his actions.

In 1919, however, he believed that social revolution was nearing Italy, and he tried to catch its winds in his sails by aligning himself with the extreme left of the revolutionary movement and outdoing the other Italian revolutionaries in fervor. If the social revolution of which everybody was speaking had materialized, there was some prospect that the more extreme revolutionaries would take advantage of the confusion unavoidable in such a crisis and overcome the more moderate Socialists. In Russia, Lenin and Trotsky had shown that in a moment of social disintegration a rigidly organized group of men, armed and ready for anything, could become the rallying center for a large mass of desperadoes. He had no hope of being again received into the Socialist camp. All that remained to him was to gather around himself as his companions in adventure men capable of responding at the same time to ultrarevolutionary and ultranationalistic slogans. These men did exist. The process of demobilization was throwing into the labor market some 160,000 discharged officers. The better elements among these went quietly back to their homes and sought work like the anonymous masses of demobilized workmen and peasants. But for some of them it was not easy to find a livelihood. They originated from the semi-intellectual lower middle classes. Before the war they had been clerks, professional men in a small way, or petty shopkeepers, and had risen to the rank of officers during the war, or they had been called to the colors at the age of nineteen or twenty and had learned no craft but that of commanding men. They had grown accustomed to having a fair amount of money to spend and had acquired a taste for command and for a life of adventure. If they had not found other men to regiment, they would have been obliged to come back to low clerical jobs or to manual labor. Of that they had not the slightest intention.

Rejected by the bourgeois intellectuals but nevertheless unwilling to lower themselves to the status of manual laborers, the semi-intellectual lower middle class in all countries furnishes the recruiting ground for professional politicians. When they fail to find service with a conservative party, they gain a livelihood in revolutionary movements. The less intelligent, less lucky, or more scrupulous remain throughout their lives, regardless of what party they are in, on the lower rungs of the political ladder; their class is the nursery of the paid wardheelers. The more intelligent, more fortunate, or less scrupulous may rise to such exalted positions as those of a royal prime minister or a Reich's chancellor.

On their return to civil life, these men could not adapt themselves to the uneventful and obscure labor of a postman, a shop assistant, or a clerk. An intelligent observer called them "the fifth estate."[6] Some of them threw in their lot with the Socialists and Communists and were jestingly called "war Socialists." Most of them went to swell the ranks of the first "fasci." War Socialists and Fascists are to be found at the head of all the worst disorders of those years.[7]

These "Fascists of the first hour," as afterwards they were termed, were convinced that the country, which owed victory to them, had the duty of providing for them now, not in proportion to their ability to work but in proportion to their glory. The war was the sole foundation of their claims. The acts of military valor which they had performed—or boasted they had performed—were their titles of nobility. They hated the Socialists and all those who had opposed the war, as they would have hated a personal enemy who was trying to deprive them of all their honors and rights. The Socialists, furthermore, were the leaders of the workers, who were then earning high wages, while they—the "saviors of the Fatherland"—were unable to find employment.

Yet their hatred of the Socialists by no means meant that they were conservative. None of them ever dreamed that one day they would become the missionaries of hierarchy, discipline, and obedience. Being hungry and dissatisfied with themselves, their neighbors, and the world in general, they imagined that they were revolutionaries. To them, both the "capitalist" who passed by in his automobile and the skilled worker who earned a good

---

[6] L. Salvatorelli, *Nazionalfascismo* (Torino: Gobetti, 1923), p. 14.

[7] G. Volpe, *Storia del movimento fascista* (Miláno: I.S.P.I., 1939), p. 16. War "pushed up high on the ladder of military bravery, men from the masses and from the small bourgeoisie, who, when the war was over, *reluctant and incapable of returning to their old ranks* (italics ours), acted as an energetic revolutionary ferment in Italian society."

wage were "sharks" exploiting the country. They hung about the towns, eaten with idleness and eager for action in any direction, capable alike of heroic acts and frightful crimes. They were naturally attracted toward the revolutionaries of the prewar vintage who formed the earlier bodyguard of Mussolini.

The most violent were those who during the war had served in the shock troops ("arditi"). Not a few of these "arditi" had, before the war, been sentenced to jail for common crimes. During the war they had been pardoned and sent to the front to rehabilitate themselves by killing as many of the enemy as possible. They had in fact rehabilitated themselves, but under the uniform of the shock troop men they had kept their aboriginal mentality of criminals. On November 10, 1918, during a patriotic demonstration through Milan in their company, Mussolini had addressed a group of "arditi" in the following terms: "Forward comrades! I have supported you while the cowardly philistines were slandering you. The gleam of your daggers and the bursting of your bombs will do away with all the vile ones who want to impede the forward advance of the greater Italy. Italy belongs to you! To you!"

During the war, in May 1918, those Revolutionary Syndicalists, Republicans, and Anarchists who supported war to the finish had founded an "Italian Labor Union" ("Unione Italiana del Lavoro"), the leader of which was Edmondo Rossoni. This man, no less than Mussolini, had before the war been a Revolutionary Syndicalist of the extreme left. He had been a militant among the Industrial Workers of the World in the United States. On June 11, 1911, a group of "prominent" Italians placed a wreath on the monument to Garibaldi in New York. Following this "patriotic" demonstration, the Italians of a revolutionary stamp staged one on their own account. The orator who held forth at the monument was none other than Rossoni, who (we read in the paper *Il Proletario* for June 12, 1911):

> With a sonorous voice that vibrates in one's ears like the string of a taut bow, lashes out against the whole filthy crew of swindlers, exploiters, counterfeiters who need the cloak of patriotism to conceal their plunder. After stating that he assumes full responsibility for his act, amidst a delirium of applause, he spits with might and main on the King's tricolor and on the wreath of the prominent citizens. Our protest has been made and we are satisfied. But not Rossoni, for he throws himself once more at the pedestal of the

monument and proposes that each one of those present file
before the wreath and decorate it with a conscientious spit,
which everyone does, applauding.[8]

When the war broke out, Rossoni, like Mussolini, suddenly discovered
that he too was a Nationalist. He returned to Italy and, in May 1918, with
other Socialists no less revolutionary and no less patriotic than he, helped
found the Italian Union of Labor with the program of "war against the
capitalist system and all the institutions upholding that system."[9]

Rossoni's tactics in 1919 were demanding more than the unions controlled by the Socialists would be contented with, thereby hoping to win
the working masses to his own ultrarevolutionary-nationalist movement. In
November 1918, the National Federation of the workers in the metal
industry, led by Socialists, had entered into a labor agreement with the
employers. Rossoni, who was heading a small group of workers in the same
trade, rejected the Socialist agreement, demanded the forty-four hour week,
a minimum wage, and the Saturday afternoon rest (which in Italy was called
"the English Saturday"), and branded the Socialist union leaders who had
been content with a forty-eight hour week as traitors of the proletariat. One
of the followers of Rossoni, in a meeting held at Milan in March 1919,
maintained that "workers must have the right to get drunk on Sunday and
stay at home on Monday without incurring punishment" (*Corriere della
Sera*, March 21, 1919).

Mussolini wholeheartedly seconded Rossoni. No doubt the forty-eight
hour week *was* a betrayal of the proletariat. The strikes were always wrong
when they were sponsored by Socialists, and always justified on the condition that they broke out without or contrary to the advice of Socialist
leaders. In March 1919, in Dalmine, a town in northern Italy, 2,000 factory
workers, who were engaged in a wages dispute with their employers, occupied the workshops. This, the first "sit-down strike" in Italy, was promoted by Mussolini's followers. Mussolini himself went to Dalmine and
addressed the men, praising their enterprise. In his newspaper he wrote:
"The Dalmine experiment is of great value as showing the potential capacity of the proletariat to manage the factories themselves" (April 1, 1919).

These demagogical maneuvers fell into the void. Mussolini, Rossoni, and

[8] The files of *Il Proletario* are available in the New York Public Library.
[9] L.R. Franck, *L'Economie Corporative Fasciste, en Doctrine et en Fait* (Paris, 1934), pp.
12–14, 25–28. This is the best study up to the present available concerning the relations
between capital and labor under the Fascist dictatorship.

the Italian Union of Labor had been in favor of war. The men who were returning from the front, in their overwhelming majority, were inimical to whoever had advocated war, whether he called himself Bissolati or Mussolini. Rossoni never succeeded in obtaining a wide influence. He was a general without soldiers.

From what source did Nationalists, Futurists, and Fascists get the money to maintain their men and to support their papers and other lesser publications?

The Futurists had no daily paper and Marinetti could support those few among his friends who lacked the means of livelihood. But the *Idea Nazionale*, the daily paper edited by the Nationalists, and the *Popolo d'Italia*, Mussolini's daily, which had a small circulation, could not have existed without considerable financial assistance.

As for the Nationalists, even the stones on the street knew that they were supported by the steel, sugar, chemical, and other industrialists who throve on armaments, protective tariffs, and government contracts.

As regards Mussolini, it seems that the subsidies from the French government ceased as soon as the war was over and the French Foreign Office no longer had need of Italian blood. In 1919, 1920, and 1921, Mussolini was violently anti-French. But other sources of revenue had been opened. In January 1919, in that tumultuous meeting at Milan, where Bissolati was prevented from speaking, Mussolini's opponents hurled in his teeth the word "Ansaldo." The Ansaldo Company was then the most important armaments firm in Italy. For the munitions firms, as for the army chiefs, the end of the war had come suddenly and just at the time when they were at the peak of their efficiency. This had been an unpleasant surprise. Everything that kept people agitated and might bring about international complications was useful to their interests. Mussolini and his Fascists, as well as the Nationalists, were the groups on whom the armaments firms and the army chiefs could count the most to keep the country in a state of disturbance.

In 1919, the Socialist paper *Avanti* stated that the military chiefs were buying up thousands of copies of the *Popolo d'Italia* and having them distributed among the soldiers. Mussolini did not deny the fact and confined himself to saying that the military chiefs were free to do as they liked. The military chiefs hoped that, reading Mussolini's paper, the soldiers would absorb the nationalistic ideas and reject the revolutionary ones. The soldiers absorbed the revolutionary and rejected the nationalistic ones.

Then the military chiefs threw on "Bolshevism" the blame for the soldiers' view instead of blaming themselves for their own stupidity.

It was a general belief in Italy that, besides the Ansaldo Company, other industrialists were subsidizing Mussolini's daily paper. In fact, as soon as the war was over, the industrialists began to demand that the government, according to *laisser faire* doctrine, abolish all the restrictions imposed on private activities during the war and give up all functions not strictly political. At the same time, they demanded that the government protect the industries with tariffs, give subsidies to the merchant marine, favor the use of national fuel to the exclusion of coal imported from without, and so forth. These demands clashed with the policy of *laisser faire*. But businessmen did not see any clash. *Laisser faire* and government intervention contradicted each other in the books of economists, not in the pockets of business men.

Mussolini supported this campaign. His services deserved a reward. If he had not been able to profit from this entry, he would not have been able to announce, on December 23, 1919, that next year the *Popolo d'Italia* would possess "the typographic equipment indispensable to a paper of large circulation."

To be sure, Mussolini's ultrarevolutionary hullaballoo did not aim at pleasing the big businessmen. However, the method of supporting ultrarevolutionary (but not numerous) elements who bore from within and from without more numerous, more moderate, better organized, and therefore more efficient radical organization is an old strategy on the part of conservative parties. Aristophanes, the Greek comic author of the fifth century B.C., introduces in his play *The Knights* the aristocratic party in Athens, which, in order to undermine the power of the demagogue Cleon, hires a sausage-seller who can shout louder than Cleon himself. "If you surpass him," they say, "the cake is ours." This explains why not only Mussolini but also scattered Fascist local groups were subsidized by businessmen.[10]

Notwithstanding the noise he was making in his paper, in 1919 Mussolini's influence in Italy was of slight or no moment. At the parliamentary elections on November 1919, the Fascist and Futurist candidates in Lom-

---

[10] One of the Fascist officials said in March 1925: "The industrialists are greatly mistaken if they think that having accepted their subsidies in 1919, 1920, and 1921, Fascism has given up protecting the workers" (quoted by L. Hautecoeur, "Le Fascisme," *L'année politique française et etrangère*, October–December 1925, p. 145).

bardy got only 5,000 votes out of a total of 350,000, of which 90,000 went to the leader of the Socialists, Turati.

AUTHOR'S NOTES TO CHAPTER 7

Mussolini's wounds have become the subject for an heroic saga. Mrs. Sarfatti wrote:

> "I remember the terrible shock when the news that he was wounded reached Milan. What fearful details! Forty-two wounds, his whole body bruised, full of splinters of every size. . . . He seemed like San Sebastian, his flesh pierced as with arrows, scarred with wounds and bathed in blood" (*Life of Benito Mussolini*, p. 230).

The London *Morning Post*, October 4, 1926, wrote: "Signor Mussolini fell on the Italian front with as many wounds as Caesar, and when lying, swathed in his bandages, had no doubt ample time to consider the true philosophy of peace."

The truth is that, according to a report given by Mussolini in his *Diary*, the forty-two wounds all together had a circumference of thirty-one and one-half inches, which means that each one was on an average less than an inch. If two of them were so large that it was possible for a man's fist to enter into them, it is obvious that these two wounds alone made up almost the whole circumference, and the other forty wounds must have been superficial and almost invisible scars. Therefore there was no reason for Mrs. Sarfatti to make such a fuss over wounds which were anything but serious during a war in which a half-million Italian soldiers had lost their lives. One has to add that Mussolini's wounds would have healed much more quickly had his blood not been stained with syphilis.

While Mussolini was in the hospital, the king went to visit him. According to the report published in Mussolini's diary, the king said to him: "And now, after so many feats of bravery, you have been wounded" (*Diary*, p. 194). Thus Mussolini was officially credited with "many feats of bravery" which had never taken place. As a consequence, Mrs. Sarfatti did not miss this opportunity for exalting her hero. She tells us that even outside his battalion the rumor spread that he was "so bold": his "specialty was to collect live bombs, a dangerous game, needing much quickness both of eye and hand." "While unsurpassed for bravery, he also knew how to be prudent" (*Life of B.M.*, p.229). She never asked why such unsurpassed bravery in catching up live bombs was never acknowledged by Mussolini's superiors and why nobody ever thought of bestowing upon such a heroic and well-known warrior a gold, or a silver, or even a brass medal.

A few days after the king's visit, Austrian airplanes bombed the hospital (*Diary*, p. 180). Mrs. Sarfatti is positively sure that the Austrians purposely bombed the hospital in order to get rid of Mussolini and to win the war: "At once, from out the sky, came an aeroplane, which proceeded to fire upon the hospital correctly identified, where lay this enemy so deeply feared and hated" (*Life*, p.231).

On February 23, 1932, the secretary of the Fascist Student Group (GUF) of Turin, while celebrating the fifteenth anniversary of the day on which Mussolini had been wounded and thus had made "his bloody offering to the Fatherland," gave the following account about what happened when the hospital was bombed:

> The Austrians, knowing that their fiercest enemy was lying bleeding in the school of Ronchi, exultant with savage glee, sent aeroplanes to finish him off. Roar of explosions, crashing of bombs, resounding of shattered walls, shrieks of the wounded, nailed to their beds by new agonies. But the enemy failed in their highest mission. Once again the crucified hand of Jesus had come down from above and sheltered the head of the man from Romagna. No human force could arrest the prodigies that Destiny was preparing for him (Turin daily *Gazzetta del Popolo*, Feb. 25, 1932).

These are trivial matters indeed. But they serve to show how sagas are concocted and end by being accepted as history.

In March 1919, addressing the first nucleus of his followers in Milan, Mussolini announced that within two months about a thousand Fascist groups would spring up all over Italy. At the beginning of July, the level of his expectations had gone down from 1000 to 300, but even these 300 branches would be born "before long" and only in the most important cities: "Fascism can not propagate itself outside the cities." In October 1919, at the first national conference of the Fascist branches in Florence, the Fascists made out that 137 branches already existed, and that 62 were in the process of formation; the membership was given as 40,000. But, according to the report submitted to the Fascist congress in November

1921, in October 1919 there were no more than 20 local branches, and those enrolled in them numbered 17,000 (*Popolo d'Italia,* November 8, 1921). This last figure was certainly invented. If it had been true, every local branch would have had on an average of 850 members, a fact which was never heard of in Italy in 1919. In a speech of March 9, 1924, Mussolini stated that at the end of 1919 the Fascists in all Italy "did not amount to 10,000" (*La Nuova Politica dell'Italia* [Milan: Alpes, 1926], p.17). In the *Popolo d'Italia,* March 23, 1929, the administrative secretary of the party officially stated that on December 31, 1919, there were in Italy 31 Fasci with only 870 members. This last figure seems to be the only correct one. The others seem to have given, not the actual members of the Fascist local branches, but a rough estimate of Fascist sympathizers.

8

The
Populist Party

A new political organization offered itself to the Italian people as the only one capable of carrying out a program of basic social and political reforms without violent upheavals: the Italian Populist party ("Partito Popolare Italiano").[1]

In the decade before the war, the Catholics had cast their votes for their own candidates only in exceptional cases. As a rule, they had voted for Conservative candidates against Socialists or other well-known anticlericals. During the war, as the discontent against the war increased in the country, the Catholics realized that it was not advisable for them to go on acting as an appendage of the old Giolittian parliamentary coalition. The soldiers were stirred up by immense expectations. The young priests, who had served in the trenches during the war as chaplains, would have bluntly refused to serve as electoral canvassers of the old politicians. The Catholic organizations of the prewar period with conservative tendencies could not mobilize the restless Italian masses on the field of political action. Therefore, in January 1919, there arose the Italian Populist party as an entirely new formation.

The Catholic organizations of the prewar period had been controlled in

---

[1] The Italian term *Partito Popolare* is usually translated in English "Italian Popular Party," but the word "popular" leads to the notion that the other Italian parties were "unpopular" or that the *Partito Popolare Italiano* claimed to be the only "popular" party in Italy. It is more to the point to translate "Partito Popolare" into "People's Party" or "Populist" Party.

each diocese by the bishops and, in the last instance, by the Vatican. The new party abstained from labeling itself "Catholic"; it even denied that it was a "religious" party; it claimed to be a "political" party, although it intended to conform its conduct to "the sound principles of Christianity." Being a political party and not religious, it was autonomous from ecclesiastical authorities.

Of the old Catholic organizations, the "Catholic Electoral Union" *(Unione elettorale cattolica)*, which before the war had supported the candidates of the Giolittian parliamentary coalition when it did not present its own, disappeared without anyone's ever asking what had happened to it. The "Economic-Social Union" *(Unione economica-sociale)*, which before the war contained the trade unions, cooperative societies, banks, and in general all the economic organizations controlled by Catholics, was officially disbanded by the Vatican, and the trade unions formed an "Italian Confederation of Workers" *(Confederazione Italiana dei lavoratori)*, while the cooperative societies gathered into three different national federations, one for the consumers, the second for production, and the third for banking. The Confederation and the three federations allied themselves with the Populist party. Outside the Populist party remained some minor organizations of the prewar period—for example, the "Society of Italian Catholic Youth" *(Società della gioventù cattolica italiana)* and the "Union of Italian Catholic Women" *(Unione delle donne cattoliche italiane)*, which were under the control of a "Central Committee for Catholic Action" *(Giunta centrale dell'Azione cattolica)* and finally of the Vatican.[2] In this way the difference between the organizations affiliated with the Populist party and autonomous from ecclesiastical authorities, and the Catholic organizations dependent on the ecclesiastical authorities, showed up clearly.

The Populist party condemned imperialism and upheld the League of Nations, disarmament, and the discarding of treaties. In domestic policies, it advocated universal suffrage, even for women; proportional representation; social legislation aimed at admitting the workers to the ownership of the means of production and increasing the number of small landowners; a more active struggle against illiteracy; and freedom for individuals, associations, and local bodies from the oppressive, bureaucratic, and centralized state. To those who condemned the war and those responsible for it, these Catholics, who had been averse to the intervention of Italy into the

---

[2] E. Vercesi, *Il movimento cattolico in Italia* (Firenze: La Voce, 1913), p.253.

war, recalled their own past and hailed Pope Benedict XV, who in 1917 had tried in vain to stop the "useless carnage" (words used by the pope himself). To those who had favored the war and were elated by victory, the military chaplains and the young men who had returned from the war showed their medals for bravery and their wounds and mutilations. If one never wanted to have another war, the program of the new party promised him a policy of peace under the wings of the League of Nations. This, however, did not prohibit the Catholics of nationalistic tendencies from demanding Dalmatia, Asia Minor, Ethiopia, and what not. Most organizers came from the secular and regular clergy, together with young men back from the army. In March 1919, in Naples, 350 canons, parish priests, and priests held a meeting in which they decided to enroll in a mass in the Populist party (*Corriere della sera*, April 1, 1919). The same thing happened all over Italy. But since the party was not Catholic, or not even religious, any non-Catholic who accepted the sound principles of Christianity might join in it. There were Jews who applied for its membership and candidly tried to become its candidates in the coming national election.

The rise of the new party was amazingly rapid. In 1914, the Catholics controlled, all over Italy, no more than 42,000 trade unionists in industry and 65,000 in agriculture.[3] At the end of October 1918, Catholic trade unionists were 162,000. In March 1919, the Italian Confederation of Workers numbered 200,000 (*Corriere della sera*, March 15, 1919). By the autumn of 1920, the membership had risen to 1,189,000.[4] In June 1919, at the first national conference of the party, 850 local branches were represented with 55,895 members. At the end of 1919, the local branches numbered 2,700 with 100,000 members.[5]

The new party was received at first with favor by the old governing groups who hoped that, no less than the Catholic electoral organizations of the prewar period, it would act as a "maneuvering mass" in their service against the Socialists.[6] Soon the "liberals" were disap-

---

[3] Vercesi, *Il movimento cattolico in Italia*, p.252.

[4] *Bollettino dell'Ufficio del Lavoro*, 34(1):523.

[5] A. De Rossi, *Il primo anno di vita del Partito Popolare Italiano* (Roma: Ferrari, 1920), pp. 72, 79.

[6] T. Tittoni, *Nuovi scritti di politica interna ed estera* (Milano: Treves, 1930), pp.281–82: "The new Populist party had aroused great hopes at its birth. Many liberals counted on it as an ally against socialism. I was one of those. . . . I no longer had any faith in the future of the liberal party, which, in my opinion, had wandered off the direct way . . . The Populist party ought to have given the assurance that it would free the country from the influence of the subversive parties. If it had done so, it would have controlled the situation and would have become predominant over all other parties. It was in a position to do so, since it was

pointed.[7] In the summer of 1919, they and the Catholic conservatives began to complain of a "black Bolshevism."[8]

They were not entirely wrong. In the Populist movement soon men came to the fore here and there who started a lively competition with the Socialists under the banner of Christ instead of that of Lenin. In August 1919, in the village of Calusco (province of Bergamo), the peasantry banded together at the sound of the bells and beseiged the sons of a Catholic landowner, Count Medolago Albani, for twelve hours until the father sent word from Bergamo that he agreed unconditionally to the terms demanded by the peasants (*Corriere della sera*, August 5, 1919). Not a few events of this kind occurred in 1919 and 1920.

Yet if one wants to examine the facts objectively, one must bear in mind that in Italy, as everywhere else, in the immediate postwar years, the conservatives themselves were often more sanguine in their utterances than many professional revolutionaries.[9] Everyone was promising everything to everybody. Whoever had advised calm and patience would have been outdone by those who shouted for extreme measures. Indulging to a certain extent the convulsions of the masses was the only means of keeping in touch

the only party which possessed the means of fighting against socialism for the conquest of the masses. If this had come to pass, I would have officially joined the Populist party." Tittoni had been foreign minister with Giolitti and ambassador to Paris. He was to become one of the highest personages in the Fascist regime. He was a big landowner in the district of Rome, where the peasantry formed the most poverty-stricken people of Italy. For the significance of the word "liberal" in Italy during the first twenty years of the current century, see Chapter 5.

[7] Tittoni adds to the words given in the preceding footnote: "But, alas!, at the first Congress which the party held in Bologna, it was clear that the majority of the assembled men had no idea of the situation which the party could have and should have taken by giving the country what it needed and the liberal parties could not give it."

[8] The Catholic O.M. Premoli (*Storia ecclesiastica contemporanea, 1900–1925* [Torino, 1925, p.110]) writes: "The saddest thing was that the clergy of the countryside and of the small towns, usually coming from peasant or working class stock, were quick to applaud this Catholic socialism and aligned themselves against the bourgeois class." Baron E. Beyens, Ambassador of Belgium to Rome from 1921 to 1925, in his book *Quatre ans à Rome* (Paris: Plon, 1934), echoes the anger of the Catholic conservatives against the Populist party.

[9] For the "revolutionary" utterances of Salandra and Orlando, see Chapter 5. To remain in the Catholic field, it is well to remember that in 1920, the bishops of the U.S.A. announced the coming "abolition of the salaried man." Cardinal Bourne wrote: "Everybody admits that a new order, new social conditions, new relations between the various social classes will arise, as a result of the destruction of the old order of things." Monsignor Deploige, president of the High Institute of Philosophy of the University of Louvain, wrote: "A new order is developing, and the world of tomorrow will be quite another thing than the world of yesterday" (Vercesi, *Il movimento cattolico italiano*, pp. 263–64). In Italy, the slogan "land to the peasants" was launched for the first time in 1918 by a "Reformist Socialist," Aurelio Drago, who afterwards became Fascist; and it was picked up and chanted by ultraconservative Marquis Tanari, who also became Fascist afterwards.

with them and of relieving their bitterness. A party like the Populist party, which was recruiting into its ranks large masses of peoples from all stations of life, was bound to show drifts towards either the extreme left or the extreme right. It is unfair, when passing judgment on the work of the Populist party, to get exercised about its extreme left, and to ignore the fact that the directorate of the party tried to keep down—and when necessary disavowed outright—its activities.[10]

The real guilt of the Populist party—an unpardonable guilt in the eyes of the conservatives, both "liberal" and Catholic—was in not joining with the wealthy classes to oppose the organizations of working people. In the eyes of the conservatives, any strikes of laborers were "Bolshevist," whether they were "white"—that is to say, instigated by Christian Democrats—or whether they were "red"—i.e., led by Socialists, even if they were not accompanied by acts of violence such as those which were experienced by the sons of Count Medolago Albani. The banner made little difference, when both of them demanded the same increase in salaries and decrease in the hours of work. If Jesus Christ refuses to serve as galley guard over those who have to earn their daily bread by the sweat of their brows, Jesus Christ also becomes a "Bolshevist." Whoever wants to drown his own dog, says that it has gone mad.

The fact is that the Populist party prevented the Socialist party from gaining an undisputed hold upon the peasantry. Out of the 1,189,000 members who were controlled by the Populist Confederation of Workers in 1920, 945,000 were metayers *(mezzadri)*, small tenants, or small landowners. Of the 2,150,000 trade unionists who, in 1920, were under Socialist leadership, no more than 750,000 came from agriculture classes. If the Populist party had not been there, the grip of the Socialists would have been overwhelming among the peasantry as well as among the city workers. The great landowners, the bankers, and the *nouveaux riches* who supported the Populist party in 1919 and 1920 did a good stroke of business and a smart thing. They placed their money and their Catholic faith at a very high rate of interest.

While it accomplished this negative although highly important task, the Populist party did not possess sufficient strength for any independent positive action. In the cities it never had any preponderant influence. Its followers were almost exclusively rural and from nothern and central Italy.

[10] L. Sturzo, *Popolarismo e Fascismo* (Torino: Gobetti, 1924) pp.23–28, 107, 122–23, 168.

Here, the rural populations are spread about the country. The parish priest lives in contact with them, knows their mentality and needs, and if he is a good man and active in the field of social services, he easily becomes the social leader of the rural community as well as the minister of the sacraments. The conditions are quite different in southern Italy. Here the peasantry is usually concentrated in fair-sized towns. The day laborers swarm out from the town in the morning to work in the fields, and they return home in the evening, or at the end of the week, or after several weeks of absence. The parish priest is unable to gain over them that hold which comes from permanent personal contact. He is unable to know, one by one, more than a small part of his overpopulated and congested parish. Furthermore, the clergy of southern Italy are less educated, less austere, more concerned with their own interests and those of their families than are the clergy of northern Italy. In this sector also, the backwardness of southern Italy shows itself. As a consequence, southern Italy, not unlike other Italian cities, was a barren field for the Catholic clergy, unless some priest of exceptional intelligence and moral character should be here and there available as social leader of the people.

Under such conditions, the Populist party never rallied under its banner more than one-fifth of the politically active population. It should have allied itself with other parties if it wished to carry out its program, or some planks of its program. Here serious difficulties arose from within and from without.

The mass of its followers was formed essentially of that class which, in Italy, is termed "popolo minuto," or "thin people." It was cut-and-dried democratic in its rank and file. Its national secretary, a Sicilian priest, Don Luigi Sturzo, shared sincerely in the feelings of his followers and enjoyed great prestige among them. But the party was also flooded by all those conservatives who, in the prewar period, had controlled the Catholic political movement. They formed only a small minority compared to the "thin people" and the lower clergy. But they enjoyed the confidence of most cardinals, bishops, and high officials of the Vatican. They were noblemen, big landowners, and other solemn personages well known for public offices previously covered up. They could sustain the expenses of electoral contests. They had time to dedicate to politics. They knew all the ways and means by which a politician appears at the right moment, at the strategical spot, any time a candidate for parliament, for a local body, or for the national executive of the party is to be chosen. They administered the banks affiliated with the party, and, through these, they controlled many cooperative societies. The most important of these banks and the most rotten was the Banco di Roma, which subsidized the two most important newspapers of the party, the *Corriere d'Italia* of Rome and the *Avvenire d'Italia* of Bologna. In the non-Catholic circles, it used to be said that the Populist party was born carrying in its stomach the cancer of the Bank of Rome. The other dailies, the *Momento* of Turin, the *Italia* of Milan, and the *Messaggero Toscano* of Pisa, were also kept alive by Catholic conservatives at the expense of the local banks. As a Catholic deputy later was to confess, "under the flag of the Italian Populist party there was not one single party but two: two Catholic parties which, in a memorable historic moment, amalgamated" (*Corriere della sera*, July 28, 1928). This twofold nature of the party was a permanent cause of internal friction and, in the last analysis, of uncertain and inefficient action. The party was a machine in which a great number of little cogs turned in one direction and a few large cogs rotated in the opposite direction, disturbing or altogether paralyzing the working of the small ones. The party never succeeded in coming down from the clouds of philosophic and moral abstractions to the terra firma of a definite program of far-reaching reforms which forced the other parties to take a stand and to fight pro or con.

Granted that the party had to ally itself with other parties if it wanted to carry on an efficient work, the conservative wing of the party was ready to come to terms with the right wing of the Giolittian parliamentary coalition, continuing the prewar Catholic policy. In May 1919, a Catholic congress held in southern Italy, in which three archbishops and fourteen bishops took part, demanded that the Catholics in the coming national election should not put forward their own candidates but support the "national" groups—in other words, the Conservatives and the Nationalists (*Corriere della sera*, May 12, 1919). If the leaders of the party had taken this way, they would have lost their army. The old Giolittian coalition was discredited and unpopular. The new party had arisen precisely because it had become necessary to break away from the tactics of the old Catholic organizations.

There remained the parties which were (or professed to be) democratic: the left wing of the Giolittian coalition, the Reformist Socialists, the Republicans, and the Official Socialists. Here insurmountable difficulties arose.

National unity and free institutions in Italy had been created and kept up during the entire nineteenth century through a bitter struggle against the Vatican, the high clergy, and that part of the lower clergy and of the population which formed the "clerical" party—a party not only conservative but outright reactionary. In the last ten years of the nineteenth century, under Leo XIII, there had been quite a promising beginning of Christian democracy. But Pius X, at the beginning of the present century, had suffocated that movement and associated the Catholic organizations with the conservative groups in all national and local elections. Therefore, the anticlerical currents, which went back to the time of the Risorgimento, were always alive and active in the democratic parties, and often they took the form of blind sectarian hatred. However much the Populist party insisted on calling itself democratic, it could not make people forget the recent past of the Catholic movement, especially when many of its old leaders occupied visible strategic positions in the new party.

There was another reason which made difficult, not to say impossible, any understanding between the Populist party and the Democratic anticlerical parties. This was the "Roman question."

Before 1859, the pope had simultaneously been head of the Catholic Church—an international religious organization—and sovereign of territories in central Italy. According to Catholic doctrine, territorial sovereignty was necessary to the pope as a guarantee of his spiritual liberty as head of the international Catholic Church. Between 1859 and 1870, all the papal territories were annexed to the Kingdom of Italy. When Rome, the capital city of the papal state, was occupied by the Italian troops in September 1870, the pope retired, together with his court, into the so-called Vatican, a complex of buildings, gardens, and other grounds covering an area of about fifty acres on the right bank of the Tiber river.

In March 1871, the Italian Parliament passed an act, "the Law of Guarantees." According to this law, the person of the pope, like that of the king, was to be sacred and inviolable. The pope was authorized to "enjoy the use" of the Vatican, of the Lateran Palace, and of a villa in the country near Rome. He was empowered to keep a guard for his person; envoys accredited to him were accorded diplomatic immunities; the Italian government should abstain from any jurisdiction over the Vatican and from interfering in the administration of the Catholic Church throughout the world. The law further provided that the pope would be offered an annuity of $600,000 for the maintenance of his court and diplomatic service.

Thus the pope remained head of the Church, but he was deprived of the territorial sovereignty which was considered a necessary guarantee of his liberty. He was a dispossessed sovereign living with his court in the heart of his ancient state, encompassed by his dispossessors. He continued to enjoy all the privileges of an independent sovereign, but he could not even claim, as his own legal property, the very palace in which he lived. The Italian government simply granted him the use of it and reserved the ownership of the property for itself. In the place of this territorial guarantee, he was offered a law which pledged the Italian government to respect his liberty. But the very Parliament that had passed the "Law of Guarantees" might repeal it and subject the pope to a new legislation which would interfere with his liberty.

Pope Pius IX refused to acknowledge as legitimate this act of legislation enacted without his consent. He let slip no opportunity to claim the territories over which he once exercised sovereignty. He refused the annuity offered him by the Italian government and appealed to Catholics throughout the world to provide the needs of the Holy See with Saint Peter's pence. When Pius IX died in February, 1878, his successor, Leo XIII, refused to give the traditional blessing of the new pope to the populace awaiting in St. Peter's Square. He declared that he regarded himself as a prisoner under enemy domination. He forbade the faithful in Italy to go to the polls or to stand in elections of candidates for representatives in Parliament. Sovereigns of Catholic countries were prohibited from coming officially to Rome to pay visits to the Italian court. Outside Italy, Catholics carried on a systematic campaign of propaganda against Italy, usurper of the rights of the Holy See. As long as the territorial sovereignty of the pope was not restored in some way, Italy was to be considered a lawless power, with no legitimate status in the commonwealth of nations. By these methods, the Vatican aimed at keeping the Roman question alive.

Despite this and many other difficulties, Italy managed to live and strengthen herself. On the other hand, all the Italian governments, regardless of the party in power, took care to respect scrupulously the liberty of the pope as head of the Catholic Church. No bishop outside Italy was ever able to complain that his communications with the pope had been hampered by the Italian government. No ambassador from foreign governments to the Holy See was ever able to assert that the Italian government placed obstacles in his relations with the pope or violated his diplomatic immunities.

Little by little, it became clear that the condition of the pope was more comfortable after 1870 than it had been before. The pope no longer had the responsibility of governing a territory peopled by subjects, a part of whom did not intend, under any consideration, to obey him. On the other hand, he enjoyed in actual fact a complete liberty, even if it was not guaranteed by territorial sovereignty. While he was immune from all the responsibilities which burden the shoulders of civil governments and really enjoyed a complete liberty, he could still complain on the ground that his very liberty was not guaranteed. He could present himself to the world with the romantic halo of a prisoner who had been the victim of an act of violence but who did not stoop to violence and who continued, on the contrary, to protest in order to maintain his rights. The pope could have found no more convenient situation than this one in any other solution of the Roman question.

These circumstances explain why Pius X (1903–14), the successor to Leo XIII, slowly began to abandon the position of intransigent protest which Pius IX and Leo XIII had maintained for thirty years. In 1904, by way of exception, he permitted Italian Catholics to take part in national elections in some constituencies. In 1909 and 1913, exceptions were multiplied. Catholics were elected deputies and took their oaths of allegiance to the constitution.

When the World War broke out, the Central Empires, on the one hand, and the Powers of the Entente, on the other, were eager to have Italy as an ally. No Catholic in either camp felt any scruple in turning to profitable account Italian cannon fodder, even though not blessed by the pope. Italy joined the Entente. As a consequence, the German and Austrian Catholics began to be very much concerned about the Roman question. The French and the British Catholics found it more convenient to ignore it. Since Germany and Austria lost the war, nobody raised the Roman question during the peace negotiations.

Having lost any hope of keeping alive the Roman question either abroad or in Italy, Benedict XV and Cardinal Gasparri, his secretary of state (foreign minister) decided to negotiate an accord with the Italian government. The negotiations were begun in the spring of 1919. The pope would be content merely with having his sovereignty over the Vatican explicitly recognized.[11] Since the Italian government had never thought of wielding

---

[11] The initiators of the negotiation, Monsignor (later cardinal) B. Cerretti, semi-official delegate of Cardinal Gasparri, and Prime Minister Orlando, have published the records of their exchange of views. Cerretti's diary was published in the Catholic review *Vita e Pensiero*, June-July 1929, pp. 411ff., and Orlando's version in V.E. Orlando, *Su alcuni miei rapporti di governo con la Santa Sede*, (Napoli, Casa editrice Sabina, 1930, pp.71 ff.)

any authority over the Vatican, Orlando agreed to the demand of the pope. The negotiations, interrupted by the fall of Orlando's cabinet in June 1919, were taken up again under the following cabinet. The way to a final settlement of the question was now open. The negotiations, however, remained absolutely secret. They were made known only in 1929. In 1919, the Roman question, although it had lost all intensity, always remained open.

To be sure, the leaders of the Populist party, more than anyone else, desired peace to be made between the Holy See and the Italian government. But they did not know that the pope was ready to renounce explicitly his sovereignty over all his old territories except the area of the Vatican. Even if they had known it, they would not have been authorized to reveal the negotiation, which was to remain secret. On the other hand, if they had flaunted the Roman question on their banner without proposing any definite solution for it, they would have aroused the suspicion that the Vatican was preparing to come out again with all its traditional claims. Violent reactions would have resulted from it in the tumultuous atmosphere of the postwar period, not only on the part of the anticlerical parties, but also of those "liberals" who had always advocated an understanding with the Catholics.

The leaders of the Populist party resolved the problem by ignoring it. They confine themselves to demanding that the relations between state and Church be reexamined and the liberty of the Church in the exercise of its spiritual mission all over the world better guaranteed—words which might say anything or nothing.

The official review of the Vatican, *Civiltà Cattolica*, in its issue of February 15, 1919, complained of the fact that the program of the new party made no "explicit mention of the full liberty, sovereignty and independence of the pope." The authors of a pamphlet published a few weeks later wrote:

> There is lacking in the program of the Populist party any explicit mention of the full liberty, sovereignty and independence which the pope is entitled to in his exalted office; there is lacking the courageous and befitting affirmation that the "Roman question" must be solved. As Catholics, we can not break away from the pope, nor ignore his present condition. A party which takes its inspiration from Christian principles, can not disregard the sorrowful fact that today,

> the independence and the spiritual liberty of the pope are
> not sufficiently guaranteed. . . . For the very glory of Italy,
> the Populist party must concern itself with the solution of
> the "Roman question."[12]

In the first national congress of the party, in June 1919, two congress-
men, Count Vincenzo Reggio d'Aci and Count Filippo Sassoli de' Bianchi,
sought to raise the issue of "the serious disagreement existing between state
and Church in Italy." Count d'Aci said:

> If the Populist party desires a Christian state, it must desire
> that this disagreement cease. It is not its task to say how.
> The Supreme Authority will take care of that. But it must
> bring home to the masses the necessity of closing this con-
> flict. There should be included in our resolution an item to
> the effect that the Roman question is still there, and we
> desire it to be settled.

L'Osservatore Romano, on June 17, 1919, at this point of the record,
inserted: "clamor, interruptions." The two counts understood and withdrew their proposal.

This silence on a question which really existed, and really ought to have
concerned the party, also aroused suspicions among anticlerical parties.
What were the leaders of the Populist party aiming at? Were they silent
today because they were waiting for the moment when they could show
their claws, or did they really consider the Roman question so out of date
that it was not worthy of their notice? The political situation could become
more favorable to the Vatican as a result of the influence that the Populist
Party had acquired in government and administration through its electoral
and parliamentarian action. What would the Vatican have done then? It
was only natural that the anticlerical parties should be suspicious of a
movement which, even on the subject of the Roman question, followed an
obscure line of conduct.

The Populist party took as its war cry the word "liberty." It demanded
"religious liberty from every kind of sectarian oppression"; "liberty for the
Church in the accomplishment of its high spiritual mission"; liberty for the
private schools maintained by the Catholics which could not stand up

---

[12] Gemelli and Olgiati, *Il programma del Partito Popolare Italiano: come non è e come
dovrebbe essere* (Milano: "Vita e Pensiero," 1919), pp. 59–60.

against the competition of the schools favored by the government; liberty for the trade unions controlled by Catholics, which could not have been able to develop if the government had favored only the Socialist unions. There was no doubt, therefore, that the Populist party demanded liberty for the Catholics. But what about the liberty of non-Catholics? Don Sturzo maintained that the Populist party demanded "liberty for all." Yet the official doctrine of the Catholic Church has never accepted "liberty for all." The Catholic Church admits only the "liberty for the good"—that is to say, for what the authorities of the Church define as "good." Freedom of conscience for all, freedom of worship for all, freedom of speech for all, freedom of the press for all, freedom of teaching for all—these "freedoms for all" have always been condemned by all the popes as liberty for evil, for error, for disorder, for anarchy, for immorality.[13] In the countries where the Catholics are not able to control the governments, the Church "tolerates" freedom for all, but the Catholics must utilize these liberties granted to all in order to gain that sway over the government which is their due. When they have gained control, they must use it to restrict and, whenever possible, to suppress entirely, the freedom of evil.[14]

The Populist party maintained that it was autonomous from the ecclesiastical authorities and from the Vatican. But its secretary general was a Catholic priest, who would have taken no initiative for the creation of the new party, nor would have become its secretary general had he foreseen that his ecclesiastical superiors might condemn him. Many of the most active members of the movement belonged to the secular or regular clergy —that is, they were men who, no less than Don Sturzo, were bound to their ecclesiastical superiors not only by the duty of obedience common to all Catholics, but also by that specific form of discipline which is peculiar to the clergy. The mass of the party was made up of practicing Catholics. The

[13] Georges Michon, *Les documents pontificaux sur la democratie et la societé moderne* (Paris: Rieder, 1929), has made a collection of the most characteristic condemnations pronounced by the popes in the nineteenth century against all the liberties which are essential to a democratic regime.

[14] See especially the encyclical *Libertas*, June 20, 1888, of Leo XIII. The declarations in favor of all liberties made by Governor Smith in 1927, in his discussion with Mr. C.C. Marshall (*Atlantic Monthly*, April and May), were "tolerated," but never explicitly "approved," by the ecclesiastical authorities of the United States of America because they were made in a country where the Constitution grants in equal measure as much to the "good"—that is to say, to the Catholic religion—as to the "evil"—that is to say, to all other religions. The day on which the authorities of the Catholic Church believed it possible to set up in the United States a monopoly for "good" and to suppress the freedom of "evil," then the declarations of Governor Smith in favor of all freedom for all, would no longer be "tolerated" and would be "condemned."

official Catholic doctrine teaches that the Catholic owes obedience to the ecclesiastical authorities in all dogmatic and moral matters, and not in political questions. But where does moral end and where does political begin? The pope is infallible when he is speaking *ex cathedra* on matters of dogma and morals. But he never speaks *ex cathedra;* instead he speaks, day in and day out, by means of encyclicals, allocutions, letters. More often than the pope, the bishops speak. To disobey the pope or the bishops is at least a sin of pride insofar as it implies mistrust towards the legitimate authorities of the Church. A non-Catholic may ask advice from the authorities of his church, but *in the last instance* it is his individual conscience which commands him to act on his own exclusive responsibility. Entirely different are the duties of the Catholic. If he does not wish to fall into sin, he must obey the "doctrinal teaching" of the pope and the bishops. At the most, he is allowed to remain silent.

Pope Benedict XV and his secretary of state, Cardinal Gasparri, neither approved nor forbade the rising of the new political party. They ignored it. By ignoring it, they allowed, or at least tolerated, it. What would happen on the day when tolerance was withdrawn? A priest-journalist summed up the situation in the following terms:

> When delicate matters are at stake, one ought to take care not to go beyond certain limits. The fact that the Populist party professes not to be a Catholic party does not change the fact that its strength mainly comes from the Catholic Church. If, therefore, on the assumption of its actually or potentially non-Catholic nature, its leaders should come to grips with the ecclesiastical authorities, many of the faithful would be forced to choose between their religious conscience and their party loyalty. They would choose the former. . . . It is wise to act with extreme caution in matters where the ecclesiastical authority can, and perhaps must, have the last word. Thus, the nonreligious nature of the Populist party must be taken with a grain of salt. Otherwise one can run up against some delusion. . . . The Populist party would be inconceivable if there was not there the permission of the Holy See.[15]

In other words, the party remained autonomous as long as it did nothing which might displease the ecclesiastical authorities; but on the day when

[15] Vercesi, *Il movimento cattolico in Italia,* pp. 183, 185, 290–91.

the latter declared that they could no longer approve its work, it would find itself at the crossroads: it had either to renounce its autonomy and obey the ecclesiastical authorities, or to assert its autonomy and face a condemnation on the part of the ecclesiastical authorities.

Don Sturzo was convinced that in a regime of freedom for all, the Catholic Church, not protected but not discredited by legal privileges, relying on the strength of its own ideas, depending on the sole force of persuasion and example, would win over to its side the spirit of the Italian people. When the hour of ill fortune struck, he gave proof of his sincerity. But in 1919, this proof had not yet been shown, and it was legitimate to wonder whether his faith in democracy and in "freedom for all" were not destined to disappear as soon as the political situation was changed. Many other Catholic priests who, after the War of 1914–18, arose in other countries of Europe as leaders of Christian democratic movements (Seipel in Austria, Joos in Germany, Korosec in Yugoslavia, Tiso in Slovakia), were to unmask themselves as insecure friends or outright traitors of democracy. In Italy, too, it was to be shown how shaky was the democratic faith of too many leaders of the Populist party, who, as soon as the wind changed, passed over bag and baggage to the Fascist party. Even those who believed in Don Sturzo's moral integrity had to keep in mind that Don Sturzo might disappear, but behind him and his party, there stood on its feet the entire organization of the Catholic Church, ready to return to the assault with its doctrinal traditions intact.

The parties which remained faithful to the anticlerical tradition of the Italian Risorgimento, therefore, were not wrong if they refused to enter with the new party into relations of good neighborliness. Certainly there was in them something more than a calm vision of real dangers. There was also unreasonable hatred. But the Populist party aroused insuperable suspicion, even among people who thought anticlerical hatreds to have become outlived and would have welcomed a democratic movement no longer chained by a narrowminded and sectarian anti-Catholic mentality.

AUTHOR'S NOTES TO CHAPTER 8

He who wishes to understand the difficulties with which the Populist party was confronted—to understand, in fact, the whole history of Italy—must give up the misconception that the population of Italy is Catholic and, as such, obedient to the pope and the clergy.

If all those who were baptized at birth in the Catholic Church are to be counted as Catholics, there is no doubt that Italy is a Catholic country. But if one understands by Catholics only those who consistently do their best to give a general Catholic tone to the society in which they live, it is then very doubtful that the majority of Italy's population can be termed Catholic in fact.

From the religious point of view, the Italians may be grouped into five classes: (1) non-Catholics; (2) indifferent; (3) idolaters; (4) Catholics proper; and (5) mystics.

To the first class belong not only the 10,000 Jews and the 125,000 Protestants of the official statistics, but also a large number of persons who were baptized in the Catholic Church but have lost all religious faith and profess anticlerical principles or even atheism.

An Italian census, in which people were asked to state their religion, was taken in 1911. In that census, 870,000 persons declared that they had "no religion," while 653,000 more did not give any answer. This silence, in all fairness, may be interpreted as an equivalent to the answer "no religion." Of these persons who implicitly or explicitly declared that they were not Catholics, 900,000 were men and 600,000 were women. Of the 870,000 Italians who explicitly declared that they had no religion, a good 200,000 or a little less than one-quarter, belonged to the provinces previously governed by the pope, though these provinces contained scarcely one-twelfth of the total population. From this section of the population, during the nineteenth and twentieth centuries, came the militant anticlericals. One of their typical representatives was Mussolini, who, up until 1921, made profession of atheism and advocated by all means the destruction of the Catholic Church.

The "indifferent" group is formed by people who were baptized in the Catholic Church and perform certain external acts of religion, such as contracting marriage according to the religious rite, christening their children, declaring themselves Catholics, and at the point of death asking for a religious funeral so as to obtain a regular ticket to heaven. But as for the rest, religion and the Church have no part in their lives. Nine-tenths of the Italian intelligentsia belong to this "baptized but indifferent" variety. One of the mental features of this class is their "anticlericalism"—that is to say, their opposition to all attempts of the clergy and of the Church to exercise any influence on the political and social life of the country and on schools and educational institutions. They refuse to be dictated to by the clergy and become fiercely anticlerical as soon as they feel themselves to be annoyed by the Church. The Italian literature of the nineteenth century is permeated by anticlerical spirit. From Alfieri to Carducci, papal Rome has been the butt of sharp attacks and vilification. When they are not out and out anti-Catholic, these "indifferent" intellectuals are Catholic, but in a negative sense—in the sense that they do not adhere to any Christian non-Catholic sect. They do not profess atheism, because there is, in their hearts and minds, a traditional attachment to certain forms of religiosity which, not infrequently, in old age or at the point of death, emerge from the depths of their consciousness. But during their lifetimes, or at least as long as they are in good health, they are not an asset, but rather a liability, for the Italian Catholic Church.

Giolitti was a typical representative of this class. On May 30, 1904, he said to the Chamber of Deputies:

> I believe that it is not a mark of weakness to look with indifference to religious questions. The State and the Church should be two parallel lines which never meet. Woe unto the Church if it should wish to invade the powers of the State. We will be as severe towards it as against anyone else who tries to usurp those powers.

When he arrived at the point of death in 1928, he declared that he wished to die, as he always had lived, within the bosom of the Catholic Church, and he stipulated that he should be given a religious funeral.

Most urban workers, when they are not out-and-out irreligious, have as a rule this indifferent mentality. It will never be possible for an Italian of this type to understand how a man of sense can lose his temper over the affairs of the pope, while he could go out to breath the fresh air and play a game of cards during his hours of leisure. Italian folklore is full of stories in which priests and monks and nuns are the object of derision. The poetry of the various Italian dialects frequently and gladly takes as the butt of its satire priests, cardinals, and popes. The common people of Rome are the most characteristic representatives of this indifference and raillery. They say, "At Rome they make faith; elsewhere they believe it."

The "idolaters" comprise the mass of the lower classes in southern Italy, the Papal States, and a good part of Tuscany. The men and women of the low people of Naples who pile abuses on the image of their patron saint, calling him "Yellow Face" when he is slow in performing the miracle of making his blood boil; the peasants who worship their Madonna but despise as inferior the Madonna of the neighboring town, or believe and practice witchcraft, or lick the floor of the sanctuary with their tongues while crawling on all fours towards the miraculous idol; the public woman who keeps a lamp ever burning before a holy image in her "workroom"; should these idolaters be counted as Catholics? One would not dare to answer in the affirmative, not only because the faith and ideals of the Catholic Church do not deserve this offense, but also because the doctrines of the Church and the teaching of the clergy have no real influence whatever over this idolatrous population. The sacraments are to them nothing but magic rites, and the priest, after he performs those rites, is for them a man like all others, if he is fortunate enough not to be looked upon as a person of doubtful morality. The pope is for them a kind of mythical being with whom they have nothing in common; and while they are as generous toward the local sanctuaries as their poverty permits, to the pope they send very little or nothing at all.

It would be wrong to believe that the idolaters are morally inferior beings. As a rule they love their families and are hardworking, temperate, and thoroughly honest. One finds among them the same proportion of moral and immoral persons as in other sections of any other population. Ignorance and superstition are maladies of the mind, not of the heart.

Now finally we come to the Catholics who are consistently so, since they accept the doctrinal and moral standards of the Church and conform their conduct thereto, so far as human frailty allows them to do so.

How many are the "Catholics proper" in Italy? It would be absurd to give definite figures. But we can get some idea of their numbers by examining the returns of the national election in 1919. This election was held under the system of universal suffrage and proportional representation, which permitted each party to mobilize under its own banner all the forces available in the country. The government brought no pressure to bear upon the electorate, so that this was the only Italian election in which the Chamber was not forced to examine any protests against government interference in the elections. The Populist party had its candidates in all constituencies and was supported by the clergy as well as by all Catholic organizations. Though it professed not to be a "Catholic party," it was the party of the Catholics. Thus the latter had a chance to express by plebiscite their will to influence national politics through a party that represented their political, social, and moral beliefs. They polled 1,170,000 out of

5,682,000 votes—i.e., about one-fifth of the total.

Two-fifths of the votes—2,400,000—went to the Socialist party, their program being essentially anticlerical and their candidates all men well known for their hostility to the Church. The remainder, 2,100,000—i.e., two-fifths of the votes—went to the other parties, among whom the Republicans, the Reformist Socialists, most "Radicals," and (last but not least) the Fascists belonged to the anticlerical tradition. The rest were mainly indifferent or idolaters.

In short, not more than one-fifth of the Italian population may be regarded as "Catholic proper."

Four sections of northern Italy (Piedmont, Liguria, Lombardy, and Venetia), which in 1919 contained one-third of the total population of the nation, contributed 613,000 voters to the Populist party—that is, one-half of the votes received by the party in all of Italy. To these 613,000 votes, the cities of major importance contributed scarcely 70,000 votes, while the smaller towns and the country districts gave 540,000 votes, or six-sevenths. In the four most characteristic regions of southern Italy (Basilicata, Calabria, Sicily, and Sardinia), which contained one-fifth of the total population, the Populist party received only 115,000 votes—that is, one-tenth of its total national vote and one-ninth of the votes in those regions. Here again, the more populous cities gave scarcely 13,000 votes, while the other nine-tenths of the votes came from the less populous centers. These figures show conclusively that the "Catholics proper" live in the rural areas, especially in northern Italy.

Not a few of these consistent Catholics belong to what we would like to call the "mystic" type. They are to be found especially among women of all classes and social conditions. The Italian low clergy not seldom provides unknown heroes who live a life of poverty and sacrifice, exposed in many districts to the hostility of irreligious surroundings. Italian missionaries in non-Christian countries have carried more than their share in the work of evangelization. Superficial observers do not notice the existence of this "mystic Italy." The foreigner who goes to Rome, and there comes in contact with the intriguing clergy of the Vatican or with the indifferent intellectuals of the lay world, concludes that all Italians are irreligiously cynical. This is a great mistake. All Italians are not in Rome. The mystic Italy, the Italy of St. Francis, of St. Catherine of Siena, and of Savonarola, is still alive; it produced Don Bosco in the nineteenth century.

The Italian mystics accept dogma without discussion. But they take no interest in it. Nor do they like others to discuss it, even for the purpose of defending it. Dogmatic controversies are not salutary to the salvation of the soul; that which matters to them is receiving the sacraments, praying to the Virgin and to the saints to take pity on unhappy and sinful humanity, and performing good works in proportion to their ability. Infinite is the number of charitable works which thrive in Italy on the free, daily contributions of people because they are kept up by mystics. It is common enough to find indifferents or anti-Catholics who contribute to these good works out of admiration for the men and women who silently devote to them treasures of abnegation and of kindness. The mystics worship the pope and would never dare to revolt against him. Protestants, if they are English, can get an idea of this devotion by remembering the feelings of the English crowds for their king. But the pope as an earthly power does not appeal to them. To them, the ideal pope would be St. Peter, who possessed only a boat and a fishing net. When, on July 25, 1929, Pope Pius XI appeared in St. Peter's Square with the pomp of an Oriental despot, one of these Italian mystics said: "It would have been better for him to carry the Viaticum to some sick person." Only half an hour before, he had spoken of the pope with emotion as of the being in whom "the mystic body of the Church took real and living form." Mystical Italy does not want to hear a word of what is happening at Rome. It believes that "it is better not to go to Rome and thus not to run the risk of losing one's faith." Mystical Italy is usually not interested in political questions, which are even less important to the salvation of the soul than dogmatic controversies. They are possessed of great moral beauty, but politically they are inert. Characters of this type are often found in Russian novels—for example, Platone Karaiew in *War and Peace.*

It sometimes happens that mystics take an interest in politics. In these cases, though never challenging the dogmatic teachings of the Church, they act with a liberty which disconcerts and terrifies the high clergy. Dante severely condemned the attempt against the life of Boniface VIII by Nogaret and Sciarra Colonna, inasmuch as Boniface was the Vicar of Christ; but he reserved a place in Hell for this same Boniface VIII, inasmuch as he considered him a simoniacal pope. Girolamo Savonarola is another typical example of this Italian mysticism. In the minds of this great race of mystics, there has always been a clearcut distinction between religious problems, in which the authority of the Church and of the pope is final, and political problems, in which the citizen must take counsel with his own conscience alone.

When Cavour was on his deathbed, although he had been excommunicated, he sent for Father Giacomo, his parish priest, and asked to be confessed. Father Giacomo gave him absolution. The priest was called to Rome to account for his action. Pius IX summoned him to acknowledge in writing that he had failed in his ecclesiastical duties. Father Giacomo answered that he had acted according to the promptings of his conscience and refused to make the declaration asked of him.[16] He was neither a theologian nor a politician by profession; he was a mystic. In absolving his penitent, he followed his own conscience and common sense and not canon law. A similar case would perhaps be impossible in Ireland, or Poland, or French Canada, or even in the United States.

Don Bosco, who founded the Order of the Salesian Friars and has been sanctified, never took any interest in the territorial sovereignty of the pope, though that sovereignty was swept away under his very eyes.

The three most eminent Italian Catholic writers of the nineteenth century were Manzoni, Rosmini, and Fogazzaro. Manzoni was a senator of the realm and voted for the abolition of the sovereignty of the pope over Rome despite the fact that the pope had excommunicated all those who would aid and abet such a "usurpation." Rosmini's works were put on the Index of Prohibited Books. Fogazzaro was indicted of "modernism," and one of his novels was put on the Index.

If it were true that Italy is a consistently Catholic country, the whole history of Italy in the nineteenth century would be an insoluble puzzle. Between 1848 and 1880, the schools were withdrawn from the control of the Catholic clergy; the religious ceremony of marriage was deprived of civil validity; the clergy lost all the privileges claimed for it by canon law, and most of its property was confiscated; the amplest liberty of discussion and of propaganda was granted to all religious faiths and organizations; and, last but not least, the pope was dispossessed of the sovereignty which he held over central Italy. The pope excommunicated all those who had a share in this anticlerical legislation. No particular attention was paid to his excommunications.

During the Risorgimento, the Italian Catholic movement drew its

---

[16] A. Comandini, *L'Italia nei cent'anni del secolo XIX* (Milan: Vallardi, 1900–42), 4: 108, 135–38.

strength (or rather its weakness) above all from the followers of the old dynasties, from the mummified high clergy, and from quarrelsome politicians who professed allegiance to the absolutistic conceptions of De Maistre. These people did not give a single martyr to the cause of the pope. In Rome during September 1870, there was staged a demonstration of affection for Pius IX on the eve of the arrival of the Italian troops. There was another demonstration after the Italian troops occupied the city. Inasmuch as Rome at that time contained 220,000 inhabitants, it was not difficult for the militant Catholics to assemble several thousand persons to demonstrate in favor of Pius IX. Nor was it difficult for the militant anticlericals to collect as many to demonstrate in favor of the Italian troops. In both cases, most of the demonstrators were probably those curious persons, always the same, who are never missing when there is the chance to help make a lot of racket. Neither of the two parties believed itself bound to provoke a conflict which would disturb the demonstration of the opposite party. The volunteers who fought under the papal flag between 1860 and 1870 were almost entirely Swiss, French, Irish, Spanish, Austrian; there were few Italians and fewer still who were inhabitants of the states of the Church.

To be sure, September 20, 1870, the day on which the Italian troops occupied Rome, was a day of mourning for Italian consistent Catholics. But not one among them shed a drop of blood to vindicate the rights of the pope. Most of them were consoled easily enough, as was the parish priest of Masserano, a small town of Piedmont, who filled two bottles with the choicest wine of his vineyard, sealed them, and decreed that they should be kept in the cellar of the parish house as a gift to the pope who made peace with Italy. The two bottles were handed over to Pius XI on September 4, 1929, according to an account published in the Italian press the next day.

In 1874, the Holy See "advised" Italian Catholics to remain aloof from national politics, and the "advice" became a categorical prohibition in 1886. Since about 40 percent of the Italian electorate habitually abstained from voting, the Vatican boasted that this was the consequence of the papal veto. But when the veto was repealed, the number of voters who went to the polls did not increase in any appreciable proportion. They had been going to the polls even when the pope forbade them to do so.

During the first twenty years of the current century, while the Holy See was still complaining against the usurpation of its former territories and Catholics the world over were complaining along with the Holy Father, the

Italian Catholic deputies uttered never a word concerning the Roman question, either during the electoral campaigns or in the Parliament.

There were in Italy, in 1929, over twelve hundred unfrocked priests, of whom more than eight hundred were teachers in public schools. The public did not pay any attention to the ecclesiastical censures and treated them as good citizens and reliable teachers. The Holy See exacted from the Italian government a special article against them in the Concordat of 1929, excluding them from holding government positions. This measure was in open violation of the constitution of the realm which guaranteed equal rights to all citizens of all faiths and denominations. After the signing of the Concordat, the protests against this proviso were so numerous that the government left most unfrocked priests unmolested, under the pretext that the law was not retroactive.

There are two Churches in Italy: the local popular Church, which is to be found in the parishes; and the Vatican, which is an international institution having its seat in Rome. The fact that the majority of the high and low officials of the Vatican Curia are Italian does not suffice to make of it an Italian institution. The non-Italian sees in the Vatican a "Roman" institution. The Italian sees in the Vatican a "cosmopolitan" institution. While the prelate of the Vatican is imbued with "Roman spirit," the parish priest is anchored to his parish and to his parishioners.

The authors of the Italian Risorgimento had a clear idea of the gap existing between cosmopolitan Vatican and the popular Italian Church. They attacked the Vatican but did not touch the parishes. These tactics explain their victories.

The Holy See holds a far greater influence upon England and the United States than upon Italy: *maior e longinquo reverentia.*

9

The
Socialist Party

The Radicals and the Republicans, like the Reformist Socialists, had wanted war, and therefore they too were unpopular. Only the Official Socialist party had uncompromisingly opposed the war. Therefore, in northern and central Italy, the workers and artisans of the cities, as they were gradually demobilized, enrolled in those trade unions which were under Socialist leadership or joined directly the local branches of the party.

The trade unions which were associated with the Socialist party formed national federations, and the latter in turn were gathered into the "General Confederation of Labor" *(Confederazione generale del lavoro)*. This had been created in 1904 and had permanent national headquarters analogous to those of the Trade Union Congress in England or the American Federation of Labor in the United States.

In the most important cities, all the unions in the city and the countryside, associations of private clerks, elementary school teachers, and lower public employees; and the cooperative societies run by Socialists formed a local confederation with a permanent staff and headquarters. This was the "Chamber of Labor" *(Camera del lavoro)*, an institution unknown in Anglo-Saxon countries but which had great importance in Italy. The Chamber of Labor was the center of lively economic, political, and social activities. The secretaries of the unions and of the associations gathered in a general assembly and transacted those local affairs which held a common interest for the entire working class. The Chamber of Labor was the new municipality of the working classes, whereas the old town hall was supposed to represent all classes. The unions and cooperative societies of the smaller towns turned for advice and help to the Chamber of Labor in the capital city in their district. The Chambers of Labor also were affiliated with the General Confederation of Labor.

In 1913, the membership of the General Confederation of Labor had been 327,302. During the war, by 1916, it dwindled down to 201,291. In 1917, a trend towards a greater activity became apparent, and the membership went up to 237,560 in 1917 and to 249,039 in 1918. It jumped to 1,159,062 in 1919 and to 2,150,000 in 1920.[1] As we have already seen, no more than 750,000 of this number were agricultural day laborers, and even these mostly were dealing with land reclamation—i.e., with public works rather than with agriculture. The Socialist movement in Italy, as in the other countries of Europe, appealed especially to city workers.

The great majority of the membership came from northern and central Italy. Here, during the preceding half-century, industry had made the most progress, and agriculture had reached its highest level by land reclamation and the use of machinery and chemical fertilizers. In southern Italy, where the political education was more backward, neither the Socialist party nor the Populist party had agents in sufficient numbers to organize the war veterans. These—in the great majority agricultural day laborers—formed associations of ex-servicemen *(ex-combattenti)*. The military authorities, the nationalists, and the conservatives favored these associations in southern Italy as well as in northern and central Italy. They hoped that the ex-servicemen, by forming associations of their own, would keep clear from the Socialist and Populist parties and would act as an electoral base for a new conservative movement of which the nationalists would be the heart and soul. Unfortunately for them, not even in southern Italy did the ex-servicemen want to hear anything more about brass hats, nationalists, or conservatives. From their sufferings and the sufferings of their families they wanted a new world to be born. What form it should take they did not know. They were waiting to be guided by someone when he came forth. If it had known how to deal with them, the Socialist party could have easily won them over.

All over Italy there were vast masses who would have liked to make a

[1] R. Rigola and L. D'Aragona, *La Confederazione Generale del Lavoro nel sessennio 1914–1920* (Milan: La Tipografica, 1921), pp. 120–22.

clean sweep of all those who had been responsible for the war. They were ready to follow the Socialists in a policy of reforms. But they took no interest in a revolution like that which had developed in Russia in 1917. The conditions of Italy were very different from those of Russia. In 1917, the Russian peasant-soldiers had deserted their regiments in confusion and on their return to their villages had expropriated the large landowners. The Italian peasant-soldiers at the end of the war were formally discharged. They did not come home as the result of military and administrative disintegration. Moreover, there were in Russia very few small landowners in proportion to the area of available land. In Italy there were big landowners only in central and western Sicily, in some exceptional sections of the South, and in Lazium; and what passed in Italy for a large estate was ridiculously small compared with those formerly existing in Russia and still found in east Prussia, Hungary, England, or Spain. The land to which the Italian peasant-soldiers returned had for centuries been divided among millions of small owners, tenants, and metayers. The small owners would have resisted stubbornly any disturbances in their tenure. The tenants and metayers wanted to become owners of the land they cultivated, not to have it "socialized."

As for the industrial workers, these knew well that the Italian population could not subsist without importing from abroad coal, iron, cotton, oil, rubber, meat, and wheat, and that a Communist revolution would have deprived the country of foreign credit (not to speak of foreign armed intervention). This fact was pointed out by one of the leaders of the right-wing Socialists, Filippo Turati, in the national convention of his party in September 1919:

> Italy does not possess the endless resources of Russia. . . . In Italy we would most certainly be starved under a Socialist government, because it would be immediately boycotted by our creditor states. We would have the immediate revolt of the starving masses in the first few days of our revolution. These are facts of common evidence.[2]

Lenin was not in disagreement with Turati. In the summer of 1920 he advised the leader of the Italian left-wing Socialists, Serrati, not to attempt a Communist revolution in Italy. "We do not want," he said, "a second

[2] G. Lazzeri, *Filippo Turati* (Milan, 1921), p. 198.

Hungary."[3] Discussing the prospect of social revolution in Italy with Angelica Balabanoff (who later told this to the writer of the present book), Lenin asked her: "Comrade, has it ever struck you that Italy has no coal?"

The danger that Italy ran of remaining without raw materials and foodstuffs in case of a Communist revolution was the subject of lively discussion in Italy. An anarchist in 1920 felt that it was necessary to prove that "all the bourgeois press, from the yellow to the red, all the economists and all the Socialists" were lying when, in order to discourage social revolution, they spread alarm over possible economic breakdown and starvation. He admitted that unless the revolutionaries could immediately organize production and distribution, the revolution would fail completely, "because of the less class-conscious proletarian mass." Thus, for one or two years Italy would have to find within herself all necessary resources. This could be done. The two million tons of coal "which certainly were to be found in her warehouses," the lignite produced in the country, charcoal, and electric power would make up for the six million tons of coal which Italy had had to import in 1919. The most serious problem was that of bread. Italy consumed 6 million tons a year of wheat, of which 1.5 million were imported from abroad. To cover this deficit, it would be necessary to ban the export of potatoes, chestnuts, fruits and vegetables, tomato paste, oranges, and lemons. It would be necessary also to do without 8.5 million tons of meat, fats, and fish which were imported from abroad. The Italian people would find the solution to this problem by eating the livestock which existed in Italy.[4] It would be useless to follow the writer in all his calculations. It is enough to note that the two million tons of coal which should have existed in the warehouses did not exist at all; that Italian lignite as a rule consists of 75 percent water; that the hydroelectric plants existing in 1920 were taxed to the utmost of their capacity, that to obtain from them more power it would have been necessary to import machinery from abroad, and that new plants could not have been created overnight; that the charcoal, even if all the trees of Italy were destroyed, would have been useless to many industries, beginning with the iron industry; that 1.5 million tons of oranges, lemons, and tomato paste would not have been the equivalent in nourishment to 1.5 tons of wheat; that Italian livestock had been severely depleted during the war and was in 1920 barely beginning

[3] A. Rossi, *La naissance du Fascisme* (Paris: Gallimard, 1938), p. 73.
[4] Epifane, *Fattori economici pel successo della rivoluzione sociale* (Milano: Libreria della Società Editrice "Umanità Nova," 1920), p. 32.

to come back to normal, and that, if it had been used for food, agriculture could not produce milk, cheese, vegetables, tomato paste, potatoes, and the other products which would have to substitute foreign wheat and not even produce domestic wheat. The survey under discussion, in its childish innocence, brings us an echo of the discussions which took place among the workers on the subject which everyone felt to be the main problem of Italian life in peace and in war, in revolution or in normal times.

In the autumn of 1920, the concern about the danger of a blockade against Italy in the event of social revolution became so widespread that Lenin felt the need of taking part in the discussion. He admitted that "the blockade of Italy, should the proletariat be victorious there, is not only possible, but even probable on the part of England, France and America." The question was "very serious." Russia had been able to withstand the blockade, thanks to the expanse of her territory and the scarcity of her population. Conditions were quite different in Italy. Therefore, the Italian revolution "would not be able to resist for very long, unless it were combined with the revolution of some other country of central Europe." "This cooperation is difficult." But since all Europe was going through a revolutionary period, cooperation was "not at all impossible." "A certain coordination, no doubt still insufficient and incomplete, was assured in Italy, and it would be necessary to fight to obtain complete coordination." Lenin said:

> The revolutionaries and Communists must not dispute the danger and the difficulties of the struggle. It is up to them to inspire in the masses greater firmness, to purge the Party of all weaklings, waverings and versatiles, to infuse in the movement more enthusiasm, more internationalism, a greater readiness to make sacrifices for a great end, and to hasten the revolution in England, in France and in America, if these countries should decide to blockade the proletarian and Soviet Republic of Italy.[5]

The Italian people always retained enough sense to realize that they could not expect a revolution in England, France, and America for the sake of Soviet Italy, and that in Italy enthusiasm, internationalism, and willingness for sacrifice would not serve for long as a substitute for bread, coal, and oil. If France, England, and the United States had discarded their

[5] Lénine, *Oeuvres complètes*, 25: 549.

capitalistic systems and plunged into communism, the Italian workers would have rushed on the bandwagon and "gone Bolshie," even against their will, in order not to starve. But Italy was the last country in which a communist revolution could be started. The Italian workers wished to make "the rich men who had willed the war" pay dearly for it. They went on strike day in and day out. They threw stones at the motorcars and voted for the Socialist candidates at elections. But even in their wildest moments they held back from irreparable absurdities.

Not only were material conditions in Italy profoundly different from those in Russia, but the mentality of the Italian Socialists, even when they called themselves revolutionaries, was very different from that of the Russian Socialists:

> In the countries living under constitutional and democratic regimes, the State did not appear as an inimical force to the majority of the Socialists. The massacres of the past had been forgotten. The State now appeared rather as a comfortable home in which there was room for everyone. It had become a national house which no one could hope to own, but which any solvent corporation had the right and the chance to rent. On the contrary the State, as it appeared to Lenin, in its dark and threatening structure, was the fortress of St. Peter and Paul, was the Winter Palace, the abode of the sanguinary autocracy which Peter the Great and Catherine II had equipped with modern big and small guns. Around it bearded Cossaks with whips and carbines. No ways of entrance for the people. From this situation Lenin's revolutionary mentality sprung. It was as different from the law-abiding mentality of his European Socialist comrades exactly as the fortress of St. Peter and Paul and the Winter Palace differed from Buckingham Palace or the Elysée. . . . While European Social Democracy had been engrossed for thirty years with cooperative societies, unions and parliamentary reforms, Lenin had been busy organizing workers in the same spirit with which a chief of staff organizes his army for war.[6]

Thus, when the Tsarist regime collapsed and its breakdown brought about a condition of universal anarchy, Lenin and Trotsky thrust themselves into the tempest prompted by hatred and a savage eagerness for

[6] E. Lussu, *Teoria dell' insurrezione*, 1936, pp. 20–22.

revenge and destruction. At the head of a few thousand armed men they crushed everyone who clung to the past, destroyed all vestiges of the old regime, and built up a new military and administrative machine under the urge of everyday needs.

The German and Italian working classes and their leaders belonged to quite a different world. The German proletariat was not that desperate multitude that had nothing to lose except chains which Marx and Engels had described in the *Communist Manifesto*. They had old-age pensions, unemployment insurance, sickness insurance, schools for their children, the assets of their trade unions and cooperative societies, and many other advantages to lose. The leaders of that proletariat—union secretaries, members of parliament, journalists, managers of cooperative societies—in the last thirty years had attained a comfortable position under the protection of the Bismarckian Empire. The German "proletariat," in January 1919, let Rosa Luxemburg and Karl Liebknecht be brutally assassinated by officers of the regular army and voted for the party of Ebert and Noske who were hand in hand with the chiefs of the regular army.

The situation was basically the same in Italy. The numerous strikes, often capricious, which took place in those years, are evidence of restlessness and not of revolutionary feelings. To abstain from going to work or to indulge in a lightning strike, and to take your dear wife by the arm and your beloved son by the hand and to go out of town to have a good time, is a different matter from feeling that kind of anger, hatred and fighting determination which makes for revolution.

Among the Italian Socialists, those who belonged to what we have termed the right wing of the party, and who saw their leader in Filippo Turati, never thought a Communist revolution possible and never worked for it. Even they made a certain display of revolutionary slogans because the slogans were part and parcel of the Marxian ritual. But their revolution only meant that radical renewal of the social and political structure which results from the development of the means of production. Their revolution was a sort of natural phenomenon, like the revolution of the earth around the sun, to which the human race must adapt itself in its sowing and reaping. The revolutionary task of the Socialists was to educate and organize the proletariat and make it ready to take over political power when the development had arrived at its final stage. But the final stage never was at hand. The revolution which had taken place in Russia did not correspond in any way to the pattern of the Marxian revolution as they had always imagined it. In their heart of hearts, they would have liked a policy of compromise and cooperation with those non-Socialist groups which had democratic leanings, in order to secure political reforms, gradually to gain control of the central and local governments through the normal channels of democratic elections, and transform political into economic democracy as it became feasible.

It is impossible to say how things would have turned out if they had gone differently. Therefore, no one can maintain with certainty that if the Socialist party had adopted this method, the Fascist movement would have had no chance of victory in Italy. The only thing that can be stated is that the method of the right-wing Socialists was never tried, because the majority of the party never allowed them to make the trial. When they broke away from the majority in the autumn of 1922, all chances for useful work had passed in vain. Furthermore, in 1919, not even the right-wing Socialists were willing to associate themselves with other parties in order to confront the crisis of the postwar period. They, too, were embittered by four years of struggle against those who had wanted the war and they announced that "the liquidation of the war had to be done by those who had wanted it": "we would be a most incautious party if we were to take their place in this moment, and thus were to free them of their responsibility."[7] And yet the best way of making those responsible for the war pay for their responsibility would have been precisely to chase them from the government and take their place, even though it meant assuming a heavy heredity. To accept the responsibility of government, the right-wing Socialists, it seems, were waiting until the budget was balanced and everyone in Italy was happy and content. Lenin and Trotsky never felt any hesitation in accepting the heredity of the Tsarist regime and the military disaster. None among the Italian right-wing Socialists had the fiber either of Lenin or of Trotsky.

The revolutionary Socialists, who were in the majority in the political organizations and in the national executive of the party, began to call themselves "Maximalists" *(Massimalisti)* in 1918. The Italian word "maximalist" corresponds to the Russian word "Bolshevist." The Russia of Lenin was their paradise. In a national congress of the party held in Rome in September 1918, by a crushing majority they adopted as the program of the party "the setting up of the Italian Socialist Republic under the dicta-

---

[7] Words of Turati, in the Socialist National Convention of September 1919: Lazzeri, *Filippo Turati*, p. 198.

torship of the proletariat." In their considered opinion, the hour of social revolution was approaching. Who was to decide when the hour had struck? The "revolutionary proletariat" whom they had trained to worship the *Communist Manifesto* of 1848. The proletariat was to take the initiative and the Socialists were to follow it. When a crisis of restlessness more widespread and acute than usual broke out, they expected the "revolutionary proletariat" to bring about the apocalypse but never did anything to bring it about with an act of their own will. Hardly had the crisis passed than they returned to announce that the hour of the apocalypse was approaching. For them, any idea of an alliance between Socialists and non-Socialists was taboo. All non-Socialists were "bourgeoisie." Among the faithful and the unfaithful, among the elect and the sinners, among the forces of good and the forces of evil, no compromise was allowed. The struggle between "capitalism" and the "proletariat" had to be a fight to the finish. When Mussolini and Marinetti shouted down Bissolati in the Scala Theater of Milan in January 1919, the Maximalists intoned that Bissolati had gotten what he deserved. Had he not wanted the war? How could he now expect a just peace? Could there be a just peace if communism did not spread from Russia to the rest of the world?

The economic and political strikes, both local and general, were hailed almost without exception by the Maximalists as manifestations of revolutionary spirit. They did not realize that in those strikes, too often repeated, the working classes were exhausting, not consolidating, their forces, and that finally they would tire and end by spurning them as futile and harmful.

They were clamoring for the adoption of the Russian Soviets in Italy. They never realized that the Russian word "soviet" means "union" in Italian, and that the Chambers of Labor, which had arisen in Italy through native and spontaneous experience, were the Italian Soviets. There was no need of importing into Italy from Russia institutions which had been born there through the breakdown of a despotic regime which had always denied to the workers the trade union right and the municipal franchise. The Italian Maximalists were like one who searches for his horse while on horseback. In their hands, the Socialist party in those years was a demented giant.

The division within the Socialist party had its effects within the Confederation of Labor. The right-wing Socialists controlled the majority of the trade unions and the central headquarters of the General Confederation of Labor. But a good many local unions were under the control of the Maximalists. They followed their own policies, taking the initiative in declaring strikes or in bringing them to an end without heeding the advice or resolutions of the national directorate of the Confederation. At the critical moments, the leaders of the Confederation worked constantly to refrain the hotheads and postpone dangerous resolutions. One of them, Ludovico D'Aragona, in an address given in Milan in September, 1922, made the following statement:

> We are perhaps responsible for having given way too much at the time of the Bolshevist madness. But we know we did all in our power to restrain the extremists. It is our glory and our pride that we prevented the outbreak of the revolution which those extremists desired. And then, after we had had the honor of preventing the revolutionary catastrophe—Fascism arrived.

D'Aragona, however, took for himself and his friends a larger share of glory, pride, and honor than they deserved. More than the right-wing Socialists, the Maximalists had prevented the revolutionary catastrophe, since they had been constantly talking of the impending revolution without doing anything but talk.

Turati hit the mark in March 1920 when, in an interview with *The Manchester Guardian*, he affirmed that there was no reason in Italy to fear a revolutionary crisis, but that the Maximalists "were fanning the fire of Soviet theories only to keep the masses awake and excited. These theories were merely legendary notions, unripe programs incapable of being put to practical use."[8]

Since the revolution which they always announced as imminent never showed itself, the Maximalists had to explain how this could ever happen. The explanation was at hand. The right-wing Socialists who controlled the national directorate of the Confederation of Labor were unwilling to start the revolution, and their "betrayal" was the key to everything. There had been "socialist traitors" even in Russia in 1917, if Lenin and Trotsky's words were to be accepted at their face value. But when they thought that the moment for action had come, neither Lenin nor Trotsky asked the opinion or the permission of the "socialist traitors." They acted on their

[8] N. Lénine, *La maladie infantile du Communisme* (Paris: Bibliothèque Communiste, 1920), p. 131.

own account against both "capitalists" and "socialist traitors." The Italian Maximalists never thought that they also should act on their own account. The revolution always was to be started and carried out by the other fellows.

There was among them a group of extremists who were analogous to the German Spartacists of 1919, and in fact were proud to call themselves "Spartacists." They were destined to break away from the Socialist party and form the Communist party in 1921. They, too, did not know what more to do than pass on to the other fellows—that is, not only to the right-wing Socialists, but also to the Maximalists—the responsibility for betraying the revolution which never came to pass. Not even they could produce a Lenin or a Trotsky who would push forward without asking anyone's permission. If they had understood that there existed no revolutionary mood in the Italian masses, they would have been less ferocious in their attacks upon the "other fellows." But they had learned in their two-cent pamphlets that the proletariat was "revolutionary" by definition, and therefore they had to search elsewhere than in the proletariat itself the reason for which the proletariat made no move. They found it in the betrayal of the leaders.

Outside the Socialist party, the Anarchists made an even greater hubbub than did the Maximalists and the Spartacists. If they had had their way, they might have brought about serious revolutionary uprisings. They worked hand in hand with Revolutionary Syndicalists, who had not followed Mussolini and Rossoni and had opposed the war. They controlled an "Italian Syndicalist Union" *(Unione sindacale italiana).* But they had little following. Moreover, their revolution was not that of the Maximalists or the Communists. It was to be a revolution that would get rid of all forms of government, starting with the Communist one. They also spent a great deal of time and energy charging right-wing Socialists, Maximalists, and Spartacists with the crime of "betraying the proletariat." Each revolutionist hated his revolutionary neighbors more than he hated "capitalism."

There was never any agreement among the different revolutionary groups for any common action. Strikes or riots never developed according to any well-knit plan. A strike declared by one group often was not supported by the other groups. When a strike on a considerable scale broke out in some private industry, or when political riots spread over any large part of the country, the public services did not strike. When a great public service went out on strike, the private industries remained quiet. The postal employees' strike ceased when the railwaymen's began. The towns struck while the country remained quiet. Strikes spread in the country while the towns were free from them. Southern Italy had few large-scale strikes, while in northern and central Italy they were a daily occurrence. Everyone talked about impending revolution. No one tried seriously to bring it about. Mussolini had good grounds, therefore, when he scorned the would-be revolutionaries as being *buoni a nulla,* ineffectual talkers.

AUTHOR'S NOTES TO CHAPTER 9

Signor Villari, in *The Awakening of Italy,* is very hard on the right-wing Socialists, who "swam with the tide":

> Turati advocated the slow process of penetration into bourgeois institutions with the object of transforming them into organs for the welfare of the community instead of trying to erect a Socialist State by revolutionary means; even the more moderate Socialists who did not desire a revolution or who disbelieved in its possibility, such as Turati and Treves, were too much afraid of losing popularity with the masses to speak their minds openly (pp. 51, 74, 116).

He has no word for the ultrarevolutionary attitude of Mussolini and his friends in these years when the tide was at its highest. He writes only: "The numbers of the adherents of the Fasci were still too limited to give the movement that national importance which it was afterwards to assume, *nor had it yet developed its social policy of reconciling capital and labor:* for the moment its chief function was to oppose bolshevism by force" (p. 105). In drawing so modest a veil over all that Mussolini did to swell that tide, he can allow the whole weight of his honorable condemnation to fall on the moderate Socialists who did not dam the tide with sufficient energy.

In the same book, he states that the Socialists program was "to promote strikes in the public services with the object of disorganizing the economic life of the country in the hope that starvation would goad the masses to revolution" (p. 79). He always takes care to jumble together Anarchists, Spartacists, Maximalists, and right-wing Socialists. If the "Socialists" had had a "revolutionary program" as imagined, the effect would have been apparent in some attempt to coordinate the strikes, which should have developed according to some organized plan. In reality, they occurred sporadically and without coordination.

The accusations of the Anarchists against the Socialists are given in the volume entitled *Sempre!*, Almanacco n. 2 (1923) di "Guerra di Classe", 2d ed. (Berlin 1923); in Luigi Fabbri, *La controrivoluzione preventiva*, in the series *Il Fascismo e i partiti politici italiani* (Bologna: Cappelli, 1924), pp. 11–19; and in Armando Borghi, *L'Italia fra due Crispi* (Paris: Libreria Internazionale, 1924), pp. 125–296.

The accusations against the right-wing Socialists and against the Maximalists were formulated by Zinoviev and Lenin in 1920 *(Le Parti Socialiste Italien et l'International Communiste: recueil de documents* [Petrograd: Editions de l'International Communiste, 1921]). After Zinoviev and Lenin, all Communists have repeated their version (R.P. Dutt, *Fascism and Social Revolution* [New York: International Publishers, 1934] pp. 95 ff.).

The version of the Anarchist, Communists, and Maximalists has in common with the Fascist version the contention that in 1919–20 there was in Italy an impending social revolution. According to the Fascists, however, that social revolution was stamped down by Mussolini, while according to the Communists and Anarchists it was betrayed by the right-wing Socialists and Maximalists; according to the latter, by the right-wing Socialists.

The first version is contradicted by the fact that during the years 1919 and 1920—that is, as long as he believed in the possibility of a revolution, Mussolini was always in the first line in inciting revolutionary movements. The second version is founded only on the romantic illusion that there existed in Italy a "revolutionary proletariat," whereas such a proletariat has never existed neither in Germany, nor in Italy, nor in any other country in the world.

10

The General Strikes of April 1919

The first months after the armistice were much less agitated in Italy than they were in France and in England, not to mention Germany. In Paris, in January 1919, the life of the city was completely disrupted by a strike in all transportation services. In England, in February and March 1919, there were strikes in the subways of London, in the metal industry in Scotland, in the electrical industries, in the railroads, in the mines, and in the shipyards. Italy, by comparison, was tranquil. The employers were willing to grant generous concessions to their employees, either because they felt morally obliged to give proof of good will or because they were afraid of provoking dangerous uprisings by resistance. On February 3, the industrialists and the representatives of the unions in the metal industry agreed on the eight-hour day, which had first been demanded in 1889 by an international Socialist congress, and against which all the economists of the *laisser faire* school had raised infinite economic, technical, moral, and other objections. The movement in favor of the eight-hour day spread rapidly and victoriously among the printers, the building industry, the textile industry, and all other industrial and agricultural categories.

At the same time, the right-wing Socialists openly disavowed the revolutionary wishful thinking of the Maximalists and the Spartacists. One of the most respected Socialists of the old generation, Prampolini, speaking at Reggio Emilia in a meeting of the Socialist organizations, deplored the fact that "many easily and lightly filled their mouths with revolutionary words":

173

The bourgeois government is making elaborate preparations to suppress every revolutionary move. The very liberty which it leaves us to speak and write should make us suspicious. The frivolity with which many shout "Long live the revolution" is frightening. People believe that revolution would be the end of their troubles. This faith in violence as the way to change history is a supersitition which disregards the horrors inherent in both war and revolution. We feel contempt for the diplomats who, coldly, seated around a table, decide on war—that is to say, on the massacre of millions of men. But our clubs and our directors, do they not resemble a little those diplomats when, because of frivolity or moral indifference, they take or support revolutionary initiatives and then go to the pub to drink a glass of wine? This horrible moral indifference, this scorn of our own lives and the lives of others is profoundly bourgeois. The classic militaristic tradition had educated us to play with the skin of our neighbor. It was for this reason that Liebknecht and Rosa Luxemburg were killed by their brothers of yesterday, just as they themselves would have done the killing had they had their way.

Prampolini ended by stating that it was not true that the bourgeoisie was a minority. It was a minority if isolated, but it had a large following (*Corriere della sera*, February 19, 1919).

The leaders of the Confederation of Labor did not dare resolutely to oppose the Maximalists who were officiating in the national executive of the Socialist party. They wanted to avoid crises in their own unions. They adopted as their own the Maximalist program. But at the same time, they made clear that "they did not intend to feed ruinous illusions on the possibility of sudden social upheavals and immediate economic changes." The revolutionary innovations advocated by the national executive of the Socialist party "implied on the part of the working classes a severe and long thought-out preparation which only could be obtained through a methodical, constant, and systematic work of organization and political education." Therefore, members of the Confederation were advised to "spread among the masses the understanding of the heavy responsibility which rested on all the workers" (*Avanti*, February 3, 1919). In other words, the Maximalist program was accepted, but the day for carrying it out was postponed to that vague and indefinite future when the severe and long thought-out preparation had arrived at the right stage of ebullition.

While they edged so adroitly around the Maximalist revolution, the leaders of the Confederation treated with contempt Rossoni and the troublemakers of the Italian Union of Labor. They refused to associate with them in negotiating with the industrialists and paid no attention to the exaggerated demands the others were putting forward, with the aim of making out that the Confederation was in accord with the bourgeoisie to betray the workers.

After the eight-hour day had become the rule in all labor agreements, the most authoritative leader of the Confederation, Rigola, while rejoicing that the workers in town and country now would have more opportunity to "enjoy life," warned them that "life can be enjoyed in various ways":

> There are low tastes and high tastes. Low tastes bring about waste of strength and contribute towards increasing the misery of the working classes. The reduction in the hours of work creates for the working mass in general, and for their unions in particular, the duty to do their best to correct what there is defective in the habits of the workers. There is much to be done in Italy from the standpoint of education, physical training and a greater refinement in the tastes of the masses. We must increase the number of schools, gymnasiums, libraries. We must organize healthful games, sports, educational trips, hikes. We must build up all the institutions which help to invigorate the body or widen the culture of the working classes (*I Problemi del Lavoro*, March 1–16, 1919, p. 83).

The Maximalists had something else on their minds. They were waiting for the "great day," and they endeavored to hasten it by encouraging, under any pretext whatsoever, every kind of strike and by transforming economic strikes into political strikes and strikes of individual groups into general strikes.

Since the peace conference in Paris delayed solving the problems which concerned Italy, the Chamber of Labor of Rome, controlled by Maximalists, with no previous agreement either with the Confederation of Labor or the Socialist party, on April 9 called a general strike for the next day, combining the protest against the peace conference, because it was not giving a "quick and just peace," with the demand that "the claims of the proletariat be instantly complied with." The general strike was to cease after twenty-four hours—that is, it was to be a simple display of "revolutionary" forces and not the beginning of a revolutionary movement on the part of those same forces. The order to strike was obeyed by workers in the larger factories and by the streetcar conductors. As long as the factories remained closed, this concerned only the employers of labor and the workers. But when the streetcar conductors struck, the whole life of the city was disorganized. The paralysis in transportation especially disturbed the officials of the ministries, who had to use the streetcars to go from the outskirts of the city to their offices. In the afternoon, while most strikers were resting at home or getting a breath of air in the country, several hundred Maximalists gathered at a meeting to hear the usual slogans blasted by their soapbox orators. When the meeting was over, they tried to gain the center of the city, shouting behind a red flag. A cordon of soldiers stopped them, the police disbanded them, and several were arrested, soon to be released. Immediately the Association of Ex-Servicemen, which in Rome was controlled by Nationalists, put up a demonstration in the center of the city in honor of the army which had enforced order. They chose the very hour when the employees of the ministries were leaving their offices and when there were no streetcars to take them home. A great crowd gathered at the cry of "Long live Italy! Down with Lenin!" "Officers and soldiers, warmaimed men and Ex-Servicemen were lifted high on the arms of the crowd and carried in triumph." "A brigadier general seized a tricolor flag, kissing it repeatedly amidst bursts of applause." A procession was formed, in which many officers in uniform took part. It made its way towards the Ministry of War. Here "all the windows were crowded with applauding officers and soldiers." A commission headed by the Nationalist representative for Rome was received by the minister of war and lay before him "the homage of the people of Rome." The demonstration broke up in front of the Royal Palace. During the entire demonstration, the "revolutionary proletariat" gave no signs of life. The strike, insofar as it had pretended to be a display of revolutionary strength, had been an utter failure.[1]

Three days later, April 13, 1919, in Milan, the Maximalists called an open-air meeting. A great crowd took part. An Anarchist got up to speak, attacking the bourgeois society and "the weaknesses and the hesitations of the Socialist party." At this point, the police unwisely set out to disband the meeting. Stones began to fly through the air. The police answered them with revolver shots. There were some dead and wounded on both sides.

---

[1] The information given above has been drawn from the issues of April 10 and 11 of two Milan dailies: the conservative *Corriere della sera* and the democratic *Secolo*.

Finally the crowd was dispersed. To protest against the behavior of the police, the Milan branch of the Socialist party and the Milan Chamber of Labor called a general strike for April 15. It was to last for no more than twenty-four hours and was to be "calm and dignified so as not to give rise to unpleasant incidents." On April 15, all public services were stalled. All the factories remained idle. The morning proceeded calmly. In the afternoon, a meeting of about 50,000 persons took place in an arena outside the center of the city. All the speakers, both right-wing Socialists and Maximalists, commended the calm and the unity with which the protest was proceeding, and they recommended the resuming of work the next day. An Anarchist proposed prolonging the strike, but he was shouted down.

While this rally was taking place, groups of officers in uniform, "arditi" in uniform, and Futurists and Fascists armed with revolvers were gathering in the center of the city, waving national flags and such banners as the "arditi" used to hoist during the war when going to the attack. In the Institute of Technology, 300 students who were officers in the army gathered and went out to join the patriotic demonstrators.

When the Socialist meeting disbanded, a part of the crowd, flaunting red and black flags and posters of Lenin and of the Anarchist Malatesta, started to march toward the center of the city. It is clear that the Spartacists and the Anarchists had agreed to stage a demonstration without the agreement of the right-wing Socialists and the Maximalists. The police knew that the other demonstration had formed in the center of the city. They had always forbidden the Socialists to hold meetings or demonstrations there. This time they allowed the crowd to proceed toward their foes.

The two demonstrations met. There were revolver shots and three dead among people who had no share in the clash. Finally firemen dispersed the combatants of both sides with violent jets of water. At this point, a group headed by Marinetti and the "ardito" Ferruccio Vecchi went to the street where the Socialist daily *Avanti* had its offices and printing presses. The police and soldiers who were on duty there left the assailants a free hand. The personnel of the paper, taken unawares, tried to resist. One soldier was killed. But the staff was overwhelmed and fled out a back door. The premises were burned down. People who knew why they had come methodically destroyed the addresses of the subscribers and put lynotypes and printing machines out of commission. "The column, master of Milan which they had now regained, retraced its steps singing 'the *Avanti* is no more!' and bearing before them as the symbol of victory the insignia of the burned paper, which was presented to Mussolini in the offices of the *Popolo d'Italia"* (Marinetti's words).

During the evening, when news of the Milan events reached Rome, the Cabinet thought it advisable to calm the wave of protest, which no doubt would spread over Italy, by sending two ministers to Milan to "carry out an exhaustive investigation." One of them was Minister for War General Caviglia, who was accompanied by his private secretary Rotigliano, a Nationalist connected with the steel industry who later was to become a pillar of the Fascist movement. The other was Minister for Public Works Bonomi, one of the two Reformist Socialists who in January had remained in the cabinet, giving their support to Orlando and Sonnino against Bissolati. In 1920 and 1921, as minister for war, he was to equip the Fascist movement with officers, arms, and ammunition. In Milan, on April 16, he summoned a meeting of trade union leaders and Socialist deputies at the town hall. The Socialists gave the responsibility for the events of the previous day to the police; some of them were so stupid as to complain that Mussolini's Fascists were carrying on a campaign of "violence and hatred" and demanded that they be declared illegal. Bonomi was deeply scandalized by such an "illiberal" demand. The government would never take any "measures which might restrict freedom of speech and action; if they put themselves on this ground, the Socialists would be disregarding their own principles." Caviglia received Mussolini, Marinetti, and Ferruccio Vecchi, and he told Marinetti, "Your battle of yesterday was, in my opinion, decisive." Then both ministers received the Conservative deputies and the representatives of the "patriotic associations" who "gave an account of the facts and responsibilities exactly opposed to those given by the Socialists" (*Secolo,* April 18, 1919).

Of course, Caviglia's congratulatory words to Marinetti were not published. But Caviglia's and Bonomi's "exhaustive investigation" had the desired effect. The Milan workers continued to strike on April 16. In Turin, Bologna, and a dozen other cities of northern Italy, solidarity strikes broke out. On April 17, the mayor of Milan, a right-wing Socialist, issued a manifesto asking the citizens and workers "to keep calm waiting for the measures the government would take." On the same day, the national executive of the Socialist party (which as we know consisted of Maximalists) summoned all organizations to collect funds to rebuild the offices of their newspaper and decided that protest strikes should come to an end everywhere. On April 18, work was resumed. Plenty of money was collected. A splendid new building arose for the *Avanti.*[2]

If a rash fool had entered a church, climbed on the altar, and broken to pieces an image of the Madonna, he would have been torn apart by women whose religious sentiments had been wounded. The women would have acted instantly, without asking their parish priest what they should do. The newspaper *Avanti* was the banner and the symbol of Italian socialism. To wreck its premises was brutally to defy the faith, the pride, and the hopes of millions of men and women. If the Italian "proletariat" had really been animated with revolutionary spirit, they would have responded to Marinetti's unheard-of challenge by an immediate general revolution, or at least by massacring the authors of the attack who were boasting of their prowess.

A few days later, the writer of the present book commented upon these events in the following terms:

> A revolutionary movement, of a more or less Bolshevist type, can not succeed in Italy. The central organ of the revolutionary movement, the beacon which the faithful look up to with religious fervor, the *Avanti,* has been brutally burned down without any immediate, spontaneous, and overwhelming revolutionary outbreak (Weekly *L'Unità,* April 26, 1919).

A year later, Mussolini wrote:

> On April 15, 1919, the Boshevists of Milan showed up in a bright light their philistine and cowardly soul. No move towards revenge was sketched or attempted. No collection of money, no victory in elections will cover over the significance of that day (*Popolo d'Italia,* April 16, 1920).

No doubt the "Bolshevists" of Milan were philistines in the sense that they were not revolutionists in dead earnest, and were cowardly in the sense that they were not gangsters. The whole history of those years may be summarized by the words of an English scholar: "Those who excelled in cruelty won."[3] But the fact is that Marinetti was not wrong when he wrote

---

[2] The same newspaper sources have been used as for the Rome disturbances of April 10 and 11, plus Marinetti's flamboyant report in his book *Futurismo e Fascismo* (Foligno: Franco Campitelli, 1924), pp. 167–70.

[3] Preface to A. Rossi, *The Rise of Italian Fascism: 1918–1922* (London: Methuen et Co., 1938), p.x.

later that "on April 15, 1919, Bolshevist arrogance had been dealt a mortal blow."[4] Those events gave the "anti-Bolshevists" for the first time the feeling that behind Italian "bolshevism" there was no real revolutionary impetus.

In the Rome and Milan events of April 1919, one finds summed up the basic features of all "revolutionary" disturbances which occurred in Italy from 1919 to 1922.

According to the Marxian doctrine as it had been elaborated in Germany before the war, the general strike was to burst forth spontaneously from the "revolutionary proletariat" in the hour of the apocalypse; it was to spread, like fire in gunpowder, through the free initiative of the masses arrived at the last stage of revolutionary saturation; and it was to develop into the social revolution. According to Lenin, the general strike was to be the immediate prologue of social revolution, but that prologue was to be provoked and controlled by a rigidly organized group of revolutionaries, the "vanguard of the proletariat." The general strikes of the postwar period in Italy were either displays of ineffectual political revolutionary fireworks or acts of protest to which the workers resorted when they believed themselves, rightly or wrongly, to be victims of an injustice. But fireworks and protests were to become laughable as soon as everybody realized that there was behind them no will or no power to mean business. Too often reiterated, they were to lose their appeal to the working classes. At the same time, they aroused anger and reprisals from other sections of the community. And since such reprisals evoked, at the most, other ineffectual protest strikes and more reprisals, the whole game boiled down to moral failures for the strikers.

Another feature in the events of April 1919 in Rome and Milan was the participation of officers of the army in "anti-Bolshevist" street demonstrations. In Novara also, on April 18, a colonel in uniform addressed a patriotic demonstration, and on April 22, groups of students, "arditi," and officers in uniform stormed the town hall which was under Socialist administration (*Corriere della sera*, April 19, 1919). The army regulations punished soldiers who took part in political demonstrations of any kind. Therefore, a general who had attended the Bissolati meeting at the Scala Theater in January and had addressed the public demanding freedom of speech for Bissolati was put on the retired list (*Corriere della sera*, January 21, 1919);

---

[4] Marinetti, *Futurismo e Fascismo*, p. 170.

in Bologna, a soldier in uniform who was taking part in a Socialist manifestation, was arrested (*Corriere della sera*, January 25, 1919); the minister for war issued a warning against officers and soldiers who meddled in public demonstrations (*Corriere della sera*, January 27, 1919); a discharged officer of Socialist sentiments, who had addressed a public manifesto to the other discharged officers, was put under arrest (*Corriere della sera*, March 9, 1919); in Lovere (province of Bergamo), the secretary of the Socialist local branch, who was under military discipline, was arrested on the charge of "carrying on propaganda incompatible with his duties as a soldier" (*Corriere della sera*, April 2, 1919). But no officer was ever reprimanded or punished for taking part in "patriotic" or "anti-Bolshevist" demonstrations. Nay more, the minister of war thought that there was no reason why such "decisive battles" as that of April 15 should be discouraged.

Still another feature of the events under consideration was the participation of young people of the middle classes in "anti-Bolshevist" demonstrations. Those young people had grown up amidst the tragic events of the war and had been fed in the schools on patriotic literature of the heroic type. Most of them were sincere and generous in their sentiments. They cherished no personal interests. Communists, Anarchists, and not a few Socialists failed to understand and respect the feelings of that youth. They pursued with their scorn, as if they were one and the same thing, both sincere national sentiments and Nationalistic brutality. They could not conceive of a sacrifice being possible or honorable unless it was made for the "proletariat." They branded the heroes of the war as criminals and praised the deserters as heroes. In certain districts a man found that to have done his duty with honor in the war, or to have returned home disabled, was regarded as a shameful thing that had to be concealed. This attitude did more harm to the revolutionary parties than any other cause. Nationalists, Fascists, and Futurists, with great shrewdness, took advantage of this mistake. One of the main sources of their appeal in their "anti-Bolshevist offensive" lay precisely in the vindication of the rights and dignity of disabled veterans and men decorated in the war. It was this appeal which caused many intellectual young men to gather round them.

Finally, we must not overlook the fact that among the intellectual classes, an acute feeling of envy and hate towards the working classes was spreading slowly. The working classes, by means of strikes, succeeded in obtaining wage increases to meet the rising cost of living. But the teachers in elementary and secondary schools and in universities, the judges, the policemen, and all other civil and military officials who had to live on fixed incomes had no means of reestablishing the balance between revenue and expenditure. If they had gone out on strike, nobody would have been afraid of them. Why should the pupils be disturbed if their teachers went out on strike? On the other hand, the government postponed as long as possible any increase in the salaries of its own employees so as not to swell the horrifying deficit in the budget. Thus, large sections of the intellectual classes were discontented with the government. But they were also envious of the workers, and the envy became hatred when a strike in transportation or in the food or light supply made their own plight worse.

In the very days of the disturbances of Rome and Milan, the Conservative newspapers began to make comparisons between the pitiful economic condition of the public officials and that of the workers. In its issue of April 8, 1919, the *Corriere della sera* wrote:

> Today there are many professional engineers, laboratory directors, professional men, public officials, judges, university professors, state councillors, who can't believe their eyes. They see foremen who demand wages which run from 1,000 to 2,000 lire a month. . . . What should members of the high judiciary demand, who, after spending the best years of their lives on books, have reached, when they are 35 or 40 years old, a salary of 600 lire a month, and the oldest ones about 1,000 lire? The humiliation among intellectual classes is general. Fathers wonder if they are not wrong to send their sons through 12 or 14 years of school after the elementary schools, and if it would not be better to send them directly into a workshop.

The Marxian doctrine of the German Socialists had taught that, by a constant progress in the technique of production, capitalist society was moving toward the concentration of wealth in an ever-diminishing number of hands, and hence towards an increasing proletarization of the middle classes. When this process had attained its climax in an extreme degree of technical perfection and concentration of wealth, the proletariat, its numbers swelled by the decayed middle classes, would seize from the handful of capitalists the means of production and distribution and would set up a classless society based on economic equality. Experience shows that there exists no rectilinear developement of capitalist society toward the concentration of wealth. Concentration in one field is offset by dispersal in others.

The large-scale motor industry had brought about the disappearance óf a host of small carriage makers, but it has given rise to a quantity of new small undertakings for repairing and housing cars and providing for the wants of motorists on the roads. Land ownership shows no signs of concentration. On the contrary, there is a strong tendency for large estates to be broken up among small owners wherever the land gives a greater yield by the intensive application of individual labor. The postwar period in Europe brought severe poverty and distress to the middle classes. But the middle classes, while being déclassé by the economic crisis, did not agree to identify themselves with the proletariat. Italian fascism and German nazism in their beginnings were essentially movements of impoverished middle-class elements who had determined not to sink to proletariat level and set out to wrest from the lower classes that share of national wealth which they had won.

Neither in Germany nor in Italy did the Marxians of the strict observance ever realize the gravity of this phenomenon and its implications. The Rome and Milan events of April shook no Maximalist sleepwalker from his Marxian slumber. On April 29, the national executive of the Socialist party issued a manifesto in which it summoned the Italian proletariat to go on a general strike on May 1, which in Europe was the traditional Labor Day, and made the following announcements: "The working class must assert that it is ready to adopt and follow the teachings of Russia, Hungary and Bavaria, where political and economic power is controlled only by those who produce and who work. . . . Everyone be ready for the great hour" (*Avanti*, April 29, 1919).

During those same days in Bavaria, the Communist Republic, proclaimed on April 4, was collapsing in a bloody reaction and giving way to a ferocious "totalitarian" regime.

11

Italy
in June 1919

Between April 14 and 23, at the Paris Peace Conference, the clash between Wilson and the Italian delegation came to a head. Orlando walked out of the conference and left for Italy on the evening of April 24. Sonnino followed him two days later. Along the way from the frontier to Rome, they were greeted with triumphal demonstrations. Numberless wild demonstrations against Wilson took place all over Italy. Even the Confederation of Labor, although declaring itself hostile to the "exorbitant demands of territorial annexations" made by Orlando and Sonnino, protested against Wilson, who "was applying his ideals in a onesided manner" since he left the way open to French and English imperialism and blamed only Italian extravagances. Turati, on April 29 in the Chamber, while he was explaining the reasons why the Socialist deputies would refuse a vote of confidence to the cabinet, did not fail to affirm that "in Fiume there was no one who did not speak Italian" (a contention rather difficult to uphold, since in the city of Fiume fifteen thousand Slavs were intermingled with twenty-four thousand Italians), and he blamed the English Laborites and the French Socialists who, while looking the other way when the territorial ambitions of their governments were concerned, "pretended to preserve their democratic and socialistic virginity by upholding Wilson only when Fiume, Dalmatia, and eastern Istria were under discussion." The Chamber voted confidence in the cabinet by 382 votes; only 40 Socialists voted against it. The Senate gave the cabinet their unanimous 191 votes. But what Orlando, Sonnino, the majority of the Chamber, and the unanimity of the Senate wanted, no one knew. Turati rightly denounced in his speech the absurd situation in which the ministers had placed themselves and the country:

> Either you know that a settlement is possible or you are not sure of the result. In the first case, why has this enormous hysteria been aroused in public opinion? In the second case, the hysteria you have provoked makes you its prisoners. It prevents you from returning to Paris without humiliation. You could have told us: "Success did not result from our good will; we are hampered by too many precedents; we can not return to Paris with dignity; let us leave our place to one whose hands are freer and who, with better fortune, can renew the negotiations which we broke up." A profound respect would have greeted the words and the gesture. Instead, you build yourselves up upon your failure as upon a pedestal. You tie to your failure the life of your country. You summon the country to show its solidarity with you up to any consequences: up to, God help us, war, a new war. A new war today. Have you ever thought of that?

While Orlando and Sonnino were collecting demonstrations and votes of confidence in Italy, in Paris Wilson, Lloyd George, and Clemenceau were settling all the problems which were still hanging. Sonnino had always obstinately and stupidly opposed the recognition of the new Serbo-Croat-Slovenian Kingdom. The three decided upon its recognition in his absence. In addition, they fixed the dates on which the peace terms were to be handed over to the delegations of Germany and Austria-Hungary and stated that if the Italians remained absent from that ceremony, the Treaty of London would become null and void.

On May 4, at a great meeting in Rome, the mayor of Rome demanded Dalmatia plus Fiume, and D'Annunzio discourteously attacked President and Mrs. Wilson, proclaiming that "a return to Paris would mean the dishonor of Italy." The evening of the same day, Sonnino and Orlando left for Paris, without demanding or obtaining any terms, merely in order to avoid the reprisals which they would provoke by their absence. They had hardly returned to Paris when Wilson, Lloyd George, and Clemenceau, without consulting them, allotted to Greece the district of Smyrna in Asia Minor, which in the agreement of St. Jean de Maurienne (April 19, 1917) had been assigned to Italy. Lloyd George and Clemenceau divided between themselves the German colonies in Africa, postponing to the future the negotiations with the Italians on the compensations which had been promised them by the Treaty of London.

Italy's international influence depends not so much on her military strength (which is not great when compared with that of other big powers) as on her ability to balance herself among the other big powers when they are at loggerheads. Her importance, great in time of conflict, vanishes as soon as one of the European powers or a coalition of powers has obtained decisive superiority. Then the promises made her in the hour of stress can be disregarded with impunity, and she can be tossed in the refuse can like a squeezed lemon. In 1915, Italy had enjoyed maximum influence. Sonnino had abused that influence and, for his intervention on the side of the anti-Germanic Entente, had wrested a price which the latter was reluctant to pay. In 1919, the war was over, Germany was powerless, and Sonnino was no longer in a position to balance himself between Germany and her foes, nor could he menace Wilson, Lloyd George, and Clemenceau with war. He could only threaten revenge for such a time when Germany would have regained her forces. This the Italian newspapers did. Such threats, instead of improving the situation of the Italian negotiators, made it worse.

Meanwhile, conditions in Italy were becoming more and more disturbed. The frontier territories, which had been the theater of war, and the former Austrian territories, which were now under the control of the Italian troops, were in a state of economic, social, and political chaos. The populations who had been forced to leave during the war had returned there and had found tremendous destruction everywhere. Trade with central Europe was paralyzed. Relations between Italians and Slavs in the mixed territories were made more difficult by the fact that the frontier between Italy and Yugoslavia was still under discussion.

In May and June, there was a steep rise in the cost of living, especially in the price of food. As a consequence, there was an increase in strikes for higher wages. The strikers in industry and agriculture, who had numbered 22,280 in January 1919, 40,103 in February, and 68,820 in March, jumped to 87,449 in April and 309,026 in May.[1] Associated with the demands for

---

[1] *Annuario statistico italiano: 1919–1921*, p.395, 398. The *Corriere della sera*, a conservative newspaper and far from biased in favor of workers who struck, in its issue of June 16, 1919, admitted that "the rise in the cost of living had made necessary to a large extent the wage increase, since it had lowered the earning capacity of the workers." It has been estimated that between 1914 and June 1919, there was an average rise of 220 per cent in agricultural

wage increases in the strikes were the demands for the introduction of a new "constitutional regime of labor" in place of the traditional regime of the employer as "master in his own house." The resistance of the employers hardened as the pressure on the part of the workers' organizations became more intense on this second point. The public was very disturbed by some of these strikes. For example, the strikes of the waiters of restaurants in Rome (June 5–13) and in Milan (June 6–22) proved extremely trying to those persons who had no families or were on business and did not know where to have their meals.

In addition to these strikes, there were those to which public officials resorted for the same economic motives. On June 11, 50,000 elementary school teachers, organized in a national association directed by Democrats and Socialists, went on strike all over Italy. On June 14, even the Catholic teachers, organized in a separate association, joined the strike; the strike ceased on June 20.

The economic strikes of one category provoked solidarity strikes in other groups through which the workers' organizations endeavored to force the employers to agree to the terms demanded by the original strikers. In Biella (Piedmont), a strike of 30,000 workers in the wool industry, which had begun May 6, caused, on June 1, a two-day solidarity strike among many other working categories; the original strike was not settled until June 11. In Naples, on June 8, the Communists succeeded in having proclaimed in the whole of the province a general solidarity strike with the workers in the steel industry. Newspapers were not published. Twenty-one towns in the province remained without any light. Streetcars, whose employees had refused to take part in the strike, were attacked. The solidarity strike ceased on June 11, and the particular strike in the metal industry, which had started on May 8, was settled on June 13.

In addition, there were food riots. On June 11, in La Spezia, the fruit and vegetable shops closed down as a protest against the town hall, which had blocked the prices for their merchandise. The workers reacted by proclaiming a strike against the traders, and they turned to looting restau-

wages, but the cost of living for a working family of five persons rose from 41.20 lire a week in the first half of 1914 to 120.05 a week in June 1919 (Bachi, *L'Italia economica nel 1919*, p.162). In other words, the rise in the cost of living, 292 percent, was higher than the increase in earnings. Signor Villari (*Awakening of Italy*, p.50) writes: "Wages had greatly increased during the war, while prices . . . had only slightly risen; it was after the armistice that prices had begun to mount rapidly, and *although they had not caught up with the increased wages*, the workers felt defrauded because they were not as well off as they had been during the war years."

rants and shops of stockings, hats, clothing, oil, cheese, and wine. The police intervened; there were two dead and seven wounded, among them a policeman. "The women were more raging and impassioned than the men. The streets where the fighting was the fiercest gave the impression of a battlefield: fragments of mirrors, windows, fixtures, foodstuffs of all kinds are scattered everywhere" (*Corriere della sera,* June 13). On June 12, the uprisings spread to the suburbs of the city, where many shops were sacked. "Police and troops did not intervene" (*Corriere della sera,* June 14). "Several shopkeepers demanded protection from the Chamber of Labor, and they were assigned guards, who did their duty very well" (*Secolo,* June 14). On June 13, in the towns of Massa and Carrara, near La Spezia, general strikes broke out to protest against the cost of living and against the police who had killed two men in La Spezia on June 11. The strikes stopped when the shopkeepers announced a reduction in the prices of foodstuffs and shoes. On June 14, the sacking of shops extended to three other towns. On June 15, at Pisa, the Chamber of Labor, directed by Syndicalists, called a twenty-four-hour general strike to protest against the behavior of the police at La Spezia and against the high cost of living. Meanwhile in La Spezia, in an imposing meeting, the Socialists and the directors of the Chamber of Labor proposed the cessation of the strike on the condition that the government, while awaiting the public trials, would release the men arrested in the riots of the preceding days and would enact a general reduction of 30 percent in prices. The Anarchists and Revolutionary Syndicalists demanded a 50 percent reduction and the release without any trial of all the arrested persons, even those who had been seized while looting merchandise from stores. The Anarchists and Syndicalists prevailed, but the population was tired. On June 16, the Chamber of Labor ordered the cessation of the strike for the next day. The Anarchists and Syndicalists, to distinguish themselves from the Socialists, ordered the strike to continue for another twenty-four hours.

Not only Anarchists, Communists, and Syndicalists, but also persons of Conservative ideas in normal conditions, were going crazy. In Genoa on June 11, the associations of industrialists and merchants proclaimed a lockout of five days to protest against the government, which was not abolishing the restrictions to which private initiative had been subjected during the war, but rather was planning to impose new ones. Since such respectable people as industrialists and merchants were striking, the Chamber of Labor called for June 12 a general strike of protest "against the increasing cost of living, against the government,and against those who were starving the people." All the democratic parties and the Association of Ex-Servicemen took part in the strike. During a meeting held by the Chamber of Labor, a group of "arditi" collided with the demonstrators, and there resulted one dead and six wounded among the civilians and four wounded among the police. Several shops were sacked; many windows were broken; an industrialist who was coming into the city in his car was forced out on the street and his car destroyed; a Conservative deputy was manhandled. Other protest meetings and demonstrations against the high cost of living took place in other cities near Genoa. The next day (June 13), disorder continued in Genoa on the part of isolated groups who, in the afternoon, imposed the cessation of streetcar service and the closing of the shops. Quiet was restored by June 14, but the lockout of the industrialists and merchants continued with businesslike punctuality until the end of the fifth day.

In Milan and Turin, on the afternoon of June 13, when the news came that the corpse of Rosa Luxemburg had been found in a canal of Berlin, "persons unknown" (most likely Communist hotheads) went around announcing that the Chambers of Labor had called a general strike of protest. Lightning strikes broke out in many factories, and in Milan the streetcar service was stopped. Here the Chamber of Labor ordered the strikers back to work the next day and was obeyed. At Turin, where Communists controlled the Chamber of Labor and the local branch of the Socialist party, the disturbances were of a much more serious nature. In the evening of June 13, 20,000 persons gathered in the center of the city, singing a song which finished with the words "Death to the King." There were numerous clashes between the police and the demonstrators. The police stormed the Chamber of Labor, pursuing the rebels from floor to floor. There were five wounded, one of whom, a policeman, was seriously hurt. As a consequence, the next day a general strike of protest took place in the city.

At Bologna, the morning of June 15, while a great Socialist parade was going across the city, a group of extremists who had joined up with the parade demanded that the national flags along the way be withdrawn. Conflicts arose. An officer was assaulted. He used his revolver and wounded a woman. In the afternoon a group of Nationalists and "arditi" staged a counterdemonstration. This is how the Nationalist daily, *Idea Nazionale* (June 17), described what happened:

Soldiers and officers associated themselves with the Nationalists and the "arditi." Violent quarrels arose between them and the Socialists, and the police had to intervene to disperse the demonstrators. . . . Then the Nationalists betook themselves, almost at a run, to the street where the headquarters of the Chamber of Labor are located, *without the police trying to stop them* [italics ours]. There were few people in the Chamber. When the demonstrators gained the entrance, one of them cried out: Forward! Forward! One "ardito" broke in, no one knows for what purpose (!!). He was soon surrounded by those present who seized his banner from him and chased him out with kicks and blows. Other "arditi" came forward to defend their comrade and revenge the insult which had been paid him. The Socialists who were in the Chamber of Labor wisely barred the entrance and took good care not to come out into the open. The demonstrators fired several revolver shots without provoking any reaction. Unfortunately, two shots struck two students who were among the "arditi" and wounded them. At the insistence of the police and the soldiers, the "arditi" broke up.

On the following day, the Chamber of Labor, controlled by right-wing Socialists, refused to proclaim a general strike. But another Chamber of Labor, newly created by Revolutionary Syndicalists and Communists, proclaimed the strike. The next day, the streetcars did not run, and many factories remained idle.

In the countryside around Padua, the tenants were striking under Socialist leadership. On June 21, a landowner was assaulted in his home and defended himself with his gun, wounding three persons, one mortally. In the district of Bergamo, the Populists were in control of the day laborers. While the Socialists were demanding "the land for the peasants," the Populists were demanding "the land rented to the peasants." Their followers gathered at the sound of the bells.

At Genoa, on June 24, the Federation of Longshoremen, which was having a dispute with the shipping companies, forbade the departure of a ship, and the personnel of the ship carried out the order. This ban was extended on June 30 to two other ships.

At Sampierdarena, in the vicinity of Genoa, on June 25, the Association of Ex-Servicemen, in agreement with the local Fascists, opposed the auction sale of the furniture of three families of ex-servicemen who had not paid their rent while the men were at the fighting front. The demonstration, threatening "death to the barbarous exploiters of those who defended the country" and revenge against the "magistrates, judges, sheriffs, lawyers, accomplices of the barbarous house owners," prevented the auctioning, summoned the other tenants to pay only half of the rent, and invaded the courtroom singing a famous patriotic anthem which began with the words, "Brothers of Italy, Italy has awakened."

At Naples, on June 28, the peasants refused to bring their products into the city, not intending to accept the prices established by the town hall. Even the priests struck. At Loreto, on May 1, six priests refused to celebrate mass, not having received the increase in salary which they had demanded, and were dismissed, but "they made immediate submission: an example of a strike, lockout and victory of the employers" (*Corriere della sera*, June 26, 1919). A strike of priests took place also at Prato for reasons which were not explained by the newspapers which gave the news (*Corriere della sera*, June 20, 1919). At Naples on July 1, 200 priests sent a letter to the newspapers threatening to strike because they could no longer live on a salary of 200 lire a month. The letter said: "We have had enough. Hunger has forced the wolf out of the forest."

To appreciate the situation in its entirety, one has to bear in mind that while the figures of the strikes for economic reasons in industry and agriculture can be regarded as complete, the solidarity strikes or the partial or general strikes promoted for political reasons were not taken into account by official statistics. The two Milan dailies from which we have taken the information on solidarity and political strikes gave a fairly diligent chronicle for northern Italy, but did not mention events in southern and central Italy unless they were particularly serious. Therefore, the country was even more agitated than the data which we have collected would lead us to believe.

In these events of June 1919, even more than in those of the preceding April, are clearly revealed several of the features which were destined to repeat themselves continually in the following years:

1. When Nationalists, Fascists, Futurists, and "arditi" attacked the headquarters of Socialist institutions, the police allowed them a free hand. The practice was illegal and immoral. But in the Socialist meetings and street demonstrations there was always someone who attacked the police with stones or revolver shots, and the police were glad to see volunteers take their revenge.

2. The Maximalists, Spartacists, and Anarchists could not ask the pro-

tection of the police while insulting, stoning, and wounding them in their demonstrations. They should have defended themselves with arms against those who attacked them with arms. But they never thought of this any more than they thought of taking a trip to the moon. Convinced that the "revolutionary proletariat" would be invincible on the "great day," they waited for the "great day" to arrive. Meanwhile, they answered the armed attacks with futile protest strikes, which they thought would train the proletariat in "revolutionary gymnastics."

3. The Nationalists, Fascists, Futurists, and "arditi" had realized how infantile was the revolutionary technique of their adversaries. Being sure of the connivance of the police, they did not fear clashes, but rather it was to their great interest to instigate them. The Nationalist newspaper commented upon the incidents in Bologna on June 15 in the following terms:

> We do not deplore these incidents. The Nationalists, followed by the true and strong Italian citizens of Bologna, reacted against the provocation and the violence of the Socialists, just as they had reacted in April in Rome and in Milan, defending the will of the people against the Bolshevist violence. . . . When a group of persons tears to pieces the National flag, insults officers and openly declares a state of civil war—all of which happened in Bologna—it is the definite and obvious duty of the citizens to react, even if this reaction takes the form of fighting with revolvers—fighting which, as far as that goes, took on very small proportions in Bologna (*Idea Nazionale*, June 17, 1919).

4. The most important fact of all was that, behind the Nationalists, Futurists, Fascists, and "arditi," a group of·generals was maneuvering.

In 1915, at the outbreak of the Italo-Austrian war, there were 142 generals in the Italian army. At the end of the war, 1,246 officers bore this title. In France in 1914, there were 360 generals. At the end of the war there were 769. Italy, therefore, had 477 more generals than France. The number of colonels and junior officers had increased proportionately. But most junior officers were civilians who had been mobilized for war and were eager to go back to civilian life. Colonels and generals had no civilian status to return to, and they did not want to be discharged. In the Chamber of Deputies on March 4, a representative called the attention of the minister of war to this situation:

Officers who in 1915 were captains and have never done any fighting, have never commanded a unit, have never seen a battle field, today are generals. Since they can not ask parliament and the country, which would rebel, for an increase in the number of the big army units, they are devising other schemes to the advantage of the high ranks. Before the war, the staff officer allotted to the command of an army corps was a colonel, now he is a brigadier general. In the same way, colonels have taken the place of lieutenant colonels, and majors of captains. The officers assigned to the general staff of the army are tripled. . . . There are 24 divisions and 12 army corps. If you put a colonel as staff officer, not at each army corps, but at each division, you create jobs for 24 instead of 12 colonels. I have been told also that every brigade, besides consisting of two regiments, should have officers of another regiment.

The minister of war, that same General Caviglia who, the following April, was to conduct the "exhaustive investigation" about the burning of the *Avanti* in Milan, did not deny any of these facts but confined himself to saying that "he, too, was giving close attention to all those problems." The pensions to which the war-maimed men and the families of the soldiers killed in war were entitled, and the medical examination of sick claimants, were granted only after exasperating delays. This was due partly to the disorder in which the records were kept, but mostly to the fact that the office staffs protracted business as long as possible to avoid demobilization. An official at the ministry of pensions who dispatched more than twelve cases a day was regarded by his colleagues as a blackleg, and his life was made impossible by their hostility. Yet it would have been possible for one single official to dispatch at least fifty cases a day if he had worked hard. The veterans and the families of the dead felt that they were being robbed of their rights by a malevolent "government" and a wicked "bourgeoisie."

The surest way for the many generals and colonels of making themselves indispensable was a new war. In 1919, the general staffs of the army and navy had in readiness plans for no less than four fresh wars: a war in Georgia against the Russian Bolshevists; a war in Asia Minor against Turkey; a war in Albania against Greece and Yugoslavia and the Albanians; and a war in Dalmatia and Slovenia against Yugoslavia.

In June 1919, rumors began to circulate of a plot for a military *coup d'état*. The Chamber of Deputies would be disbanded, "those responsible for the disaster of the country" arrested, the workers' organizations declared illegal, and war against Yugoslavia started. The Duke of Aosta (cousin of the king), General Giardino, D'Annunzio, Federzoni, and Mussolini were supposedly among the plotters. The fighting forces were to consist of "arditi" and officers. Giardino, Federzoni, D'Annunzio, and Mussolini denied that "idiotic rumor," that "mad invention." But Giardino, interviewed by the *Corriere della sera*, admitted that, in his private talks at the Senate with his colleagues, he had upheld the necessity of "listening to the voice of the people," of "preventing rash initiatives," and of giving the people "definite assurances that it would have the right and the means to express its will by legally electing its political representation." "Is this clear? I have nothing else to say" (*Corriere della sera*, June 12, 1919). It was not the least bit clear, since he did not explain whether all those measures were to be taken by a cabinet regularly appointed by the king according to constitutional rules, or by a cabinet created by that military *coup d'état* of which he had been named as one of the leaders. His silence on this point, far from dispelling suspicion, confirmed it. D'Annunzio announced that he did not fabricate plots, but that "in the name of the true people" he was ready to undertake any daring initiative and that "with the sole force of the true people Italy would gain her fifteenth victory." He had counted fourteen victories in the Italo-Austrian war. Where and against whom was the fifteenth victory to be won? In Rome and against Parliament? Or outside Italy and against Yugoslavia? Whoever revolts against a legal government always speaks in the name of the "true people." Mussolini made the following announcement: "That which must happen will happen."

The writers of the conservative *Corriere della sera* could not explicitly accuse a prince of the Royal House and a high-ranking officer in the army. Therefore, they maintained that the rumors of the military conspiracy had no grounds. But they were glad that "a tempest of ridicule had drowned and smothered that invention"; "to paint the devil on the wall sometimes does good." Then they took care to explain why the country would react with "scorn and revolt" against any attempt at a military coup d'état:

> The wish to recommence the war in one way or another has been expressed too often in meetings and in newspapers. . . . When a great army is mobilized and there is no war, it is natural that someone, in academic discussions, should

consider giving such a big machine a task, within or outside Italy. On the other hand, the people suffers from the immense burden placed upon it by the state of war while there is no war. There is only one remedy: peace, demobilization, opening of foreign trade, return to confidence and work. . . . This is just the opposite of those dictatorial and warlike plans which are attributed to the fantastic military conspiracy. (*Corriere della sera*, June 14, 1919).

The political activities of the "arditi" have to be related to the political maneuvers of the military black hand. The military administration, while delaying as much as possible the demobilization with the pretext that the problem of the Italo-Yugoslav frontier was still unsolved, was granting leave to thousands of "arditi," who were present in political demonstrations in uniform, with their daggers on their hips, shouting their war cry, "To us!" The military authorities did nothing to discourage these illegal acts. The "arditi" did not confine themselves to political demonstrations. The Socialist daily *Avanti* published whole columns every day of common crimes committed all over Italy by "arditi." The Nationalist newspaper protested vigorously that the *Avanti* was using individual acts of violence as a pretext to slander the "arditi":

> The *Avanti*, by exposing this or that individual case of delinquency, tries to defame that spirit of victory which assumes in the "arditi" a more perspicuous form. . . . But the "arditi," purged and organized, shall remain and will perpetuate in the Italy of tomorrow, that very spirit of national and military education, from which the present active and efficient resistance to the criminal endeavors of the enemies of the country has sprung. . . . Italy will never allow her best sons to be wickedly offended (*Idea Nazionale*, May 18, 31, 1919).

The best way of putting an end to the campaign of the *Avanti* was to disband the regiments of the "arditi" now that the war was at an end, to forbid the use of military uniforms to all those who were no longer under the colors, and to leave the police to deal with any common criminals. Instead, on June 17, the newspapers came out with the news that a general had been appointed inspector of the "arditi," with the task of reorganizing and disciplining them. The *Idea Nazionale* had been well informed in May when it had asserted that the "arditi" would not be disbanded.

The Italian military authorities had before their eyes the "Frei Korps" which in Germany, from December 1918 onwards, had been carrying on civil war under the leadership of officers of the former Imperial army. In Italy, the "arditi" were to be the counterpart of the German "Frei Korps."

AUTHOR'S NOTES TO CHAPTER 11

When one reads descriptions of postwar disorders in Italy, one is never told that the situation was equally serious in England, France, the United States of America, Belgium, and Switzerland. He is led to believe that the Italians were the only people who, in the postwar years, went crazy, on account of their "backwardness" or the "emotional nature" so different from that of more civilized and more steady people.

The fact is that in England, at the beginning of June, the policemen of London, Liverpool, Birmingham, Manchester, and other important cities threatened a strike to get not only an increase in their salaries but also the right to form trade unions and to go out on sympathetic strikes with any other union. In London 20,000 policemen marched to Hyde Park, and 100,000 persons joined their demonstration. Speakers attacked the ministers and announced that the official ballot on the question of a strike had been 44,539 in favor of and 4,324 against a walkout, but the walkout was postponed until after the peace was signed. In Plymouth, on June 8, 1,500 troops refused to entrain for an isolation camp, and the authorities had to give in. In Liverpool, Cardiff, and other cities on June 12 and 13, violent fights occurred between Negro laborers and the population: there were dead and wounded; houses were stoned, set afire, or looted. On June 16, rioting soldiers wrecked a camp, looted the officers' mess and shops, took safes and other valuables, tried to fire a bank and two other buildings, and destroyed a theater with a capacity of 2,000 persons. In July, as a result of a strike in Yorkshire, 200,000 miners were out of work, 6 mines were flooded, and 17 were in danger of a similar disaster. In August, the policemen of London and Liverpool attempted a strike but failed. One hundred fifty shops were looted in Liverpool; the soldiers who were keeping order were stoned, and there were many wounded. In London, the subway operators and the street cleaners went on strike, and many cities were threatened with lack of bread because of a strike of the bakers.

In Switzerland, at Basel and Zurich, there were general strikes in August against the high cost of living, in which even public officials participated; 5 were killed in a street riot at Basel.

In France, at the beginning of June, there were 500,000 workers on strike, of whom 200,000 were in the metal trade in the Paris region. On June 2, the subway employees, the taxi drivers, and the autobus drivers went on strike. On June 17, in Brest, 200 sailors, carrying a red flag, attempted to enter the naval jail to rescue imprisoned sailors.

In the United States, strikes were on a gigantic scale. In June, drivers, teamsters, porters, postal clerks, telegraph and telephone operators, and electrical workers went on strike. Bombs exploded in Washington, Boston, and New York City. In July, a strike of dockers kept 500 ships idle in New York's port and 700 in other harbors. In Chicago, 30,000 workers in the building trades went on strike. Boston was paralyzed by a strike in the subways and streetcars. In August, the railway traffic between New York and Boston came to a standstill.

In Italy, no strike of policemen was ever threatened or attempted. At the beginning of August, Prime Minister Nitti received a summons through a sheriff from prison guards who asked for an increase in their salaries, and this was regarded as an intolerable scandal.

The basic difference between the disturbances which occurred in Italy and those in other countries arose from the fact that in other countries, and especially in England, disturbances were toned down or altogether hushed up by the press, while the Italian press devoted a vast amount of space to those events, thereby creating greater excitement and worry. What especially matters in politics is not what really happens but what people believe is happening. The Italian press was always more vociferous than the press of other countries, thus giving the impression of greater excitement and actually creating excitement even when it might have been avoided if news had been more wisely handled.

In General Giardino's book *Piccole faci nella bufera* (Milan: Mondadori, 1924), p.50, we learn that the plot which was divulged in June 1919, and other "famous plots," were "invented to defame military chiefs, not excluding princes of the royal blood" and that "at various times he was shadowed by the police." Giardino does not "defend himself from such dirt," and only states that he "feels highly honored by such stories" and "when the political trend was changed, an official inquiry showed that the charges had been framed by a dirty police agent." At any rate, we learn that "at different times" he was shadowed. If there had not been serious reason to suspect a man who was an army chief, a former minister of war, and a senator, why would the police have wasted time on him? If there were grounds for suspicions, it was natural that the investigation should be entrusted to police agents. Therefore it is difficult to understand Giardino's scorn for men who were only doing their duty and without whose services no government can get along.

The "princes of the royal house" whom Giardino mentions were "one prince of the royal house," the Duke of Aosta, cousin of the king. We shall see that the duke really had a hand in the military conspiracy which was to lead to the *coup d'état* of October 1922.

12

From
Orlando to Nitti

Orlando's failure at the peace conference sealed the doom of his cabinet. Those who had opposed the war were against him because he belonged to the war party. Those who had advocated a more intelligent policy at the peace conference were against him because of his inept attitude. Those who expected him to bring back Dalmatia plus Fiume in his pockets from Paris were against him since he had not dared to annex Dalmatia and Fiume to Italy, in the teeth of Wilson, Clemenceau, and Lloyd George. What would have happened to Italy if England had stopped shipping her coal and the United States had stopped shipping her grain, they did not ask. Politics for them was not the art of the possible; it was the dream of the desirable. When he returned to the Chamber of Deputies to give an account of recent events, Orlando received only 78 votes of confidence; 259 deputies voted against him, while 171 stayed away from the sitting (June 21, 1919).

Orlando was succeeded in the premiership by Francesco Saverio Nitti. No prime minister in Italy had ever been confronted with a more difficult heritage.

To the disorderly movements, which up to this time had occurred in Italy because of the postwar economic and moral upheavals common to the whole world, was added now the hysteria produced by the failure in the peace conference. Everyone shouted against the peace conference and against the Treaty of Versailles. The Maximalists, Communists, and Anarchists shouted because shouting was bringing the "great day" nearer.

The right-wing Socialists, who during the war were demanding "any peace whatsoever," now that they had peace were not content with that kind of peace. Those democrats who had willed the war in the hope of getting a just peace shouted because that was not the just peace they had anticipated. The Nationalists shouted because they had remained with empty hands. Those who had opposed the war shouted because in this way they could also shout against those who had willed the war.

The most vociferous were the Nationalists. They had supported Orlando and Sonnino to the bitter end. Now that utter disaster had shipwrecked their men of confidence, they were not honest enough to admit their errors. No self-respecting politician ever does so. They searched for scapegoats on whom to heap the blame for the "humiliation" that Italy had suffered. It was not difficult to locate them. It was not Orlando and Sonnino, nor those who had supported them, who were responsible, but those Italians who through lack of discipline and of patriotism had not supported Orlando and Sonnino against the "foreigner." If all Italians had stood behind their representatives during the peace negotiations, Wilson and the Allies would never have dared to deny Italy the fulfillment of her "national aspirations." The "traitors" of "parliamentary democracy" had "stabbed Italy in the back".

Mussolini, as is his custom, was the most violent of all. He cursed the men in power as cowardly and urged the Italian people to crush all "traitors"—Catholics, democrats, and above all "Bolshevists"—and lend a helping hand to Russia, Germany, Hungary, and Bulgaria, which he called the "proletarian nations," in a new "revolutionary war" against the "capitalistic nations." Italy would never obtain pity from the American, English, and French "wolves, foxes and jackals" so long as she stood before them with humble and fawning air. To disarm her "terrible" allies, she should show them dire teeth and not whimper when they treated her lightly.[1]

This uproar about "mutilated victory" affected primarily the young people of the middle classes. The idea that Italy, after so many sufferings, was the victim of criminal injustice and ingratitude created in them a desire for violent action against all those in Italy and outside of Italy who were responsible for her débâcle. They came to believe that the old politicians should be thrown out of power even at the cost of a revolution and that the affronts suffered by the country in the peace conference should be avenged even at the cost of a new war.

[1] *Popolo d'Italia,* September 15, 1919.

They would have protested indignantly against the accusation that they were antirevolutionary. They would never have given their support to any political movement serving conservative interests and ideals. Mussolini satisfied their confused restlessness by presenting himself to them as the only authentic revolutionist at that time existing in Italy. As a Fascist writer has remarked, one could find among Mussolini's followers "the republican and the anarchist, the syndicalist and the revolutionary, the college student and the futurist, all actuated by the dynamic nature of the 'arditi.' A happy combination of values and forces until then dispersed, now were united by a common mentality which had found in war its first school."[2] In other words, all mentalities except the conservative were to be found among Mussolini's followers. The Fascist movement was not a defense against the revolutionary aftermath of the war, but was itself a revolutionary aftermath. To be sure, Mussolini fought against the Socialists and the Communists. But the Anarchists, too, fought against them, and even the Communists were continually at loggerheads with the Socialists, though forming part of the same party until the end of 1920. These were struggles, not between conservatives and revolutionists, but between men who claimed to be more revolutionary than others.

The sole political group which in those years had the courage to declare itself to be out-and-out conservative and antirevolutionary and frankly advocated repression was the Nationalist party. The intellectuals of the well-to-do classes and the officers of the regular army who were interested in politics adhered, not to the Fascist movement, but to the Nationalist movement. Nobody would then have guessed that some day Mussolini would become the leader of a party to which the Nationalists would give almost all their ideas. What could there be in common between the heavy and pedantic authoritarian doctrine of the Nationalists and the unbridled clamors of Mussolini? The abyss which yawned between the Nationalists and the Fascists seemed at that time unbridgeable.

Nationalists, Fascists, and Futurists attacked Nitti with extreme violence. He had been minister for the treasury under Orlando from November 1917 (after the defeat of Caporetto) to the end of the war, and as long as he had served under Orlando, the Nationalists had favored him wholeheartedly.[3] But in January 1919, Nitti had resigned because Orlando and Sonnino had rejected his plan for rapid demobilization. From that moment,

[2] C. Pellizzi, *Problemi e Realtà del Fascismo* (Florence, 1924), p. 163.
[3] Praises of Nitti were published in the *Idea Nazionale* issues of December 20, 1917; January 31, March 8, April 27, May 27, July 20, 1918; January 15, 1919.

he was one of the "traitors" who had stabbed Italy in the back.[4] When the overthrow of the Orlando cabinet began to appear possible, and Nitti's name was being given as the prospective successor, the Nationalists mobilized D'Annunzio against him. In the newspapers, on May 26, D'Annunzio denounced a "plot" headed by Giolitti and Nitti and invoked against them "a punishment as direct as the jet from the fire thrower of our arditi." According to him, Nitti was "hatched by the big American bankers." The latter had other things to do than hatching Nitti. But whoever charges a politician with being in the service of bankers has a fair chance of being believed.

As soon as Orlando was defeated in the Chamber, demonstrations were staged in Rome, in Torino, and in Milan; demonstrators shouted, "Down with Giolitti, down with Nitti, long live Italy, long live the army." Nitti took great pains to announce that he did not intend "to carry the standard of Giolitti". He reminded people that he had served the country as minister of the treasury from the ruins of Caporetto to the victorious end of the war and that the only one of his sons who was able to serve as a soldier had gone to war as a volunteer. He was talking to the wind.

When he came to power, a military expedition for Georgia was ready to leave. Wilson, Lloyd George, and Clemenceau, while they were defeating Orlando and Sonnino in all their endeavors, had encouraged them to run to the assistance of the Tsarist generals who were attacking Soviet Russia. Orlando and Sonnino had fallen into the trap, hoping to find in Georgia the territorial acquisitions they had missed in Africa and in Asia Minor, and the Italian military chiefs were eager "to serve their Fatherland" in Georgia. Nitti vetoed their plans and ordered demobilization to be carried out as speedily as possible. If one does not take into account the hatred that the military chiefs felt for Nitti, one does not understand the unceasing bitterness with which this man was attacked.

On June 22—that is to say, the very day on which Nitti announced his new ministry—the Association of War Veterans held their first national congress in Rome. Six hundred thousand members were represented. A Nationalist, Giunta, invoked "a great movement of opposition" against "the policy which was then being followed in Italy." He was shouted down. The next day, the "ardito" Ferruccio Vecchi was lifted bodily and thrown out of the hall. Giunta tried once more to lead the congress to a demonstra-

---

[4] Violent articles against Nitti in the *Idea Nazionale*, March 8 and 10, 1919.

tion against the parliament and invoked "a constituent assembly, the only way which gives the people the right to govern itself." The constituent assembly had been one of the war cries of Mazzini from 1831 to 1870, during the Risorgimento: the people should proclaim a republic in all Italy, and a constituent assembly elected by universal suffrage should draw up the constitution of the newborn republic. The Republicans had always demanded a constituent assembly, which would do away with monarchical institutions and establish a republic. In 1919, the Republicans continued to insist upon their old idea. Giunta, by adopting now the same war cry, was expressing his friends' discontent with the king who had summoned Nitti to the premiership. The Congress of the War Veterans did not listen to Giunta. Someone asked that Mussolini and D'Annunzio, who were in Rome, be invited to come and speak. The congress voted down the proposal. It was clear that the war veterans wanted nothing to do with either Nationalists, Fascists, or "arditi."

Not for this did Nationalists and Fascists give up the struggle. On the evening of June 28, they called a meeting of protest in Rome against Nitti. The minister of war forbade the officers to intervene. Many officers in uniform went just the same. One of the Nationalist leaders, Corradini, spoke violently against "the parliamentary clique" which "was dominating the nation and all its institutions, from the most humble to the higher ones, even to those which in vain were at the top." This was an allusion to the king who had entrusted the government to Nitti. Another speaker said, "Let us gather with one sole will around our foremost soldier, Gabriele D'Annunzio. Veterans, are we ready to listen to the voice of D'Annunzio, of our highest commander, when he summons us for the salvation of Italy?" Another speaker: "Enough of applause and boos. Let us have facts and not words." At this point a voice announced, "The meeting is adjourned. It will be resumed at Piazza Barberini." The crowd shouted, "To Piazza Barberini!" This was where Nitti lived.

D'Annunzio was to have participated in the meeting. At the last minute he failed to appear. But in the *Idea Nazionale* of July 1, he published the address he was to have made had he not thought it prudent not to make it. In that speech, he reproached the crowd that let its meeting be controlled by policemen:

> What have you been doing while I was relentlessly preparing in silence something of which I hope you will soon hear?

> What arms do you give me? . . . I have come here to measure your patience, which seems to be boundless. . . . If I followed my own instinct, I would go and burn the Home Office tonight with cans of gasoline. With an iron club I would go and do away with Nitti. With my old airplane I would let a load of bombs loose over the Chamber of Deputies. . . . You think, however, that it is better to go to bed. . . . Very well then, go home and put your head down between two pillows. And send me once and for all to the devil.

It is clear that the meeting had been planned with the idea that it should finish with an attack against Nitti in Piazza Barberini, and that the policemen and the carabineers[5] would let the officers in uniform pass because military discipline bound them to respect the officers as their superiors.

The policemen and carabineers, however, had received orders to interpret their military duties differently. They prevented the attack on the residence of Nitti, handing out blows and beatings to both civilians and officers in uniform. There were no dead or wounded, which shows that the police acted with forbearance under the circumstances, while the officers were prompted by no heroic urge.

The methods which the police used to break up demonstrations—blows, beatings, and even shots of revolvers and rifles—had never raised any objections on the part of the Nationalists as long as they had been used against "subversives." This time it was Nationalists, Fascists, and officers in uniform who had been manhandled. This was an unpardonable crime for which Nitti was responsible. He had "attacked, insulted, violated and struck down in the streets," not a certain number of seditious officers, but "the war veterans." The war veterans were not those who had refused to let D'Annunzio and Mussolini speak in their congress, but those who wanted to assault Nitti. The *Idea Nazionale* wrote in its issue of June 30:

> We speak in the name of the war veterans. We announce that we are ready to resort to any acts of extreme violence. Never, never will we tolerate that a man of doubtful origins and discredited reputation subject war veterans to shameful treatment and unloose civil war to defend himself. Nitti

---

[5] There were two organized bodies in Italy for the maintenance of peace: the police, who depended on the Home Office, and the "carabineers," who depended on the War Department.

must be forced out of the body of our nation like a malignant cancer which threatens it with rottenness.

The Nationalist deputy of Rome, Signor Federzoni, raised a protest against the police, who, "by unheard of violence," had dared without cause to "manhandle officers in uniform, thus violating military discipline." It was not the officers who had violated military discipline by taking part in an illegal manifestation, but it was the police who had stopped them from attacking the house of the prime minister. D'Annunzio proclaimed that, on the evening of June 28, the men who had been killed in war had been killed a second time: "They were killed by the Italian club just like those who, under the atrocious Austrian maces, had gasped out their last breath." In its issue of July 2, the *Idea Nazionale* published a letter signed by "many officers," which read, "Do the ministry and the Parliament want civil war? So be it. We are ready, we are determined for anything. . . . Let us have leaders and a general appeal to the veterans. . . . We have weapons. We have the army with us. At the preordained moment, all the soldiers will follow us." In its July 3 issue, the same newspaper published a letter signed by "an officer who has fought in the war." He said, "Let us take up our revolvers and defend our honor, our dignity . . . If an officer has the right to kill a soldier, who attacks him, so much greater is his right when faced with a carabineer. If our honor is not vindicated, if our superiors do not vindicate it, we are entitled to rebel against them."

These and other equally seditious letters, published without individual signatures, were forbidden by military regulations. Most likely they had been cooked up by the staffs of the paper. But Salandra's son, who was a lawyer by trade, undertook to expound in a signed letter the rights and privileges of officers in uniform. To be sure, they were not permitted to participate in political demonstrations, but the task of enforcing the law was up to their superiors and not to the police or the carabineers. An officer could be arrested only by an officer of higher, or at least of the same, rank. As a consequence, a carabineer or policeman who struck an officer committed a "serious act of insubordination." For his own part, Salandra's son would "react by any method whatsoever, none excluded, against an inferior, carabineer or not, who threatened the dignity of his rank," and he did not doubt that all his fellow officers were of the same opinion (*Idea Nazionale,* July 3). In other words, officers in uniform had the right to participate in any seditious movement whatsoever; the police would merely take their names, if they could succeed in getting them, and denounce them to their superiors so that the latter could decide whether it was the case to punish them or not, after the seditious movement had been carried out.

According to these new theories of constitutional law, the Nationalists held a protest meeting on July 4, in which participated "many hundreds of officers, war veterans, and citizens," under the chairmanship of war veteran Giuriati, who in later years was to become secretary general of the Fascist party and minister for public works under Mussolini. Nitti was made the butt of the day, and the meeting also voted "a warning to the Crown, the Government and the Parliament" (*Corriere della sera*, July 5, 1919). For Nationalists and Fascists, as well as for Maximalists, Spartacists, and Anarchists, there were no more laws. The latter dreamed of a proletarian revolution which never came to pass. The former worked for a military coup d'état, which in the end was bound to come.

This storm of words had hardly begun to calm down when an unprecedented wave of food riots convulsed a large part of Italy. The riots began at Forlí, in Romagna, on the morning of June 30, when the crowd, exasperated by the mounting prices of vegetables, eggs, fruits, and fish, destroyed in the market place everything which had been put out for sale—a method certainly not conducive to reducing the cost of living. The workers' organizations also wanted to do something to diminish the cost of living and called, for the following day, a general strike to protest against the profiteers and against the government which did nothing to stop "profiteering." Even the mayor of the city wanted to do his part, and he ordered all prices to be cut in half. The following day, during the strike, a shopkeeper fired a shot at a group of persons who had gathered in front of his shop. The shop was sacked, and, when the news of the event spread, other shops of cloth, foodstuffs, and shoes were looted. The shopkeepers who wanted to avoid being looted attached placards to the fronts of their shops saying, "I have given over my keys to the representatives of the people," or "The merchandise has been placed at the disposal of the Chamber of Labor," or "The keys have been handed over to the mayor." Something on the same order had taken place at La Spezia two weeks before, and the news of what had happened at La Spezia served as a model for the strikers, the mayor, and the shopkeepers of Forlí. Here, however, the strikers did not grab for themselves the merchandise which was not destroyed; they "requisitioned" it, and, piling it on automobiles and trucks also "requisitioned," they carried it to the Chamber of Labor. In this way the wealth was not "privately appropriated," but "socialized."

On July 2, at the news of the events of Forlí, general strikes against the "profiteers" and the government which did not tie the hands and feet of the "profiteers" broke out in three cities close to and north of Forlí: Faenza, Meldola, and Imola. At Imola the crowd sacked the shops as in Forlí. The police resorted to arms and killed four persons. On July 3, the general strikes spread to the cities south of Forlí: Cesena, Senigallia, Falconara, Ancona, Chiaravalle, Iesi. Automobiles "requisitioned" by "red guards" carried the news from city to city that the "great day" had arrived. On July 4, the whole of Romagna and the adjoining section of the Marches were the theater of general strikes, forced reductions in prices, and "requisitions."

At the same time, on July 3, the news of the events of Forlí and Imola, given in the newspapers, provoked the looting of shops in Florence and, on July 4, in Prato near Florence and in Turin and Voghera in northern Italy. On July 5, the lootings spread to Brescia, Alessandria, Pinerolo, and Novi Ligure in northern Italy; Pisa, Leghorn, Piombino, and Siena in central Italy; and Taranto and Palermo in southern Italy. On July 6 and 7, there was plundering in Milan, Sesto San Giovanni (near Milan), Vicenza (between Milan and Venice), Genoa, Rome, Naples, and Catania (in Sicily). In the town of Grottaglie (southern Italy), the crowd set the town hall on fire. At the same time, general strikes and scuffles with the police occurred in many other cities.

Most likely, the riots and general strikes which took place in minor towns were not recorded by the daily press. But even if the disorder had engulfed several cities and towns besides those enumerated above, one must bear in mind that there are about 7,500 cities and towns in Italy. This means that the country remained quiet in its huge majority. Only in Romagna and in the neighboring Marches did the upheaval cover a vast and compact area. The Italy of July 1919 was different from the Russia of 1917, when millions of soldiers, with their guns, deserted the front and disorganized the whole administrative and political structure of the country. But among the cities which were in convulsions at the beginning of July 1919, many of the most important were included: Milan, Turin, Leghorn, Florence, Ancona, Rome, Palermo. The vital centers of the country were here. If, in those larger cities, the food riots had evolved into revolutionary movements, the minor cities would certainly have followed their example. It seemed in those days that a revolution on the Russian pattern was going on and that nothing could stop it.

Nothing of this kind happened. The General Confederation of Labor kept aloof from the movement and did nothing to give it a political or revolutionary goal. The employees in the railway, telegraph, telephone, and postal services did not strike. Gradually the storm died down by itself and by July 13, conditions had returned to normal all over Italy—that is to say, there were no more strikes or other incidents than in normal times.

During the whole crisis, the police and the carabineers, obviously under orders from Nitti, everywhere abstained from acts of violent repression. They resorted to defensive tactics. They protected against assault the banks, the most important sections of the large cities, and all vital centers of governmental activities, and they left to their own resources the outskirts of the large cities, the countryside, and the smaller towns. It would have been difficult for them to do otherwise. The carabineers, to whom in normal times belonged the task of maintaining order, were reduced to no more than 28,000 in number, owing to losses incurred in the war. On the other hand, the soldiers of the regular army were in sympathy with the rioters and could not be utilized for repression without running the risk of unruly reactions on their part. Under such conditions, had Nitti given orders for a bloody repression on a huge scale, he would not have been at all sure of carrying it out successfully; at the same time, he would have forced the General Confederation of Labor out of their inaction into some nationwide protest—that is to say, into an even vaster upheaval. Perhaps the final push would have been given to that leap in the dark that the extremists were waiting for. Prudence was, for Nitti, the better part of valor.

Here and there clashes occurred between the police and the rioters. There were victims: four dead in Imola; one in Florence; two in Brescia; two in Genoa; one in Catanzaro; five in Taranto; two in Rome; four in Spilimbergo; eight in Lucera. But given the extent and the violence of the upheaval, all in all the police and the carabineers handled the situation with wisdom.

13

Conservatives
and Revolutionaries

The food riots of July 1919, more than any other event, help us to understand the mentality of the Italian population and the aims of the different parties during the first postwar years. The Florence riots were both the most serious and the most significant.

In Florence, the local branch of the Socialist party, the official paper of the party, *La Difesa,* and the Chamber of Labor were all under the control of Maximalists. On June 21, 1919, *La Difesa* announced that "action was imminent":

> Proletarians, the hour has come to pass from words to deeds. The threads of an immense net of sacrifices and incitements to struggle are being drawn together. Woe to those who believe that they can appease popular wrath by some general strike contained within time limits. Our generous people want nothing but action. To action they have been trained. In action they have been led to place every hope. But it must be true and conclusive action. Comrades, let us arise. The great hour is about to strike.

When, however, the news of the riots in Forlí was first given in the press on July 2, it was not the Maximalists who incited the crowd to "true and conclusive action." It was that same Nationalist, Giunta, who a few days earlier in Rome had endeavored to stir up the war veterans against the government. On the evening of July 2, in a meeting of war veterans, he waved a pair of shoes, shouting that he had to pay forty-eight lire for them and urging his comrades to sack the shops. On the morning of July 3, the ultraconservative daily of Florence, *La Nazione*, devoted two columns to describing the "disciplined" revolt of Forlí, Faenza, Imola, and other cities, and half a column to attacking fiercely war profiteers:

> Truly it is an unsavory task to give vent to our indignation against people who for good or ill still belong to the Italian family. But disgust and anger raise our gorge. Is it possible that even today, after the terrible lesson of the war, we find men so obstinate and persevering in evil doing? Do these wretches realize nothing of what is happening around them? Do they not know that the patience of the people has its limits, behind which lie the most cruel and unknown possibilities? Have they brains, have they blood, have they nerves, these maleficent citizens? We will add no more. We still have a vague hope that certain examples of yesterday may bring more wisdom to these perverted individuals. If this hope also proves vain, then indeed we should not be the ones to deplore an outburst of collective indignation, provoked, as it would be, in every possible manner.

When an ultraconsèrvative paper wrote in this manner, what else could the crowd do than follow the "examples" indicated? The sacking of shops actually began the very afternoon of July 3. During that afternoon, the whole night, and the morning of the next day, the outer sections of the city and the country around were left to the "requisitioning" done by self-appointed authorities. It was never known how many shops were looted. They ran into the hundreds.

The writer of the present book, who was living at that time in Florence, roamed through the streets during the days of the tumult to learn "how a revolution is made." When the crisis was over, he published the following account:

> Whoever walked through the streets of Florence during the days of the upheaval and tried to understand what the people was thinking and wanting, did not find anywhere the idea of a social reorganization along communistic lines. Even less was there a desire for fighting or sacrifice. We never saw anywhere in the world so many people armed with

flasks of wine as we saw in the streets of Florence in those days. Men, women, boys, girls, old people, young people, all went around carrying one, two, three flasks of wine. Florence was not hungry, it was thirsty. The crowds were made up of goodnatured, jolly people, who went peacefully home, happy at last to have gotten a flask for two lire, or even free of charge, and anticipating the jubilee the family would enjoy on that little godsend. When they were wiser than the average, they deposited their first haul at home and returned to provide for more at half price or to "requisition" it altogether. Second to flasks of wine, the most sought-after merchandise were shoes. There was no heroic and revolutionary exaltation in anyone. There was no will to set up a new social organization in place of the old authorities. . . . Everywhere there are corwds ready to revolt. There does not exist anywhere a class equal to a revolution. Nor should it be said that the revolution did not take place because an all-out movement was not yet in readiness. When it is ready in the spirits of the people, the all-out movement bursts forth as soon as a local incident gives a push. It cannot be prepared for a fixed date.[1]

That was the state of mind of the crowd. What about its leaders? At 3:00 P.M. on July 3, thousands of workers flocked instinctively to the Chamber of Labor. Here was their general staff, and here they came to ask what they should do. The editor of the Maximalist newspaper was conspicuous by his absence. He was not there to repeat to the "masses" that "the great hour had struck." The task of leading the "proletariat" fell on the shoulders of the secretary of the Chamber of Labor. The unfortunate man, having to say something to that crowd, told them that "the working class *was forced* to head an energetic and resolute movement against the greed of the food profiteers," and he proposed to the workers that they proclaim a general strike. Thus, the general strike which had already begun before it was proclaimed, was now proclaimed. Meanwhile, the "requisitions" had begun in the shops, and that merchandise which had not been destroyed or had not ended up in the homes of the "requisitioners" was carried to the Chamber of Labor, which suddenly found itself laden down with cheese, pieces of cloth, shoes, flasks of wine, hams—a confused heap of every sort of good. At 6:00 P.M., the secretary of the Chamber of Labor went to the prefect of the province, not to tell him that he was dismissed from his post

[1] Weekly *L'Unità*, July 10, 1919.

and that "the dictatorship of the proletariat" had set in, but to consult with him on the appointment of "a committee which would devise the best way *to discipline the movement.*"

On the following day, July 4, the Maximalist paper published a triumphal article: "The hour has come, not for half measures, but for energetic and radical decisions. Let him who must understand it . . . The dictatorship of the proletariat has shown how great its efficiency is. Direct action has triumphed. Forward! Forward! Towards Communism."

The conservative newspaper came out with six columns devoted to the events of the preceding day under an enormous headline which read: "Yesterday, in Florence, the inevitable came to pass." For two years the newspaper had foreseen that "inevitable." The fault was with that "shady organization" which was bleeding the Italian people. The paper expressed satisfaction for the movement which had developed "with a certain discipline and seriousness, except, of course, for some isolated cases unavoidable in popular uprisings when disturbed elements came in." What mattered was that the Chamber of Labor had taken on the responsibility for the "requisitions." "The Chamber of Labor must not forget that having taken on that responsibility, it has a duty to see that it does not become looting."

The Chamber of Labor was doing everything possible to instill a little order into the chaos. At 9:00 A.M., the committee, appointed the previous day in agreement with the prefect and made up of representatives of all the workers' organizations, from those of the Socialist party to those directed by Revolutionary Syndicalists and Anarchists, convened in the Chamber of Labor. Since the strike was going on without permission from anyone, the committee decided that the strike should go on, but the workers in the gas, electric, and other public services and the nurses should not take part in it. Furthermore, the shopkeepers would receive posters stamped by the Chamber of Labor to be attached to the doors of their shops telling the public that the shops were "at the disposal of the Chamber of Labor." Nobody should "requisition" the shops protected with those talismans. Private property was put under the protection of the Maximalist Chamber of Labor. In this way the committee began "to discipline the movement."

On July 5, the Maximalist paper was still shouting its empty slogans:

> The struggle is not yet over. It has hardly begun, it must spread. It must become more intense. All the hopes of the

workers must be fulfilled. Communism, which is still a hope, must become a reality. Who does not realize that our aims are ever further ahead, ever higher?

While the writers of the Maximalist paper were getting drunk on words, the writers of the conservative paper, on July 5, stopped expressing satisfaction with "the discipline and seriousness" of the movement and insisted more strongly on the fact that the responsibility for what was taking place belonged to the Chamber of Labor. It was its duty now to "clear up the juridical muddle which it created by the requisitions." Its directors' responsibilities would be both commercial and criminal. At the present time, they had in addition a responsibility toward mankind, since the feeding of the city had become their duty. Thus, if supplies were to run short, the Chamber of Labor would be responsible.

The committee of the Chamber of Labor had other things to do than to pay attention to such insinuations. The population was getting tired of aimless and wasteful riots. Therefore, they issued an order to the effect that the strike should cease at 12:00 P.M. of the coming night. This order was published in the same issue of the Maximalist paper which was announcing that the struggle had not yet come to an end, nay was at its beginning. Since July 5 was a Saturday, the strike was to cease on a Sunday. The committee was sure of being obeyed by everyone, for on a Sunday all factories were shut whether or not the workers wished to strike. In the meantime, another day of reflection would help people to find the path of common sense again. In fact, on Monday, July 7, work was resumed everywhere.

Now, on July 7 the conservative paper found out that people who desired a political revolution were pushing the country to starvation and misery; during the food riots they had not succeeded in their endeavor, but they would try again. All those who loved their country must draw closer together to defend it against internal enemies. Thus, in Florence, an "Anti-Bolshevist Alliance" arose. And Giunta, that same Nationalist who, on the evening of July 2, had waved the forty-eight-lire pair of shoes, was one of its primary founders. Of course the shopkeepers and peasants whose produce had been "requisitioned" were enthusiastic about this newborn alliance.

All over Italy, those newspapers which worked hand-in-hand with the Nationalist clique followed the same line as in Florence. In Rome, the daily *Giornale d'Italia*, which was the organ of Salandra, Sonnino, and the army and navy chiefs, had published violent articles against the food profiteers. When the tumult calmed down, the same paper attacked the "Bolshevists" for stirring up disorder and invoked a coalition of all good citizens against the enemies of the Fatherland, foremost among whom was Nitti. The *Idea Nazionale*, in its issue of July 3, gave the news of the disorders of Forlí without a single word of condemnation. On July 4, it blamed the food profiteers for everything which was happening. On July 5, it protested against the "fabulous prohibitive prices of wine"; incited the war veterans, not to come to grips with the carabineers, but to rebel against Nitti; and published a proclamation in which D'Annunzio asserted that the enemy of Italy was in Rome: "We will chase him out." On July 6, the *Idea Nazionale* explained that to the high cost of living a "super-high cost" of living was being added and that the liberal state was guilty of not preventing this second evil. The night between July 6 and 7 at about 2:00 A.M., a group of about thirty persons appeared before a barracks and tried to induce a battalion of "arditi" quartered there to take part in a *coup de main* aimed at getting hold of strategical points in the city. They failed; some of them were arrested, but their leader, a certain Argo Secondari, escaped. They were all "arditi" (*Idea Nazionale*, September 19, 1919). At last, on July 7, food riots broke out in Rome also, and went on for three days. Immediately the Nationalist paper began to attack Nitti violently for not having maintained order. On July 9, while food riots were still going on, a group of Fascists, Futurists, and "arditi," led by Marinetti, tried to stir up a demonstration against Nitti in the heart of Rome.

In Bologna, where the Chamber of Labor and the municipality had succeeded in avoiding disturbance, the military authorities themselves hastened to put at the service of the Chamber of Labor forty trucks which would serve eventually to requisition the products from the peasants (*Idea Nazionale*, July 5, 1919). If the Chamber of Labor had made use of those trucks, it would have created an abyss of hatred between the workers of the city on the one hand, and the tenants and small landowners in the country around the city on the other.

As was to be expected, Mussolini was the most violent of all in attacking the food profiteers. The *Popolo d'Italia* wrote on July 4:

> In Romagna the people have revolted vigorously against the greed of the speculators and have already succeeded in obtaining a great reduction in prices. Requisitions and control

of prices are having the desired effect. We are witnessing the revolt of the working classes against those primarily and directly responsible for the intolerable food situation. It is not the Socialist party which has provoked and directed these demonstrations. It lacks the will to lead a movement which may disrupt the parliamentary game of trickery, past and present. For our part we explicitly affirm the fundamental justice of the popular protest.

And on July 5:

I hope that the masses in the exercise of their sacred right will strike at the criminals, not only in their goods, but in their persons. A few food-hogs hanging from the lamp-posts would be a good example. The Fascist central committee proclaims its absolute solidarity with the masses who have risen against the famine-makers, welcomes the movement of requisitioning by the people, and pledges the Fascists to promote and support the agitation.

In Milan, the food riots began on July 6 and lasted for two days without reaching the seriousness of those of Florence, because in Milan the police had gathered sufficient force to check the storm and made 2,200 arrests among the underworld. In Milan, too, as soon as the storm was over, "anti-Bolshevist" initiatives multiplied, promoted by those same persons and by those same groups who, a few days before, had been at the fore in inciting the crowds against the food profiteers. Mussolini was in the first row again in this new "anti-Bolshevist" upsurge.

All these facts lead us to the conclusion that the food riots in July began spontaneously in Romagna, as in La Spezia and the neighboring towns in the middle of June. But now the political groups who were working against Nitti set out to fan the flame, in the hope that Nitti, overcome by the disturbances, would be forced to cede the government to a ministry of generals, or that, to reestablish order, he would resort to a policy of violent suppression which would create an abyss of hatred between him and the Socialists. Nitti avoided both alternatives and gave the country the impression that he did not intend to profit from the food riots to inaugurate a reactionary policy. Thus the clashes, even if there were dead and wounded, remained unfortunate local incidents, unavoidable in such a vast upheaval.

The Chamber of Deputies reopened on July 9—that is to say, when the worst of the crisis was past. The Socialist deputies, although retaining their attitude of uncompromising opposition to any "bourgeois" government, abstained from attacking the new prime minister with too violent criticism, and on July 14, 1919, the Chamber gave him 257 votes of confidence. Of the 111 votes against him, no more than 25 came from the Socialists, because 15 of them did not participate in the vote in order to make the position of the cabinet less difficult. The rest of the opponents were deputies who had supported Orlando and Sonnino to the bitter end. Even among the latter, however, two score joined the majority in their vote of confidence.

While the Conservatives, during the food riots, were exasperating the unrest everywhere, the right-wing and Maximalist Socialists did everything possible to put an end to food riots and strikes, not only in Florence, but all over Italy. Even in Turin, where the Socialist party and the trade unions were controlled by extremists, the unions summoned the workers back to work and disavowed every attempt at unauthorized strikes (*Secolo*, July 10, 1919). Unfortunately for them, the Maximalists were not capable of reconciling their wishful thinking with their actual activities. On July 5, the committee of the Florence Chamber of Labor, on announcing that the strike was to cease, declared itself certain "that no one would fail to respond to the call which would be launched in good time for the final conquests." Similar nonsense was reiterated everywhere.

The writer of the present book, who had observed the Florence food riots, noticed the fact that the reactionary groups in Italy were willing to resort to brutal violence but could not do so unless the country first grew tired of the aimless disorder which was upsetting the life of the country:

> Everything which piles up hatred against the city workers in the other classes of the population paves the way for reaction. What could better further reaction than the "requisitions" at the expense of the shopkeepers and the peasants? This is why the food riots were stirred up, or at least were accepted with sympathy, for not more than one or two days, by certain newspapers. When weariness has become universal against this state of affairs, then the police will no longer be indulgent as at the present time. Then machine guns will blaze in the streets (Weekly *L'Unità*, July 10, 1919).

By persisting in the use of revolutionary rhetoric while not being possessed of either revolutionary mentality or revolutionary aims, the Maximalists were exasperating the postwar neurasthenia and playing into the hands of the reactionary groups:

> From such incoherent and inconclusive ups and downs of urgings, tumults and returns to quiet, nothing can come except anger among the damaged and disturbed classes, disappointment and apathy among the less wild sections of the working people, a growing nervousness among the groups less amenable to the control of the trade unions, and in the end, a terrific reaction through martial law and military courts (*L'Unità*, July 10, 1919).

A new evidence for the fact that no revolutionary situation existed in the country was given on July 21. On that day, a "general demonstration" against the military intervention in Russia and Hungary on the part of the western powers was to take place in England, in France, and in Italy. The "general demonstration" had been decided upon on June 27 at an international conference held at Southport (England) by the representatives of the Socialist parties and trade unions of the three countries. Every country was to carry out its own demonstration "in the form and by the methods best suited to the conditions of each country." This meant that the English workers would remain as law-abiding as ever; the French woud hold meetings with thunderous addresses, provided that Clemenceau allowed them to do so; and the Italians were at liberty to try the "great day." The most zealous in preparing the demonstration were precisely the Italian Maximalists—that is, the citizens of a country whose government had no intention of intervening either in Russia or in Hungary, while Great Britain and France actually were intervening in Russia. When the Maximalists, in the days of the food riots, announced that the "great day" had not yet arrived, but was coming, they thought immediately of the demonstration decided upon at Southport. In a new meeting held at Paris on July 4, the leaders of the French and Italian Confederations of Labor decided that the demonstration should take the form of a general strike on Monday, July 21. But the Maximalists who controlled the Italian Socialist party would not agree to one single day and decided that in Italy the general strike was to last for two days—that is, from Sunday, July 20, through Monday, July 21, as if people were unable to realize that a general strike on a Sunday was but childish humbug. The leaders of the General Confederation of Labor did not have the courage to oppose this new excess of foolishness. They consented to proclaiming not only that the strike was to be "a first and solemn mobilization of the international forces," but also: that the French would participate in the strike; that the English would not strike but would "show their tendency to resort to the use of the direct action of their powerful trade unions" if the necessity should present itself; that the Swiss, Dutch, Swedes, and Danes "would join the general movement" and that in this way "would be begun in the world the international action of the proletariat against the interests of capitalism" (*Avanti*, July 7, 13, 1919). The national organization of the railwaymen and that of the employees in the postal and telegraph services promised that they would join in the strike. This was an absolutely new factor of which it was not possible to foresee the consequences. Was the "great hour" really about to break?

The "great hour" did not break even now. The leaders of the Confederation of Labor, after siding with the Maximalists in putting up the bluff of the two-day strike that was really only a one-day strike, reminded their membership that the strike was to be "disciplined and calm," that "it was folly to hope that now in Italy the Maximalist ideas might be carried out," and that the "more extreme elements" should not be allowed to prolong the strike (*Corriere della sera*, July 15, 1919). The national directorate of the Socialist party itself exhorted all comrades "not to accept provocations of any sort," to "bridle the generous impatience which at this hour could be of no use and only have tragic consequence," and to remain happy with the thought that the strike would serve to "keep the way open to revolution in all of Europe, and especially in Italy" (*Avanti*, July 17, 1919). A new cold shower fell on the heads of the extremists when the national executive of the railwaymen revoked the decision to participate in the strike without giving any clear reasons for this unexpected change. The final blow was dealt by the French General Confederation of Labor, which, on July 19, "suspended" the strike. The "general demonstration" of July 20 and 21 was reduced to a series of uncoordinated and inconclusive strikes with a few acts of violence here and there. The strike failed especially in the railways and in the postal and telegraph services. This did not hinder the Communist Bombacci (who in later years was to put himself at the service of the Fascist government), from announcing "the imminent victory of the proletariat" (*Corriere della sera*, July 22, 1919).

The one who profited from the "general demonstration" was Nitti.

Having safely weathered even this storm, he was greeted with applause in the Chamber of Deputies on July 22. Nay more, in the Senate, made up in its great majority of old Conservatives, he received a vote of confidence from all the 102 who were present, amidst continuous enthusiastic applause (July 26).

The food riots of the first ten days of July and the unsuccessful general strike of July 20 and 21 left the working classes with a sense of disillusionment and weariness. Many hopes and many enthusiasms vanished in that month. Having wasted their strength in those movements, the workers were not in a position to make any protest when a protest would have been to the point.

On the Sunday of August 3, 1919, in Trieste, 1,600 boys and girls whose parents were enrolled in the Socialist trade unions made an excursion to the country. Returning to the city that evening, the procession was halted by a group of police who wanted to keep them from going on. Confusion arose. The men and women protested, shouted, cursed; the children cried. To intimidate the crowd, the police began to shoot in the air. No one was wounded. The following morning a general strike of protest broke out. The leaders of the unions, in the afternoon, meeting in the Chamber of Labor, decided that the strike should cease the following day. Leaving the hall, all 430 of them were arrested. Immediately afterwards, the Chamber was invaded by Nationalists, "arditi," and officers in uniform and was looted. The same fate was suffered by the warehouses and libraries of the cooperative societies and the buildings of the Slav schools and organizations. These acts of violence would have provoked an immediate revolution in Trieste and in Italy if there had really existed a "revolutionary proletariat." Instead, the Maximalist leaders of the Socialist movement in Trieste, who had been released, exerted themselves to try to persuade the workers to put an end to the strike, "since its continuance would result in all kinds of reprisals." The workers, though slowly and unwillingly, obeyed.[2] No protest broke out in the rest of Italy.

A few weeks later, in September, in the national convention of the Socialist party, Filippo Turati served to his comrades the following warning:

> When our enemies find it opportune to take us seriously, our appeal for violence will be accepted by them, a hundred

[2] Report in the weekly *L'Unità*, September 11, 1919.

> times better armed than we. . . . It is the most absurd thing in the world to speak continually of violence and to put it always off until tomorrow. That only serves the purpose of arming, provoking, nay justifying the violence of our foes, a thousand times stronger than ours.[3]

The Italian Maximalists and Spartacists did not have the necessary intelligence to understand these warnings. Nothing could shake them from the certainty that "the proletariat" was there, ready to rise up, and that when the "great hour" would strike, nothing could stand in the way of its triumph.

AUTHOR'S NOTES TO CHAPTER 13

The accusations which Villari (*Awakening of Italy*, pp. 58–59) makes against Nitti in connection with the food riots of July 1919 are worth mentioning because they give a perfect idea of the Nationalist point of view:

> The government did absolutely nothing to stop the disturbances; the authorities were in fact instructed to take no energetic measures. . . . The enemies of Signor Nitti declared that these riots were actually promoted by the government, because, as he was unable to reduce the cost of living or even prevent its further rise by legal means, he deemed it advisable in his ignorance of economic laws, to entrust the task to mob action. It was also said and firmly believed that Nitti contemplated the riots with satisfaction, as he hoped that they would terrify the bourgeoisie into supporting his government as its only bulwark against real revolution. This view is probably an exaggeration, but there is no doubt that Nitti did encourage, and to some extent justify the rioting once it had started. . . . Even if this conviction were unfounded, the mere fact that it was widely diffused constitutes a serious charge against Nitti's policy.

Villari gives as "widely diffused" the conviction which his political friends were trying to spread. Moreover, he takes good care to ignore the following facts:

[3] Lazzeri, *Filippo Turati*, p. 206.

1 In July 1919, Nitti did nothing more nor less than what Orlando had done a few weeks before when the food riots had occurred at La Spezia and neighboring towns.

2 The rioting was encouraged not by Nitti, but by the Nationalists, the Fascists, and Orlando's and Sonnino's followers.

3 In July 1919, the ultraconservative Senate gave Nitti a unanimous vote of confidence, despite the noise which was being made by the Nationalists, the Fascists, and Sonnino's and Orlando's followers.

14

The "Land to the Peasants" and D'Annunzio in Fiume

There was much talk about the need for a new political constitution in place of the one which dated back to 1848. But no one plan was ever agreed upon by a nationwide body of opinion.

The Maximalists and Spartacists were committed to importing into Italy the institutions of Soviet Russia. The national executive of the Socialist party entrusted comrade Bombacci, an elementary school teacher who later was to become a Fascist, with drawing up a plan, which was to be discussed by the party and then given its final shape by the national executive itself. Comrade Bombacci issued his plan in January 1920. Local soviets, or "councils of workers and peasants," were forthwith to be created in all cities, towns and villages. A "national institution" consisting of central councils of workmen and peasants was to lead the local soviets in their struggle "against the bourgeois regime and its democratic delusion, Parliament." The central soviets, as well as the local soviets, were to operate under the "close inspection" of the "vanguard of the proletariat"—that is to say, of commissioners appointed by the Socialist party, who were to take care that only "men effectively tied to the working classes" should become members of the councils and were to prevent the "bourgeoisie from undermining the free expression of the will of the working classes." Local and central soviets were to be ready to take over the direction of all "economic, social and political, both internal and external, relations" and to establish the dictatorship of the proletariat and carry out social revolution. This masterpiece of idiocy was published in the daily *Avanti* on January 23, 1920, and was the beginning and the end of Italian local and central soviets. Nobody discussed the plan, the national executive had no time to give it the final shape, and the bourgeois regime carried on as best it could.

The Republicans conscientiously went on repeating their age-old war cry of the constituent assembly. The Fascists made as much noise as possible with the same war cry, and there were a few moments when even the Nationalists hoped to frighten the king by joining the Republicans and Fascists in demanding a constituent assembly (see Chapter 12). But it was easy to object to them that the Chamber of Deputies could always reform the constitution in unessential details, with the agreement of the Senate and the king, and this agreement would never be lacking as long as the reforms were backed by a wide enough current of opinion in the country. If, instead, the Republicans intended to abolish monarchic institutions and proclaim a republic, then they could not expect that the king and his followers would give up without fighting. First a Republican revolution should triumph, and then the necessity of a constituent assembly would arise. To be sure, Maximalists and Spartacists were for a republic. But they would never have cooperated, even for the sake of a revolution, with the Republicans, who had committed the irreparable sin of advocating the war. Furthermore, they wanted something more vast than a simple political revolution for a republic. They wanted a social revolution and the dictatorship of the proletariat. This dictatorship embodied the republic as the whole embodies all the parts. They were not prepared to concern themselves with the part when the whole was within the reach of their hands. The Anarchists alone were ready to participate in a Republican revolution. It was their intention to join in with any revolutionary movement whatsoever, spread it, eliminate their allies at the right moment, and ultimately arrive at the total overthrow of any brand of government whatsoever. But since they accepted no constitution, they were not interested in any constitutional reform, and, in any case, their influence was appreciable only in some limited areas of central Italy. Thus, Republicans and Fascists were never able to set up a republic. The very fact that they did not dare to advocate frankly a republic, but took the side issue of the constituent assembly, showed that their war cry did not arouse wide response.

A rough draft for a constitutional reform was drawn up by the General Confederation of Labor. The National Council of Labor, which up until that time had consisted of members appointed by the government, and had only had advisory powers, should be elected by employers and workers and endowed with legislative powers.[1] This might have been a first step toward a more intelligent division of labor among different legislative bodies, taking the place of one single parliament in the central government. But the Maximalists, who controlled the Socialist party, never took any interest in such trifling matters, and the leaders of the Confederation themselves, overwhelmed as they were with a steady flood of big strikes, had no time for pressing constitutional reforms.

All the talking which was done for constitutional reforms was reduced to substituting the system of proportional representation for the single-member system in the coming national election. Proportional representation had always been one of the planks in Socialist platforms in all countries of Europe. A nonpartisan association for proportional representation had been in existence in Italy for many years. The newborn German and Austrian republics had adopted it in their elections. Rapidly in 1919, proportional representation was accepted in Italy by politicians of all shades of opinion. During March, a conference of Democrats, Populists, Nationalists, and Reformists was held in Rome to demand proportional representation. Some of the most authoritative "Liberals"—i.e., Conservatives like Senator Tittoni and Senator Ponti—declared themselves in favor of it.[2] The "Liberal" (Conservative) Association of Milan put forward the same demand. So did the National Congress of the Nationalist party (*Idea Nazionale*, March 20, 1919), the National Congress of the Populist party (*Corriere della sera*, June 15, 1919), a meeting of those deputies who had supported Orlando and Sonnino to the bitter end (*Corriere della sera*, June 20, 1919), and the National Congress of War Veterans. The Fascists, following their usual custom, raised the greatest furor about this and threatened to "hinder with every means, even violence," national elections if they were carried out by the old method.[3] Everyone advocated proportional representation for different reasons. The Democrats and right-wing Socialists were true to their traditional tenet. The Conservatives and the Nationalists felt themselves menaced by the discontent of the masses, were afraid that under the single-member system they would fail to be elected, and thought that proportional representation would at least secure them

---

[1] Bachi, *L'Italia economica nel 1919*, pp. 397–98.
[2] F. Ruffini, *Guerra e Riforme Costituzionali* (Torino: Paravia, 1920), p. 76, n. 23; p. 84, n. 106.
[3] *Secolo*, June 8, 1919. See V. Nitti, *L'opera di Nitti*, (Torino, Gobetti, 1924), pp. 111–120.

minority seats. The Populists wanted to have no electoral links with either the Conservatives or Democrats, and proportional representation would allow them to go their own way without compromising with anyone else. Those who had no partisan aims and only wanted to put an end to government-"manipulated" elections hoped that proportional representation would make more difficult, nay impossible, this scandal. The Maximalists and Spartacists did not realize that proportional representation was incompatible with the "dictatorship of the proletariat," since the proletariat must not allow any "bourgeois" minority to enjoy the advantages of any proportional representation and so block the work of the dictatorship. Lenin in Russia had never thought of proportional representation, but his admirers in Italy were never used to thinking. They did not prevent their right-wing comrades in the Chamber from "cooperating" with the other parties in demanding proportional representation. Nitti, on coming to power, saw that it was impossible to stem the tide. So the electoral reform was passed by Parliament in August.

Under the new system, Italy was divided no longer into single-member constituencies but into districts, each of which was to elect from five to twenty deputies. The voter had to choose no longer one single name from among the contesting candidates, but one list from among those which any group of no less than three hundred citizens was entitled to lay before the electorate. In addition, the voter was entitled to designate the man whom he preferred within the list he had chosen. Each list was to be allotted a number of seats proportionate to the number of votes it had received, and these seats were to be assigned to the men who within the list had gotten the highest number of preferential votes.

The Act of 1912 had enfranchised all those male citizens who had been soldiers. Since all Italians had been soldiers during the war of 1915–18, the quasi-universal suffrage of 1912 now became universal suffrage. In 1919, the franchise was extended to all those who had served in the war even if they had not yet reached twenty-one years of age, and so 700,000 youngsters were added to the registered citizens. The electorate which had leaped from 3,329,000 (9.28 percent of the population) to 8,672,000 in 1912 (24.2 percent of the population), now went up to 11,915,000 (29.3 percent of the population). The extension of the franchise to the minors who had been under the colors during the war was advocated by Salandra. Salandra had always been opposed to universal suffrage, but now he was hoping that the young men coming fom the fighting front would add to the Nationalist and

Conservative vote. This was the only reform for which he took the initiative, whereas in November 1918 he had predicted nothing less than a revolution.

Toward the middle of August, while the parties were preparing themselves for the coming elections, in several parts of Apulia the agricultural day laborers who were unemployed or who were striking for higher wages began to seize the lands (*Corriere della sera*, August 12, 22, 1919). Before the end of the month, the peasantry in most districts of Latium, where latifundia were owned by noble Roman families, followed their example. Soon the laborers of Sicily did the same. The promise of "land to the peasants," made and repeated during the war, was bearing its fruits. The movement mainly affected large estates which were given over to grain growing or grazing. The idea was that the owners of uncultivated or badly cultivated lands were to hand them over to laborers, and these, by better farming, would increase production. Not infrequently, however, the laborers found more to their liking lands which were already highly cultivated.[4] War veterans were in the forefront of the movement. When led by Populists or by the directors of the local branches of their national association, they marched with the Italian tricolor flag and to the sound of patriotic music and declared their readiness to pay an annual rent. When led by Socialists, they paraded red flags, sounded proletarian songs, and did not mind about rents. But as a rule, the Socialists abstained from supporting this kind of initiative. It would have resulted in the creation of a more numerous class of small tenant farmers and landowners, while the socialists aimed at the "socialization of all means of production."

The soldiers were in sympathy with the land raids by war veterans. In some places they refused to come out against them. If the government had attempted repression, wider disturbances might have ensued. Here again Nitti resorted to the strategy of wearing down. On September 2, he issued a royal decree which granted the prefects of provinces the power to authorize the temporary occupation of uncultivated or badly cultivated lands by associations of laborers; within the next four years, committees of experts and arbitrators would decide whether the occupation should become permanent and what indemnity should be paid to the old owners. Thus the raids on land developed almost everywhere in a peaceable and jolly mood. Only in the town of Corneto Tarquinia (Latium) did the crowd kill a police

[4] Bachi, *L'Italia economica nel 1919*, pp. 274, 418; *L'Italia economica nel 1920*, p. 296.

commissioner and seriously wound five carabineers who were trying to resist the movement (*Secolo*, September 29, 1919); and in Sicily the police killed seven persons at Riesi and two at Terranova (*Secolo*, October 10, 13, 1919).

One year later, the minister of agriculture stated that 79,000 acres of land had been seized without the consent of the owners, 34,000 being in Latium, and that about 172,000 acres had been seized after friendly agreements.[5] Even if one guesses that seldom were these "friendly" agreements "free" agreements, the fact remains that 250,000 acres represent no more than one-third of 1 percent in a country with 76.6 million acres of land. Even if we take as the basis of our comparison only those two sections of Italy in which the phenomenon occurred on a vaster scale than in the others —that is, Latium and Sicily, we find that 250,000 acres represent 2.3 percent of the 10.6 million acres, the total surface of those sections of Italy. Italy was not Russia. Yet the right of private ownership had been violated without the government resorting to bloodshed to uphold it. Therefore, Nitti was charged with being an accomplice of "rural Bolshevism."

This was not the worst of his trials. On September 12, in order to prevent the city of Fiume from being left to British and French troops, D'Annunzio, at the head of a regiment of regular army and groups of "arditi," who had gotten hold of guns and tanks, occupied the city. Behind him there rushed upon Fiume many generous young men, intoxicated with the frenzy of the "mutilated victory," who sought no personal profit and would have made any sacrifice in order to serve their patriotic ideal. But there rushed, also, a mixed crowd of adventurers who preferred to honest and humble daily work the carefree parasitic life of military service without the risks of actual war, half-crazy revolutionists who thought that D'Annunzio would be a western Lenin, businessmen with shady pasts, cocaine addicts, and harlots. Within a few days, D'Annunzio had under his command fifteen thousand men with artillery, airplanes, and four warships. Three generals, Maggiotto, Ceccherini and Tamajo, openly passed over to him.

At first sight, this was a "private war" against England, France, and the United States, captained by a poet destitute of both moral and common sense: a medieval pageant, which did not end in tragedy solely because nobody outside Italy took it seriously. But behind D'Annunzio were the

[5] Interview given by Micheli, minister of agriculture, to the Rome daily *Tribuna*, October 22, 1920. Villari, *Awakening of Italy*, p. 101: "In Sicily, many land estates were seized, but the conflicts were usually the result of action by the ex-combatants' associations and by organizations of laborers who really wanted land to cultivate: settlements were sometimes effected by agreements with the landlords."

chiefs of the army and the navy. To reach Fiume, D'Annunzio had had to cross Istria, which was under the control of the Italian military authorities. The latter knew in advance what D'Annunzio was preparing, and they let him proceed unmolested, pretending that they were unable to stop him.

The Fascist historian Signor Volpe gives unstinted praise to the Italian pre-Fascist regime for having created an army which was the "well disciplined and faithful instrument of the nation. Politics and factions, seditions and dictatorial ideas, were things altogether unknown in the Italian army."[6] In 1919, this tradition came to an end. Officers of the army and navy, who were bound by an oath of allegiance to the king, deserted their posts, joined D'Annunzio at Fiume, and publicly took an oath which pledged them to disobey their king. D'Annunzio's "legionaries" in Fiume sang an "official" anthem in which they threatened to go from Fiume "to Rome," fighting against everyone, even "in the Quirinal"—that is, in the palace of the king, to "throw bombs on the Parliament," to "clean the Home Office," and to "do away" with Nitti.[7]

Guglielmo Ferrero, the well-known historian, in an article of September 27, 1919, pointed out that D'Annunzio in Fiume was surrounded "by fragments of the Italian army which had ceased obeying the law" and set forth the dangers that were implicit in the situation:

> Until now Europe seemed threatened by the red revolution. Italy is the first of the victorious countries to find herself between two fires: the red revolution and the white revolution. There are those who are striving to make of the army a battering-ram for civil wars. . . . I believe that Italy is, among European countries, the one that has least to fear the red revolution. . . . What if the example of breaking the tablets of the law comes from on high, from those classes and those parties that have the greatest duty to respect them?[8]

The significance of these portents was to reveal itself within three years. The same clique of superior officers and politicians who, in 1919, favored D'Annunzio, was to favor Mussolini in 1921 and 1922. The "march on Fiume" in 1919 was the precedent for the "march on Rome" of 1922.

---

[6] Volpe, L'Italia in Cammino, p. 60.
[7] N. Papafava, Appunti militari: 1919–1921 (Ferrara: S.T.E.T., 1921), pp. 152–53.
[8] G. Ferrero, Da Fiume a Roma (Milano, 1923), pp. 10, 13.

In Fiume, the supplies which had once been the property of the Austrian government, and which at the end of the war were heaped up in the military storehouses, fell into the hands of D'Annunzio's "courtiers." Three thousand Italian citizens of Fiume became employees of the "government" in a city of 39,000 inhabitants, of which 15,000 were Slavs. Those three thousand "government employees" clamored for the annexation of the city to Italy, because the city would not have been able to maintain them from its own resources alone, while annexation would saddle their salaries upon the backs of the Italian taxpayers.

During the fifteen months in which Fiume was under D'Annunzio's control, those three thousand employees and those who flocked to Fiume from all parts of Italy formed the so-called Italian party in Fiume. In Fiume, D'Annunzio founded a "totalitarian" state. A single party alone was allowed to exist—D'Annunzio's. A "plebiscite" was cooked up in October in such a way as to give a "unanimous" vote in favor of D'Annunzio in a city in which there were 15,000 Slavs hostile to him. When, in December, another "plebiscite" was on the point of telling D'Annunzio that the population was tired of him, the "arditi" seized the ballot boxes and prevented the counting. An immediate penalty of death was decreed for anyone in the city "who professed sentiments hostile to Fiume." The practice of forcing to drink castor oil those who harbored in their hearts impure feelings was invented by D'Annunzio's "legionaries" in Fiume. The fez, the black shirt, the dagger, and the spiked mace had been the distinctive apparel of the "arditi" during the war. The "arditi" imported that apparel to Fiume, only replacing the cruel spiked mace with a more gentle bludgeon (manganello). The song "Giovinezza" ("O Youth!") and the so-called Roman salute, made by raising the right hand in the air,[9] were the song and the salute of the "arditi" during the war and were adopted in Fiume. The meetings in the open air, where the leader asks questions and the crowd raise their right hands and shout "yes" or other prearranged answers, were used by D'Annunzio at Fiume. The city anticipated down to the smallest detail what Italy was to become after the Fascist conquest.

Those who profited most from D'Annunzio's *coup de main* were the Socialists. They could affirm that another war was imminent, a war of which D'Annunzio had given the signal by occupying Fiume. Many who were beginning to weary of the inconclusive disorder provoked by the Socialists

---

[9] In classical antiquity it was the slaves who saluted their masters by raising the right hand. Free men greeted one another by shaking hands.

were now forced to choose between the disorder brought about the Socialists and a new war which would certainly result from a military dictatorship.
They thought that the Socialists were less dangerous than the army chiefs.
D'Annunzio not only fed the spirit of sedition in the army and made it
impossible for the civil government to make use of the military forces to
maintain order, but also increased in the civil population the turmoil of
suspicion, discontent, and hysteria.

A few days after D'Annunzio's raid on Fiume, at the beginning of
October, the National Congress of the Socialist party was held in Bologna.
The right-wing Socialists, led by Turati, maintained that they must remain
faithful to the tradition of the party and participate in the coming elections
and in the work of the future Chamber, with the aim of wresting from the
men in power the greatest possible number of immediate reforms useful to
the working classes. The Maximalists upheld that the social revolution must
do away with Parliament as with all other bourgeois institutions, but that
the Socialist party must take part in the electoral campaign to increase the
revolutionary disquiet; the Socialist deputies must go to Parliament to
sabotage from within this "bourgeois institution" and in this way hurry up
the hour in which the "revolutionary proletariat" would construct the
Republic of the Soviets. The Spartacists maintained that the "revolutionary
proletariat" should abstain fom the elections and stir up without delay
social revolution according to the pattern of Soviet Russia. The right-wing
Socialists carried 14,880 votes, the Maximalists 48,411, and the Spartacists
3,417.

During the electoral campaign, the Spartacists did not put up any candidates, but they joined with the Maximalists in disturbing the meetings of
the other candidates and in giving, with their yells, an idea of what they
thought the dictatorship of the proletariat should be.

Mussolini did not limit himself to yelling. During this electoral campaign
there appeared in Milan and neighboring cities groups of armed men, paid
at the rate of thirty lire a day and ready to fight the Socialists not only with
yells but also with revolver shots.[10] Mussolini took the funds to maintain

---

[10] This fact was disclosed before a committee of Milanese journalists by two subeditors of
the *Popolo d'Italia* who were at loggerheads with Mussolini. See *Avanti*, February 12,
1920, and *Il Secolo*, February 14, 1920. *La Civiltà Cattolica*, (March 6, 1920, pp.
472–74) commented on the disclosure in the following terms: "A little light on the
subject. It is very little. But this faint gleam is enough for us to be able to say: 'What
a cesspool! In the hands of such people rests the banner of patriotism and of national
honor!' "

those men from the sum of one million lire which had been collected among the Italians of the United States to be sent to D'Annunzio at Fiume through Mussolini. Mussolini kept 480,000 lire for himself and sent the rest to D'Annunzio. The latter had never in his life had overpowering scruples in matters of money, but on that occasion he was very scandalized by the financial operation which Mussolini had carried out without D'Annunzio's permission.[11]

On November 13, 1919, at Lodi, Mussolini's men, as a reprisal against Maximalists who had broken up a previous meeting, fired revolver shots into a meeting held in a theater, killing three and wounding eight. The Maximalists did not react even by a general strike. They were getting used to having the proletarians killed while the "dictatorship of the proletariat" was on the way.

The national elections were held on November 16. Nitti abstained from interfering in them. This was the first and only case in Italy in which no charge was leveled against the government for "manipulating" elections. The Maximalists and extremists, who had disturbed the meetings of the other parties, did nothing on election day to hinder the freedom of the vote. The returns, therefore, represented the exact state of mind of the Italian people at that moment. As a consequence, they were disastrous for those political groups—"Liberals" (i.e., Conservatives) and Democrats—who had formed the majority in the Chamber of 1913–19. Those electors who had promoted or accepted the war voted against the deputies going out of office because they had been neutralists or half-hearted supporters of the war. And those who had opposed the war blacklisted the deputies going out of office because they had never dared to vote against the war and had assumed, no matter how unwillingly, the responsibility for it.

The gravity of the disaster is realized if one compares the results of the elections of 1913 with those of 1919:[12]

---

[11] The Chief of Staff of D'Annunzio, Major Reina, was present when D'Annunzio had an outburst of anger, terming Mussolini a "thief". The writer of the present book got the incident from Major Reina himself. Being a representative, he denounced the fact in the Chamber (August 7, 1920). Mussolini endeavored to silence him, challenging him to a duel. His seconds demanded that an investigation be made to ascertain whether the fact was true or not; only if the fact were not true would the duel take place. Mussolini's seconds rejected any investigation. So no drop of blood was lost by anyone. The documents of this funny dispute were published by the weekly *L'Unità*, August 19, 1920.

[12] U. Giusti, *Le correnti politiche italiane attraverso due riforme elettorali dal 1909 al 1921* (Firenze: Alfani e Venturi, 1922), pp. 21, 29. Some minor discrepancies in the number of seats between our data and those given by Giusti depend on the fact that our data belong to November 1919 and Giusti's to August 1920, when some deputies had been dead.

		VOTES		SEATS	
		1913	1919	1913	1919
I.	Giolittian Coalition:				
	a). "Liberals" and Nationalists			a} 310	
				b}	23
	b). Democrats	3,392,000	1,779,000		91
	c). Radicals			73	57
	d). Reformists			27	22
II.	War veterans		320,000		33
III.	Catholics	302,000		29	
IV.	Populists		1,167,000		100
V.	Republicans				9
VI.	Independents	437,000	581,000	17	17
VII.	Socialists	883,000	1,835,000	52	156
	Total	5,014,000	5,682,000	508	508

The "Liberals," Nationalists, and Democrats went down from 310 to 114 seats, losing 196. Sonnino was not elected. Salandra was elected; the Nationalists obtained scarcely a half a dozen seats and were saved from total destruction only because the elections were held under a system of proportional representation which prevented minorities from being crushed under the weight of the stronger parties. Bissolati was only elected because of proportional representation. Under the single-member system, many other seats in northern and central Italy would have fallen to the Socialists.[13] The other groups would have survived mainly in southern Italy, and a dangerous gap would thus have been created between northern and southern Italy. Proportional representation prevented this development.[14]

There is no doubt that in the months of September, October, and November 1919, universal suffrage contributed much to avoiding more violent disorders. Electoral right is not the source of sovereignty, as men learned in democratic ideologies repeat and men learned in oligarchical

[13] If we take as an example the province of Florence, we find that the single member system would have given twelve Socialist deputies and only two non-Socialist deputies, whereas the province elected eight Socialists, three Populists, and three "Liberals" (Giusti, Le correnti politiche Italiane, pp. 39–41). To be sure, under the single-member system, the electors, forced to choose between no more than two candidates, would have acted differently than under the new system. But given the hostility that the mass of the Populist party felt towards all old political leaders, including Salandra and Giolitti, one may state without danger of error that that mass, if it had not been able to vote for the Populist candidates, would have voted for the Socialists rather than for the old politicians.

[14] I. Bonomi, From Socialism to Fascism (London: Hopkinson and Co., 1924), pp. 78–79.

ideologies take great trouble to deny. Electoral right is a means—rather crude but quite accommodating—given to the citizens to declare every so often whether or not they are satisfied with the men at the head of the government. If they are satisfied, they vote for the candidates who are in favor of the government. If they are not satisfied, they vote for the opposition. To give elections a greater task than this is absurd. But this task is very useful and important. Electoral institutions force the men in power to pay attention to the discontent which their action might provoke in the electorate. Universal suffrage forces the ruling classes to stay on the alert and to take cognizance of every symptom of discontent. At the same time it lets the citizens express their discontent without violence. Ballots take the place of bullets. Universal suffrage is the best preventative against revolutionary crises. In times of crisis, an election by universal suffrage is an abortive revolution. It would have been much more difficult for the Italian government to cross over the war, if Italy, in 1912, had not become a country of universal suffrage—that is, if the propagandists of peace at all costs had been able to tell the people that the German and Austrian workers and peasants enjoyed the electoral right, whereas the Italian workers and peasants were deprived of that right while shedding their blood in the war. Even the crisis of 1919 would have been much more serious if the general discontent had not been tempered by the prospect of making a cheap revolution on election day. Most likely, without the safety valve of universal suffrage, the mass of peasants and workers would have had recourse to direct action. In 1919, they waited for the national elections; and after the elections, they waited, all through 1920, to see what the newly elected deputies would do. Thus the two most dangerous years of the postwar crisis were tided over. The Anarchists are not wrong when they maintain that elections lull the revolutionary spirit and that therefore the true revolutionaries must abstain from them.

Proportional representation, joining universal suffrage in 1919, lessened the bitterness of the electoral contest. Under the single-member system, the electorate is forced in every constituency to divide itself among no more than two factions, one of which must put the other out of commission. Proportional representation permits each party to show its own electoral strength without being entirely cast aside if in a minority. Each party thinks more of increasing its own votes than of destroying those of its opponents. Even under a regime of proportional representation, the electoral struggle assumed here and there the form of uncivilized throat-cutting because of the Maximalists and Spartacists. But under a single member system, it would have degenerated into civil war.

No one had expected such a great triumph for the Socialists. The Maximalists saw in it the proof that the "great hour" was drawing near. If they had possessed more brains, they would have found much food for thought when, in Milan, two of Mussolini's henchmen, Virtuani and Volpi, hurled a bomb at a procession which was celebrating the Socialist victory in the election, and nine persons were seriously injured (November 17). The Socialists proclaimed for the following day the ritual general protest strike. The police displayed commendable solicitude by arresting Mussolini, Marinetti, Vecchi, and about ten others who had taken no part in the crime. The bench found that there was no proof against the accused men and, with equally laudable solicitude, released them. The Socialists were left with their nine wounded men, their general strike, and the following challenge by Mussolini: "It is one thing to drop a ballot into a box, and another thing to hurl bombs from street corners, or, what is worse, to get them in your own mug."[15]

[15] G. Cipriani-Avolio, *Una volontà: Benito Mussolini* (Roma, 1932), p. 114.

15

The Breakdown of Parliament

When a new House entered in service, Italian tradition required that the king inaugurate it with the intervention of the deputies and the senators. The constitutional deputies swore an oath of faith to the king and the constitution. The king, after receiving the oath, read a short address which did not say anything, and so the performance was over. The Socialist and Republican deputies had always stayed away from this ceremony. They took their oaths on the following days, with the understanding that they did not attach any importance to that rite imposed upon them by a law which, in their opinion, was illegitimate. In 1919, the Maximalist deputies found that this procedure was not "revolutionary" enough. Therefore, they decided to intervene *en masse* in the sitting and to leave the hall *en masse* when the king appeared.

From the time the king had taken the throne in 1900, he had never given any sign of being a reactionary. The years which had not yet come were to show that he was neither a reactionary nor a democrat. He was merely a man without any force of will, who desired one single thing: to leave every responsibility for whatever happened to Parliament and to the prime minister designated by any parliamentary majority whatsoever. He chose for prime minister the man who was backed for that office by the majority of the leading politicians whom he consulted according to the rules of the protocol. If the new prime minister received a vote of confidence from the House, the king, from that time on, meekly signed all the papers which the prime minister lay before him, until the moment when the majority of the Chamber forced the prime minister to resign. Then the king would choose a new prime minister by the usual procedure, and the signing of the papers began again. The portrait that Borgese has made of King Victor Emmanuel is worth reading:

> His subnormally small stature had impressed his moral character, from early adolescence onward, with the marks of discomfort and bitterness, and although not at all wicked or foolish he had learned from a physical inferiority, always present to his consciousness and to other people's eyes, an unforgettable lesson of diffidence and shyness. . . . Had he suffered only from such a personal drawback, added to the disturbances of the time, his task would have proved hardly gratifying. But he had been brought up, at that, as the only child of an insignificant king . . . and of an exceedingly significant queen, whose front-page popularity and literary vanity the scion could not like, being shaped by nature to anything but literature and rhetoric. This environment, or loneliness, had made his dryness drier; his education was strict, and the teacher particularly entrusted with the office of molding his mind did not a single day neglect to inculcate in him the theory that a constitutional monarch has nothing to do but obey and express the will of the people and the Parliament: in shorter words, that he has nothing to do. His father, King Humbert, after a mildly reactionary attempt into which he had been dragged almost unawares, died of an Anarchist's bullet: a lesson more eloquent to young Victor Emmanuel than all the hours he had spent with his teacher of constitutional law. . . . He did not love the crown; he submitted to it. . . . His leisure was spent in the most harmless of hobbies, namely, numismatics, or the systematic collection of old coins. . . . His frame of mind was sceptical, and yet his daily routine was blameless. A good husband, a loving and assiduous father, a conscientious bureaucrat, he embodied the ideals—especially tidiness, thrift, and modesty—of the Italian bourgeois of his generation, on a throne, indeed, too high for his legs. . . . This king did not care for glory and power; nothing was more alien to his mind than the bloodthirsty glamour of D'Annunzio's poems and speeches. . . . At the end of the war he could think, altogether grey-haired and grey-moustached although not yet in his fifties, of starting again his ordinary life . . . with his daily schedule suitably balanced between the signing busi-

ness of the constitutional monarch and the sapient leisure of the numismatist, but, in truth, with the real fibres of his heart wholly devoted to the task he really loved. It was not the task of shooting predestined gemsboks, neither was it the purpose of strutting, on ideal stilts, before clanking armies or cheering crowds: vanities of vanities which he inwardly minimized, in the spirit, say, of Ecclesiastes. His nearest next was what he really loved; the task which really absorbed him was that of head of the family: of a family, now, whose hereditary estate had increased through a trial by combat as perilous and fortunate as it had been unexpected and dreaded.[1]

From June 1919 on, the king had been made the target for the attacks of the Fascists and for the more or less veiled threats of the Nationalists, because he had opposed his stolid inertia to every plan for a military *coup d'état*. The military chiefs spoke openly of the need to substitute the Duke of Aosta for him. The *New York Times*, in its issue of December 7, 1919, published "a photograph of Her Royal Highness Duchess of Aosta, who is expected to become queen of Italy in the event of the abdication of King Victor Emmanuel III and his queen." If the king had been a man capable of a *coup d'état*, he would have replied to the defiance of the Maximalist deputies by having them all arrested on the night preceeding the opening of the Chamber and would have proceeded to the inauguration of the new Chamber without them. In their turn, the Maximalists either should have summoned their "revolutionary proletariat" to start their revolution on the day of the inauguration by the king and should have come to the sitting and remained in the hall and proclaimed their "republic of the Soviets," or else they should have absented themselves from the ceremony and spared themselves an act of vulgar discourtesy. Neither the king nor Nitti were men capable of a *coup d'état*, and as for the Maximalists, they were persuaded that it was not up to them but to the "revolutionary proletariat" to provoke the "great hour." Their sole task was to make noise and to wait for the "great hour." They did not even think of refusing to swear the oath on the following days. They put before the House a bill for the abolition of the oath. Then they forgot all about it and it never came under discussion.

The morning of December 1, when leaving the royal palace with his

[1] Borgese, *Goliath*, pp. 233 ff.

retinue to go to the House of Parliament, the king was cheered by 2,000 officers in uniform, including eight generals, who accompanied the retinue to the Parliament and from the Parliament to the royal palace after the ceremony.

The author of this book was present at the royal sitting. The king entered the hall, limping, surrounded by the princes of the royal house, including the Duke of Aosta, all much taller than he and therefore making him appear smaller than ever. The Socialists, in a compact group, covered three sections of the extreme left. The right-wingers, forced by discipline, were present with the Maximalists. The few Republicans occupied the seats near the Socialists. Hardly had the king reached the throne than the Socialists and the Republicans rose in a body and left by a side door, the Maximalists shouting, "Long live socialism," the right-wingers and the Republicans shouting nothing. Little by little, as they left, the deputies and senators of the other parties occupied their places. The king, standing up on a stool which had been prepared before his chair to make him seem less small, with his hands crossed on the hilt of his sword, tried to assume a majestic air, but he did not succeed; his startled and uncertain eyes seemed those of a dog who emerges from the water where he almost drowned. When the clamor of the deputies who were leaving and the applause of the deputies and senators who remained had calmed down, the ceremony began and was concluded without further incident.

After the king had reentered the royal palace, clashes began to break out in the streets between officers and Socialists. As usual, the Socialists, disarmed and prepared only for strikes and elections, suffered the worst of it everywhere. One Socialist deputy was seriously, four others slightly, wounded.

Then the national executive of the Socialist party called a general strike all over Italy to protest "against the injury inflicted upon the representatives of the proletariat." The leaders of the Confederation of Labor joined in that deliberation, not because they considered it reasonable, but because their tactics were to let themselves be drawn along by the Maximalists and at the same time to slow them down in their course. No date was fixed for the end of this strike, whereas the one in July 1919 had been announced for only two days. This meant that this strike was to last as long as the "revolutionary proletariat" wished, with the above-mentioned proletariat being entitled, if he willed it so, to precipitate the "great hour" during the strike. The Maximalists had wanted the strike to be so, and the leaders of the Confederation had let themselves be towed along in this.

On December 2 and 3, the strike spread over all the most important Italian cities. The railwaymen alone made an exception and went to work. As usual, the Anarchists intervened everywhere to provoke clashes with the police. In all of Italy there were eight dead, two of whom were among the police, and many wounded. The most serious incidents occurred in Mantua. Here, on December 3, a few hundred extremists and Anarchists, waving a banner on which was inscribed the name of Spartacus, burned down the railway station, forced open the door of the prison, set free the prisoners, took over the guns belonging to the guards, and sacked a store selling firearms and other shops. At the end of the day, there were five dead, including a soldier and a woman.

Not even on this occasion did the "great hour" strike. On the afternoon of December 3, the Confederation of Labor got the upper hand over the national executive of the Socialist party, and both institutions summoned the party and the trade unions all over Italy to return to work the following day, keeping themselves ready, however, "to fight effectively everywhere any reactionary attempt on the part of professional militarism." On December 4, the Chamber of Labor of Mantua condemned "the criminals and thieves" who had perpetrated the disorders of the previous day, but, in a new clash with the police, the insurgents suffered two dead. By December 5, the agitation had died down everywhere. Once again the general strike, while it never developed into a decisive revolutionary movement, left in its wake a certain number of dead and an immense and useless waste of energy.

After those days, the "Liberals," Nationalists, and Fascists could employ a formidable argument in their propaganda against the "Bolshevists." Since April 1919, officers in uniform, violating the duties of military discipline, had participated in many political demonstrations, and extremist Socialists and Anarchists had here and there maltreated officers in uniform. But these were sporadic cases which were given no importance. On December 1, 2,000 officers in uniform took part in the royalist demonstration of Rome, and during the general strike of the following days, many officers were mobbed in all parts of Italy. In Turin, a colonel was wounded so seriously that he died. "Liberals," Nationalists, and Fascists had never protested against the scandal of officers who were taking part in political demonstrations in the streets; in fact, they had encouraged the scandal. Now they began loudly to protest every time officers in uniform became involved in unfortunate incidents, and their propaganda found fertile ground, thanks to the blindness of extremists and Anarchists, who assaulted and maltreated officers even when they were going peacefully about their business.

The Socialists continued in vain to dream with their eyes open. The *Avanti*, in its issue of December 5, wrote: "The war has precipitated the course of inevitable events. The masses are changing their mentality with such rapidity that even we may find ourselves carried away by the swift avalanche of unpredictable events and imponderable factors."

On the following day, the same paper published a letter from Lenin. Lenin never had had any direct experience of Italian life and had no information in Russia of what was happening in Italy. But two things he considered sure: (1) that the Socialists who did not adhere to the Communist International were "betrayers of the masses," "a general staff without a party," and should be treated everywhere as enemies by the Communists; and (2) that "the dictatorship of the proletariat and the soviet system had already won a moral victory in all the world" and "the final victory, notwithstanding the white terror of the bourgeoisie, etc., would truly come to pass, unavoidable, in all the countries of the world."[2] After the Maximalists at the Congress of Bologna had won their victory (see Chapter 14), Lenin, on October 29, wrote to Serrati to express satisfaction with the Italian Communists and to approve the decision to participate in the coming elections. Certainly "the open or veiled opportunists, who were numerous among the Italian Socialist parliamentarians" would try to steer the party away from the Communist line accepted by the Congress of Bologna: "the struggle against those tendencies was not yet over." Yet Lenin added:

> Given the international situation of Italy, the Italian proletariat has very difficult tasks yet to perform. It may be that England and France, helped by the Italian bourgeoisie, will try to incite the Italian proletariat to a premature insurrection, in order to stamp down on it more easily. But they will not succeed in their aim. The wonderful work which the Italian Communists have done guarantees to us that they will win over to the cause of Communism all the industrial and agricultural proletariat, as well as the small landowners; and then—if they choose the opportune moment from the

[2] Letter from Lenin to Serrati, director of the *Avanti*, and Lazzari, secretary general of the Italian Socialist Party, August 19, 1919; published in *Avanti* September 2, 1919. *Lenin's Works* (Russian edition) 17:430.

point of view of the international situation—the dictatorship of the Italian proletariat will achieve decisive victory.[3]

This letter had been written on October 29, before the Italian elections
of November 16. Most likely after these elections, Lenin would not have
advised prudence, but would have encouraged the Italian Communists to
be more daring. At any rate, the letter, published in Italy on December 6,
was considered by all a cold shower poured by Lenin on the heads of the
Italian extremists, insofar as the latter were advised to abstain from premature revolutionary attempts, to win over first, not only the industrial and
agricultural proletariat, but also the small landowners, and to await "the
opportune moment from the international point of view." Serrati had
published the letter of Lenin on December 6 because he had not received
it before that time, and any journalist would have published a letter of
Lenin whatever the content had been. But the Nationalists maintained that
the letter was a forgery, that Lenin could not have given advice of that kind,
and that Serrati was endeavoring to put a brake on the revolutionary
exaltation of his own followers: "After making use of the magnificent name
of Lenin to urge the masses on towards violence, they again make use of
it to quiet them down" (*Idea Nazionale,* December 7, 1919). Even if the
letter had been faked and its purpose had been to calm down the masses,
the Nationalists should have rejoiced over this unexpected evidence of
wisdom. They were disappointed. They had lost all hope of controlling the
new Chamber by legal means. They could not attain their ends except by
a military *coup d'état.* This could not be carried out unless the disorder in
the country had reached such a climax as to force the king to make his own
choice: either a Communist revolution or the military dictatorship. If
Lenin now advised caution, all their last hopes would be shipwrecked.

Nitti would have needed a solid majority in the Chamber capable of
resisting, at the same time, the extremists of socialism and the extremists

---

[3] The letter was published in its integral text in the first edition of the Italian Socialist paper.
The censor stupidly suppressed the last part of it, beginning with the words, "It may be,"
etc. But other papers—for example, the Populist *Corriere d'Italia* of Rome (December 8),
reproduced the entire text from the first edition of the *Avanti.* The Russian edition of the
works of Lenin (24: 504) gives the incomplete text of the second edition of the *Avanti.*
We cannot say whether the editors did not take the trouble to search out the complete
text, or whether they deemed it prudent to cover with a modest veil the fact that Lenin,
in October 1919, advised the Italian comrades not to let themselves be betrayed by
premature revolutionary attempts and to wait for an "opportune moment" which was
never destined to arrive.

of the reaction. But the new Chamber was split up into three sections: 100 Populists, 156 Socialists, and 252 deputies neither Socialist nor Populist. In the latter section were 33 representatives of the war veterans and 17 independents. They had no common platform. Some were Reformist and some Nationalist, some Democratic and some Conservative, and some nothing at all. Each one was following his own calling. They carried no weight. The 9 Republicans would have been willing to vote in favor of the government only if it had been the government of a republic, and anyhow they were lost in the middle of the other 508 deputies. The 23 "Liberals" and Nationalists formed a compact group but were unpopular, and they carried little weight. When these small factions, heterogeneous and unable to unite among themselves, had been eliminated from the number of the influential groups, there remained 100 Populists, 156 Socialists, and 170 Democrats-Radicals-Reformists.

The Populists had a place analogous to that of the Catholic Center in Germany. In Germany, the Center had been in alliance with the Conservatives before the war, had broken away from them during the war, and now formed, with the Democrats and Social Democrats (analogous to the Italian right-wing Socialists) the parliamentary coalition upon which the new-born Weimar Republic was based. In Italy, in 1919, an alliance of the Populists with the "Liberals" and Nationalists would not have been permitted by the bulk of the Populist voters or by Don Sturzo, and, even if it had been possible, it would not have given a sufficient foundation for a new cabinet. The Populists, by allying themselves with Democrats, Radicals, and Reformists, could contribute to the formation of a bulk of 270 members—that is, little more than half the Chamber—and resist the opposition of the 156 Socialists and the 23 "Liberals" and Nationalists. But such a parliamentary coalition would have had to be compact and prepared to confront the Socialists resolutely. Instead, the Democrats who had survived the disastrous election were divided between followers of Nitti and followers of Giolitti. A part of them realized the necessity of a compromise with Yugoslavia on the Adriatic question, and part of them remained blindly tied to the ideas of Orlando and Sonnino and demanded the annexation of Dalmatia as well as Fiume. One part suspected the other, and all distrusted the Populists.

Under these conditions, no efficient coalition government was possible unless the 156 Socialists were willing to cooperate. Among them, 50 came from the preceeding Chamber and had been reelected because they had always voted against the war. Almost all of them being right-wingers, they would have associated themselves with the Democrats, Radicals, and Reformists to uphold Nitti. But most of the 100 newly elected members were Maximalists. The Russian revolution of which every one talked, but about which no one knew anything, had an extraordinary fascination for them. Parliamentary action had lost all prestige in their eyes. The presence of 156 Socialist deputies in the Chamber would have been of no importance whatsoever, if they did not "bring about the revolution." What was meant by "bringing about the revolution," no one knew. But all were agreed that if they took part in a "bourgeois" government instead of "bringing about the revolution," they would be betraying the proletariat. They had come to the Chamber with the sole aim of sabotaging from within this "bourgeois" institution by shouting and provoking disorders. The two sections of the Chamber which they occupied on the extreme left were always like a cage of shrieking monkeys, violent and vulgar. The right-wingers had taken part in the electoral struggle side by side with them—had been elected together with them on the same lists and on a platform of uncompromising opposition to all "bourgeois" parties, and their colleagues and the national executive of the party left them no freedom of movement. For thirty years the Socialist party had fought for and advocated "the conquest of political power" through electoral and parliamentarian tactics. And behold, just at the moment when they had become strong enough to control any government whatsoever, the party shut itself within the ivory tower of revolutionary intransigence and renounced any influence on the government.

A democratic regime can function only so long as the citizens are willing to accept the verdict of the majority as final, to join in electing by ballots representatives whose majority shall form the executive, and to abide by the law even if judicial penalties have to enforce it. When no clear majority exists among the representatives, the different groups must be ready to compromise and form a coalition capable of carrying on. There is no need of unanimity; neither would it be possible to have it. There will always be people who refuse to cooperate and to abide by the law. But as long as there are no more than small minorities, the democratic regime stands. A crisis arises when those minorities are no longer small and when they withhold their cooperation after it has become indispensable. Such was the case of Italy in 1919–20. The Maximalists maintained that the proletariat is a compact class engaged in a fight to the finish with the capitalist class. In expectation of the millenium, they were not allowed to come to any compromise with the political representatives of the capitalist class. As long as Socialist deputies had been few in number, their Marxian mentality did not disturb the working of parliamentary institutions. They gave expression to the distress of the toiling multitudes and acted as a useful alarm-signal that prevented the conservative parties from going to sleep in their self-complacency. But now they formed almost one-third of a House where no coalition government could be formed without their cooperation. They were not numerous enough to form a cabinet by themselves alone, but their Marxian prejudice, averse to compromise, forbade them to ally themselves with any "bourgeois" party and to help them to form a cabinet. The system could not help but break down.

This breakdown occurred at a time when the seditious attitude of the army chiefs made a firm government more than ever necessary. Those who had not yet understood the seriousness of the military conspiracy should have understood it on November 23, when the government let the newspapers publish the news that on November 14, D'Annunzio had left Fiume on a warship for Zara, the capital city of Dalmatia, without the Italian fleet's doing anything to arrest him, and that in Zara, Vice-Admiral Millo, governor of Dalmatia on behalf of the Italian government, had received him with sovereign honors and had publicly given his word of honor that he would never relinquish Dalmatia. The censor had kept the news secret until after the election of November 19 was held. As the *Osservatore Romano*, official daily of the Vatican, observed (November 23), if the government had let the news out before the election, the so-called patriotic parties would have suffered an even more disastrous defeat. In the newly formed House, in the session of December 21, a deputy raised the question of the relations between the civil government and the highest military authorities. He asked if it were true that the danger of undisciplined acts on the part of the troops stationed a short distance from Fiume had been referred in time to the chief of staff, General Diaz, and if this fact were true, why the civil government had not punished General Diaz, who had not prevented the raid on Fiume; he asked why no sanctions had been taken against those army chiefs who were responsible for the discipline in those regiments to which the soldiers had belonged who had accompanied D'Annunzio to Fiume; and why Vice-Admiral Millo, after giving his word of honor to D'Annunzio, had remained governor of Dalmatia instead of being deprived of his position and punished:

Here is not the case of a public official, who, feeling an irreconcilable clash between his duties as a public official and his convictions, resigns from office, cedes his post to a person who enjoys the trust of the responsible government, and having regained the status of a free citizen, follows the line of political conduct which his conscience dictates to him. Here we have a high military official, who continues to hold the office which was entrusted to him by the responsible government, and at the same time takes on the obligation of eventually disobeying the responsible government. It is an obvious case of sedition. Yet the Vice-Admiral and Governor Millo is left in his post. Therefore, it is our right and our duty to ask whether in Italy sovereignty is vested in Parliament and in the cabinet which has the trust of Parliament, or whether we are living under a regime of dual civil-military sovereignty, in which there exists a right of veto on the part of the high-ranking navy and army officers against the will of Parliament and of the government. . . . We are like that character in the novel of Manzoni who, having been infected with the plague, did not dare to look at the spot of himself which was swollen for fear of finding the signs of his sickness.

These words fell on deaf ears. The Maximalists saw the threat of the military dictatorship, and they denounced it in their newspapers and addresses. But in their childish mentality, they were persuaded that everything which weakened Parliament—an institution of the capitalistic world —hurried the total collapse of that world. If the military chiefs attacked that "bourgeois" institution from the outside while the Maximalists sabotaged it from within, so much gained for the preparation of the "great day." The "revolutionary proletariat" would make a clean sweep of both the military chiefs and Parliament. The Maximalists sawed through the branch of the tree on which they were sitting.

Nitti never had any stable majority at his beck and call. He had to rely upon the remains of that majority which, at the time of Giolitti, before the war, had seemed unshakable and which now formed only a minority in the Chamber, and on the half-hearted support of the Populist deputies who voted for him only because they did not know of any other man who could gather around himself any majority at all. His tactics were to gain time, to live from hand to mouth, to profit from the division between the Socialists and Populists which paralyzed both of them, and to make the minimum of concessions to either of them.

He should have forced the deputies to face their responsibilities; laid before them a plan of sweeping financial, administrative, and social reforms; and forced them to discuss them, to amend them if necessary, or to reject them if they had the courage. The Maximalists would have aroused the indignation of vast sections of the working classes if, for example, they had hindered the discussion of bills which established the eight-hour day, old-age pensions, or unemployment insurance, or which provided for a vast plan of land reclamation. The right-wingers and the Confederation of Labor would have been able to break away from them, vindicating their right and their duty to serve the cause of the working classes by constructive action and not by disorderly clamor. At least fifty Socialist deputies would have joined in a movement of positive legislation.

Instead of remaining at his post in Rome and confronting the Chamber with definite proposals to discuss, accept, or reject, Nitti left Italy time and time again to go to Paris to discuss the eternal question of the Adriatic and the eternal question of colonial compensations. He made use of these trips as a pretext to ask the Chamber to defer their sessions for as long as the prime minister was absent. The deputies, who had nothing to discuss because the government gave them nothing to discuss and who did not dare to provoke a crisis because they did not know what cabinet should follow that of Nitti, willingly deferred their sessions. But when they convened again, they always found themselves with nothing to do except listen to the violent recriminations of the Socialists against the responsibilities of the last strikes and of the last bloody clashes between demonstrators and police, or hear the accounts of the last unsuccessful negotiations on the eternal Fiume affair. The parliamentarian paralysis was made worse by the fact that Nitti had chosen Orlando as chairman of the House—a man who had lost all prestige during the peace conference and who was absolutely lacking that energy which would have been necessary to discipline the discussions of those 500 persons, among whom there were about 100 who seemed like patients who had escaped from a lunatic asylum.

The dealings with the Vatican on the Roman question had reached such a point that Nitti could have laid before Parliament the treaty of conciliation between the Holy See and Italy, showing that the Holy See was content that Italy should recognize the sovereignty of the pope over the Basilica of St. Peter and the Vatican—that is, over 100 acres over which, since 1871, the Italian government had never exercised (or thought of exercising) any jurisdiction. In this way, Nitti would have allayed the suspicions of those who considered the Vatican an irreconcilable enemy of the unity of Italy; he would have assured for himself the loyalty of the hundred Populist deputies, and he would have put the other deputies face to face with an issue of national interest. Besides this, he would have given an evident proof that the war had not been won in vain if it had ended a dispute which had seemed insoluble half a century before. But Nitti did not dare to take any courageous initiative in his, or in any other, field.

When D'Annunzio seized Fiume, Nitti had a burst of anger and before the House denounced that undertaking as a criminal blow which had been planned by "militarism." He was right. But he should not have stopped there. After trying the method of persuasion to induce those of D'Annunzio's followers who had been impelled by an urge of generosity to return to obedience, he should have firmly suppressed that crime of military sedition and punished those who continued to disobey. It would have been enough for him to blockade Fiume and to force D'Annunzio to surrender because of hunger. Before taking this step, Nitti should have put an end to the eternal Adriatic question by annexing to Italy outright Gorizia, Trieste, Istria, and Fiume, announcing at the same time that he was ready to hand over Dalmatia to Yugoslavia as soon as the latter had ceased arguing with Italy about the other territories. Lloyd George had so many other difficulties to deal with that he hardly would have taken upon himself the added burden of a conflict with Italy over a little city of no importance. President Wilson had been struck with paralysis in September 1919. He would certainly not have declared war upon Italy on account of Fiume and would have closed this unfortunate chapter with a platonic protest at the most. Clemenceau had gone out of power in January 1920 and could no longer display his brutal arrogance on this (as on all other) points. As for Yugoslavia, she was in the first and most difficult phase of her internal organization and could think of anything but of attacking Italy. A year later, the Belgrade government gave up Fiume because at last it stood before a clear and resolute Italian will, not because it would not have preferred another solution. Nitti should have put his plan before Parliament so that all groups would have been confronted with the responsibility of choosing between a compromise with Yugoslavia or a fresh war on the Adriatic question.

He knew that the heads of the army and navy were in accord with D'Annunzio and would disobey any government which renounced Dalmatia. Since the military chiefs were disloyal, Nitti should have challenged them either to obey or to face openly their own responsibilities by assuming power. But this would have meant precipitating the country into the abyss of a military dictatorship. On the other hand, after the first irritation which he felt at the news of the march on Fiume, Nitti thought that, at bottom, D'Annunzio, encamped in Fiume, was a useful pawn in the attempts to find a favorable compromise in the Fiume question. Thus, he chose to play, on this ground also, a waiting game. He let the supplies necessary for the population of the city pass from Italy to Fiume. Meanwhile he endeavored to bribe the military chiefs by agreeing that the army in time of peace should consist of fifteen army corps (rather than twelve as before the war) and would keep many useless generals, inspectors, and other brass hats.[4] Nitti was endowed with the soul of an appeaser, and not that of a fighter. He was a sensible man, but he never gave the feeling that there was somebody at the helm, leading the country with a stern hand through the storm.

At this point, one may ask how momentous steps towards financial and economic recovery could have been taken while Parliament was paralyzed and unable to work.

The answer to this question is found when one realizes that Parliament is not in charge of daily administration. Its function is legislative and political. It passes the legislation and, in countries like England and pre-Fascist Italy, designates the prime minister who has to form a cabinet. The burden of the daily administration falls on the permanent officials, high and low, who operate the machinery. Whether a cabinet has a short or a long life, whether parliamentary control breaks down or not, the officials of the administration remain at their posts. During the war and the years that followed, by virtue of the extraordinary powers granted by Parliament to the executive, the estimates and bills which the Chamber did not discuss or pass were enacted by "orders in council" ("royal decrees"). The government was not at all hindered by Parliament in legislation or administration. Never before in the history of Italy did the executive have so free a hand in finance, either for good or for evil, as during those years of parliamentary paralysis.[5]

Suppose that an American Guy Fawkes should succeed in blowing up

---

[4] Papafava, *Appunti militari*, p. 154.

[5] From 1895 to 1913, the number of royal decrees varied from a minimum of one to a maximum of twenty-four a year. The war augmented the number of these exceptional measures. Thus, there were 100 in 1914; 221 in 1915; 173 in 1916; 337 in 1917; 348 in 1918; 1029 in 1919; 545 in 1920; 350 in 1921 (debate in the Senate, December 12, 1925).

the Washington Capitol while both Houses were in session, so that all the representatives and all the senators were suddenly wiped out. The Congress of the United States would then be paralyzed—in fact, destroyed. But the taxes would not cease to be collected; the railways and mines would not stop working; shipping would not be held up; and the banks would not be closed except on the funeral day. Parliament is not the whole of the country. It is the voice of the country. One can have a disease of the throat, of the nose, or of the mouth, that interferes for a time with one's speech, while the rest of one's body is healthy. Italy's health had not broken down, though her Parliament was not working. An intelligent student of public administration, Ubaldo Formentini, wrote in 1922: "The bureaus which do not die and do not change, govern. . . . It is not true that the state is weak: it is very strong and it is becoming stronger all the time. The truth is that certain powers of the state are extraordinarily weakened in comparison with certain others."[6]

By royal decrees, 3.3 billion lire were appropriated for public works to avoid unemployment (November 17, 1918), insurance against incapacity and for old age (January 5, 1919) and unemployment insurance (October 14, 1919) were set up. Taxation was radically reformed by royal decree. The effects could not follow at once, for administrative machinery had to be created for the carrying out of the new measures.[7] The revenues, which for the budget of 1918–19 had brought in 9.6 billion lire, brought in 15.2 billion in 1919–20 and 18.8 billion in 1920–21.[8] The national loan of January 1920, which brought in 18 billion lire—a tremendous sum for Italy —was floated by royal decree. The forces for the maintenance of public peace were reorganized by royal decrees. As we have seen, when the war ended, the carabineers numbered only 28,000. By June 1920, their numbers had risen to 60,000. Moreover, an auxiliary police body, the "Royal Guard," had been created, which in June 1920 numbered 25,000 men.[9] One Socialist deputy, a carter by trade, earned great popularity by interrupting the ministerial speeches in season and out of season with the cry: "Dissolve the Royal Guard." The Royal Guard went on increasing.

But when all this has been said, the fact remains that as a result of the election of November 1919, Parliament had become a paralytic body. It

[6] "La crisi ministeriale e la Costituzione," *Rivoluzione liberale*, February 19, 1922.
[7] E. Flores, *Eredità di Guerra* (Naples: Ceccoli, 1925), pp. 129 ff.
[8] Bachi, *L'Italia economica nel 1921*, pp. 258 ff.
[9] Nitti, *L'opera di Nitti*, p. 165.

represented the country perfectly because it had been elected freely under a system which made it an exact mirror of the country. But it had been elected in an abnormal period, and therefore it worked in an abnormal way. A situation of this kind could not endure forever. Either Parliament would perform its legislative duties, or it would be eliminated from the Italian political body as a useless—nay troublesome—organ.

16

Italian
"Bolshevism"
in 1920

During the first half of 1920, the number of strikers for economic reasons (foremost among which was the rising cost of living) jumped to 1,769,000, as against 877,000 in the second half of 1919.[1] Figures are not available for solidarity strikes, for general (either local or national) strikes, or for dead and wounded in street riots. From a perusal of the daily press, however, one draws the positive conclusion that they increased in the same proportions as the economic strikes, if not more markedly. Strikes in agriculture gave place to the seizure of land, not only in southern Italy, but also in northern Italy, and to the abandoning of starving or unmilked cattle in their stalls, criminal fires of haylofts and stalls, the cutting down of trees, and clashes between strikers on the one hand and "blacklegs" and police on the other.

The election of November 1919 had shown that the Populist party was the only efficient bulwark against the Socialists among the peasantry. Socialist attacks on the Populist trade union leaders and members became more and more bitter. The Populists answered in kind. Fights and blows were frequent. This division between Populists and Socialists delighted the other parties, but it did not help to calm the universal restlessness. On the other hand, in some sections of Lombardy and Venetia, the Populist peasantry vied with the Socialist peasantry in going on strike, starving the cattle and attacking landowners and farmers. With the passing of time,

---

[1] *Annuario Statistico Italiano: 1919–1921*, pp. 385, 398.

some of the Populist agitators of 1920 went over to the Communist party.

Railwaymen and employees in the postal, telegraph, and telephone services had never struck during 1919, and their wisdom was highly commended by the government for not participating in the July 20–21 general strike. But they could not live on wisdom, praises, and their old wages. In his turn, Nitti was concerned with the enormous expenditure which was needed to increase their wages and to grant them the eight-hour day; he tackled this problem, like all other problems, by delaying as long as possible any solution. As a consequence, those employees began to hold protest meetings; then they practiced slow-down methods; and at last, in January 1920, the employees of the postal, telegraph, and telephone services went on strike. Only now did the government make concessions to them; if they had been made before, they would have avoided the strike. Soon the railwaymen came in, and, after two weeks of strike (January 6–20), they got what they demanded: an increase in wages, the eight-hour day, and protection against arbitrary treatment on the part of their superiors. But Revolutionary Syndicalists and Anarchists during the crisis got control of their national organization, and from now on discipline went to the dogs. On May Day, traffic was practically suspended all over the country. About fifty strikes of a more or less extensive nature occurred up until June 1920. Some of the strikers broke out to hold up trains of soldiers, carabineers, and royal guards. On April 15, at the station of Leghorn, a train of royal guards bound for Turin was held up. On April 22, at the stations of Pavia, Domodossola, Novara, the railwaymen refused to convey the troops summoned to Turin to restore order there, and at the stations of Florence and Rome there was a stay-in strike. On June 8, the railwaymen of Cremona station refused to convey a train of war ammunitions, which they thought was destined for Poland to be made use of against Soviet Russia. A station official managed to get the train dispatched. The strikers demanded his transfer to another station. This demand having been refused, the strike spread to Milan and to eastern Lombardy. The strike ended on June 24, without the transfer being obtained.

Italian railway strikes were much less serious than those which occurred in England at that time. In September 1919, half a million men struck for nine days and entirely paralyzed the traffic throughout England. In Italy, in January 1920, no more than 72,000 out of 198,000 went to strike; in southern Italy, 90 percent of the employees abstained from striking. Almost all the other strikes were of short duration. But a strike in a railroad center like Verona, Milan, Turin, Genoa, or Bologna, even though it was merely local, disorganized the services on all the lines radiating from the center. The discomfort among the public was great, and the railwaymen were to pay dearly for their extravagances when reaction set in. The cases of stoppage in military trains amounted to no more than a dozen during the whole year. But they became a commonplace in "anti-Bolshevist" propaganda, and people, hearing them eternally talked of, ended by believing that that intolerable scandal was occurring every day and everywhere and must be stopped at any cost.

In December 1919, the Anarchist Errico Malatesta came back from England. He was sixty-seven years old and had behind him a half-century of revolutionary activities. In the spring of 1914, he had been connected with a rather serious uprising which had broken out in central Italy—the so-called Red Week—and, to escape arrest, had taken refuge in England. A general amnesty had reopened the gates of Italy to him, but he had not been allowed to cross over into France, and when he tried to go by sea, the English government had forbidden all ships, whether English or not, to take him on board. He succeeded in stowing away aboard an Italian ship. When the news spread that he was in Genoa, the entire working population suspended work to show their joy and received him as a conquering hero. In February 1920, an Anarchist daily, *Umanità Nuova*, was started in Milan under Malatesta's editorship.

Malatesta, like Lenin, was revolutionary in dead earnest, and his long, consistent, and fearless past, his unselfishness, his personal charm and youthful energy gave him an immense prestige. But he had been brought up in southern Italy between 1860 and 1880. In 1884 he had been forced to go into exile to escape imprisonment, and from then on he had lived outside Italy until 1913, except for several clandestine visits of a few months duration in 1896 and 1897, when he was only in contact with few friends. When he was able to return freely, from August 1913 to June 1914, he spent those ten months among the anarchistic elements in the Marches and Romagna. He had no deep acquaintance with northern Italy, in which industry had been greatly developed in the past forty years and where the Socialist party controlled the city workers. Others who had never been forced into exile and who had always lived in Italy should have known better than Malatesta. But the Anarchists continued to live in the idealistic atmosphere of Bakunin, just as the Socialists lived in that of Marx and the Republicans in that of Mazzini. The "people" or the "proletariat" of the twentieth century was no longer that which the romantic revolutionaries of the nineteenth century had imagined, loved, and glorified.

Men and women flocked to listen to Malatesta and read his paper, hoping to find in him the savior, the liberator, the leader, a new Garibaldi, the Italian Lenin. But he was not Lenin, the Communist. He was Malatesta, the Anarchist. According to his doctrine of anarchistic individualism, whoever set himself up as a leader instead of remaining humbly among the rank and file would be guilty of the crime of dictatorship. He was ready to take part in any revolutionary attempt, but never as the leader of his fellow men. All men ought to be free and equal, and he did not feel entitled to enslave them by issuing orders to them, not even orders for a revolution. He was saddened rather than elated when people expected leadership from him—a deplorable leftover from the respect for authority which had been planted in people's minds by bourgeois miseducation. Nettlau, who shared Malatesta's political faith, writes:

> He was willing to face any kind of sacrifice, but not to seize political power. Even if they had placed dictatorship at his feet, he would not have accepted it. . . . This misunderstanding, the fruit of the cult of authority which is common to all advanced parties except the Anarchists, is truly tragic. . . . The people awaited a signal, an order. But the signal and the order never came, nor could they have come. . . . The people applauded and then returned to their own homes. The slightest popular initiative would have set the avalanche in motion and a new chapter of history would probably have begun. But this was not to be.[2]

According to Nettlau and the Anarchists, "this was not to be," because the Socialist "leaders," whether right-wingers, Maximalists, or Extremists, not only gave no signal, no order (and in this they remained within the bounds of their duty, because they had no right to give any), but they smothered revolutionary initiatives as soon as they manifested themselves, instead of furthering them, spreading them, and aggravating them, always and everywhere.[3] The same charge was leveled by the Extremists against the Maximalists, and by both of them against the right-wing Socialists. The

---

[2] M. Nettlau, *Errico Malatesta* (New York: Casa Editrice Il Martello, 1921), pp. 300–01.
[3] An explanation similar to that given by Nettlau is found in A. Borghi, *Errico Malatesta in 60 anni di lotte anarchiche* (New York: Edizioni Sociali, 1933), pp. 184–89.

root of the accusation was the same for all: the notion that there existed a "revolutionary proletariat," eager to rebel and capable of triumphing, if somewhere there had not been somebody who betrayed it and paralyzed its natural impulses. That "slightest popular initiative," which Malatesta desired and awaited, never materialized, not because the "leaders" betrayed the proletariat, but because the "revolutionary proletariat" was a figment of their imagination. Even though Malatesta did not believe that he had a right to give orders and went to the popular meetings unarmed, many of his followers took part in the meetings well supplied with rocks, clubs, and revolvers, incited immediate struggle, and provoked clashes with the police. If the "proletariat" had been the revolutionary mass which only needed a signal, an order to "set the avalanche in motion," as Nettlau writes, they had plenty of such signals and orders, even too many. The orders always fell on deaf ears. The "proletariat"—that is to say, those who attended the meetings and the demonstrations—had a choice between those Anarchists who incited them to rise up, Malatesta who gave no orders, and the Maximalists, who advised them to wait for the "great hour." The proletariat applauded the most bombastic addresses, gave vent by their applause to their nebulous hopes for a better world, and returned home, waiting for that better world to fall into their laps from the heavens. Only a very small minority set up to direct and immediate action, assaulted the police, and left a certain number of dead on the battlefield—often people who were there just by chance and were killed without knowing why. Then the "proletariat" would call a general protest strike, and all would finish like this, ready to begin again on the first occasion. Even in Germany, in January 1919, the "proletariat," forced to choose between Ebert and Noske on the one hand, and Rosa Luxemburg and Karl Liebknecht on the other, chose the former. Yet in Germany at that time, the objective conditions for social revolution were infinitely more favorable than in Italy, had the Marxist doctrine been correct. These were the harsh realities stripped of their ideological illusions. The Socialists and Anarchists of all schools did not see them and were beating the air with their wings.

Given the Italian situation, and given his individualistic and anti-dictatorial mentality, Malatesta was destined to add fuel to the fire of Italian restlessness without increasing in the slightest the chances of social revolution. The Anarchist movement became more aggressive, but not more effective. More often than before, meetings ended in clashes between the crowd and the police with dead and wounded. Some bomb outrages had been made by Anarchists in Milan in September 1919. In 1920, bomb outrages multiplied. Whoever wished to furnish himself with bombs had only to go and pick them up at the former fighting front, where they had been left unexploded with criminal carelessness by the military authorities at the moment of the demobilization.

When clashes with the police and bomb outrages occurred, the Maximalists hurried to blame the Anarchists as "irresponsible" promoters of discouragement among the rank and file of the revolutionary army. On April 5, in a riot which Anarchists had promoted at Decima di Persiceto, near Bologna, there were nine dead. During the protest strikes of the following days, in which, in many sections of Italy, the railwaymen participated, there were six dead in Modena and more than thirty wounded in Andria. The national executive of the Socialist party refused to call a national protest strike. The Anarchists charged the Maximalists with betraying the proletariat. The *Avanti,* April 10, 1920, had a flash of sense: "Let us put an end to words. Arms are needed. Have you got them? Where are they? Why do you not make use of them? You are but talkers. During these last years you have done nothing but talk. Yes, as long as talks are needed, you are strong." The Maximalists saw the beam in the eyes of the Anarchists, but not in their own.

While "ruling" Fiume, D'Annunzio tried to stir up disorder or to take advantage of spontaneous disorder everywhere. Malatesta was able to reach Italy thanks to the help he received from the secretary national of the Italian longshoremen, Giulietti, who was working hand and glove with D'Annunzio. On October 26, 1920, the *Avanti* gave the following cryptic item: "There was a time when D'Annunzio endeavored to take advantage of the foolishness of some trade union leader, and to sell himself as the champion of socialism and of a Socialist republic, made speeches with a Bolshevist flavor, and even concerned himself in railway strikes."

We are in a position to throw some light on these words. At the beginning of 1920, a secret meeting was held in Florence. Giulietti announced that all the army chiefs who commanded the regiments between Fiume and Rome were loyal to D'Annunzio and ready to march on Rome; the Republican deputies and some Socialist deputies had agreed; the secret organization which was organizing the March on Rome was termed "the Sacred Lamp" ("Sagra Lampa"). The other fellows maintained that the movement could not succeed if the General Confederation of Labor did not second it. Giulietti took it upon himself to feel out the ground. One of the

Confederation's leaders agreed. The others refused. Thus the "Sacred Lamp" was extinguished.[4] But D'Annunzio was not discouraged by this. Between June 26 and 29, 1920, in Ancona, the soldiers refused to leave for Albania. On June 28, an emissary of D'Annunzio, Lieutenant Claudio Mariani, went to Ancona bearing letters from D'Annunzio, General Ceccherini, and Major Santini, in which D'Annunzio put at the disposal of the revolting soldiers "all the Communist [sic] forces of Fiume."[5]

In 1920, in Florence, an officer of the seventieth infantry regiment, who claimed to be an Anarchist and a secret service agent of England, offered the Anarchists funds for their paper *Il Grido della Rivolta*. The Anarchists kept a watch over him and discovered him to be a government spy. In Florence again, shortly afterwards, a senior officer of the Florence garrison offered assistance in bringing off a *coup de main* against a military barracks. The Anarchists, suspecting a trap, did not act.[6]

There was much talk in those years of a formidable propaganda carried on all over Italy by agents of Russian bolshevism. Excited imaginations saw sinister Bolshevist agents everywhere. There is no doubt that the Russian government had a certain number of agents in Italy, as elsewhere. But it is difficult to estimate the precise extent of the Russian ramifications. Anyhow, one of the most active Bolshevist agents, a certain Ferrari, who spoke several languages, had huge funds at his disposal, and was on intimate terms with Serrati, formed the subject of a question asked in the Chamber by the Nationalist deputy Signor Federzoni: Why did the government leave this dangerous Bolshevist at large? The government gave no reply. But one fine day the Socialists discovered that this most dangerous Bolshevist was a secret agent of the Italian police. Whatever authentic Bolshevist propaganda there was in Italy, there was also a trumped-up "bolshevism," either because the police fabricated it to spy upon authentic "bolshevism" or because men like D'Annunzio were stirring up pretexts for military reaction.

Mussolini, who was to attribute to himself and his Fascists the merit of having stamped down "bolshevism" in Italy, in the last months of 1919 and

---

[4] The writer of this book was informed about this maneuver by one of those who attended the meeting. Malatesta also was approached: A. Borghi, *L'Italia tra due Crispi* (Paris: Libreria Internazionale, 1924), p. 103.

[5] *Umanità Nuova*, July 1, 1920; quoted from Borghi, *L'Italia tra due Crispi*, p. 234, n. 1.

[6] Camillo Berneri, the Anarchist who was murdered by the Communists in Barcelona in 1938, and who in 1920 was a student at the University of Florence, gave this information to the writer of the present book.

the first six months of 1920 abandoned himself to the most unbridled revolutionary manifestations. When D'Annunzio occupied Fiume, Mussolini glorified that "coup" as an "intrepid cutting of the Gordian knot tied around Italy's neck by the western plutocrats," as "the only great gesture of revolt against the plutocratic oligarchy which had made the Treaty of Versailles," and as the "only evidence in Europe of a will which, straight like the blade of a Latin sword, did not bend under the coercion of Versailles." The revolution was on the march: "commenced at Fiume, it can be concluded only at Rome."[7] On the eve of the elections of November 16, he tried to reconcile the voters to him by declaring himself opposed to any dictatorship whatsoever:

> We maintain that if, tomorrow, our wildest foes were the victims of illegal repression, we would uprise, because we are in favor of all liberties against any tyranny whatsoever. . . . There is no one in Italy who wishes to be governed by anyone who claims to be a Messiah, a Tsar, or the Almighty Father. We want liberty for all. We want to be ruled by the will of all, and not by the will of a group or a man, whatever he may be.[8]

Since he had not been elected, he forthwith advocated the abolition of Parliament. When Malatesta came to Italy, Mussolini hailed the old revolutionary:

> We do not know whether the fact that we were interventionists and have the courage to be proud of it, is such as to procure us excomunications from the old Anarchist agitator. Perhaps he is much less uncompromising than the idiotic and mischievous members of the Socialist party. We are far from agreeing with his ideas. We do not believe in any revelations. We do not believe in the possibility of creating earthly paradises by means of laws and machine guns. We do not believe any longer in magical changes. We have another concept—strictly individualistic—of life and of the elites, which have to rule. We are always ready to admire those unselfish men who profess a faith for which they are ready to die. Therefore our ideas do not keep us from sending our cordial welcome to Malatesta. We do so in the hope

[7] *Popolo d'Italia*, September 13, 14, and 25, 1919.
[8] *Popolo d'Italia*, November 11 and 14, 1919.

that the vast experience of his long life will help to unmask the merchants of revolution, the vendors of Bolshevist smoke, those who are preparing for a new tyranny which, after a short while, would leave the people prey to a frightful reaction (*Popolo d'Italia,* Dec. 27, 1919).

His scorn for every religious faith still accompanied his ultrarevolutionary fireworks. In the *Popolo d'Italia* of December 12, 1919, he wrote:

We profoundly detest all forms of Christianism, that of Jesus as much as that of Marx. We greet with extraordinary sympathy the revival in modern life of the pagan cult of force and audacity. . . . Enough, red and black theologians, of all churches. No more false and sly promises of a heaven which will never come! Enough, ridiculous saviors of the human race. The human race does not give a damn for your infallible prescriptions granting happiness. Leave the path open to the primal forces of the individual. No other human reality exists except that of the individual.

On January 1, 1920, he wrote: "Let us return to the individual. Two religions are contending today for the dominion of the souls, the black and the red. From two Vaticans come encyclicals, from that of Rome and that of Moscow. We are the heretics of both religions."

On that same day, he commented in the following words upon the strikes the employees in the postal, telegraph and telephone services were threatening: "We want a fight to the finish for bringing about greater equality in salaries, the increase of bonuses for night work and extra work, and the right to a regular career for the employees. We demand our rights against false patriots and war sharks."

A few weeks later, the General Confederation of Labor refused to support the strike in the railway service. The Fascist Lanzillo, who later was to become a solemn personage in the Fascist regime, wrote in the *Popolo d'Italia* (January 24, 1920):

The strike is the work of a formidable mass of employees who undeniably act in good faith and with the persuasion that they are within their rights. In the controversy of the railwaymen, the Socialist party and the General Confederation of Labor have abandoned the railway employees until they were near defeat. After so many years of Socialist domi-

nation, these strikes are the first which have been planned
and carried on outside and in spite of the tyrannical will of
the Socialist party. The days of working class violence have
a revivifying value and are a thousand times superior to the
paltry methods of the mischief mongers.

In April 1920, the government introduced the daylight savings time. The
Communists found out that this new method of counting the hours had
been invented by the "bourgeoisie" to render even more pitiless the sweat-
ing of the proletarian. In some Turin factories there were strikes in protest.
Mussolini applauded those strikes. The Italian state as it then was—the
wretched, democratic state in which people struck even against the daylight
saving bill—was, in Mussolini's opinion, too active, too oppressive, intolerable:

> I, too, am against the daylight saving bill. It represents
> another form of state intervention and coercion. The state
> with its enormous bureaucratic machine induces a feeling of
> suffocation. The state was tolerable to the individual so long
> as it contented itself with being a soldier and a policeman.
> But today, the state is everything: banker, usurer, gambler,
> navigator, procurer, insurance agent, postman, railwayman,
> impresario, manufacturer, schoolmaster, college professor,
> tobacconist, and innumerable other things, besides being, as
> always, policeman, judge, gaoler, and tax collector. The
> state, this Moloch of fearsome aspect, does everything, con-
> trols everything, and sends everything to perdition. Every
> state undertaking is a calamity. State art, state schools, state
> postal services, state shipping, state trading, alike are disas-
> trous—the litany could go to infinity. The future prospects
> are terrifying. Socialism is merely an amplification, multi-
> plication, and perfection of the state. The bourgeois state
> now controls nine-tenths of your life and of your activities.
> Tomorrow the Socialist state will control your every mo-
> ment, your every deed or movement. Today you are obliged
> to declare the number of your children, but tomorrow you
> will be forced to declare the exact number of your amorous
> adventures. Under the Socialist regime, even love will be
> standardized, tailored and mapped out for the use, conven-
> ience and pleasure of the hundred thousand Socialist offi-
> cials who will spring up under state socialism. If men had
> even a vague apprehension of the abyss which awaits them,
> the number of suicides would be increased. We are ap-

proaching the complete destruction of human personality. This state is the gigantic machine which swallows living men and casts them forth again as dead ciphers. Human life has no longer any privacy or intimacy, either material or spiritual; all corners are explored, all movements timed, every man is pigeonholed on his particular "shelf" and numbered like a convict. The great curse which fell upon the human race in the misty beginnings of its history and has pursued it throughout the centuries has been to build up the state and to be perpetually crushed by the state! . . . I start from the individual and strike at the state. Down with the state in all its phases and incarnations. The state of yesterday, of today and of tomorrow. The bourgeois state and the Socialist state. In the gloom of today and the darkness of tomorrow the only faith which remains to us individualists destined to die is the at present absurd, but ever consoling religion of anarchy (*Popolo d'Italia*, April 6, 1920).

He was in full sympathy with the peasants who here and there were seizing the land. On May 25, 1920, he wrote: "The peasants who rise up today to solve the land question, must not meet with our hostility. They may, perhaps, commit excesses, but I beg you to remember that the war was fought by peasants."[9]

If then the revolutionary wave did not break the dikes even in the first half of 1920, the reason is not to be sought in Mussolini's activities, not only because he did everything possible so that the wave would break through the dikes, but because his influence at that time was not yet remarkable. In October 1919, the Fascists claimed to have 40,000 adherents to their political movement in all Italy and 160,000 members in their unions.[10] But these figures were imaginary. We have seen that in the elections of November 1919, Mussolini did not even receive 6,000 votes in the whole of Lombardy, whereas the Socialists received 138,000 and the Populists 61,000. According to the report given to a Fascist national conference in November 1921, there were at that time in Italy only 17,000 Fascists, (*Popolo d'Italia*, November 8, 1921), but according to a speech by Mussolini on March 24, 1924, "there were not even 10,000," and according to an official communiqué published in the *Popolo d'Italia* on

---

[9] This article as well as the two of December 12, 1919, and April 6, 1920, have been suppressed in the official collection of Mussolini's *Scritti e discorsi.*
[10] Figures given at the National Conference of the Fighting Fasci held at Florence and at the Congress of the Italian Union of Labor held in Forlì.

March 23, 1929, there were a mere 870. The latter seems to be the most probable figure. Such influence as Mussolini had only served to make the prevailing restlessness more acute.

Italian "postwar neurasthenia" was termed "bolshevism," not only because the Russian Revolution had made bolshevism fashionable and agitators actually had tried to use the crisis to bring about a Bolshevist revolution, but also because the politicians who had made war badly and peace worse—the *nouveaux riches* who aroused general indignation by their insensate luxury, the military chiefs and Nationalists who had created the poisonous myth of the "mutilated victory" and had planted the seeds of sedition in the army by the raid of Fiume—all these found it convenient to trace the people's unrest to "Bolshevist" propaganda. In politics, as in other matters, we do not like to look for the causes of evil in our own faults; it is always more comfortable to lay the responsiblity at other people's doors. And if any strike, any street riot, any uproar is to be dignified with the name of bolshevism, then there is no doubt that Italy in 1919 and 1920 was in the throes of bolshevism. Italians are a noisy people. They cannot do anything without a great noise, and often they make a great noise without doing anything. But if the term "bolshevism" is to be applied only to a social revolution which overthrows the well-to-do classes and deprives them of political power, then Italy never was in the throes of bolshevism during those years. And if, by "bolshevism," one means economic breakdown resulting from political disorder, no economic breakdown ever existed.

There is no need to belittle the discomfort caused by strikes, expecially those affecting the railways and other public services, or to minimize the responsibility of aggressive radical elements who indulged in the costly game of creating trouble in the hope that trouble would breed revolution. There is plenty of evidence that among the masses during the first half of 1920, there was truly the expectation of an impending social revolution. But when all this has been taken into account, the fact remains that there were many disturbances, strikes, riots, and much noise and confusion, but the fatal crisis never came.

The people who, with bated breath and upturned eyes, spoke of bolshevism during those years were for the most part not insincere. In 1919 and 1920, they were terrified by the tragedy of Russia. They were in a state of blue funk, waiting for the social revolution as sheep wait to be led to the slaughterhouse. If fear, bewilderment, and cowardice in the wealthy classes were enough to bring about a Communist revolution, the Italian people, in 1919 and 1920, could have made as many Communist revolutions as they desired. Unless we take that panic into account, we shall not be able to understand the ferocity of the following Fascist reaction. Moreover, one has to remember the patriotic bitterness and yearning for revenge which really existed in large sections of the Italian middle classes against the English, French, and Americans who "had mutilated Italian victory," against those Italian politicians of the old school who "had won the war but lost the peace," and against all those Italians who had refused to countenance Sonnino and were opposed to fresh international warlike adventures. The Socialists formed the most powerful section of the antiwar groups, and against them, therefore, Nationalists and Fascists focused most of their hatred. They were termed "Bolshevists" even when they professed the mildest possible brand of socialism. Thus originated the slogan that the Fascists were fighting against bolshevism. But just as it is not advisable to take the word of a man under the influence of wine, it is also not advisable to take the word of a man under the influence of panic or anger. If the psychological reflexes of the postwar crisis are checked by the objective indices of economic and social life, every unprejudiced inquirer must come to the conclusion that the so-called Italian bolshevism of 1919–20 was nothing worse than an outbreak of uncoordinated unrest among large sections of the Italian people, to which the worst elements of the ruling classes replied by an exhibition of cowardice and bitterness out of all proportion to the actual danger.[11]

A striking example of Italian anti-Bolshevist frenzy is Pantaleoni's book *Bolscevismo Italiano* (Bari: Laterza, 1922). In the eyes of Pantaleoni, anyone who was not an uncompromising advocate of the *laisser faire* economic doctrine was either a "Bolshevist" or a "crypto-Bolshevist." Anarchists, Communists, Socialists, Republicans of the Mazzinian tradition, the members of the Populist party—all were "Bolshevist." Those democrats who did not fight the Socialists with sufficient fury were not "Bolshevists," but "crypto-Bolshevists" ("bolscevisti sornioni"). Jumbling together all the conflicting groups into a single entity called "bolshevism" and attributing to this single entity all the acts and all the responsibilities of the different groups, Pantaleoni makes his readers believe in the existence of a Bolshevist

[11] A fair-minded resumé of the causes of the general unrest is given by Giorgio Mortara, *Prospettive economiche 1923* (Citta' di Castello, 1923). pp. 421–22; see also Mowrer, *Immortal Italy*, pp. 317–29. The book of this intelligent and honest American eyewitness was written before the Fascist legend was concocted; it is therefore a valuable and trustworthy source of information.

movement that was compact, intelligent, coordinate, and appalling in its strength.

England, in 1919 and 1920, labored under even greater discomfort than Italy. Yet never did it occur to Englishmen to fall into convulsions of fear that England was going "bolshie."

17

The Occupation of the Factories

In June 1920, Nitti resigned, because the deputies of the Populist party had deserted him. Orlando had discredited himself during the peace conference. No other politician was available for the premiership except Giolitti, the leader of those deputies who in 1915 had opposed Italy's entrance into the war. This fact contributed greatly to spread the feeling that the war had been a failure.

Soon Giolitti had to face not only the usual wave of strikes and street riots, but also a mutiny of soldiers in Ancona. They had been commanded to leave for Albania to quell a revolt that had broken out there against the Italians. The soldiers refused to leave. Many officers of the regular army had disobeyed the civil government in September 1919, siding with D'Annunzio in the Fiume affair. This time it was the soldiers who disobeyed their officers, refusing to go to war in Albania. The seeds of military sedition sown during the preceding year by the Nationalists bore their fruit. The Anarchists and Republicans, who were strong in Ancona, tried to take advantage of this movement. But the soldiers did not follow them. They submitted to their officers and took part in stamping down a revolutionary attempt in the city, in which twenty-five persons lost their lives (June 26–27). The usual outbreak of disconnected general strikes took place.

The national executive of the Socialist party met to decide whether it was the time to widen the movement and bring about the long-heralded social revolution. The members of the executive, who were all either Maximalists or Extremists, split up into two equal parts: three against three. To have a plurality, they asked the representative of the deputies, who according to the constitution of the party attended the meeting without the right to vote, to vote just the same. Everybody knew that he would cast his vote against widening the movement, and so he did. Thus again the "great hour" was postponed. But now the Extremists were in a position to maintain that it had not struck because the proletariat had been betrayed by the four people who had not cast their votes for revolution.[1]

A few days later, trouble broke out in another quarter. Giolitti had chosen as his foreign minister Count Sforza, who had always condemned the plan of annexing Dalmatia to Italy and was willing to reach an Italo-Yugoslav compromise on the Adriatic question. At Trieste, on July 13, a group of Nationalists and Fascists burned down the headquarters of all the political, economic, and cultural organizations of the Slavs in the city, called the "Narodni Dom"—an outrage resulting in damages of about $200,000. The incendiaries procured from a neighboring military barracks the benzine necessary for their job. They had hoped thus to wreck the negotiations between Sforza and the Belgrade government. At the head of this feat was to be found that same Giunta whom we have met, in June and July 1919, as a troublemaker in Rome and in Florence.

Meanwhile, among the upper and middle classes, a new state of mind had been slowly maturing. The industrialists, who during the war had manufactured munitions or army cloth, had not until now actually suffered as a result of the disorders and strikes. The fear of the disorders which might result from unemployment prevented the government from stopping the production of war material. Then the industrialists protested that they could not go on paying the wages demanded by the workers unless the government raised the price of goods. The government, in order to pay its way, increased the circulation of paper money. As a result prices soared; there were new strikes, a renewed fear of disorder, and new orders for war material.

But the government could not continue indefinitely to order useless war material. The industrialists, in their turn, could not pass from uneconomic to economic prices without either giving up profits or lowering wages, and they could not lower their wages without a fierce struggle against the economic organization and the political influence of the working classes.

[1] This fact was made public in October 1920 (*Civiltà Cattolica*, November 20, 1920, p. 374). Neither the Maximalists nor the Extremists denied it.

In lower Lombardy, Emilia, Tuscany, and Apulia, where the pressure of the Socialist and Populist unions was at its height, the employers of agricultural labor were kept in a state of constant fear for themselves and their families, often isolated in the open country and without means of defense. In the first year after the war, they had put up with these trials, hoping they would soon blow over; the peasants were nearly all demobilized soldiers, and it was necessary to look with forbearance on the extravagances of the "saviors of the country." But as time passed, the honeymoon with the "saviors of the country" waned and irritation grew. The hail of new taxation made it increasingly difficult for the landowners to bear the burden of high wages and of the unessential or even wasteful work they were obliged to provide for the unemployed. Those who were most exasperated were not the big landowners, who did not come into contact with the laborers and metayers, but the farmers, the stewards, the owners of medium-sized estates, and the small holders. Bitterest of all were the small owners who had bought land with what they had saved during the war and who had now to defend their property.

Besides the "antibolshevism" of the industrialists and landowners, there was that of the shopkeepers and tradesmen. Many of these had been opposed to the war, and in 1919 they had sympathized with the "Bolshevist" protests against those responsible for the war. But as soon as this "bolshevism" began to fix prices, to loot shops, to break shop windows, they too became fiercely "anti-Bolshevist." Moreover, the retail cooperative stores of the Socialists and Christian Democrats competed with the small shopkeepers. For these people, "antibolshevism" meant putting an end (a) to street disorder, (b) to regulation of food prices, and (c) to the competition of the Socialist and Christian-Democratic cooperatives.

The public servants also had their "antibolshevism." The workers, the landless peasants, and those public servants who could strike—such as railwaymen and post office and telegraph employees—had up until then defended themselves against inflation and the consequent rise in prices, by exacting higher wages and higher salaries. In contrast, the magistrates, army officers, teachers, retired officials, and others with fixed incomes were living a life of great hardship. A great many of these, too, had been "Bolshevists" in 1919. During 1920, comparing their increasing poverty with the increasing wages of the manual workers, they too became "anti-Bolshevists." They attributed their troubles solely to the secondary, but more obtrusive, fact of the strikes, instead of tracing it to its primary, but less obvious, cause—inflation.

A subsection of this bureaucratic "antibolshevism" was the "antibolshevism" of the carabineers, of the royal guards, and of the police, who were forced to rush hither and thither to stop disorders; were insulted in the papers and at revolutionary meetings; were exposed to continual danger of wounds or death; and were exasperated by the very necessity of the frequent use of arms against tumultuous crowds. The Extremists of a small city of Tuscany, Abbadia San Salvadore (Siena), certainly did not diminish the strength of this "anti-Bolshevist" current in August 1920 when they assaulted a religious procession, clashed with the carabineers who tried to keep order, killed one of them, suffered one dead in their turn, and for revenge killed a friar and wounded two priests. Two other persons and a baby lost their lives in the fray. In Rome, on July 20, the streetcar men wanted to celebrate their victory in a strike, adorning the streetcars with red flags. The public reacted against and manhandled employees so badly that some of them had to be taken to hospitals. The Chamber of Labor called for a general protest strike. Clashes occurred between Socialists and Nationalists. The premises where the Roman edition of the *Avanti* was published were looted. Three Socialist deputies were rather seriously wounded. After four days of strike and street fighting, the tide subsided. There is no doubt that the attack on the workers was led by Nationalists, but there is no doubt either that large sections of the population were exasperated with the streetcar men and either took part in or approved of the reaction.[2]

The general staff of the army was carefully watching over these symptoms of reaction. During the summer of 1920, a Colonel A.R., a "military expert in civil war," was sent by the War Office for a tour of inspection all over Italy. His report was published a year later by the Communist paper *Ordine Nuovo* (October 2, 1921), and its authenticity was never contradicted. Colonel A.R. did not think it possible for the Italian revolutionists to achieve anything serious:

[2] For this slow growth of the "anti-Bolshevist" mentality in the different classes before the autumn of 1920, see the remarks of Guglielmo Ferrero, *Da Fiume a Roma*, pp. 91–93. See also in the volume *Il fascismo e partiti politici italiani* (Bologna, 1924) the studies of Luigi Fabbri, *Controrivoluzione preventiva*, pp. 21 ff.; Mario Missiroli, *Il fascismo e la crisi italiana*, pp. 14 ff.; and Giovanni Zibordi, *Critica socialista del fascismo*, pp. 16–42. The studies collected in this volume are the work of men of the most widely divergent political views. They were written in the second half of 1921 and first half of 1922. Thus, taken as a whole, they form a first-rate source of information on the origins of the Fascist movement.

Discontented and revolutionary-minded people are not capable of organization. They act in heterogeneous masses under the impulse of passing emotion. The arms in their possession are scarce and unevenly distributed. They have no organized bodies capable of making use of them. Their equipment is necessarily inadequate, particularly for prolonged resistance. The political groups that help to keep up mass excitement possess clever and courageous men, but these are interspersed with senseless braggarts, and they all have a very limited grasp of tactics, the use of arms, discipline, cooperation, and even action itself. The very conditions of life of these subversive elements allow them only extremely limited resources; any attempt at coordinated preparation remains local, or at best extends to the district. . . . Long and far-sighted preparation is impossible for them. The more fanatical meet together, spur each other on, choose leaders, issue instructions; most of the others remain undecided, passive, without initiative. Hypnotized by noise and crowds they delude themselves as to their strength and their prospects. Their first reverse will be followed by disillusion and disorder.

According to Colonel A.R., an army based on compulsory universal service was not fit for large-scale repression. The privates were part of the populace and shared its mentality. "A solid framework of long service officers and noncommissioned officers, well paid and carefully chosen on a voluntary basis," would be more to the point. Not even this voluntary army would suffice:

We must add to our conscript army and the 250,000 mercenaries which we shall soon possess a militia of idealists, consisting of the most expert, brave, strong and warlike from amongst us to support and control their action. This militia must be capable of being used both for defensive action and for political purposes, and must be able at this critical period to put fresh blood and life into the national forces and lead them to victory.

Officers of the regular army should join and command those men. The local groups should be under the control of a central staff consisting of political and military experts:

Minor engagements with the object of chastising the insolence of the more subversive centers will give a fine schooling to our militia and serve to break up and demoralize the enemy at the same time. But care must always be taken to have one or more bases as starting points and as centers for concentrating our resources. These bases must be at a reasonable distance from the place where the blow is to be struck, so that it is possible to return to them without arousing suspicion and to reorganize there in the event of a temporary setback. This is the procedure to be followed when local punitive action is undertaken.[3]

This plan was to be carried out in its entirety during the following year. To pave the way to its acceptance, some further big revolutionary scare was still needed, and it came.

In July the workers in the metal industry had demanded a further increase in wages and threatened to strike. The employers now were determined to withstand the workers' organization until its unconditional surrender. That same Rotigliano who in April 1919 was General Caviglia's secretary was now the representative of the employers.

Occasional acts of sabotage took place in various factories. On August 30, one of the firms declared a lockout. The men's leaders, to prevent the other firms from closing down, called a "lock-in," or, as it is now termed in the United States, a "sit-down" strike. The movement spread to other industries. Half a million workers all over Italy occupied the factories in which they were accustomed to work, both government and employers being powerless to offer resistance.

Labriola, a former Revolutionary Syndicalist who had grown wise and was now minister of labor in Giolitti's cabinet, expressed the opinion in 1924 that in September 1920 the leaders of the Socialist party might have seized political power without remarkable opposition.[4] As a matter of fact, the workers, in shutting themselves up in the factories, had walked into a trap. Had they really been revolutionaries, they would have seized not the workshops, but the government offices, the telegraph and telephone services, and the railroads. As long as they remained in the factories, the government could afford to sit still and wait until they got tired.

The employers protested that the workers were violating the right of

---

[3] Rossi, *The Rise of Italian Fascism*, pp. 97–99.
[4] A. Labriola, *Le due politiche: Fascismo e Riformismo* (Naples: A. Morano, 1924), p. 164.

private ownership and demanded that the government should eject them from the factories by force. This Giolitti refused to do. A bloody repression at that moment would have forced all the groups of the extreme parties to take sides with the occupants of the factories and would have created that coalition of revolutionary forces which the revolutionaries themselves had been unable to achieve.

While the workers were waiting, nobody knew for what, the Socialists were quarreling among themselves. At a national Conference of Labor, the Communists and the more hot-headed Maximalists demanded that "the crisis should be extended" and given definitely revolutionary aims. The right-wingers declared themselves willing to leave the leadership of the movement to the national directorate of the Socialist party. Then the extremists would provoke the revolutionary uprising and the Confederation of Labor would follow in their wake. The representative of Turin—that is to say, of the most active Communist center in Italy—gave such a disheartening report of the conditions prevailing in that city from a revolutionary standpoint that the extremists, confronted face to face with their responsibilities, did not dare accept the proposals of the Confederations.[5] On September 11, after a day an a half of heated debate, the Maximalists split up between right-wingers and extremists, and the former defeated the latter by 591,000 votes to 409,000.[6] Now the extremists were again in a position to maintain that social revolution had been impossible because the other fellows had not willed it. The social revolution had to be carried out by the right-wing Socialists, who did not believe that it was possible, and not by the extremists, who were promising it day in and day out. What the latter actually wanted was to take advantage of the crisis to discredit the right-wingers and put them out of the way before the "great hour" struck when

[5] *Le Parti Socialiste Italien et l'Internationale Communiste* (Petrograd: Éditions de l'Internationale Communiste, 1921), pp. 25, 87; A. Rossi, *The Rise of Italian Fascism*, pp. 75 ff. Rossi is a pen name of Angelo Tasca, who was the Communist representative of Turin at the conference. His is, therefore, firsthand evidence. He writes: "Armed insurrection was out of the question, for nothing was ready. The workers felt safe behind the factory walls, not on account of their arms, often ancient and inadequate, but because they looked on the factories as hostages which the government would hesitate to shell to bits in order to dislodge the occupants. It was a long step from this defensive attitude to open street fighting, as the workers were, if confusedly, aware. Even in Turin, where there was a venturesome advance guard, better armed than elsewhere, the Communist leaders took no active steps, and restrained the groups which had prepared lorries for a sortie from the Fiat works."

[6] See the *Corriere della sera*, September 28, 1920: "Italy has been in peril of collapse. There has been no revolution, not because there was anyone to bar its way, but because the General Confederation of Labor has not willed it."

the "revolutionary proletariat" was to take care of itself.

As the days passed, the men saw that without technical guidance, raw materials, or the confidence of foreign markets the occupation of the factories was useless. By shutting themselves up in the factories, they had shut themselves in a trap. The government had only to wait till the men were tired. When tiredness set in, Giolitti came in and brought about an agreement between employers and workers, as a result of which the workers went home but "representatives of labor were to have the right to inquire into every phase of industry, including the finances, so as to know the true conditions in the industry in which they were employed, enabling them to demand increased wages when earnings justified the advance; the converse of this was that they should not oppose a reduction in wages when earnings declined."[7]

A French scholar who was an eyewitness to these events, Monsieur Albert Dauzat of the Sorbonne, wrote a few weeks later:

> Weeks and months have passed, and the revolution, hoped for by some, feared by others, has not taken place, and according to all evidence, will never take place. The hour is past. The strikes have not attained the political results which the extremists were hoping for. The capitalist society has shown itself to be singularly resistant. The occupation of the factories seems to have marked the turning point of the crisis. The social and political order has safely emerged from it. . . . The password was above all to avoid the spilling of blood, which might bring about the irreparable. In their turn, the Socialist and trade union leaders always advised their followers to keep calm. This attitude is to the credit of the Italian population and the political leaders. The government left the reins slack, without, however, letting them go altogether. This was a dangerous method according to the Conservatives. To be sure there are risks involved, but no greater than in the opposite method.[8]

Giolitti could congratulate himself that his wait-and-see policy had been successful beyond all expectation.[9]

---

[7] H. C. MacLean, *Labor, Wages and Unemployment in Italy* (United States Department of Commerce, Washington, D.C., 1925), p. 3.

[8] A. Dauzat, "La crise sociale en Italie," in the *Revue Mondiale*, December 15, 1920.

[9] Of the crisis, which is termed "occupation of the factories," we have the account given by Minister of Labor Labriola in the Senate, on December 20, 1920 (*Le due politiche,*

This method of the "sit-down" or "stay-in" strike was imitated in France by millions of workers in June 1936. The French government did not bomb the workers out, if for no other reason than it would have damaged the plants had it done so. Of course, the French employers protested that the strikers were holding their plants unlawfully. Yet no sane man proclaimed that France in 1936 was in the throes of a Bolshevist revolution. On the contrary, the *New York Times* of January 6, 1937, commented as follows: "It (the movement of sit-down strikes) testifies to the reserves of prudence and self-control of the French people that so little violence should have marked the seizure of shops and factories." The method of the sit-down strike spread to the United States in January 1937. Governor Murphy of Michigan refused to put out the workers by force in Detroit, Flint, and nearby towns. It is to be hoped that after this American experience, the occupation of the factories in Italy in 1920 will cease to be advertized as a most terrible exhibition of "Italian bolshevism."

One of the misrepresentations which has been widespread in English-speaking countries in connection with this event hangs solely upon a mistaken translation of the Italian word "controllo." The word "controllo" does not mean "control"—that is, ownership and management. It means "checking of the accounts." The workers demanded higher wages to meet the increasing cost of living. The employers retorted that the output of their industry did not allow higher wages. The workers maintained that their trades were flourishing. The automobile industry, for instance, had exported as many motorcars in 1919 as in 1913, on the eve of the war; in 1920, the year of the occupation of the factories, the export of cars had risen to eight times what it had been in the previous year. While the employers maintained that their concerns were in a state of distress, the workers knew that unemployment was on the decrease in the metal trade, which meant that business was good.[10] The workers therefore demanded

pp. 297–311), and two immediate and detailed descriptions. One was published in the "Studies and Reports" of the International Labor Office, Series A, Number 11, November 5, 1920. The other is the work of one of the most intelligent authorities on Italian economic and social life, R. Bachi (*L'Italia economica nel 1920*, p. 347). Other good accounts are given by Vercesi (*Il movimento cattolico in Italia*, pp. 254 ff); Borghi (*L'Italia tra due Crispi*, pp. 248–96); Mowrer (*Immortal Italy*, pp. 329–34); Odon Por (*Fascism* [London: Labour Publishing Co., 1923], pp. 66 ff); C. Beals (*Rome or Death: The Story of Fascism* [London: John Long, 1923], pp. 35–38); P.H. Box (*Three Master Builders* [London: Jarrolds, 1925], pp. 135–37).
[10] Labriola, *Le due politiche*, p. 304–05.

that the accounts of the firms should be audited and made public. They also demanded that in each factory the workers should elect a committee to represent them in disciplinary disputes and in carrying out labor agreements. In order to induce them to leave the factories and return home, Giolitti promised them that he would introduce into parliament a bill providing for the "controllo delle Fabbriche"—that is, giving the representatives of the unions the right to get authentic information about the actual financial condition of the firms and the right to have a voice in matters of internal discipline in each factory. The British commercial attachés in Rome, Messrs. E.C. Cure and J.H. Henderson, in their *General Report on the Commercial, Industrial and Economic Situation in Italy in December 1920* (p. 19), wrote:

> The employees refuse to work because they believe that they are being exploited, even although many would accept a system under which the rights of the capital were recognized, provided that they were satisfied that it was being equitably administered. It is to be hoped that this difficulty will in part be removed by the introduction of the method of *Controllo operaio* put forward in the course of the recent metal workers' dispute and conceded in principle by the final agreement. *Controllo operaio*, strictly speaking, connotes a right to audit and investigation by the workmen rather than a share in management. . . . Negotiations have broken down on account of a demand by the workmen to extend the meaning of the word, and in particular to make it include a right on their part of having a voice in the engagement and dismissal of employees.

The Fascist agents and those "scholars" who have lapped up their "propaganda" have translated the Italian "controllo" by the English word "control," and so the saga has been created that the workers demanded the ownership, or at least the management, of the factories.

During the crisis in Turin, the strikers murdered a young Nationalist and a prison warden, and killed in street fightings three royal guards and a carabineer.[11] The two first crimes were of a peculiarly atrocious nature. There is no social upheaval in which the creeping in of crazy or criminal elements can be avoided. All over the rest of Italy no other bloodshed

[11] For these crimes, eleven people in March 1922 received sentences ranging from one year to thirty years imprisonment.

occurred. An American manufacturer, owner of a large plant in northern Italy, related his personal experience:

> The workers were simple enough to believe that in occupying the factories they had started a world revolution. At our place they did no malicious damage to the machinery. They tried to run the factory instead. During their theatricals I went out to play golf every day. Though I crossed the factory district in my car I was not molested (*Survey Graphic of New York*, March, 1927).

Turin was regarded as the citadel of the Italian Communists, and the Fiat motor car factory was one of the most rampant hotbeds of communism in Turin. On September 20, its manager, Signor Agnelli, went to the main factory ("Fiat Centro") to take it over again from the "Internal Commission" which had managed it during the occupation. The *Corriere della Sera* (October 1, 1920) writes: "His arrival was greeted with applause. On the table of his office lay a large bunch of red carnations (the Socialist emblem). On one wall the Soviet emblem, the sickle and hammer."

Signor Agnelli did not consider the applause sufficient compensation for the Communist sickle and hammer, and announced in the papers that he would resign his position of general manager of the company. A month later his mother died. We read in the *Corriere della Sera* (October 31, 1920):

> Three thousand workmen of the Fiat followed the funeral. In sign of mourning the trade union leaders called a stoppage of work during the funeral in all the fourteen factories of the concern. As the coffin was carried out of the church, one of the members of the "Internal Commission" of the main factory, who is a Socialist member of the county council, went up to Signor Agnelli and said so that all could hear: "Do come back to us." A representative of the clerical staff on behalf of all his fellows expressed the same desire, Signor Agnelli, overcome with emotion, did not speak, but gave a long handshake to the two men.

Such was Italian "bolshevism" in 1919–20: a childish bacchanal of applause, red carnations, Communist emblems, strikes, and demonstrations, lasting over twenty months and stained with the blood of about three hundred people killed in riots.

Mussolini approved of the occupation of the factories, but he charged the Socialist leaders with not being willing to strike a decisive blow. Michele Bianchi, one of his comrades, wrote:

> Our attitude from the first moment has been one of sympathy with the masses. . . . Today we say that the occupation is a formidable mistake, unless the organizers know how to use it as a stepping stone to another and infinitely vaster scheme. Must it be used for a social upheaval? If so, it would be a proof of admirable political sense and would be logical. But they (the organizers) have too mean a mentality to undertake such a task.[12]

During the days of the occupation of the factories, Mussolini sought out Bruno Buozzi, the leader of the movement. Their meeting took place at a hotel in Milan, in the presence of Manlio Morgagni of the *Popolo d'Italia* and his colleague Guarnieri. Mussolini made no "offer" of any kind, but he asked to be informed of the aims of the movement. He expressed the opinion that the workers ought never to be ejected from the factories again by force. If the aims of the agitation were purely economic, the Fascists would care little whether the factories belonged to the employers or the workers, but they would oppose with all their strength any experiment in Bolshevist government.[13]

On September 28, three days after the workers had left the factories, Mussolini maintained that Giolitti was responsible for the seizure of the factories; the dispute had been dragging on for many weeks, and Giolitti had never intervened to cut the knot: "An early intervention on the part of Giolitti could have put a stop to the foolish quibbles into which the industrialists had hardened themselves." Thus Giolitti should have cut the knot against the industrialists. Moreover, Giolitti "perhaps" could have

---

[12] *Popolo d'Italia*, September 2, 1920.

[13] This account was given by the daily *Giustizia*, a right-wing Socialist paper, on December 13, 1922. It was textually reprinted by the Conservative daily *Corriere della sera*, May 11, 1923, in a controversy with the *Popolo d'Italia*. Mussolini did not contradict it. Buozzi, in the spring of 1926, in London, granted its accuracy in a talk with the writer of the present book. It is not clear what Mussolini meant in threatening to oppose an experiment in Bolshevist government after saying that he did not care whether the factories belonged to the workers or the employers. Probably he was keeping a foot in either stirrup. If things were to go well for the workers, he would recall the first part of his speech to prove that he had been in favor of the workers; if things went ill with them —as actually happened—he could claim the merit of having opposed the Bolshevist danger.

prevented the seizure. Mussolini did not say how. Most likely he meant by ordering the army to occupy the factories:

> Twenty-four hours after the movement had been started, the task had become more doubtful. Everyday increased the difficulty of evicting the workers from the factories by force. The evils brought about by this passive attitude of the government have certainly been very serious, but nobody is in a position to maintain that the strong arm method would not have started a fire which would have been infinitely more dangerous. When different methods of repression have to be weighed, one must coldly examine whether the end is worth the means.

Anyhow, a revolution had taken place in Italy and the credit for it had to go—to whom? To Mussolini:

> What has happened in Italy in the September that is now ending has been a revolution, or, to be more precise, a phase of the revolution started—*by us*—in May 1915. There has been no street fighting, no barricades, nor anything of the theatrical appurtenances of revolution such as thrill us in Victor Hugo's *Les Misérables*. But a revolution has nonetheless been achieved, and we may add, a great revolution. A right, which has been sacred for centuries, has been broken down.

The reverse was the truth. The occupation of the factories was for the Italian workers a great practical lesson, in politics and in economics. They were brought up against the hard fact that their manual labor in conjunction with machinery was not enough to produce wealth. They needed technical direction, credit, and commercial organization.[14] The occupation of the factories marked the climax and then the beginning of the decline in the Italian postwar excitement.

In war, an army begins to win when its opponents cease to believe in victory and begin to retreat. Then those who might have fled, had the enemy resisted ten minutes longer, feel themselves as strong as lions and charge in pursuit. This was the case with the Italian employers. A Commu-

---

[14] "The failure of the experiment," wrote the above-quoted observer a few months later, "had a conspicuous historical importance. The working classes have learnt much in these weeks" (Bachi, *L'Italia economica nel 1920*, p. 348).

nist who gives the Maximalists the responsibility for all the mishaps which occurred during those years, but ignores as best he can the responsibility of the extremists, writes:

> The occupation of the factories marked the decline of the working-class movement, and the inglorious end of "maximalism," though its corpse continued to litter the ground until the Fascists swept it up. A distinct change soon came over the workers' psychology, "the beginnings of wisdom," in the words of Mussolini. Instead of disarming their adversaries, it had the effect of making them more agressive and drove them to reprisals. How and why did such a phenomenon occur? Because the occupation of the factories gave the *bourgeoisie* a psychological shock, which explains their fury and guided their successive steps. The sense of property and the authority of the industrialists was hit; evicted from their factories, they saw work going on, for better or for worse, in their absence. Now that the shadow of death had passed away, life flowed back into them. After a few days of bitterness and uncertainty, during which their chief feeling was a deep grudge against Giolitti, who had "failed to back them up" and had forced control of their industries on them by decree, their reaction took the form of a fight to the death against the working class and the "liberal state".[15]

Giolitti felt that now he could strike a big coup. On October 17, he had Malatesta arrested in Milan. No serious reaction broke out.

On October 20, a circular emanating from the army general staff urged the divisional commanders to favor the Fascists. The plan which had been drawn up by "the military expert in civil war" had been adopted by the War Office.[16]

---

[15] A. Rossi, *The Rise of Italian Fascism*, p. 76.

[16] This fact was revealed in 1921 by Giuseppe De Falco in *Il Fascismo milizia di classe*, p. 26 (in the volume *Il Fascismo e i partiti politici italiani*). Bonomi, secretary of war in 1920 in Giolitti's cabinet, explained the fact in 1924 as follows: "In October, 1920, one of the many departments of the general staff, without asking either the chief of the general staff or the War Office, requested information about the first Fasci di combattimento, in terms which might have been construed as favorable towards those first Fasci, which were then rather followers of D'Annunzio than Mussolini. A commandant in central Italy—or rather, as was subsequently ascertained, one of his subordinates—interpreting this request for information as an intimation to join the Fascists, drew up and sent out a circular eulogizing the Fascists, and directed it to the dependent military commands and to the three prefects of the region. The cabinet gave me, then minister for war, due notice of the circular; and in agreement with General Badoglio, chief of the general staff, I sent out a clearly-worded circular, signed by him, to all the military

AUTHOR'S NOTE TO CHAPTER 17

The fantasy of the Fascist agents has woven itself around the occupation of the factories more than any other incident.

Sir Percival Phillips, special correspondent of the notorious *Daily Mail,* in his book *The Red Dragon and the Black Shirts: How Italy Found her Soul: the True Story of the Fascist Movement* (London: Carmelite House, 1923, p. 13), says: "Communist policy is flinging men alive into blast-furnaces, as was done by a Red tribunal composed of women at Turin." We do not know whether in Russia or anywhere else Communist policy ever flung men alive into blast furnaces. What we do know is that at Turin no such thing ever happened. It is bad enough that during the occupation of the factories there a Red tribunal should have talked wild words about throwing two unfortunate men named Scimula and Sonzini into a blast furnace before it sentenced them to be shot (*Corriere della sera,* March 2, 3, 4, 1922). Why exaggerate facts in themselves terrible?

The French paper *L'Oeuvre,* November 18, 1926, reproduced from a French weekly a description of the following incident:

> The March on Rome, which put an end to this terrible regime is due to M. Fiat. The workers, not content with occupying his factory, gagged the great Italian industrialist, and outraged his wife and daughters before his eyes. Indignant, the great industrialist placed at Mussolini's disposal the necessary funds for overthrowing the regime.

L'Oeuvre observed that M. Fiat is no other than the F(abbrica) I(taliana) A(utomobili) T(orino) (The Italian Motorcar Company of Tu-

commands in Italy, pointing out the serious mistake which someone had committed and reaffirming that the army was and must remain outside any party competition" (*L'Azione*, a review of political, social and literary culture, Rome, March 9, 1924). In the weekly *La Rivoluzione Liberale* of Turin, March 18, 1924, Gobetti replied: "Bonomi expects us to be extraordinarily idiotic." Already in 1919 the plan of organizing a "white guard" against the "Bolshevists" existed among army chiefs. In December 1919, two men who had returned from the war, a teacher in Genoa and a railway executive in Florence, were requested by their former commanding officers to gather around them groups of white guards, to whom the military authorities would supply arms and money. Both refused. It is more than probable that in 1919 and 1920 a certain number of Fascist groups were organized in this way. But during the time Signor Nitti was prime minister, the military officials had no such orders from the minister of war, and therefore not many officials acted on their own initiative. Only when Signor Giolitti succeeded Signor Nitti, and after the occupation of the factories, were the high military authorities given a free hand to execute the plan they had had in readiness for a year.

rin); this company had neither wife nor daughters who could have been outraged. The journalist paid to write this piece of propaganda evidently knew nothing of the world-famous motor factory. As regards Signor Agnelli, manager of the Fiat Company, no one ever broke into his house, nor were his wife or daughters ever outraged.

Villari (*Awakening of Italy,* pp. 94–97), while describing the crisis, omits any reference to the writings and actions of Mussolini and his friends in those days. He makes no distinction between the attitude of the moderate Socialists and that of the others: "The Socialists regarded this form of direct action as 'beginning the long-hoped-for dictatorship of the proletariat' "; "the Socialist party attempted to gain control of the whole movement in the hope of converting it into a definite revolution and instituting a Soviet Republic." He states that the occupation of the factories was ordered by the Communist deputy Bombacci and other leaders of the F.I.O.M. (Italian Federation of Engineering Workers); that the proposal to give the occupation a revolutionary character was defended by the "Socialist party" and opposed by the General Confederation of Labor.

The statement that the Communist deputy Bombacci, together with other leaders of the F.I.O.M., ordered the occupation of the factories is sheer invention. Bombacci was not among the leaders of the F.I.O.M. and took no part in the unfortunate decision—if for no other reason than that, during the summer of 1920, he was in Russia.

Villari represents a half-million workers as a mass of assassins, drunkards, and thieves. Bachi, who had no brief for the workers, writes:

> The workmen's leaders tried to prevent acts of violence, sabotage and theft. Acts of violence against individuals were not numerous, but some of them were of exceptional gravity. Subsequently it was ascertained that the material damage to plant and the waste of raw material and manufactured goods had been rather extensive, but the very nature of the industries concerned, and the timely measures taken by the union leaders, kept theft within relatively narrow limits.[17]

[17] Bachi, *L'Italia economica nel 1920,* p. 347.

Villari asserts that as a result of the occupation of the factory, "the value of the lira on the Swiss exchange fell to 25 centimes; it had been 74 at the beginning of the year." Had he been an honest man and not a propaganda agent, he would have compared the rate of exchange of the lira in September and October of 1920, not only with January of 1920, but with the intervening and following months. He would then have shown that the lira had been falling steadily ever since 1919, owing to continual inflation, and that in September and October 1920, its fall was no more precipitous than the previous and following months. The purchasing price of 100 Swiss francs in Italian lire was: 1919: March, 132.30 lire; June, 151.32 lire; September, 174.86 lire; December, 241.67 lire; 1920: March, 321.24 lire; April, 410.50 lire; May, 352.78 lire; June, 309.98 lire; July, 305.53 lire; August, 341.98 lire; September, 373.74 lire; October, 408.33 lire; November, 427.55 lire; December, 441.02 lire; 1921: March, 446.86 lire; June, 339.64 lire (Bachi, *L'Italia economica nel 1919*, p. 106; *L'Italia economica nel 1920*, p. 119; *L'Italia economica nel 1921*, p. 100).

18

The "Anti-Bolshevist" Reaction

In August and September 1920, a commission of delegates from the Italian Socialist party, the Confederation of Labor, and the Italian cooperative movement was in Russia to discover the promised land:

> Even in material details, the Italian delegation proved its comprehension and solidarity. They had brought with them about a hundred enormous cases filled with food—canned goods, rice, oil, sugar, etc., medicines and soap, needles for the tailors' cooperatives, and other much-needed supplies. One needed to have witnessed the sufferings of the Russian people to judge how welcome these contributions were. Of the many delegations which came to Russia in this and subsequent periods, the Italians and the Swedes were the only ones who proved their fraternal solidarity in this manner.[1]

Between Serrati, who was the leader of the Italian Maximalists and, as editor-in-chief of the *Avanti*, the most influential man in the Italian Socialist party, and Lenin and Zinoviev, president of the Communist International, a sharp dissension made itself felt when they came to discuss the ways and means to bring about social revolution in Italy. Lenin had solved the problem as long ago as the autumn of 1919 in the letter published by

[1] A. Balabanoff, *My life as a Rebel* (New York: Harper & Row, Publishers, 1938), p. 262.

the *Avanti* at that time (see Chapter 15): it was necessary to expel from the Socialist party Turati and the other "parliamentary opportunists." In May 1920, he developed this idea more fully in a booklet on *The Infantile Malady of Communism*, in which he not only accused the right-wing Socialists of having betrayed the proletariat, but blamed the Italian Socialist party for being "inconsistent" in its refusal to expel Turati and his followers.[2] Zinoviev, naturally, was in agreement with Lenin. Both of them were like doctors who cured sick people by standing down in the street, calling them to the window to stick out their tongues, and prescribing medicine from below. Serrati knew that it was impossible to expel Turati and his followers from the Socialist party without creating a deep gash, not only within the party, but also in the trade unions. The Confederation of Labor would have lost its most able directors and would have been thrown into a dangerous crisis, which would turn out to the advantage of the employers and the anti-Socialist parties. Therefore, Serrati refused to be dragged down a street which he thought disastrous.[3] A Communist who opposed Lenin at that moment would have had to be a man of exceptional stubbornness. Serrati was not a man of great intelligence. But he was courageous and honest, and he held his ground. Angelica Balabanoff was then in Russia among the leaders of the Third International. She had lived in Italy for many years. She stood with Serrati. She was shocked by the low tricks by means of which Lenin and Zinoviev endeavored to abuse Serrati's devotion to Soviet Russia in order to make him a tool of division in his own country. Lenin and Zinoviev succeeded in winning over only two of the Italians: Bombacci, the emptyheaded elementary school teacher, who afterwards was to go over to fascism; and an ambitious university professor of economics, Graziadei, who had once been a right-winger and afterwards, when the Fascist reaction set in, withdrew into his shell, managed to save his skin, and is now quietly living in Italy:

> These two individuals had been chosen, rather than others, because of their weakness and vanity, their inability to resist flattery and applause. They had been received and flattered in the Kremlin, the ex-residence of the Tsar, in a setting

[2] N. Lenine, *La maladie infantile du Communisme* (Paris, Bibliotheque Communiste, 1920), p. 78, 131 ff.

[3] The documents of the controversy between Serrati on the one hand, and Zinoviev and Lenin on the other, are found in the volume *Le Parti Socialiste Italien et l'Internationale Communiste* (Petrograd: Editions de l'Internationale Communiste, 1921).

which spoke of power and money! Whereas Lenin looked upon these two men as tools whom he could use and then get rid of, the two pilgrims themselves imagined that they were chosen for their positive qualities to be the leaders of the Italian movement, under the Bolshevik wing. While we were absent, they were shown to Russian audiences as authentic representatives of the revolution—in opposition to Serrati, who had "betrayed" it. Their speeches were translated into whatever Zinoviev wished them to say. They became completely inebriated with the ovations of the crowds and the flattery of Zinoviev's satraps.[4]

When Moscow's pilgrims came back to Italy, the delegates from the Confederation of Labor and the cooperative societies, all right-wingers, did not keep for themselves their own findings. Though (to the great horror of Angelica Balabanoff and Emma Goldman) they had been made to travel on boats and trains all spotlessly clean, well-equipped, and stocked with the best of food, they had not been fooled. They told harrowing tales of the conditions among the Russian people. Serrati did not say anything about what he had seen. His silence was significant enough. The Bolshevist myth received a severe blow.

The controversy between the extremists and Serrati grew violent. Serrati went on insisting that the "unity of the Italian proletariat" must not be jeopardized by unsound measures planned without foresight. The occupation of the factories had been a grandiose movement, but it had been directed by right-wing Socialists. It had had economic, and not political, ends, developing peacefully everywhere, with the exception of a few local incidents. To be sure, Italy was in a revolutionary situation. But "the revolution cannot result from a magic signal given by a chief, although personal influence is not without effect. The revolution depends on very complex circumstances and numerous factors which, at a given moment, provoke the crisis." The task of the Socialist party was not so much to push the mass towards violent struggle as it was to "prepare all the forces of the future Socialist order, to consolidate the new regime and to lead it to its final triumph." With this aim, the party could not do without those men who, for many long years, had managed unions, cooperative societies, and municipalities. These were the only men capable of conducting the affairs of the new society when the old had fallen. "Picture to yourselves the city

4 Balabanoff, *My life as a Rebel*, pp. 265–66.

of Milan under the direction of a handful of inept parvenus who have waited for the last moment to profess themselves as fervent Communists."[5] These controversies were not devised to keep the revolutionary temperature high in Italy.

Two facts in the autumn of 1920 showed that a new frame of mind had already been created in Italy among the non-Socialist parties. At the municipal elections which took place in September and October all over the country, the Socialists only won 2,022 municipalities (24.3 percent); the Populists 1,613 (19.4 percent); and all the other parties which had formed "patriotic" or "anti-Bolshevist" blocks, 4,692 (56.3 percent).[6] The Socialists showed particular strength in Lombardy and Emilia, and the Populists in Venetia. But all over Italy and even in northern Italy, the Socialists were beaten in almost all the most important cities: Venice, Turin, Genoa, Florence, Rome, Naples, Palermo. In Turin they were defeated by a narrow margin—48,899 against 48,792 votes—thanks to the Populists who, making this sole exception to their tactics of independence, joined the "anti-Bolshevist" block and saved the situation. In Milan the Socialists won with barely a 3,000-vote plurality, on a poll of 144,000 votes. Both in Turin and in Milan the working people formed the clear majority of the population. Obviously part of them had voted "anti-Bolshevist." The only overwhelming Socialist victory in a big town was at Bologna. As far as one went, from northern to central and southern Italy, "anti-Bolshevist" and "patriotic blocks" carried the day. A few days after the municipal elections were over, on November 4 Armistice Day was solemnly celebrated all over Italy. The previous year, no celebration had been held. The country was upset by the electoral campaign, and Nitti, not wrongly, feared that the celebration would give rise to protests against the war and dangerous street riots. In 1920, no Anarchist, Communist, or Socialist thought of disturbing the ceremony. The wave of antipatriotism that for nearly two years seemed to have submerged the country had now clearly subsided. On November 10, the *Popolo d'Italia* remarked that "the Italian domestic situation was improving daily."

Now the moment was ripe for the government to resume its proper functions—to maintain public peace and respect for the law as opposed to any form of disorder. Once the respect for law and order had been restored, it would have been necessary to wait patiently until the healing process had

---

[5] *Le Parti Socialiste Italien et l'Internationale Communiste*, pp. 14, 24, 28, 87.
[6] Giusti, *Le correnti politiche italiane*, pp. 32–33.

done its work and the people had, little by little, found their way back to the path of common sense. Restoration of public peace had become an easy task, since the left-wing parties were disheartened.

It is true that the gate could not all at once be put back upon its hinges. Time is the only healer of certain diseases. And it would have been a great and precious lesson to our people if they could have rid themselves of Communist dreams and revolutionary illusions by free experience and spontaneous conviction. Some credit was due to them, for they had shown much firmness and spirit of sacrifice after Caporetto. Patience and calm was the obvious duty, especially for those politicians who had known neither how to make war nor how to make peace, and who were mainly and directly responsible for the postwar neurasthenia with which the Italian people were afflicted.

It was the misfortune of Italy that a man like Giolitti happened to be in power just at that moment. Experience had shown that the Chamber of Deputies, as elected in November 1919, was not workable. A new national election was needed if a less disorderly house was to be had at hand. Before the World War, Giolitti had been accustomed to "manage" parliamentary elections without any scruples and with complete success. He thought that the Fascists would help him to reduce the number of deputies in the Chamber belonging to the Socialist party. The Fascists were eager to "teach the Bolshevists a lesson." Let them teach that lesson. When the job had been done, the Fascists could easily be disposed of. After all, they formed only a small minority in the country. The military chiefs also were willing to lend a helping hand in stamping down the "Bolshevists." On the condition they ceased disobeying the civil government in the question of Fiume, they would be useful when cooperationg with it for a common purpose. The only thing needed was to leave them to equip the Fascists with rifles, machine guns, bombs, and trucks, and place in command of them retired officers and officers on leave. As far as the police and the judiciary were concerned, it would be enough for them to take no notice of disturbances started by the Fascists and to intervene only when it was a question of disarming, trying, and sentencing those who attempted to resist. Fresh national elections could not be "manipulated" overnight. Several months were needed to prepare them.

A first effect of the understanding between Giolitti and the Fascists was seen at Trieste on October 14. Here, inside the Socialist party, the extremists prevailed. They had announced a meeting of protest in favor of Russia.

Giunta, on behalf of the Fascists, intimated that "no meeting would be held either today or tomorrow, because it would be against Italy. We are determined to shoot, if necessary, whoever withstands our shock; we are ready to kill and to die" (*Avanti*, October 16, 1920). The police forbade the meeting. The extremist daily, *Il Lavoratore*, summoned the proletariat "to come down into the streets against the enemy." The workers left the factories. Street fighting occurred here and there. The Fascists attacked the premises of *Il Lavoratore*, and burned down everything. The police were conspicuous by their absence. The general strike, as usual, died down. The maneuver had been planned by Giunta in agreement with Giolitti, who had called him to Rome to give him instructions about what to do.[7]

At this point a horrible massacre in Bologna, on November 21, 1920, precipitated the "anti-Bolshevist" reaction.

The municipal elections in Bologna, had, as we have said, given the Socialists a sweeping victory. A group of Fascists, exasperated by this victory, on November 4 attacked the Chamber of Labor. The secretary of the Chamber, a Communist named Bucco, who had wearied and irritated the city by his overbearingness, showed himself on this occasion a coward unable to organize resistance. After having abused the police for two years, he telephoned to them for help against the Fascist assault. The police arrived and confiscated a store of arms and explosives. Whilst the police were searching the premises, the Fascists looted them.

To retrieve this moral setback, the Socialists decided to celebrate the opening meeting of the new town council by a grand demonstration, to take place on November 21. An "anti-Bolshevist" paper of the city, *Il Progresso* started a campaign to prevent the Socialists from waving red flags in their demonstration. The police induced the Socialists and Fascists to come to a compromise: the Socialists renounced their procession and confined themselves to holding a meeting in front of the town hall (Palazzo d'Accursio); the red flags were to appear on the balcony of the town hall only while the new mayor and the other official speakers were making their speeches; as soon as the speeches were over the flags would be taken away and the meeting would dissolve.

Notwithstanding this agreement, the populace remained suspicious and excited. Dark rumors of assaults and counterassaults were circulated. On

---

[7] The source of this information is, for us, Guglielmo Ferrero. He got it from Olindo Malagodi, editor of the Rome daily *La Tribuna*, who belonged to Giolitti's most intimate circle.

the afternoon of Saturday, November 20, the directorate of the Fascio circulated the following typewritten manifesto:

> Citizens, the Reds, beaten and disbanded in all the squares and streets of our city, call up their hordes from the country-side, to take their revenge and hoist their red rag on the town hall. We shall not endure this insult! It is an insult to every Italian citizen, and to our country, which will have nothing to do with Lenin and with bolshevism. On Sunday, the women and all those who love peace and quiet, are requested to stay at home, and, if they wish to deserve well of their country, to hang out of their windows the Italian flag. On Sunday in the streets of Bologna there shall be only Fascists and anti-Fascists. It will be the test! The great test in the name of Italy.

On Sunday, November 21, at 3:00 P.M., the new municipal councillors met to elect the new mayor. The hall was full of people, and in the square outside thousands were gathered. Cordons of troops on foot and on horseback, carabineers, and royal guards closed all the streets leading to the square, to prevent the Fascists and Nationalists from coming into contact with the crowd gathered there.

At 3:30 P.M., a group of about five hundred Fascists, Nationalists, and army officers in uniform flung themselves against one barrier of soldiers and broke through. They reached the entrance to the square and tried to break through the second barrier, just as the new mayor came to the window, accompanied by the red flags, to speak to the crowd. Three revolver shots rang out from the assailants. These shots, in the general nervousness, produced a wave of panic. Some carabineers and royal guards opened fire on the town hall. The crowd in the square rushed for shelter to the inner courtyard of the town hall. Onto the terrified mass fell bombs from a window of the town hall. Among the crowd, ten were killed and fifty-eight wounded. Some were victims of the firing of the carabineers and royal guards. The greater number were struck by fragments of the bombs.

Meanwhile, in the council chamber, shouting and disorder reigned. Some struggled to the doors to escape, some threw themselves on the floor to avoid bullets coming in at the windows. Suddenly two men armed with revolvers (or perhaps only one who changed places as he shot) came forward toward the bench occupied by members of the anti-Socialist minority and began to shoot at them. One of the minority, a distinguished officer in the war, was killed; two others were wounded.

When the town hall was searched by the police, they discovered that a Communist, a certain Martelli, one of those unbalanced fellows who are only too numerous among revolutionary parties, had laid in a store of bombs in case the town hall was stormed. He was an intimate friend of an agent provocateur, a certain Galli, who, a short time afterward, killed his mistress and burned her body, but was never prosecuted for this crime. Was it he who dropped the bombs on the crowd?

These are the facts, as they can be reconstructed today, in cold blood, from the records of the public trial, which took place in Milan from January 30 to March 14, 1923.[8] In November 1920, under the immediate impression of the tragedy, it was not possible to distribute the responsibility dispassionately. Political bias had free play. The "anti-Bolshevist" parties and papers shifted the responsibilities from the actual authors of the crime to their party as a whole. All the Socialists, whether right-wingers, Maximalists, or extremists, were, without distinction, involved in a storm of moral indignation. Giolitti caught the ball on the fly and dissolved the municipal council. The city was now managed by a commissioner who worked hand in hand with Nationalists and Fascists. The judiciary, by issuing warrants of arrest for hundreds of people who rightly or wrongly were charged with responsibility in the massacre, did the rest. Nationalists and Fascists became the masters of the city. They banned from the city all the leaders of the Socialist party and kept the working people in a permanent state of terror.

A few weeks later, the city of Ferrara witnessed a perfect replica of what had happened at Bologna. On December 19, two Socialist attorneys, who were deputies, had been manhandled in Bologna while leaving the court where they had acted as counsel for defense for workers. As soon as the news of the attack reached Ferrara, during the night, the Socialist leaders summoned all the organizations of the city and neighboring villages and towns to a mass protest meeting for the afternoon of the following day. The police did not forbid the meeting, but on the morning of December 20, 1,000 Fascists gathered in the city on trucks from nearby and far-away districts. The trucks had been provided by employers and military authorities. The police allowed them to enter the city. They plastered posters saying, "An eye for an eye, a tooth for a tooth, blood for blood." At 2:00

---

[8] They were published in full by the press of the time. We have used the record in the *Corriere della sera.*

P.M., 4,000 people were gathered in the theater, and a great crowd, for which there was no room in the theater, was waiting outside. The Fascists marched toward them. The people opened their ranks, allowing them to pass. A red flag was in the crowd. The Fascists tried to get hold of it. A fight around the flag ensued. A revolver shot was fired. Then, from a nearby municipal building, a communist began firing blindly upon the crowd. There resulted three dead and three wounded among the Fascists, two dead and six wounded among the Socialists. Then the police came in and arrested seventy-six secretaries of unions and Socialist mayors in the district of Ferrara. When the leaders were thus put out of the way, the Fascists attacked the towns of the province one after another. Every Monday, market day in Ferrara, hundreds of peasants who were coming from the surrounding countryside were beaten up. The police gave the Fascists the names of the persons who were to be assaulted.

In a few weeks, the reaction got hold of the provinces of Bologna, Ferrara, and Cremona—that is, of the richest agricultural sections of Italy, in which the unions of the day laborers were the most powerful and the most exacting. From now on, the small landowners and tenant farmers refused to grant the demands of the unions and withdrew the concessions they had made during the preceding two years; their economic interests sharpened their spirit of revenge. The large landowners soon joined. Following the example of the landowners and farmers of the Valley of the Po, those of western Lombardy, Tuscany, Apulia, and Sicily stiffened their resistance against their day laborers and metayers. The industrial employers also began not only to refuse any further increase in wages, but to impose wage cuts and to enforce a more rigid discipline in the factories. No one said anything further about "controllo" in the factories.

At the same time the question of Fiume petered out. In November 1920, Sforza, in agreement with the representatives of Yugoslavia, had settled the Adriatic question by the Treaty of Rapallo. To everybody's amazement, Mussolini, on November 13, 1920, announced that, under present conditions, it was necessary to accept the Treaty of Rapallo; the problems could be taken up again in the future.[9] Giolitti, asked what Mussolini would do at the moment of the final crisis, smiled and rubbed his thumb against his

---

[9] "Even the organ of fascism, which, with the greatest violence, has agitated the question of Dalmatia for two years, becomes pliant, abjures its thesis, preaches resignation, abandons D'Annunzio" Attilio Tamaro, "Il Trattato di Rapallo," in *Politica* 6 (November 1920): 246.

index finger, a gesture which the Italians make when they want to indicate "money." An overwhelming majority in the Chamber of Deputies and the Senate gave their sanction to the Treaty of Rapallo in December 1920. D'Annunzio protested that he would die rather than surrender. Giolitti knew how to take care of him. He reminded the king that he, as a constitutional monarch and as supreme chief of the armed forces, was in duty bound to summon the military chiefs to their oath of loyalty to himself and the constitution. The king did his duty. Millo forgot that he had given D'Annunzio his word of honor and submitted. The other military chiefs did not dare to disobey. Some of D'Annunzio's soldiers died in a clash with the Italian regular army. When he realized that the regular army meant business, D'Annunzio announced that Italy "was not worthy that he should die for her" and vanished from the scene. In Italy no serious disturbance occurred. This Cape of Storms also was safely navigated.

Mussolini, with that sense of the psychological moment which he possessed to a high degree, wrote as follows on December 31:

> It is honest to add that during the last three months—to be exact since the referendum which led to the ending of the occupation of the factories and since the return of the mission to Russia—the psychology of the working classes in Italy has changed profoundly. The wave of idleness and shirking seems to have died down. The working masses seem convinced that the fundamental problem of the moment is that of production. A clear symptom of this state of mind is the comparative ease with which agreements lately have been reached after peaceful negotiations in the important trades of textiles and chemicals.

The *Corriere della sera*, on December 31, 1920, said: "In the last few months, a spontaneous reaction on the part of the Italian people has succeeded in greatly diminishing Socialist tyranny. The high-water mark of revolutionism, represented by the occupation of the factories, has been followed by a rapid decline."

In January, at the National Congress of the Socialist party held in Leghorn, the attacks of the extremists against right-wingers and Maximalists came to a head. The right-wingers got 14,625 votes, the Maximalists 98,028 votes, and the extremists 58,183 votes. If one compares the situation as shown by the Congress of Bologna in October 1919 with that of January

1921, one finds that during the intervening year, the strength of the right-wing Socialists had been neither increased nor diminished. They were 14,880 in October 1919, and they were still 14,625 in January 1921. But the Maximalists had swelled from 48,411 to 98,028, and the extremists from 3,417 to 58,183. Most Maximalists and extremists were converts of the last year, improvised "war-Socialists." During the following months, they went out as easily as they had come in. Those who withstood the Fascist tide with greater stubbornness were mainly men of the "old guard."

As a result of the Leghorn Congress, the extremists left the Socialist party and formed the "Italian Communist party." This split among Socialists, coming after the occupation of the factories, the information brought from Russia by the trade union and cooperative leaders, and the moral disasters of Bologna and Ferrara, did not foster more sanguine hopes among the workers in city and town. The idea spread that revolution had become impossible.

At the beginning of 1921, Mussolini shifted his fighting front. As long as social revolution had seemed possible, he had attacked from the left the Socialists and Communists, charging them with being inefficient revolutionaries. When social revolution proved to be impossible, he began to attack the Socialists and Communists from the right, charging them with being responsible for strikes and political disorder. He scented the new direction of the wind and adapted his tactics to the changed situation. Now that Mussolini's "revolution" was openly directed, not against capitalist society, but against the Socialist movement, the Italian industrialists and big landowners generalized the method of subsidies. To be sure, the Fascists were still making a display of revolutionary fireworks. But nothing was more natural than the formation of a *union sacrée* against the common foe between those who were willing to attack it from the right and those who for two years had fought it from the left. Thus the Fascist local branches became the rallying point of all the "anti-Bolshevist" forces seeking to organize themselves.

The "arditi," who until December 1920 had been with D'Annunzio in Fiume and had been forced to leave the city, now were out of a job. Part of them found in the Fascist ranks fresh and well-paid employment. They imported into the Fascist movement the black shirt, the dagger, the club, the song "Giovinezza," the Roman salute, the castor oil, the cruelty—all their implements, slogans, and practices.

Not only half-starved discharged army officers, but also unemployed workers, found in Fascist activities a means of livelihood. In Italy, as elsewhere, an industrial crisis was setting in and leading to unemployment. Unemployment, as always, undermined the fighting spirit of the workers. Employers and Fascists took advantage of this situation. Many war-Socialists now found their true souls and joined the Fascist movement. The certainty of impunity was added to the love of adventure and to the allurement of good pay.[10]

To these elements, which all in all represented, but on a larger scale, the situation prevailing during the previous two years, were added now elements which originated from the classes of the landowners, shopkeepers, and artisans. In the summer of 1921, a careful observer wrote:

> After a few months nearly everywhere in the country districts, in Emilia, in Venetia, in Apulia, the greater part of the Fasci were formed by protégés of the agrarians. Fascism changed markedly from what it was before October, 1920. The undergraduate element was no longer its main strength. Even the leadership of the Fascists here and there changed hands. Not even in the towns were their adherents the same as they used to be. The earlier Fascists were for the most part more disinterested and were moved by the patriotic spirit which had been fanned and exaggerated by the war—a patriotism undoubtedly ill-understood and vague, but sincere. They were reduced to a minority by the influx of new elements.[11]

Such a vast and rapid influx of wealthy and conservative people into an organization of impecunious youths who believed themselves revolutionaries bewildered and scandalized many "Fascists of the first hour." One may see in Umberto Banchelli's book[12] the protests against the "sons and hangers-on of the bigwigs," who, if they came in great numbers to the meetings of the Fascists, were never in the dangerous expeditions:

---

[10] Por, *Fascism*, p. 107: "They joined the Fascists, not only because they were without political training, but also because they wanted to have a hand in what was going on, and saw no prospect of realizing their Communist hopes."

[11] Fabbri, *Controrivoluzione preventiva*, p. 37.

[12] *Memorie di un Fascista*, (Florence, ed. Sassaiola Fiorentina, 1922), p. 12, 15, 35. This book is a typical document showing the incredible mental and moral confusion created in many intelligent and generous young men by the chaotic propaganda of such men as D'Annunzio and Mussolini.

> They had come into the Fascio for their own ends, one of
> which was to exercise class justice, that is to carry out repris-
> als, not as Fascists, but as sons of the lawyer, of the doctor,
> or the war profiteer. If they met men in working clothes,
> they fell on them and began beating them. Their mentality
> was on a par with that of the Communists, who had beaten
> and murdered anybody who was decently dressed. One saw
> on arriving at the Fascist headquarters the well-known surly
> and rapacious faces of war profiteers; these were shabbily
> clothed and shod, but all had the inevitable diamond on
> their finger, and we were obliged to accept their money
> because we needed it to stifle an evil worse than they.[13]

The Italian capitalist class was of recent formation. Most of it owed its
wealth primarily to protective duties and government contracts, and it had
not yet acquired by a long political and economic experience a consciousness of its social dignity, of its rights and obligations. In particular the "new
rich" of the war—the *pescicani* or "sharks" as they were called in Italy—
were people of scant intellectual or moral refinement. Having achieved
wealth and power more often by luck than by merit, they were incapable
of holding their ground in a system of free competition and political liberty.
These profiteers, who formed the bulk of the capitalist classes in Italy at
that time, when their terror of "bolshevism" had turned to anger, were not
content to lead the workers back to a more reasonable frame of mind. On
the contrary, they purposed to exploit their victory to the utmost and to
destroy the workers' organization. Even more savage than the industrialists
were the landowners, accustomed by secular tradition to consider themselves absolute masters of their lands and to treat the peasants as beasts of
burden with no civil rights and no sense of human dignity. They, too, were
not content to defend their own liberty and property: what they wanted
was revenge on the serfs who had dreamed of becoming masters. "We will
put you to draw the plough with the oxen!" said the farmers of Cremona
to their laborers, and they set off to enroll themselves among the Fascists.
If the danger of revolution had never been great, the fear of it had been
great, and it lasted well after 1920. Fear is a bad counsellor.

---

[13] Signor Villari wrote in the *Manchester Guardian*, March 27, 1926, as follows: "Nor did
many of the capitalists sympathize with Fascism; at all events, they were certainly not
the organizers of the movement." The equivocation consists precisely in the use of the
word *many*. It is quite true that not *all* the capitalists, without exception, subsidized
Fascism. As to the "organizers of the movement," we shall see who they were.

The professional soldiers who armed and officered the Fascist bands imported their mentality into the Fascist movement, and with it that methodical ferocity which was unknown to Italian political struggles before 1921. It was the military authorities who gave the Fascists their strongly hierarchical organization. Without this aid, the armed organization of the Fascist force could never have come into being, nor would the Fascist party machine have differed essentially from that of any other Italian party.

19

The
Red Dragon
and
the Blackshirt

Wherever there was a conflict between employers and laborers, "Blackshirt squadrons" ("squadre") made their appearance, attacking the secretaries of the unions, beating them up, murdering them, looting their houses, forcing them to flee or hide, and thus breaking the backbone of the working-class organizations. Members of Parliament and editors of papers were confronted with the same fate as trade union leaders. All working-class organizations were branded as "Bolshevist" and subjected to indiscriminate attack. The offensive, which at the beginning had involved the Socialist unions, in the spring of 1921 began to invest also those unions which were controlled by the Populists. At the same time, the offensive passed from the unions to the consumers' cooperative societies. Shopkeepers, joining up with the Fascist movement, brought into it their hatred for those institutions which were their rivals. It was "a pitiless counterrevolution to a revolution which had failed" (Por, *Fascism*, p. 106). It was "the harshest, the most inexorable, the most scientific of violences" (C. Malaparte, *La Technique du Coup d'État* [Paris: Grasset, 1931], p. 221).

Luigi Fabbri, who lived in Bologna, one of the most lively centers of the Fascist movement, wrote, in the summer of 1921, the following description of the Fascist offensive:

> Where, as in Reggio-Emilia and Modena, the right-wing
> Socialist organizations prevailed, these were the ones at-

tacked; at Bologna and Ferrara, those of the Maximalists; at Treviso, the Republicans; in the province of Bergamo, the Populists; at Carrara and in Valdarno, the Anarchists; at Piacenza, Sestri and Parma, the Syndicalist organizations, not excepting those that had taken part in the war and favored D'Annunzio; at Turin, it was the Communist organizations; in some places—Padua, for instance—even the totally nonpolitical cooperative associations, directed by Conservatives, were not spared. The fury of destruction made no distinction between the various institutions; it was enough that they were run by working men, whether they were unions or federations, libraries or newspapers, retailers' or producers' cooperatives, working men's clubs or recreation halls, cafes and taverns or private houses. The pretexts vary from place to place. At Bologna or around Reggio they tell you that they had to scatter the Socialists, the cowards who could not or would not make a revolution; at Carrara and in the Valdarno they proclaim that it is time to have done with the Anarchists who threaten fresh upheavals; at Turin or Florence they declaim against the Russian Communist myth; at Rome or Milan against the Reformist Socialists and against Nitti. And so they go on, in every district, sparing only the minority groups, who, because they are minorities—whether Socialists, Anarchists, Republicans, or Populists—have nothing to defend but ideas, and do not represent any concrete interests to be destroyed.[1]

During the two years of their "tyranny," the "Bolshevists" did not once sack an office of any association belonging to industrialists, agrarians, or traders; they never forcibly compelled the resignation of any local council controlled by the Conservative parties; they did not burn a single newspaper printing press; they never looted a single house belonging to a political adversary. Such deeds of "heroism" were introduced into Italian life by the "anti-Bolshevists." It should further be noted that, while the "Bolshevist" crimes of 1919–20 were nearly always the work of an excited populace, the "heroic" deeds of the "anti-Bolshevists" were too often planned and carried out in cold blood by members of the better classes, who claimed to be the custodians of civilization.[2]

[1] Fabbri, *La Controrivoluzione preventiva*, p. 55; Mowrer, *Immortal Italy*, pp. 357–60.
[2] "If Socialist violence often verged on the bounds of criminality and sometimes overstepped them in the barbarity of its reprisals, our civilized conscience took refuge in the thought that the masses could be slowly educated and raised above the blind cruelty of instinct and of obtuse selfishness. But no excuses, no consolation come to our aid when we think of

Luigi Fabbri, in the summer of 1922, wrote:

> The hatred which the Fascists are sowing by their daily bludgeonings, by destroying the offices of labor organizations, by violating all freedom of assembly, of speech, of the press, by rendering the working of political parties in certain districts difficult or impossible, by preventing even the normal evening amusements of working men, attacking them in cafés or in taverns and forcing them to go home, by breaking into their homes, etc.—this daily growing hatred can find no vent in the light of day. Open reprisals would require that relative impunity, that freedom of movement, for defense or offense, which the Fascists enjoy by the connivance or tolerance of the police. Moreover the workers realize that they run the risk of death whether they use the cudgel or revolver, because the Fascists go to extremes at the smallest resistance. The workers know that if they make use of force in self-defense, they will inevitably be arrested. They lack means of communication, transport, rapid mobilization; for the most part they are taken by surprise. They cannot leave permanent guards to defend their villages while they are at work. The sackings are carried out either by day, when all the workers are away from the village at their work, or in the dead of night, when all are asleep. The workers, driven by passion and despair, act as best they can, whenever they find themselves in equal or superior numbers and wherever there is no probability of the intervention of the police. Since open fighting is forbidden and practically impossible, hatred finds a vent in the so-called ambushes. Let it be noted, moreover, that the partisan press very often gives the name of "ambush" to fair fights on open ground, to acts of legitimate and spontaneous defense on the part of the workers who are attacked and have no choice but to kill or be killed. The word "ambush" has been used even in the case of a Fascist who, having forced his way into a private house by breaking the door, was killed by the inmates in their desperate attempt to defend themselves.[3]

acts of premeditated and armed violence—callously perpetrated by well-to-do men whose superior training, education, social position, habits, standards of life, did not restrain them from murder, and what is even worse, from bludgeoning. If an ambush of trade unionists is always a shameful thing, a punitive expedition officered by university men, who have learned by heart Carducci's "Song of Love," brings a chill solitude to the heart." Missiroli, *Il Fascismo e la crisi italiana*, 1921, in the book *Il Fascismo e i partiti politici italiani*, p. 36. Missiroli later became one of Mussolini's henchmen.

[3] Fabbri, *La Controrivoluzione preventiva*, pp. 59–61.

Fabbri is an Anarchist, and therefore colors events so as to throw all the blame on the Fascists and exonerate the anti-Fascists. But an American eyewitness, who was not an Anarchist, wrote in 1921:

> The Italian common people are ignorant, long-suffering and easily bullied, but they are not cowards. After the first surprise they would have held their own with the Fascists, had not the latter been aided by the police. It was only against the carabineers and royal guards that they proved, once they awakened to the situation, entirely helpless. Then they began to use the universal weapon of the hopelessly oppressed, assassination.[4]

Villari (The *Awakening of Italy*, pp. 113, 115) describes the Fascist exploits as follows:

> The Fascists, armed with bludgeons or revolvers, would enter the town or village where the crime had been committed, arrest the murderers when they could find them, kill them if they resisted, and if not, hand them over to the carabineers. If the actual authors of the deed were not discovered, the leading Socialists or Communists of the place would be seized, and soundly thrashed, and sometimes the *Camera del Lavoro*, or other red institutions burnt down, or at all events, the records and furniture thrown into the street and set on fire. . . . What struck all observers was the manly bearing of these youths, their cleanliness and good manners.

Not only were those who resisted murdered, but so were persons who had had no part in the original conflict; the Fascists followed the plan of taking hostages, like armies of occupation in enemy countries. The Chambers of Labor and the other institutions of the working people were burnt, not *sometimes*, but *always:* the whole aim of the offensive, whether or not provoked by previous incidents between Fascists and anti-Fascists, was nothing but to destroy the workers' organizations by burning their records, looting the cooperative shops, and killing or banishing their organizers. Nor were the offices of the organizations the only places sacked; frequently the private houses of the leading Socialists, Communists, or Populists were burnt and their owners murdered, even when "the actual authors of the

---

[4] Mowrer, *Immortal Italy,* p. 369.

deed," used as a pretext for reprisals, were discovered.

Wherever Fascist pressure showed itself, the workers' organizations collapsed like castles made of cards. At the same time, new Fascist unions were being created which were called "economic syndicates." Their chief organizer was Edmondo Rossoni. Their budgets, as well as the salaries paid their officials, were shrouded in mystery. It is scarcely too much to trace the larger portion of their income to subsidies from industrialists, landowners, shopkeepers, and bankers. The first of these "syndicates" arose in February 1921 in the little town of San Bartolomeo in Bosco, in the province of Ferrara. These early specimens of Fascist trade unionism were facetiously dubbed "prisoners of war." Speaking of them on May 6, 1928, Mussolini admitted that "a member of them had no clear idea of where they were going."

The Fascist movement now took on a new character. Until the autumn of 1920, the cities had been the field of action for the Fascists, and their struggle against Communists and Socialists had developed on political grounds. Now the movement spread from the cities into the country, and it was no longer a mere political "anti-Bolshevist" movement; it became also an economic movement against all the workers' organizations regardless of party. All of them were indiscriminately branded as "Bolshevist."

The Nationalist leaders gave their followers the pass word to enter the Fascist groups *en masse*, without, however, giving up their affiliation with the Nationalist party. What the Nationalists thought at that time about fascism, and their purpose in associating themselves with it, was clearly stated in February 1922 by one of them, Balbino Giuliano, who later was to be minister of education in Mussolini's cabinet:

> Fascism is nationalism not yet well understood. . . . Fascism owes its popularity not only to the truth which it contains, but also to the defects which dim its light. Without their republican verbiage, without their empty revolutionary talk, without their vain threats against bourgeoisie and their *beau geste* of romantic rebellion, the Fascists would have shared the same unpopularity that nationalism only now is beginning to overcome. But now more than ever, we must preserve pure and intact our nationalistic program. We may come out in the open field side by side with the Fascists any time that it is necessary to defend those fundamental principles which we have both in common, but we must remain distinct from them and must continue our work of clarifica-

tion, without assuming the responsibility, either of the facts which have given to fascism its great popularity, or of the facts which might rob it of its popularity tomorrow.[5]

The Nationalist leaders aimed at securing control of the movement without assuming direct responsibility for the acts of violence that the Fascist bands were committing. Officially, they were not Fascist. In actual fact, they pulled the strings behind the scenes in accord with big business and the army chiefs.

How many Fascists there were in Italy at the end of 1920 is not easy to ascertain. On November 8, 1921, Mussolini's newspaper stated that the Fascists had been 30,000 in May 1920. But in a speech of March 9, 1924, Mussolini affirmed that on December 31, 1920, they had been 20,615. In 1932, the official statistics given by the administrative office of the Fascist party gave 60,000 members for December 1920. To try to find the truth in this sea of conflicting statements is a hopeless task. One thing however is clear: even if we accept as true the number of 60,000, this number represents a ridiculous force when compared with the 2,150,000 members of the unions affiliated with the Socialist party and the 1,200,000 in the unions affiliated with the Populist party. How was it possible for 60,000 men to reduce to a heap of ruins in a few months the organizations of more than 3 million men?

The Fascist historians have at hand a simple answer: the Fascists were all heroes, and the Socialists, Communists, and Populists were all cowards. By sheer heroism, the forces of Fascist civilization overcame the powers of "Bolshevist" darkness. An English journalist described the Fascist exploits as if he were a medieval poet chanting the deeds of knights-errant in a *chanson de geste:*

> A writer of the Middle Ages would relate the story of this awakening with fine imagery, for it contains all the elements of a great romance. You have a valiant knight going out singlehanded, jeered at by enemies and despaired of by faint-hearted friends, to fight a red dragon which is steadily increasing in size and strength. The entire country is in

---

[5] B. Giuliano, *L'esperienza politica dell'Italia* (Fireuze: Vallecchi, 1924), pp. 185–86. In the words of Rocco: "Fascism is merely unconscious nationalism. We have an organic doctrine and a complete conception of the state. The Fascists have their heart and their patriotic sentiment. . . . One must not give too much importance to verbal excesses of fascism" (*Idea Nazionale*, May 27, 1921).

> danger. The struggle is long and painful, and at times the
> dragon is well-nigh victorious. Gradually the knight's band
> of followers increases, and when the people see that their
> rescue is possible, they flock to his banner. And so the
> dragon is slain, and the valiant knight—who was no more
> than the son of the village blacksmith—becomes the king's
> first minister.[6]

Nothing appeals more to the imagination of the people than such simplification of history, such personification of forces and principles at war one against the other, with the destiny of a nation and perhaps of the whole mankind at stake. Myths are created that no efforts of historians nor analysis of documentary evidence can ever destroy. Yet let us see by what methods the Blackshirt managed to slay the Red Dragon.

In a village two Blackshirts enter a room where fifty workmen are assembled. They cover them with their revolvers, shouting "hands up," and then order them to stand up and leave the room two by two. As the workmen do so, Fascists waiting at the entry fall on them and club them. The fifty workmen attempt no resistance. On one side, two heroes; on the other, fifty cowards. The matter is not quite so simple. The fifty cowards, who obey the two heroes, are unarmed; the heroes know this, as the police have beforehand searched the men for arms and since carrying arms would have been grounds for arrest. Moreover, the fifty cowards know well that if they object and disobey, the two heroes will not hesitate to fire. The fifty cowards know further that the sound of the shots would bring the police on the scene and that the police would arrest, not the armed heroes, but the unarmed cowards. Most weighty of all: the fifty cowards know that should a Blackshirt by chance be killed in an affray, the Fascist directorate of the district will at once be told by telephone; a few hours later hundreds of Fascists from the neighboring villages, summoned by telephone, will arrive in motorlorries, sack their houses and those of their neighbors, burn their furniture, and indiscriminately club old men, women, and children. This time the police will not appear until everything is over, and will then arrest as murderers the men who had acted in self-defense. This is the true picture. Looking at this picture, everyone must recognize that among the two armed and fifty unarmed men, there were no heroes or cowards; there were only two gangsters.

[6] Sir Percival Phillips, *The Red Dragon and the Black Shirts*, pp. 11–13.

It is far from our minds to turn the Fascist legend upside down and make out all the Fascists to be cowards. There were, no doubt, men of courage among them, especially among the younger ones—men who were ready to give up their lives for their ideal. During 1919, 1920, and the first months of 1921—that is, while Socialist and Populist organizations had not yet been wholly devastated and dismantled—a Fascist had to possess an uncommon amount of courage. He had to face unpopularity. He ran a risk of wounds or death—a risk not as widespread as Fascist "propaganda" would have us believe, but real enough to damp the ardor of the ordinary man. The Anarchist Luigi Fabbri, whom we have quoted already, wrote in the summer of 1921:

> The assistance, moral, material and financial, of industrial and landed capitalism, the connivance of the public forces, and the adhesion of all the supine worshippers of success, would not alone have sufficed to give strength to fascism. Rather, all these coefficients would have been absent if there had not been from the beginning a nucleus of men endowed with strength of will and the spirit of sacrifice, who at their own risk broke the ice of indifference and hostility, urged on into the struggle by inward strength and careless of their own safety. Some of them met their deaths. These few, the most obscure, urging on the many, set in motion the whole machinery, which now appears so strong.[7]

We are even ready to admit that the "anti-Bolshevist" reaction was natural and might have been helpful to the workers and peasants themselves. For two years they had faced nothing but the fear and cowardice of the upper classes and had lost all sense of proportion. They had become like spoiled children, and their own leaders were often unable to control them. A virile resistance on the part of the Conservatives would have forced them to take a juster view of their capacities and responsibilities.

In subsidizing the Fascists, the industrialists, landowners, and bankers were not going beyond their rights. Capital is a social force like labor, and it was as natural that the capitalists should assist their "white guard" with funds as that the workers and peasants should contribute to the support of their propagandists and organizers.

Even the acts of violence committed by the Fascists during the first few

---

[7] Fabbri, *La Controrivoluzione preventiva*, pp. 96–97.

months of their counteroffensive can be viewed with a certain indulgence. Since the police and magistrates were powerless to defend private citizens from the capricious and overbearing power of the trade unions, such citizens might well seek to defend themselves by illegal methods.

But when all this has been said, the fact remains that (especially since the beginning of 1921), in the majority of cases, to speak of a Fascist killed or wounded in the civil war as a "hero" or "martyr" is as absurd as to apply these terms to a gangster who is killed unexpectedly by his intended victim. No doubt it needs courage to be a gangster, but this courage is not to be confused with heroism. The truth is that on both sides there were attackers and attacked, assassins and victims, ambushes and open assaults, acts of courage and acts of treachery; but the Fascists enjoyed overpowering strength, being backed economically by big business, landowners, and shopkeepers, and politically by the police, the bench, and the army chiefs.

To make our point clear, let us take an actual episode of this terrible civil war, which, in the words of Dr. Nicholas Murray Butler, president of Columbia University, has to be termed "a silent and bloodless revolution."[8]

In the municipal elections of 1920, the municipal administration had been won by the Socialists at Foiano della Chiana, as it had been in many other communes. At the beginning of April 1921, the Socialist mayor received a letter from Marchese Perrone Compagni, general secretary of the Fasci for Tuscany, inviting the mayor and his councilors to resign within the week if they did not wish to expose themselves and their families to Fascist reprisals.[9] The mayor and the councilors did not obey.

On April 12, 1921, more than 200 Fascists collected in lorries from Arezzo, Florence, and the intermediate towns and made an "expedition of propaganda" to the little town—i.e., they looted the town hall, the Chamber of Labor, and the premises of the Peasants' Union, throwing the furniture into the street and burning it. They seized the cooperative stores, distributing the goods to all and sundry and setting fire to what remained. On April 17, a second "expedition of propaganda" was carried out. This time there were barely twenty Fascists in a single lorry. They confiscated the red flag which the "Communists" usually ran up over the town hall

---

[8] In his preface to A. Rocco, *The Political Doctrine of Fascism* (New York: Carnegie Endowment, 1926). A somewhat compressed, but objective description of life in Italy during 1921–22 containing many valuable particulars, is to be found in Beals, *Rome or Death*, pp. 45–60, 105–08, 131–41.

[9] Examination of Galliano Gervasi during the trial at Arezzo, *Corriere della sera*, October 17, 1924.

instead of the national flag, burnt it together with the records of the Socialist club, and then proceeded to the village of Marciano on another "propagandist trip." On their return, several Fascists stayed at Foiano to form a local "Fascio" while the rest in the lorry took the road back to Arezzo.

A short distance out of Foiano, a group of about fifty peasants armed with guns, scythes, hatchets, and pistols were lying in wait behind a hedge. The lorry was met with a hail of bullets. The driver fell wounded, the lorry swerved and ran against a tree. While the Fascists were thrown to the ground, the peasants in hiding leaped forward upon them. They cut off the head of the driver with a hatchet blow. Two Fascists were killed, and another had three fingers severed by an axe. The remainder managed to escape.

At the sound of the shots, the carabineers, who until then had remained inactive, woke up and rushed out from Foiano together with those Fascists who had remained in the town. The peasants, seeing the carabineers approaching, took flight in their turn.

Now began the reprisals. The farmhouses near the place of the ambush were set on fire. A peasant, Burri, who was discovered in an attic, was shot through the head with a revolver.

The next day reprisals continued on a larger scale. Five lorry-loads of Fascists left Florence in the early morning. Other lorries left Arezzo and the neighboring towns and all concentrated in Foiano. The authorities, as usual, left the Fascists a free hand. The best-known "Communists" of Foiano had already left their homes. The Fascists gave themselves up to ransacking, wrecking, and burning private houses. A workman, Cino Milani, who had not bethought himself to escape, was dragged into the square: he was required to promise to resign from membership of the Socialist party; he refused. He was required to declare that he deplored the ambush of the day before; he again refused. He was shot. A peasant, one Gherardi, guilty of being the brother of a "Communist," was shot at and killed while he was trying to escape. The Fascists of Arezzo had brought with them as prisoner to Foiano the ex-deputy Bernardini, editor of the Socialist paper of Arezzo. The prisoner was forced, under threat of death, to pronounce from the window of a house a speech against the "violence of the Socialists," while the mass of Fascists howled and hooted in the street below. Thanks to this act of cowardice, which dishonors his jailers no less than himself, his life was spared.

When they wearied of tormenting the people of Foiano, the Fascists repaired to the place of the "ambush" of the day before. The peasant Caciolli was seriously wounded. Two other peasants, who were wounded as they fled, were not found; probably their injuries were not serious and they managed to hide. But this was not enough. In the night, toward 1:00 A.M., the Fascists returned to this place; they ransacked the farmhouses one by one, terrifying women, children, and old people, and reduced other houses to smoking ruins. A woman, Luisa Bracciali, who was accused of having wounded a Fascist in the "ambush" with a pitchfork, was found in her home and shot dead with revolvers. The peasant Nocciolini was killed while trying to flee. Another peasant, Alfredo Rampi, hearing that the Fascists were on his track, killed himself.

Operations continued throughout the next day, April 19. The house of Mayor Nucci, who had fled, was invaded and set on fire. The Communist club of Bettolle was sacked and burnt. Finally the Fascists collected a "spontaneous" meeting of peasants, took down their names, and declared the Fascio of Foiano founded. After having thus converted the "Communists" of Foiano to the "national faith," the Fascists, glorious and triumphant, abandoned the scene of their victory.

Needless to say, the civil and military authorities were conspicuous by their absence. They were engaged in "rounding up the Communists" who had hidden themselves in the country around Foiano. Of those guilty of the "ambuscade" who had not been killed in the reprisals, four were sentenced to thirty years' imprisonment, three to twenty-five years, two to twenty years, six to ten years, and three to from seven to ten years.[10] None of the Fascists who took part in the operations described suffered in any way whatsoever.[11]

Two basic facts must be born in mind if the Fascist victory is to be understood. The first is that the Fascist movement—we mean not the badly organized, inefficient, ultrarevolutionary movement of 1919–20, but the well-organized, and thoroughly efficient anti-trade unionist movement of 1921—began to develop after the postwar unrest in the country had begun to die down. Toward the end of 1920, the worst of the postwar crisis was over.[12] As little by little the shock of the war grew less acute, the Italian

[10] *Corriere della sera*, December 13, 1924.
[11] In our account we have followed the version of *Corriere della sera* of April 13, 19 and 20, 1921. We have not made use of anti-Fascist papers because the atrocious details they give could be suspected of exaggeration.
[12] Many witnesses could be gathered to prove this fact, which is essential for whoever wants

people recovered from the "postwar neurasthenia." The military authorities, by arming the Fascists, and the police and the magistrates, by assuring them impunity, prevented the Italian people from freely working out its own salvation. It was not pacified by reason; it was coerced by fire and sword. Fascism was no cure for the malady of bolshevism. It was a new and more appalling disease—civil war—which took the place of the revolutionary excitement, which was already on the wane; rather, it was a new and more appalling phase of the same disease from which all countries were suffering, some more, some less: the postwar neurasthenia.

The second point is even more essential to explaining the victory of the Fascists. The military authorities, the police, and the judiciary never interfered with Fascist activities; they aided and abetted them. Without this circumstance, the victory of the Fascists would become a mystery worthy of being related, not in a history book, but in a mystery story. When the question is raised whether a Fascist movement would be possible or desirable in other countries, fascism is continually confused with a conservative movement. For a conservative movement to become a Fascist movement, two conditions are necessary. In the first place, the conservatives would have to plunge into lawlessness and bloodshed. Second, they would then have to find a sufficient number of high military authorities, police, and

to understand the origins of Fascism. Among the immediate witnesses whose writings were published in 1921 and 1922, it is enough to remember Mowrer (*Immortal Italy*, pp. 343–47); Missiroli (*Il Fascismo e la crisi italiana*, p. 14); Fabbri (*La Controrivoluzione preventiva*, p. 21); and C. Degli Occhi (*Che cosa ho pensato del Fascismo quando ero popolare* [Bologna: Cappelli, 1923], p. 21). Among the witnesses who wrote after the March on Rome, we will remember only three: (1) The Jesuit fathers of the *Civiltà Cattolica* wrote in their January 24, 1924, issue: "When the danger of a revolution was the greatest, that is to say, during the first two years after the armistice, Fascism was barely born. . . . When the Fascists were able to start their attack, and this happened in 1921, and to be more precise in the spring of 1921, the danger of a revolution for several reasons could be considered as already past and overcome. When, therefore, the Fascists boast that they were the saviors of Italy, they adorn themselves with feathers not belonging to them. What they pretend to have saved was saved already." (2) More concisely and with a deeper insight into the meaning of those events, G. Prezzolini (now at Columbia University and a willing collaborator in Fascist policies in America) stated in 1925: "Fascism was rather the effect than the cause of the decay of communism in Italy" (*Le Fascisme* [Paris: Bossard, 1925], p. 236). (3) Senator G. Fortunato, a man beyond any suspicion of partiality by nobility of intellect and character, wrote in 1926 a pamphlet, *Nel Regime Fascista*, of which the Fascists forbade the publication, but of which clandestine copies were circulated: "Already the danger of revolt from the left had been overcome when the attack from the right, favored by plutocracy and militarism, so unexpectedly and rapidly developed." The English writer P.H. Box, to whom we are indebted for a most penetrating study on the origins of fascism, also clearly states that "revolutionary communism was already defeated by the good sense of the Italian people before the triumphant Fascists fell on its disordered forces" (*Three Master Builders* [London: Jarrolds, 1925], preface and pp. 18–19).

judges lost to all sense of law and honor and willing to employ the impartial power entrusted to them by law in the service of the wealthy against the working classes. Unless these two conditions exist, there is no sense in applying the name of fascism to a conservative movement.

When one wonders what the right-wing Socialists, the Maximalists, the Communists, and the Anarchists could have done in the first half of 1921 to withstand the Fascist onslaught, one has to take stock of the fact that all legal channels to obtain justice were blocked by the treacherous behavior of the police, the bench, and the army chiefs. While Maximalists, Communists, and Anarchists waited for their "revolutionary proletariat" to take revenge, the right-wing Socialists demanded that the government impose respect for law upon all. But they, together with the Maximalists, were members of a party whose national executive invoked, even though only by words, social revolution and considered an enemy any "bourgeois" government whatsoever, even if it imposed respect for law upon everybody. If a home secretary had done what the right-wing Socialists asked, he would have found himself between two fires: the reactionaries on the one side, and the Socialists on the other. As long as they did not break away from the Maximalists, the right-wing Socialists had no bargaining power in the game of parliamentary give and take.

No other way remained than to oppose force with force. The Anarchists followed this policy and threw bombs. This method proved utterly disastrous. Persons belonging to the general public—sometimes women and children—were killed or wounded. General indignation was aroused. The Fascists retorted by fierce reprisals against persons who had not the least responsibility for the outrages, and the sense of terror by which the working people were paralyzed grew more acute.

Two experiences should have opened everybody's eyes.

At Florence,[13] on the morning of Sunday, February 27, 1921, a group of about one hundred university and secondary school students of both sexes, flanked by about sixty carabineers, were passing through the streets of the city singing patriotic songs after having attended the ceremonies of

---

[13] We have reconstructed these facts with the help of the *Corriere della sera*, February 28, March 1, 2, 3, 4, 5, 1921. The *Corriere della sera*, in 1921, was in favor of the Fascists, only deploring their more scandalous excesses and calling on the government to awaken from its inertia and restore public peace. The correspondent in Florence was frankly pro-Fascist and colored his reports of the civil war in such a way as to put the anti-Fascists always in an unfavorable light. We can, therefore, be sure that, in basing our account on the reports given in the *Corriere*, we shall not unduly weight any charges against the Fascists.

the inauguration of a flag. At the top of Via Tornabuoni, two men were awaiting the procession in a narrow side street. One fired his revolver five or six times at the procession; the other threw a bomb into the middle of the group. One carabineer was killed on the spot, and sixteen people were wounded more or less seriously; one of them, a university student, died some days later. The dead carabineer and his wounded companions were put into a carriage and taken to a hospital; citizens who met the vehicle were asked to raise their hats. In the Piazza del Duomo, a railwayman who was walking along, reading a newspaper, ignorant of what had happened and therefore not lifting his hat, was shot with a musket by one of the carabineers who was escorting his dead companion and was in "a state of great excitement."[14]

Shortly after these unforeseen episodes, the Fascists entered the scene, while armored cars, carabineers, royal guards, and soldiers patrolled the streets and occupied the headquarters of the local Trade Unions Council ("Chamber of Labor") to prevent any gathering of the working masses. In the afternoon, a squad of Fascists appeared at the offices of the Communist Union of Disabled Soldiers, where the secretary of the union, Spartaco Lavagnini, a Communist railwayman and a city councilor, was alone. Part of the squad posted themselves in the street, while four of them entered the premises and shot Lavagnini dead. Thereupon they wrecked the premises without any interference on the part of the police, whose activity was limited to arresting "revolutionaries" *en masse*.

As a protest against the murder of Lavagnini and against the authorities who were systematically leaving crimes of this sort unpunished, the railwaymen, that same evening, called a lightning strike in the whole district. The tramwaymen, newspaper printers, and electricians followed suit. In the city and suburbs, numerous conflicts took place between Fascists and workers. During the night, telephone and telegraph lines were cut.

On Monday, February 28, the strike spread to all categories of workers.

[14] The correspondent of the *Corriere della sera*, February 28, 1921, while mentioning this "state of great excitement" of the carabineer, added that the man who had not lifted his hat had said: "If a carabineer is dead, there is one less of them," and that the carabineer fired on hearing these words. We can deny this detail on the authority of a teacher, a friend of the author, who was standing close beside the man who was killed. Though at that time very favorable to the Fascist movement, the teacher, as an honorable man, told the author later in the same day that the railwayman never said these words. One can, however, understand and even excuse the carabineer for losing self-control on the death of his companion and thinking that one who failed to lift his hat showed contempt.

On their side, the Fascists issued proclamations inviting the population to rise against the red terror. The prefect forbade all gatherings and processions as well as the circulation of motorcars; but, in actual fact, the Fascists had a completely free hand to hunt the workmen, especially the railwaymen, through the streets.

Their first offensive against the popular quarter of San Frediano was unsuccessful. The workmen and the women had torn up the roadway and barricaded the streets to prevent the entrance of the armed lorries. They fired and threw down tiles and furniture from the windows at those who tried to enter these narrow streets. In the afternoon, the Fascists returned, accompanied by a large patrol of royal guards, a battalion of infantry, numerous carabineers, and two armored cars. Every outlet of the quarters was blocked. The armored cars forced an entry across the barricades into the streets, firing up at the windows and forcing the population to shut themselves up in the houses. As in each street the resistance was beaten down, the Fascists and police invaded the houses, venting their fury. Hundreds of men and women were wounded at haphazard. The official report speaks of three workmen killed and fifty wounded.

Here and there, in other parts of the city, numerous other isolated collisions took place. The pro-Fascist correspondent of the *Corriere della sera*, wrote on March 1:

> At the entrance to Via Lamarmora a group of Fascists was hooted by some individuals, who, when the Fascists turned round, took to their heels, running towards Piazza Cavour. It seemed to the Fascists that one of them had taken refuge in the shop of a certain Angelico Bonini. They entered and fired their revolvers, killing Bonini. A man named Donatello Sanesi, who, frightened by the firing, was running under the colonnade of the square, was struck by a bullet and killed on the spot.

Toward evening, a lad of sixteen, named Giovanni Berta, the son of a well-known manufacturer, "wearing the Fascist badge in his button-hole" (*Corriere della sera*, March 1, 1921), tried to make his way on his bicycle through a crowd of workmen gathered on a bridge over the Arno.[15] The crowd, maddened by the happenings of those days, irritated by the Fascist

---

[15] These details came to light in the course of the trial at the Florence Assizes in the autumn of 1922.

badge, and believing the lad to be a cyclist in the service of the Fascist party, surrounded and stabbed him and threw him into the river. In a suburb of the city, a royal guard was, during the night, brutally murdered by a crowd.

The strike lasted into the following day. Police operations were transferred from the quarter of San Frediano to the other popular quarter, Santa Croce. In the afternoon, a squad of Fascists wrecked the premises of the Chamber of Labor, left at their mercy by the police who had occupied them during the two preceding days. Another squad invaded and sacked the offices of the Engineers' Union. In the suburb the police repressed, with the help of artillery, every sign of protest and revolt, while everywhere the Fascists continued their work of sacking and burning the premises of the workmen's organizations. By the afternoon, comparative calm was restored in Florence.

During those days, according to the official report, sixteen people were killed and one hundred wounded. Among the dead were two Fascists and four members of the police services. The actual number of dead and wounded among the workers was probably much higher than was stated in the official report.

That same afternoon of March 1, at an hour's distance by rail from Florence, a horrible massacre took place. To replace the strikers, the government had dispatched from Leghorn to Florence two lorries with forty-five marines and fourteen carabineers. The marines were not in uniform, in order not to draw attention on the roads. But the lorries were noticed by a man who, thinking they were carrying Fascists and carabineers, telephoned to Empoli (halfway between Leghorn and Florence) that a "punitive expedition" was on the way. As the Fascists of Florence, Leghorn, and Pisa had repeatedly threatened a "punitive expedition" against the Empoli Chamber of Labor, the news caused the assembly of a great crowd already excited by the news from Florence.[16] When the two lorries arrived in the marketplace, they were surrounded on every side: nine of the men were killed and ten more or less seriously wounded. Several corpses were thrown into the river.

In the following days, the town and district of Empoli were subjected to atrocious reprisals. The Fascists concentrated at Empoli from all the district around, wrecked the Chamber of Labor and numerous shops, while

[16] These details came to light in the course of the trial at the Florence Assizes.

the police made 218 arrests. Three lorries full of Fascists, followed by an armored car, scoured the district, wrecking trade union premises and the houses of well-known Socialists. Wherever resistance was encountered, the armored car was brought into action. At Siena, the Fascists and police attacked the Chamber of Labor. For an hour the workers put up resistance, but when the artillery fired eight shells against the door, the besieged surrendered. Ten among them were injured more or less seriously; two were mortally wounded. The Chamber of Labor was sacked and burned down.

In Florence, on March 2, the men began to trickle back to work. In Scandicci, a neighboring village, the peasants attacked with bombs a lorry of carabineers and barricaded the bridge at the entrance to the village. A column of artillery with armored cars and fieldpieces stamped out the revolt. As usual, after order had been restored, a punitive expedition of Fascists from Florence arrived and destroyed the premises of the workers' organization in the village. The *Corriere della sera* correspondent wrote, on the night of March 2:

> This evening about 6:00 P.M. there passed through the principal streets of Florence some fieldpieces, which had been in action at Scandicci. Amid the applause of the citizens, a most imposing procession then formed, in which were three lorries laden with soldiers and Fascists. They were all singing patriotic songs and waving large tricolor flags, while flowers were thrown down on the procession from the windows. The soldiers and Fascists were carrying as trophies the red flags and other subversive emblems carried off from the premises of the Mutual Benefit Society of Scandicci. The demonstration, which was not disturbed by any incident, broke up at the seat of the Fascist headquarters.

Those guilty of bomb throwing and other outrages received pitiless sentences; three were sentenced to thirty years, two to twenty-one years, one to seventeen years, seven to sentences ranging from two to twelve years. Two who had escaped were sentenced to penal servitude for life (*Corriere della sera*, July 1, 1922). The murderers of Berta were sentenced to periods of imprisonment varying from ten to eighteen years. For the outrages at Empoli, eighteen persons were sentenced to imprisonment for periods of from twenty to thirty years; thirty-two of from fourteen to seventeen years; thirty of from five to twelve years. Similar sentences were given for all the other crimes. But no Fascists were ever sentenced for the murder of Lavagnini, of Bonini, of Sanesi, nor for the wreckings, reprisals, or innumerable other acts of violence committed by them in those days.

A few weeks later, another more dastardly bomb outrage had more ruinous results. Malatesta and other Anarchists had been arrested on October 17. They never were brought to trial. The government wanted to keep them locked up as long as possible, and the public prosecutor and the examining judge were doing their best to please the government.[17] Malatesta and his friends, to protest against this unfair treatment, went on a hunger strike. It was so obvious that the treatment was unfair that the Democratic press started a campaign in their favor.[18] On the evening of March 23, three Anarchists exploded a bomb at the Diana Theater, causing the death of twenty persons and the wounding of two hundred, including women and children.[19] At the same time, a group of other Anarchists approached the building of the Socialist paper *Avanti*, intending to throw bombs on it to protest against the indifference the Socialists were showing towards the treatment of Malatesta and the other Anarchist prisoners. Half an hour later, the Fascists burned down the premises of the Anarchist paper *Umanità Nuova*, looted the headquarters of the "Italian Syndicalist Union" run by Revolutionary Syndicalists and Anarchists, the home of the Anarchist Molinari, and a Socialist club which had nothing to do with the Anarchists, and tried to attack with hand grenades the premises of the *Avanti*— which ran the risk of being wrecked twice in the same night, first by Anarchists and then by Fascists. But this time the police protected the paper.

[17] Italian judicial procedure in criminal cases was as follows: (a) an examining judge *(giudice istruttore)* assisted by a public prosecutor *(procuratore del Re)* questioned the defendant and the witnesses, whose answers and evidence were written down; (b) the public prosecutor, as a consequence of the evidence collected in this preliminary inquiry *(istruttoria)*, made his proposal *(requisitoria)* that the accused be either acquitted or committed for trial; (c) the counsel for the defense made themselves acquainted with the contents of the preliminary inquiry and made their objections to the proposals of the public prosecutor; (d) an "accusing section" *(sezione d'accusa)*, formed of three judges, made a first pronouncement—i.e., either acquitted the defendant or declared that there was sufficient evidence against him for the case to be tried; (e) in the latter case there ensued the public trial before three judges who passed the sentence in minor cases, and before a presiding judge and a jury in important cases; the defendant and the witnesses were again questioned and cross-examined; the case was argued between the public prosecutor, the counsel for the defense, and the counsel for the injured party *(parte civile)*; (f) the jury gave a final verdict as to the guilt or innocence of the defendant; (g) the presiding judge passed the sentence.

[18] A. Borghi, *Errico Malatesta*, p. 241.

[19] Of the three men responsible for this crime, two were sentenced to life imprisonment, one for thirty years; three other people were sentenced to twelve year imprisonment, and many others to minor terms.

The disgust for the bombing of the Diana Theater was enormous. Borghi, who was in prison with Malatesta, writes:

> In twenty-four hours the entire situation seemed to have turned against us. No one, who was not an Anarchist, dared admit having known us. Everyone who had exchanged a word with us felt himself to be in danger. The terror in Milan reached its zenith. The best among us had to fly to avoid imprisonment and the hunt against the Anarchists.[20]

Malatesta and the other prisoners realized that the movement of protest had been wrecked, and they desisted from their hunger strike.[21] The Diana Theater bombs were from now on steadily thrown in the face of all "Bolshevists."

The Maximalists and Communists condemned the method of bomb throwing and reacted against Fascist violence by proclaiming general strikes. Strikes were no more effective than bombs. A general strike, if it is not the beginning of a real revolutionary upheaval, is destined to die out from spontaneous extinction. A revolutionary upheaval had not come about in 1919 or 1920. It would have been folly to think of one in 1921. When a general strike took place, the Fascists, in reprisal, multiplied acts of violence against the political and trade union leaders, and after one, two, or three days, the workers, one by one, returned to work, more disheartened than ever.

Many times the workers, abandoned to their own devices, came to battle with the Fascists. A certain number of Fascists—about 300 in 1921 and 1922—fell in open battles or ambushes. But further punitive expeditions and reprisals were the result of these local frays. About 3,000 persons lost their lives at the hands of the Fascists during the two years of civil war.

Perhaps, to put an end to the struggle, one method would have been

[20] A. Borghi, *Errico Malatesta*, p. 239. It is interesting what Borghi writes about what Malatesta, he, and the other prisoners expected in prison while the Fascist attack was triumphantly going on: "To Errico it seemed incredible what we read secretly and what we learned from visitors. The burning of trade union headquarters in Bologna, the killings in Florence, the massacres everywhere, compared with the force the proletariat had shown only a few months ago, seemed to him ugly jokes of fantasy. We thought that from one day to the next we would hear the happy news of the general insurrection. We expected it every morning. We felt sure of it" (p. 232). The source of this unfounded hope was always the same: that of all revolutionaries in Italy and outside, yesterday, today, and we are afraid, always: the illusion that the proletariat is a revolutionary class.
[21] In the public trial which took place in July 1921, all the defendants were acquitted.

effective: opposing a methodical and intelligent terrorism to Fascist terrorism. The Fascists concentrated their violence especially against the leaders of the local groups: trade union secretaries, managers of cooperative societies, mayors, councilors and town clerks of municipalities, editors of papers and other men of influence among the working people: "Smite the shepherd and the flock will be scattered." No one punished this crime of keeping the country in a terrifying state of civil war, because those whose duty it was to punish it were the ones most responsible for it. Every act of violence perpetrated by Anarchists, Communists, Socialists, or Populists, on the other hand, was immediately and ruthlessly suppressed. The Socialists might have imitated the Fascists and taken reprisals, not against the small fry forming their squadrons, but against the higher-ups and against the high civil and military officials who were really responsible for Fascist lawlessness: Mussolini, Prime Minister Giolitti, the minister of justice, a couple of generals, and a couple of high judges. If those who had been responsible for the civil war had paid personally for the civil war, it is probable that the rest would have ordered the police and the judiciary to effectively suppress Fascist lawlessness. A dozen anti-Fascists who had intelligently sacrificed their lives would have saved many hundreds of lives and would have put an end to civil war.

Such an idea occurred to no one in Italy in those years. If it had presented itself to some spirit, it would probably have been rejected with horror. Victory went to those who were not shackled with scruples of a moral nature.

20

The
Military Conspiracy

While "authorized lawlessness" was making the country run with blood, Giolitti dissolved the Chamber, set the national elections for May 15, 1921, and waited for the Fascist "squadrons" to reduce the number of Populist, Socialist, and Communist deputies. The elections were held in an atmosphere of civil war. On the polling day alone forty were killed and seventy were wounded here and there.[1]

Giolitti had counted his chickens before they were hatched. He was eighty-two years old. He had always been able to manipulate elections successfully. At his age he could not realize that the methods which had been effective under the single-member system, were no longer adequate under a system of proportional representation. Under this system, he was confronted with hundreds of thousands of voters in hundreds of cities, towns, and villages. He did not know where to strike in order to turn minorities into pluralities and vice versa. Fascist "squadrons" could suppress some thousand votes here, steal some thousand votes there, but the bulk of the enemy could not be suppressed as easily as it had been at the happy time of the single-member system. He went on repeating: "I do not know how to deal with this wretched proportional representation."

On the other hand, Socialists and Communists, under the tempest of Fascist violence, forgot their quarrels and only determined to stem the

[1] Mowrer, *Immortal Italy*, p. 364.

316

Fascist tide. The Italian people never understood the controversies between Socialists and Communists and everywhere gave their votes, not to the ticket of either party, but to those candidates who were more violently attacked by the Fascists or were more courageous in opposing them. Many nonpartisan citizens who were disgusted with the Socialists in 1920, now voted the Socialist ticket as a protest against the Fascists, giving their preferential vote to right-wing Socialists. The Populists also profited from anti-Fascist violence, since they also were its butt.

The electorate returned 122 Socialists and 107 Populists. The Communists who had seceded from the Socialists won only 16 seats. This was all the strength they had at a moment when, according to the "romantic" Fascist historiography, the Blackshirt was needed to slay the Red Dragon. In the new Chamber, the proportions of the different groups were nearly the same as in the previous Chamber.

But the psychological situation had changed for the worse. The right-wing Socialists, who had always advocated abandoning the tactics of uncompromising opposition and taking part in the government with the Democrats, could not now ally themselves with the "Democrats" as long as these were led by Giolitti, who had employed the Fascists to "make the elections" with revolvers and bludgeons. All the intransigency of 1919, which in 1920 was beginning to fade away, was exasperated in 1921.

The Populists also, who would have liked to pursue a policy of collaboration, had been forced by Fascist violence to stand in the elections as opponents of the government. They returned to the Chamber elated by their victory and angry with Giolitti for having caused their electors to be bludgeoned by the Fascists, after inviting their leaders to join his cabinet.

Among the mass of deputies, neither Socialist, Communist, nor Populist, which the government regarded as its majority, was a group of thirty-five Fascists, young and violent, who had behind them outside the Chamber an armed organization ready for any excess. Giolitti had burned a forest to cook an egg.

When the new Chamber met in June 1921, the Communists, the Socialists, and the Populists, angry because of the wave of violence Giolitti had unloosed during the electoral campaign; and the Fascists and Nationalists who could not pardon Sforza's peace with Yugoslavia and D'Annunzio's expulsion from Fiume, combined and overthrew the cabinet.

At that time not even a shadow remained of the "Bolshevist" peril in Italy. On July 2, 1921, Mussolini wrote: "To say that there exists a Bolshevist peril in Italy is for interested motives to substitute fears for reality. Bolshevism has been vanquished. Nay more, it has been disowned by the leaders and the masses. The Italy of 1921 is fundamentally different from that of 1919. This has been said and proved a thousand times." From the summer of 1921 on, so-called Bolshevists were a defeated army, defending itself confusedly, without any connected plan and without the least chance of success.[2]

Giolitti's successor, Bonomi, had been Bissolati's most intimate friend before the war of 1914–18. During the war, he had drifted away from Bissolati and supported Sonnino's policies. In December 1919, when Bissolati resigned from Orlando's cabinet, Bonomi did not follow him. As war minister in Giolitti's cabinet, he had had a large share of responsibility in the pro-Fascist activities of the military chiefs. Neither he nor Giolitti had ever thought of destroying the parliamentary regime or wiping out political liberties in Italy. He also had thought that the forces of illegal violence could be brought back under leash as soon as "Bolshevist" danger had vanished. The Fascist "squadrons" might have been easily disbanded if they had not been supported by any other factor than their own strength. On July 21, 1921, at Sarzana, 6 carabineers were enough to disperse 500 Fascists who had attempted to rescue certain of their companions from prison; 20 of the scattered Fascists were savagely lynched by the populace, and many others were wounded.[3]

---

[2] Many witnesses besides Mussolini could be enumerated. Let us remember Bachi, *L'Italia Economica nel 1921*, pp. 225, 330, 339; I. Bonomi, *Dal socialismo al fascismo* (Roma: Formiggini, 1924), pp. 39. Speaking at Dundee on September 26, 1921, Mr. Winston Churchill announced to his public that Italy was no longer threatened by "bolshevism." The *Corriere della sera* and many other newspapers of September 27 reproduced Mr. Churchill's statement without questioning in any way its accuracy. In May 1922, the Nationalist Giuliano wrote: "Faced with the menace of the revolution, it was natural that the revolutionary exploits of fascism were in the best interests of all the nation. But it is also natural that this is no longer true now that the threat has diminished" (*L'Esperienza politica dell'Italia*, p. 191). Mr. Simon Strunsky, in the *New York Times Book Review*, February 6, 1927, made the following remarks: "If Italy had not accepted fascism in October, 1922, she must have succumbed to bolshevism. This is a common statement of the case, but not a complete statement. The American public has been amazingly forgetful of the highly pertinent fact that bolshevism in Italy had made its threat and been beaten back two years before Mussolini came into power. It may be that in 1922 another Bolshevist threat was preparing, but the day-by-day record of the times does not indicate it, and the extraordinary episode of the seizure and surrender of the factories in September 1920, is a prima facie argument against it. That the same Italian people would have thrown itself into the arms of bolshevism two years later and was only saved from suicide by the Fascist intervention, is conjecturable, but on the basis of faith rather than of known evidence."

[3] Banchelli, *Memorie di un Fascista*, p. 218; G.A. Chiurco, *Storia della rivoluzione fascista*, 5 vols. (Florence: Vallecchi, 1929), 3:459–66.

But while Giolitti had enjoyed a great personal prestige, which might have served either for good or for evil and had served for evil, Bonomi was a man devoid of all personal authority, incapable of doing either good or evil. He had to reckon with the army chiefs. The latter, up until that time, had obeyed Giolitti, furnishing officers, arms, munitions, and trucks to the Fascists. But as the Fascist organization gradually extended and consolidated itself, they came to realize that it might serve, in their hands, as a formidable weapon for ensuring greater influence to their caste. Under Bonomi they ceased to obey the civil government and went their own way.

The pivot of the military conspiracy was the Duke of Aosta, the king's cousin. This man was endowed with very little intelligence and awareness. But he was prompted by his wife, Hélène de France. The hand of this woman can be guessed behind all the military seditious movements which followed the war. She hoped that the Fascist movement would lead to the abdication of the king and a change of dynasty, by which her son might profit. In her veins ran the treacherous blood of the House of Orleans. To be sure, it would be unsafe to credit with overflowing intelligence the Duke of Aosta, or his wife, or General Diaz, or General Gandolfo, or General De Bono, or Admiral Thaon de Revel, or the other exalted personages who, betraying their oath to the constitution, had a share in the military conspiracy. Just as the politicians, who in 1920 authorized the military authorities to arm the Fascists, did not foresee that after six months the military authorities would be acting on their own account, so the generals, who in the second half of 1921, began to act on their own account, did not foresee the developments of 1922, and still less those of the following years. In order to take the first step in certain crimes, an intelligence above the mean is not necessary; all that is required is an absence of scruples above the normal. When the first step is taken, the succeeding ones are still unforeseen; but he who has begun to sin must go on sinning, to avoid the consequences of his first sin. Only when the chain of cause and effect has reached its end do the men who stumble forward towards unforeseen results appear to have guided events towards a devised goal.

Moreover, it should not be forgotten that, from 1910 on, a clique of Nationalist politicians, leaders of war industries and military men, always acted in the background in Italy. The Duke of Aosta and company, in taking the first steps in 1921 and 1922, needed to make no unusual expenditure of cerebral matter: it was enough to let themselves be advised by men like Federzoni, Rocco, and Forges-Davanzati, who led the Nationalist movement and were by no means stupid men.[4]

The conspiracy of the army chiefs had a decisive effect on the subsequent development of fascism. In 1919–20, fascism had been a political anti-Socialist movement carried on by uprooted members of the middle classes imbued with ultrarevolutionary feelings, and by college students seething with nationalistic excitement. In the first half of 1921, it had become an economic anti-trade unionist movement fostered by capitalists, landowners, and army chiefs. In the second half of 1921, it became an antiparliamentary movement in the service of a military black hand.

While he could not rely upon the army chiefs, Bonomi had to realize that even the police was no longer the obedient instrument which it had once been. The police had their hands tied because of the fact that in the preceding months they had aided and abetted too many Fascist crimes. Every time that Bonomi tried to set the police in motion against them, the Fascists threatened to publish the proofs that the police and Bonomi himself had aided and abetted their activities. One of the most notorious Fascist firebrands, Farinacci of Cremona, in the summer of 1921 reminded Bonomi that he had been the candidate of the Fascists in the election of May 1921:

> Among the many episodes, let us recall one. We were at Mantua one evening, when news reached us of the acts of violence committed by the Socialists at Poggio Rusco. It was the Minister Bonomi—our candidate—who placed his motorcar at the disposal of the Fascists, who that very same night were to destroy the cooperative stores of Poggio Rusco. And in the marvelous days of the electioneering struggle of 1921, we saw him marching under our standards and we attended his meetings and guarded him with our bold "Blackshirts."

In the summer of 1921, the new phase of the Fascist movement was marked by a new type of operations. Thousands of Fascists, according to plans of "mobilization" thought out in advance, would concentrate on a

---

[4] Not all the army chiefs had a share in the conspiracy. Badoglio, as chief of the general staff, had played his part in arming the Fascists at the beginning, because Giolitti and Bonomi had authorized this practice. In February 1921, he resigned his post. He did not wish to embroil himself in politics. His place was taken by General Vaccari, a protégé of the Duke of Aosta. Other generals refrained from taking any part in the intrigue, but, having no instructions from headquarters, they remained passive spectators of events. The majority took an active part, more or less overtly, in the sedition.

town or city, sometimes from great distances, traveling on motor lorries or enjoying free passes on the railroads. Headquarters of unions, premises of cooperative societies, popular libraries, private houses of "Bolshevists"— that is, of Communists, left-wing or right-wing Socialists, or Populists— everything was looted. Mayors and town councilors were forced to resign under threats that they would be murdered. When they had resigned, the prefect of the province came in and appointed Fascist commissioners to manage the "conquered" municipalities.

One of the earliest operations of this kind was the "conquest" of the town of Roccastrada. This is a small agricultural town, like Foiano della Chiana. In the municipal elections of November 1920, the administration had been won by the Socialists. On April 6, 1921, the mayor received the following letter:

> Italian Fighting Fasci of Tuscany
> Political Secretariat
> Florence, April 6, 1921
>
> To the Mayor of the Commune of Roccastrada,
> Prov. of Grosseto.
>
> Seeing that Italy must belong to Italians and cannot therefore be adminis-tered by individuals such as you, I, voicing the feelings of the citizens of your town, advise you to resign by Sunday, the 17th. Otherwise you will be responsible for anything that may happen to persons and to property. If you appeal to the authorities against this kind and humane advice of mine, the above date will be changed to Wednesday, the 13th, a lucky number indeed.
>
> (Signed) Dino Perrone Compagni

The mayor did not take this hint. For a couple of months the threats were not followed up. But on July 1, 1921, at about 4:00 P.M., two lorries of Fascists arrived. According to the correspondent of the *Corriere della sera* (July 26, 1921), they "confined themselves to blud-geoning several people and throwing out of the windows the furniture of several houses of subversive peasants." The Socialist paper *Avanti* states that the Fascists, shouting and letting off their revolvers into the air to frighten the women and children—the men being still out at work in the fields—set fire to the premises of the peasants' club and woodcutters' union and of the cooperative stores. Furthermore, they wrecked the mayor's house and that of the secretary of one of the unions, departing before the men came home from the fields.

Some days later, the mayor, while speaking with the prefect at Grosseto, was seized by the Fascists, taken to the Fascio, and obliged to sign a letter of resignation and to promise never to return to the town.

On July 24, 1921, about dawn, nearly seventy Fascists started from Grosseto in lorries, passing before the police headquarters unopposed. They reached Roccastrada at 4:30 A.M. The little town was wrapped in sleep. They set up a fusillade, shouting that the inhabitants must hang out the national flag, stopping the peasants who came out of their houses and bludgeoning them.

The inhabitants, wakened suddenly out of sleep, could offer no resistance. There was a general stampede. Several houses were wrecked and burned. Vandalism raged for three hours. About 8:00 A.M., the Fascists got into their lorries once more and left for Sassofortino, where they intended to continue their "national propaganda."

A short distance outside the town, three peasants, hidden behind a hedge, fired on the lorries and ran off. One Fascist was killed on the spot. The others, not being able to capture the fugitives, went back to the town. The pro-Fascist correspondent of the *Secolo* wrote, on July 26:

> Along the road they met a peasant and his son and shot them dead. Then they ran into the town shouting: "Who fired that shot?" They broke into several houses, shouting and stabbing four men. One of these, an old man of sixty-eight, was killed at his daughter's side. Three others were mortally injured in the streets, fifty others more or less seriously injured, and seventeen houses were reduced to a heap of smouldering ruins.

The nine dead were not members of any organization. Only one was known to have Anarchist leanings.

The thirteen carabineers stationed in the little town remained absolutely inactive, shut up in their quarters: they only telephoned to Grosseto what was happening. Needless to say no arrest was made among the Fascists, although the name of their leader, Castellani, general secretary of the Fasci for the province of Grosseto, was on everybody's lips. The three men guilty of the ambush were arrested and severely sentenced. Many other inhabitants of the town were arrested without reason and detained in prison for a considerable time.

Roccastrada was a small town. Treviso was an important city. The "punitive expedition" against Treviso, on July 12, 1921, was aimed not at Communists or Socialists, but at Populists who had taken the part of some laborers against two landowners who were subscribers of the Fascist organization. The American journalist Mowrer writes:

> Fifteen hundred men, brought together from districts as remote as Tuscany and Trieste, armed with rifles, handgrenades, machine-guns and steel helmets, part of which had been supplied by the regular troops, arrived before Treviso late, in a hundred camions, preceeded by a white motor car. Under cover of darkness they surrounded the walled town and penetrated into the streets. Their plan was complete, their enemy "whoever isn't a Fascist." First they broke into and sacked the offices of the Christian-Democratic (Populist) newspaper *Il Piave,* and then those of the Republican *Riscossa,* where a few defenders were overcome after some hours of seige. Dawn found the Fascists masters of the town, for the police and soldiers had assumed an attitude of "benevolent neutrality." So for a few hours the Fascists tyrannized the place, sacking a few shops and houses, and then withdrew.[5]

In September 1921, the sixth centenary of Dante's death was to be celebrated at Ravenna. The city would be thronged with strangers from every part of the world. It was the moment for all parties to lay aside their petty rivalries and to spare the visitors any undignified exhibition of violence. But the Fascist deputy of Bologna, Signor Grandi, thought otherwise; a month before the celebrations, he proposed that the Fascists should, on that date, make a "march on Ravenna." The pro-Fascist paper *Resto del Carlino* of Bologna wrote on September 13, 1921:

> It seemed that the idea was to stage a great demonstration of those Fascist forces that were opposed to peace with the Socialists. The leaders had in mind a spectacular march past in close formation with flags flying, that would begin at Bologna, make its way along the Via Emilia as far as Imola and double back towards Lugo before reaching Ravenna. Thus the new forces of Italy, marching in column—so it seemed to the minds of those who framed the scheme—

[5] Mowrer, *Immortal Italy,* p. 367.

should pass through the classic territory of communism and be received with open arms by the former Republican towns and villages.

Signor Baldini, the right-wing Socialist deputy of Ravenna, personally called the attention of Signor Bonomi to the disturbances which would certainly ensue if the Fascists were allowed to concentrate at Ravenna. Signor Bonomi gave his word of honor that the march of the Fascists on the city should be forbidden at all costs.[6] It is evident that in making this promise he was sincere. Even he could not fail to grasp the necessity for avoiding a scandal occurring on such an occasion, and in the presence of so many foreigners.

But Signor Bonomi had to reckon with General Sani, the commandant of the army corps of Bologna, who included Ravenna in his command. It was he who should have prevented the "March on Ravenna," which was generously advertised beforehand.[7] But on the day of the celebration, while the Fascists were advancing on the city, he went instead to Ravenna, to pay homage to Dante. He was notoriously one of those generals who, during the years of civil war, most actively helped the Fascists in his district, giving them arms and allowing the officers under him to take part in punitive expeditions.

The path was thus clear for this unheard-of demonstration. On September 9, squads of Blackshirts with flags flying began to gather freely at Bologna from Rovigo, Reggio, Modena, Carpi, Finale, etc. At 6:00 A.M. on September 10, a column 450 strong with trumpets at its head took the road (*Resto del Carlino*, September 11, 1921). The column had the delicacy to avoid Imola, the Socialists' center, and, going by way of Medicina, marched directly on Lugo. At the same time another column, 500 strong, set out from Ferrara, proceeding by way of Argenta. The two columns met at Lugo in the afternoon of September 11 (*Resto del Carlino*, September 12). As they proceeded, their numbers naturally increased. Four lorries full of royal guards followed the march (*Resto del Carlino*, September 13). On the

---

6 Signor Baldini himself described to the author of the present book the promise made him by Signor Bonomi.
7 According to the *Regolamento per il servizio territoriale*, of July 8, 1883, (Art. 30, par. 218), the military authorities could not take any initiative in the suppression of disorders, unless requested beforehand by the police. But the Appendix to these Regulations, issued in 1899 and still in force in 1922 (see the edition of 1922), made it incumbent upon the military authorities to take the necessary repressive measures in the case of grave disorders, even without any previous request by the police.

morning of September 12, 3,000 Fascists invaded Ravenna.

The events of September 12 at Ravenna were recounted by the correspondent of the *Giornale d'Italia*[8] on September 22, 1921, as follows:

> The Fascists reached Ravenna at 11 o'clock on September 12, and marched through the principal streets of the city singing their hymns, while the crowds greeted them with clapping and with cheers. The Fascists compelled everyone to uncover, exercising their cudgels upon the deaf and absent-minded. However, no incident worthy of note occurred.
>
> In the afternoon, while a group of Fascists were sitting in a café, insulting remarks were addressed to them by a Communist, who suddenly fired a revolver-shot amongst them without hitting anyone. The Fascists rose up to pursue their assailant, when a second Communist appeared before them and fired a second shot. In the confusion that followed the two Communists succeeded in disappearing.[9] The news of this encounter spread rapidly among the Fascist mass. The Fascists, divided into powerful bands, wrecked the premises of five Socialist clubs in the suburbs. The Chamber of Labor was likewise wrecked. In the square, pictures, papers, and benches were piled together and set on fire.
>
> *The authorities had taken praiseworthy precautions; troops were stationed here and there, strong bands of carabineers and royal guards guarded the most important points of the city; lorries full of policemen were waiting ready in the courtyard of the Prefecture to hasten wherever they were needed, and an armored car was stationed at its entrance; but the*

---

[8] It should be borne in mind that the *Giornale d'Italia* was favorable to the Fascists and protested against the "exaggerated reports" circulated regarding the Ravenna incidents.

[9] This part of the account must be taken with a grain of salt. In the reports which Fascist and pro-Fascist newspapers give of these "expeditions", encounters always begin with Communist shots or provocations. Is it possible in this case that the two Communists could have disappeared after having shot twice at the Fascists without hurting anyone? Luigi Fabbri, (*La Controrivoluzione preventiva*, pp. 66–67) gives the facts as follows: "The Fascists, en route for Ravenna, looted the Clubs of Godo and San Michele Fornace. At Ravenna, they at once began to compel the people to uncover at the passing of the Fascist colors, beating those who refused. Amongst those who were beaten, there happened also to be some foreigners who had come for the celebration. The Fascists broke into an inn, demanding that all present should show their personal papers. One, Colombo by name, found to be in possession of the membership-card of the Chamber of Labor, was violently beaten; he took flight; the Fascists chased him with their sticks uplifted. At last, a revolver shot rang out. The pretext had been found. In the afternoon, the punitive expeditions began." Between the Fascist and the anti-Fascist version, it is impossible to arrive at the exact truth.

attack on the various clubs was so sudden and so unexpected that it could not be prevented. Four or five thousand is a large number. The police force wisely confined itself to interfering only to prevent further damage. An attack by them would have resulted in a massacre. The city and its suburbs seethed with a crowd whose like had never been seen at Ravenna.

The premises of the Federation of the Cooperative Societies situated in Via Mazzini were guarded by a large force of police. A band of Fascists gathered in the street shouting: "Out with the Flag! Out with the Tricolor!" The police stationed there assured them that the flag would be hung out; but while they parleyed with the mass of Fascists, some of these, having climbed up like squirrels on the iron gratings of the windows and later on a ladder, succeeded in entering the building and hanging out the flag. Registers and bundles of papers were thrown down from the windows and were soon burnt to ashes.

In the evening, while a lorry full of Fascists was passing in front of a café, a young man seated at a table threw a plate or a glass at it. A Fascist jumped down from the lorry and gave the rash youth a blow with his cudgel. Revolver shots sounded from the café. The Fascists replied. Then entering the café, they completely wrecked it, smashing furniture, mirrors, glasses, china, and bottles of spirit.

The authorities succeeded in sending back the Fascists the next day by three special trains.

That the military authorities connived at the Fascist behavior is evident, even if we accept the version that attributes to the so-called Communists the responsibility for the first provocation. In these cases, sooner or later, a revolver shot is always fired, and the one party invariably tries to throw the responsibility for the shot upon its opponents. The real responsibility lies with those who created, or allowed others to create, the situation in which that shot could not but be fired. To permit more than 3,000 armed persons to congregate in a city, and then to protest that a massacre would ensue if they were interfered with (and this in a country where a year's experience had shown how such gatherings began and ended)—what else was this but deliberately to promote violence, knowing quite well beforehand what would happen?

A few days later, September 25, a deputy, Di Vagno, was killed at Mola di Bari by a band of sixteen Fascists who attacked him with revolver shots outside the town while he was going for a walk, unarmed, with friends (*Corriere della sera*, September 27, 1921). A little earlier, he had made a public speech to the peasants. There had been no disorder and no violence which could have provoked reprisals. The ambush was premeditated and carried out in cold blood. The assassins were known to everybody. Not one of them was arrested. The only thing they had to do was go and live elsewhere.

Italo Balbo, who in September 1921 led the column which "marched on Ravenna" from Ferrara, in a speech at Milan on April 23, 1923, said:

> It was in September 1921 that Fascist "squadrism" assumed a regular military formation. On September 12, 3,000 Blackshirted Fascists entered Ravenna. It was a small army, divided into regiments, batallions, and platoons; an army which had been three days on the march. At Ravenna the Blackshirts raised the cry of "to Rome! to Rome!" The experiment was a complete success. Squadrism could be transformed from a local phenomenon into a national phenomenon (*Popolo d'Italia*, April 24, 1923).

The idea of a "march on Rome" had emanated fom D'Annunzio at the end of 1919 while he was in Fiume. Mussolini, at that time, did not think that the enterprise would be successful.[10] Eighteen months later, on May 31, 1921 he wrote in his paper: "From this moment the Fascists of Latium, Umbria, the Abruzzi, Tuscany and Campania, are morally and materially pledged to concentrate in Rome at the first call sent out by the directing authorities of our movement."

What was to be the *coup d'état* of October 1922 had been originally fixed for November 1921. A large number of Fascists were to assemble in Rome with the pretext of celebrating the anniversary of the Italian Victory (November 4). D'Annunzio was to appear, to deliver a record-making speech, to place himself at the head of the Fascists, to dismiss from their posts the ministers, and be proclaimed a dictator. But at the last moment the poet failed to appear. Bonomi had bribed him with a large sum of money with which he was to succor the veterans of Fiume. He was the most prominent veteran. He kept all the money for himself. The Fascists gathered in Rome without the prearranged leader and committed excesses of

[10] Pronouncement of the Arbitration Committee of the Lombard Journalists' Association, February 1920, in the *Secolo*, February 14, 1920.

every kind, until they were expelled from the popular quarters of the city after bitter street fighting.

The Fascist National Congress of November 1921 decided that their "movement" should transform itself into a "political party," the "National Fascist party" ("Partito Nazionale Fascista"). This would be "a voluntary militia put to the service of the nation" and would conform to three basic principles: "order, discipline, leadership." The local branches were entitled to elect their own directors, but these were to be "bound by chains of absolute discipline" to the national directorate of the party and "follow their instructions without discussing them." Each branch was to have a "fighting squadron" ("squadra di combattimento") ready to march at the command of the national executive of the party.

How many were the Fascists at the end of 1921 we do not know. Mussolini, in an interview given to the *Giornale d'Italia*, May 22, 1921, had stated the Fascist membership to be no less than half a million. But according to the report laid before the Congress of November 1921, the members of the Fascist branches had risen from 30,000 in May 1920 to 230,000 in November 1921 (*Popolo d'Italia*, November 18, 1921). In 1924, Mussolini affirmed that the Fascists had increased from 20,615 at the end of 1920 to 248,000 by the end of 1921 (*La Nuova politica dell'Italia* [Milan: Alpes, 1925], p. 18). The administrative secretary of the party in 1929 gave the following figures: 20,615 at the end of 1920; 248,936 on December 31, 1921; 299,867 at the end of 1922 (*Popolo d'Italia*, March 23, 1929). Is it possible that during 1922, a year of extraordinarily good fortune, politically speaking, the Fascists had increased only from 248,000 to 300,000? Fascist statistics always show discrepancies and improbable features, as can but be the case with figures cooked up by imagination. As for the number organized into Fascist unions, they were given as 64,000 in November 1921 and as 250,000 in January 1922 (Pantaleoni, *Bolscevismo Italiano*, p. xxxi; Chiurco, *Storia della Rivoluzione Fascista*, 4:33).

In January 1922, under the direction of General Gandolfo, a national organization of the local squadrons was created. Zones of command were established with a centralized hierarchy. An illegal army was formed under the very eyes of the civil government, ready to revolt against it with the connivance of the chief of the regular army. There were two governments in Italy: a public government made up of the cabinet ministers, and a clandestine government made up of a group of army chiefs, who controlled local Fascist branches by means of Nationalists, discharged officers, and officers on leave.[11]

Fascist historiography gives the name of "bolshevism" not only to the events of 1919 and 1920 but also to those of 1921 and 1922, as if a homogeneous stream of acts of violence lasted from the spring of 1919 to the autumn of 1922. The truth is that one must make a sharp distinction between the period 1919–20 and the period 1921–22. In the first biennium, the disorders were almost always provoked by so-called Bolshevists. In the second period, the Fascists took the offensive and overwhelmed their adversaries. If the name of "bolshevism" is given to the first period, the second period must receive a different name: that of "anti-Bolshevist reaction." But the Italian disorders of 1919–20 do not deserve either the excess of honor or the indignity of being recorded in history under the name of "bolshevism." And the Italian reaction of 1921–22 had none of those formidable difficulties to overcome which in Russia frustrated every attempt at reaction. Between Russia and the Italy of 1919–22 there is the same difference as between a tornado which devastates a whole continent and a gale which breaks some windows and blows down some trees and chimney-pots. It would be more appropriate to speak of "postwar neurasthenia" in 1919–20 and of "civil war" in 1921–22. Moreover, two secondary periods must be distinguished in the civil war of 1921–22: the anti-trade union reaction, from the autumn of 1920 to the summer of 1921; and the military conspiracy, from the summer of 1921 to the autumn of 1922.

[11] G. Alessio, professor at the University of Padua in the Faculty of Law, and minister of justice from June 1920 to June 1921, stated publicly in 1925, without anyone's contesting his statement: "Generals who were discontented with their pensions which were not equal to their services, organized the disorderly forces" (*Per una nuova democrazia*, atti del Congresso dell'Unione Nazionale [Roma: Società Italiana di Edizioni, 1925], p. 89).

21

"A Leader Who Leads and Does Not Follow"

During the spring and summer of 1921, Mussolini grew uneasy about the situation which was developing under his own eyes. Each Fascist branch, controlled by its local leaders, followed its own policies according to local circumstances and paid little attention to suggestions or injunctions from any central committee. Though Mussolini was the nominal head of the movement, in fact his authority was very limited. He saw that the Nationalists, by infiltrating themselves among the Fascists, were becoming the real masters of what he considered his men. He defined the Nationalists as "the sharks of fascism" or as "mice who were nibbling the Fascist cheese and growing fat on it."

Among the Fascists, many who took seriously Mussolini's revolutionary fireworks were bewildered by the vast and rapid influx of wealthy and conservative people into their organization. An impecunious young man, Dino Grandi, who was destined to become Italian ambassador to the Court of St. James, in February 1921 complained that for the purpose of self-defense "the bourgeoisie was trying to obtain full control of the chaotic, aggressive Fascist formations" and expressed the hope that after this "transitory phenomenon," a new "socialism with new men would become stronger than ever."[1]

Perhaps from time to time Mussolini's incoherent and changeable spirit

---

[1] Letter to Missiroli, published in the Fascist magazine *Il Carroccio*, of New York, January 1928, p. 12, with facsimile. See also Chapter 18.

returned to his antibourgeois past. He could not have been so blinded by passion that he did not say to himself from time to time that if there was one man who had no right to treat the Italian working people with a cudgel and a revolver, that man was Mussolini. Before the war, none had contributed more than he to the spread of revolutionary and antinational socialism in Italy. He had launched among the masses the slogan of revolutionary neutrality in the face of the World War. During the war, none had made more lavish promises of peasant ownership and workers' control as a result of the "revolutionary war." None, in 1919–20, had contributed more to the revolutionary frenzy which led to the occupation of the factories.

On the other hand, he felt that vaster and vaster sections of the country were beginning to tire of the civil war; after damning the Socialists, they threatened now to revolt against the Fascists. Here is a fact which gives evidence for this new mood. On September 26, 1921, some Fascists in Modena were killed in an affray with the police. The Fascists of Florence endeavored to get up a demonstration of public mourning. The city remained indifferent. On September 30, the Fascists posted a manifesto in which they complained of the "open and overt hostility on the part of the citizens and especially of the bourgeoisie"; "very few citizens have felt it their duty to hang out flags of mourning for the tragic events of Modena. No shopkeepers closed their doors." This state of mind had begun to be noticeable immediately after the elections of May. Mussolini sensed it. Therefore, as soon as he was elected deputy, he tried to extricate himself from the clutches of the Nationalists.

He thought that he could solve the problem by stressing the republican character of the Fascist movement, offering his alliance to the moderate Socialists and to the Populists, and thus burn the bridges between Fascists and Nationalists. In an interview with the *Giornale d'Italia* of May 22, he declared:

> Fascism is republican in tendency ("è tendenzialmente repubblicano"). In this it differs distinctly from nationalism which is monarchist by definition. . . . In the field of social legislation and of improvement in the standard of life of the working classes, the Socialists may find unexpected allies within fascism. The salvation of the country may be assured not by suppressing the antithesis between fascism and socialism, but by reconciling them within Parliament. . . . It is

> evident that the coexistence of revolutionary and right-wing Socialists in the same party will, in the course of time, become impossible.

He ended by advocating a cabinet under the leadership of a Populist deputy: "In short, if at a given moment it pays us to do so, we shall support the government and even join it."

His interview aroused a wave of protest in the pro-Fascist conservative papers and widespread revolt among that part of the Fascist rank and file which was under Nationalist influence.[2] Mussolini at first thought that he could face the storm. In the *Popolo d'Italia* of May 24, 1921, he wrote:

> I shall not allow fascism to be altered and made unrecognizable by changing from republican in tendency, as I founded it, and as it ought to remain, to a monarchical, nay more, a dynastic movement. Our symbol is not the escutcheon of the House of Savoy; it is the Roman, and, with your permission, republican lictorial fascio. The Fascist abstention from the opening of Parliament is an act of plain logic. It is not permissible to preach one thing and practice another. If by chance these ideas of mine should not meet with the approval of fascism, it makes no difference to me. I am a chief who leads and not a chief who follows.

The next day, faced with the growing protest of his followers, "the chief who leads and does not follow" began to lower his sails:

> Fascism is superior to monarchy and republic. If fascism is monarchical, it is no longer fascism. If fascism is republican, it is no longer fascism. We do not mean to step into the shoes of the republican party, but we do not mean, either, to kneel before the throne. Nobody can swear that the destinies of Italy are bound up with the cause of monarchy, as the Nationalists will have it, or to the establishment of a republic, as the republicans believe. The future is uncertain, and the absolute does not exist. Those who would draw the conclusion that fascism espouses the republican cause, and regards the setting up of the republic as a prime necessity ("pregiudiziale repubblicana") reveal a lamentable want of

---

[2] Mowrer, *Immortal Italy*, p. 367.

understanding. In speaking of fascism as republican in tendency I only meant—speaking now for myself alone—to make a commotion in the stagnant waters and disturb certain frogs. The magnificent flame of Fascist youth runs the risk of being extinguished in the pool of conservatism and selfishness. Nests of cowardice are hidden within fascism—i.e. people who jeered at others or who jeered at us. Selfish elements, rapacious and rebellious against every aspiration towards national concord, have slipped into fascism. Others have taken advantage of Fascist violence, to satisfy paltry personal ambition.

He was confronted with a violent rebellion from the Nationalists who were bent upon destroying, to the last one, all Socialist and Populist organizations.[3] One of the leaders of this revolt was that same Grandi, who in February 1921 was so particular about the danger that the reactionary bourgeoisie was becoming master of the Fascist movement. Grandi, like Mussolini, passed from the right to the left, or from the left to the right, with wondrous versatility.

Mussolini did not give in. On July 13, 1921, he wrote:

> Until now we have used strong remedies to mend the ways of the Italian working people. But an able physician knows how to adapt the medicine to the course of the sickness. To speak of an Italian working class that now goes Bolshevist is absurd. Everyone knows that the mentality of the workers as a whole is basically different from what it was two years ago. Now is the moment to change the cure and to approach our working people with the aim of persuading them that Socialist doctrines are fallacious. . . . If we hold that we bear a truth, we ought to be ready to resort to other methods of competition. If we intend to remain always on the level of violence, this will show that we possess no truth, but we are only a negative phenomenon. I once was ready to consent to the use of violence. But now for national reasons, and above all for human reasons also, I am against it.

When the clash between the Fascists and carabineers occurred at Sarzana, Mussolini deplored the lack of discipline among his followers:

---

[3] See an article of July 1921, by Maffeo Pantaleoni, denouncing the "Bolshevist" degeneracy of Fascism: *Bolscevismo Italiano*, pp. 214 ff.

> There have flown into our organization thousands of individuals that see in fascism but a defense of their personal interests or an organization of violence for the sake of violence. A number of times in these columns have we said that violence must be chivalrous, aristocratic, surgical, and hence in a certain sense, humane. We spoke in vain. . . . We have to reestablish immediately individual and collective discipline. In a country like Italy, anarchic in tendency and spirit, fascism announced itself as a movement to restore discipline. Now if one is not capable of self-discipline, one can not pretend to impose discipline on the nation (*Popolo d'Italia*, July 24, 1921)."

On August 3, 1921, the representatives of the Fascist party and the Confederation of Labor signed an agreement, in which "they undertook at once to stop threats, acts of violence, reprisals, punishments, vendettas, pressures, and outrages of every kind." Things went from bad to worse. Sixty secretaries of Fascist branches representing 160,000 members met at Bologna and repudiated the agreement.[4] Mussolini took offence and resigned from the national executive of the Fasci. "Fascism," he wrote on August 7, 1921, "is no longer liberation, but tyranny; no longer the safeguard of the nation, but the upholding of private interests and of the most grovelling and unenlightened classes existing in Italy."

In the *Popolo d'Italia* of August 18, 1921, he asked:

> How is peace to come about? Perhaps you think you can get it by wiping out the two million citizens who voted for the Socialist party? But are you not running the risk of perpetrating civil war? Or of finding yourselves in rebellion against the whole spirit of the nation? Or of being obliged to submit to a Socialist peace tomorrow, owing to some other quite probable turn of the tables? Do you not see signs of this? Will not the united anti-Fascist front, destroyed by the agreement, form up again tomorrow almost automatically? I lay down the leadership. I remain, and hope to be able to remain, a simple member of the Fascio of Milan.

Cesare Rossi, the intimate collaborator of Mussolini, followed suit on August 20, 1921:

---

[4] Beals, *Rome or Death*, p. 64.

Since I have been one of the warmest advocates of the treaty of peace and also one of its signatories, I can no longer earnestly and honestly remain among the leaders of the Fascist organization, when, in noisy conferences and what is worse, by everyday happenings, it shows its determined hostility to the treaty. The early character of fascism has been swamped by the influx of latecomers who joined mainly when the enemy was beating a retreat. Innumerable grand panjandrums, who once formed the clerical-agrarian and conservative fraternities, have flooded fascism. Our courageous minority of 1919 has been overwhelmed by later waves of reinforcements, which brought in insincere or hysterical states of mind or interest of caste, class or local cliques. Fascism under the pressure of its rank and file, has become an absolutely conservative and reactionary movement. It is not the reaction we preached and practiced when Italy was really in danger of falling under the dictatorship of the Socialist party. It is the foolish, cruel and purposeless reaction against everything that points to the orderly, peaceable and necessary progress of the working classes today. The Fascists of the fighting zones wish, for instance, to eliminate strikes—a phenomenon which we may indeed try to render less frequent and less harmful, but which is also an economic reality and cannot be suppressed; but in actual fact they end by obstructing the liberty of assembly, the freedom of the press and the right of association of their opponents. That very mentality of petty, tyrannical, overbearing bullying, of which we used to accuse the Socialist party in the days of their arrogance, has now been wholly transferred to the rank and file of the Fascist movement. Have you ever asked yourselves, for instance, how many sacred affections are associated with those houses and their furniture, which our followers burn with such an easy conscience in some parts of the Po Valley, only because they are the homes of their opponents? The motion passed during the occupation of the factories in September 1920, against a political development of the movement, the breach between Socialists and Communists at the congress of Leghorn, the present crusade of the Communists against the Socialist party and the Confederation of Labor, the disillusionment about bolshevism in the minds of the working classes, the patriotic revival in the last municipal elections, the Fascist counteroffensive, the new cleavage between right-wingers and Maximalists: all these facts do not exist and have no value for those thoughtless ones, who are in the

habit of muddling up everything. We plunge forward one
time consecrating a flag and another invading a town, without any coherent plan, without discipline, incapable of re-
flecting, incapable of facing the problems of the hour. The
Fasci have carefully refrained from establishing one single
popular library. The most they do is to burn down those of
their opponents. Those who rejected the treaty of peace did
not understand that it met a national necessity, was a patriotic duty and for Fascism in particular represented an immediate and future advantage.

Words thrown to the winds! The industrialists, the agrarians, and the
military clique did not wish to listen; and the Fascist rank and file which
carried out punitive expeditions—excited by the fighting, pleased to hunt
down "Bolshevist" peasants like wild beasts, well-paid and sure of impunity
—were even less disposed to listen than those who cool-headedly pulled the
strings.

Under such circumstances what could "the leader who leads and does
not follow" do? If he had continued to condemn the "foolish, cruel and
purposeless reaction," Mussolini would have been left a general of a melting
army, without the subsidies of the businessmen. His paper would have gone
bankrupt. He was determined at all costs not to let things come to this.
"The Rubicon cannot be passed twice," he said several years ago to Briand.
He ceased to swim against the tide. He devoted himself to philosophical
meditations and discovered that fascism did not possess a doctrine of its
own and that this inconvenience must be remedied without delay: "Italian
fascism," he wrote on August 27, 1921, "in order to avoid death, or worse,
suicide, must give itself a body of doctrines. . . . I wish and hope that in
the next two months before our national congress assembles, the philosophy
of Italian fascism is created."

The actual fact was that the Nationalists did not need to create any
philosophy, since they had had their own philosophy for more than ten
years, and the Fascists had other things to do besides creating a philosophy.

After having indulged in philosophical meditations until November
1921, Mussolini appeared at the Congress of Rome as if nothing had ever
happened to induce him to resign from the leadership of the movement.
No one spoke of that affair. Mussolini and Grandi kissed each other, and
the leader who leads went on following his own followers. The Nationalists

exulted: "The Fascist is of our blood. When he has come more clearly to know himself, when he has arrived . . . to a more conscious maturity, he will be glad to come to the side of this father" (*Idea Nazionale*, November 27, 1921).

The moment selected by Mussolini to follow his followers had been well chosen. Until the autumn of 1921, the first role as hero of the Fascists had fallen to D'Annunzio. After D'Annunzio had deserted his post as condottiere of the Blackshirts in the projected *coup de main* of November 1921, Mussolini jumped to the forefront. From now on, he became the sole and undisputed leader—"the Duce." The army chiefs and Nationalists who pulled the strings behind the scenes had need of someone who would assume the public responsibility for the antiparliamentary movement. They were bound to the king and to the constitution by an oath of loyalty which they did not dare to violate openly and brutally. The Fascists, by attacking the Parliament and threatening the king who had refused to carry out a *coup d'état* against Parliament, allowed the generals to appear as mediators between the king, to whom they made a pretense of remaining loyal, and the Fascists, whose movement they claimed to be overpowering and invincible. For this maneuver to succeed it was necessary that the Fascist movement should publicly be led by a man who, consistent with his own past, could threaten and frighten the king.

Mussolini's task was not an easy one. If one surveys the groups which were jumbled together in the Fascist movement, one finds that the first Fasci of 1919–20 had included elements of three different origins: (1) old revolutionists who, in the autumn of 1914, had revealed a more or less confused Nationalist mentality, although continuing to call themselves revolutionists; (2) ex-servicemen of the lower middle classes, who had been uprooted by the war and who revolted in a disorderly way against the material sufferings and the moral delusions inherent in the transition from war to peace; and (3) young men of the intellectual classes, who intended to oppose antipatriotic propaganda and strikes. Left to themselves, these first groups would never have been able to form a permanent political movement of national importance. Little by little, as the postwar neurasthenia calmed down, everyone would have been reabsorbed by his own social group and would have gone his own way.

In 1921, the great majority of the newcomers who joined in with the meager nucleus of the first hour continued to come from those same lower middle classes who already formed the rank and file of the movement. But the old revolutionists and the students, who, in the two preceding years had furnished almost all the leaders of the local groups, soon found themselves reduced to a minority by a new social element, the officers of the regular army and the agents of the industrialists and the landowners. The Fascist movement was no longer merely a patriotic reaction, more or less convulsed, against the political action of the Socialists and Communists. It became the instrument of a methodical capitalistic reaction, which aimed at demolishing all the economic institutions which the Italian working classes had built up for their defense and betterment during the half-century of the free regime. Besides this, in 1921, the local actions, at first uncoordinated, began to obey a higher political direction, and in 1922 they fused into a true and proper movement of national character.

All social classes contributed to swell this movement. On the other side, men from every social class were also found among all the anti-Fascist groups, just as men from every social class were found among the vast mass of indifferents who went on minding their own business. Political history is made not by social classes, but by political parties, which consist of men who come from different social strata but are knit together by a common aim: the conquest of political power. Even when the proclaimed aim of a political party is that of fostering the interests or rights of one class against the others, the party still remains as a political organization which is not to be confused with that social class.

No doubt capitalists were to be found in the Fascist movement. If capitalists had not supported the movement with their money, the movement would have exhausted itself in inefficient clamors. On the other hand, if they had been left to themselves, the Fascists and the capitalists might at most have created a new political party—one among many others, and their rapid overwhelming victory would remain a miracle, an unfathomable mystery. This victory is to be explained by the fact that the army chiefs equipped the movement with weapons and leadership, and a section of the Italian public officials—the police and the judiciary—gave it the privilege of immunity. Big business—or, as the Marxists call it, "capitalism"—occupied, and still occupies, a prominent place in the Fascist structure. But if one ignores the other factors of that structure: the middle and lower middle class elements who provided the rank and file, the army chiefs, the Nationalist leaders, the police, and the judges, one is unable to understand the working of the whole system.

This movement (we do not mean the pseudorevolutionary inefficient movement of 1919–20, but the anti-trade unionist and antiparliamentarist efficient movement of 1921–22) was not Mussolini's creation. The Fascist branches in the various cities, towns, and villages were founded by retired officers, officers on leave, agents of businessmen, and students. The movement included men of the most diverse origins and mentality: employers of labor, who provided funds, and Syndicalists, who but yesterday had led revolutionary strikes against these very employers; army officers, schooled in monarchical ideas, and republicans, who would have nothing to do with monarchy; landowners, who took up arms to defend their property, and half-starved intellectual proletarians, with nothing to lose and everything to gain; boys of good families, playing truant from the schools to join in punitive expeditions, under the illusion that they were doing a patriotic thing, and criminals, who took advantage of these same expeditions to gratify their lust for violence.

The official historian of fascism, Signor Volpe, described Mussolini's movement such as it was in 1921–22 in the following terms:

> There were among them persons who had survived shipwrecks of various groups and parties, and deserted from other allegiances, newcomers belonging to no party and with no political past, and men who had come fresh from the trenches and from Fiume. Their essential and central thought was a war had been fought and won. . . . They were thirsty for order, productive labor, command and obedience. . . . Also, if you please, they were moved by lust for adventure, by the fascination of rapid and dangerous punitive expeditions as in time of war, by their youthful love of parades and flags stirring in the wind. Let us add, also, the class interests and the calculations of war profiteers and of scared bourgeois disposed to give money for blood and eager to solicit and to accept from others, from anyone, that salvation which they were unable to secure themselves. Neither must we exclude vile passions, the spirit of violence and of oppression, old and never dying factional selfishness, the rush of people with no occupation and no means, and other more or less pathological and physiological manifestations. . . . From its followers fascism at the beginning asked little or nothing in the matter of ideas. The doors were wide open. Everybody could enter, the wildest Communists not excluded. It was a question of action, of fighting, of demolishing, of smashing the organizations of the Italians with

Bolshevist tendencies; everybody who felt called to such activity was welcome in the Fascist ranks.[5]

The Fascist historian prudently refrained from pointing out in what proportion these contrasting elements stood in the Fascist formation: the thirst for order and the love of adventure, the rush of people with no occupation and no means and the thirst of productive labor, the disinterested patriotic faith and the vile passions. Another Fascist writer has been more precise on this point:

> The early squadrons, still in full disorder and chaotic, were formed from very strange and very different elements: former arditi, legionaries from Fiume, Anarchists who had been in the war, many unemployed of various types, a few young intellectuals and idealists lost in the crowd, and a scum of scoundrels. Yes, of scoundrels I say, of that type of scoundrels to whom the future dedicates monuments, bandits like those who first built Rome, pirates like those who laid the foundations of the Republic of Venice or of British power; adventurers like certain nobles of the Crusades. Sublime scoundrels who found redemption in an ideal which at least in its initial stage was moral, in the fire of a common spirit, in discipline, obedience and sacrifice.[6]

Each local group not only was formed of heterogeneous social elements, but followed impulses of its own according to local situations. An American student to whom we owe the best work known to us on the origins of the Fascist movement has observed that "in Romagna the Fasci were marching against the king, in Cremona against the pope, in Venetia against the Slavs, in the Tyrol against the Germans. All were against the 'Bolshevists,' but 'Bolshevists' might be the proletarians in one part, bourgeoisie in another."[7]

Holding these diverse elements together and justifying their work and their association required no ordinary amount of skill. Collective political action is only possible when those taking part in it can hoist the banner of some common faith which appeals to their better feelings, even if their

---

[5] G. Volpe, *Lo sviluppo storico del Fascismo*, in *La Civiltà Fascista* (Torino: U.T.E.T., 1928), pp. 12–14.

[6] Pellizzi, *Problemi e realtà del Fascismo*, p. 101.

[7] C. Yarrow, in his unfortunately yet unpublished PhD. dissertation, *Ideological Origins of Italian Fascism* (Yale University, 1934), p. 184.

activities spring from baser motives. It might well have seemed an impossibility to find a common faith for such a motley crowd. A Nationalist wrote in 1923:

> It was necessary to enact an out-and-out conservative program without any open clash with the demagogical prejudices that beset the political mentality of the nation, to feign to go towards the left while going towards the right, to assume an aesthetic pose of demagogy and conclude with a thesis of realistic good sense. It was necessary to perform a masterpiece of seduction on a whole people.[8]

Mussolini performed this masterpiece of seduction. He came from the lower middle classes, being the son of a blacksmith and an elementary school teacher who lived in a village of Romagna, and in his adolescence he had become an elementary school teacher. Thus he possessed firsthand experience in the mentality of those who made up the mass of his followers. He had been a jobless day laborer and was thus acquainted with the mentality of the starving unemployed worker. He had been a journalist, first of the extreme left and then of the extreme right, and thus he had gained wide knowledge of the leading personnel in the various Italian political parties. He was endowed with exceptional quickness of assimilation and a sharp intuition of the feelings of his public at any given moment. He possessed a peculiar ability in improvising catchwords and slogans, empty of meaning but resounding, which gave to the crowd the illusion of ideas which suddenly became clear. To these brilliant gifts was added an absolute moral indifference in the choice of ways and means to attain his ends. Above all, he possessed a strong, tenacious will to self-assertion, which seems to be an essential requirement in a politician who wants success, be he a genius or a makeshift, the most honest of men or the lowest of scoundrels. Of that proteiform multitude which was flowing into the Fascist movement, he was the proteiform journalist, propagandist, and animator. He stood in the limelight arousing the enthusiasm of the younger men by his daily articles, urging ever new offensive movements and boasting that he was the author of everything that was happening and not happening everywhere. From the incoherent concoction of anti-Bolshevist, Nationalist, Syndicalist, Anarchist, antiparliamentarian, revolutionary and vice versa

---

[8] Giuliano, *L'esperienza politica dell'Italia,* p. 307.

formulae which made up his intellectual baggage and that of his followers, he was quick to pick up from day to day some formula or scrap of a formula with which to please some without displeasing others, encourage some without disheartening the rest. He would unsay today what he said yesterday. He would contradict himself on the same day, on different pages of the same paper, in different sentences of the same article.

There was among the younger generation a blind eagerness to assert one's own personality against everybody else and at any cost; a fury of what may be called "intellectual abdication," a deep dislike of any effort to explore and bring light by means of logic and reflection into that dark zone which exists in our spirit and where the lower instincts of our nature are kept in check. Mussolini was proud to define himself as antirational, instinctive, anti-intellectual, pragmatic. He disparaged reason and logic as signs of spiritual poverty and creators of weakness of will. In November 1921, Einstein came to Italy to lecture on his theory of relativity, and gentlemen and ladies in every drawing room were discussing Einstein's relativity without in the least understanding the subject. Mussolini immediately seized upon the new incomprehensible word and proclaimed that he himself had already discovered and applied the principle of relativity in the field of politics before Einstein discovered and applied it in the field of science:

> Fascism has been a super-relativist movement. It has gone ahead by means of fragmentary intuitions. Everything which I have said and done in these past years has been relativism by intuition. The fact that we have taken from other parties all that which pleased and helped us, the fact that we have cast aside all that which did not please us and harmed us, are so many documents of our relativistic mentality.[9]

The mercenaries who formed the rank and file of the movement felt no need of a logically woven political doctrine; they had an immediate and profitable task before them—to knock down all who offered resistance and to get their salaries from such honorable conduct. To young intellectuals who cared for ideals, Mussolini offered Syndicalist fireworks. Many would never have followed him if they had realized that they were furthering

[9] *Popolo d'Italia*, November 22, 1921.

selfish and reactionary interests. These Mussolini fooled into believing that they were bringing about a new and more noble form of civilization. To the industrialists, landowners, bankers, and shopkeepers who did not receive salaries but paid them out, and who would not be content with fireworks, he offered the punitive expeditions, the devastation of the workers' organizations, and the killing or banishing of the organizers. To the republicans, he declared himself to be a potential republican. To the officers of the army and the seditious generals who accredited the movement, he promised that he would become a monarchist as soon as the king became more monarchical.

One of his most successful verbal tricks—destined for a great future, in Italy and outside—was that of bestowing the magical name of "revolution" upon the movement of lawless violence which his followers were carrying on with the connivance of the army chiefs, the bench, and the police. When lawless violence is carried on by the forces of the regular government against organizations or individuals who are outside the government, this lawlessness is not "revolution"—it is "terrorism." Mussolini succeeded wonderfully in turning all notions topsy-turvy so well that there were people who never suspected that under a curtain of "revolutionary" words a capitalist-militarist undertaking was being carried out.[10] He used to say: "The greater the confusion the better." By terming as a "revolution"—nay, a "great revolution," or, still better, the "greatest revolution in history"—the Fascist movement, he created the most skillful alibi for his defense against the charge of inconsistency and opportunism. He was in a position to maintain that he always had been a revolutionary, with no breach of continuity from his youthful escapades in Romagna and in Switzerland to the heights of power. If his followers looted, burned, and murdered, this happened because they were carrying on a "revolution." Even such an admirer of St. Francis of Assisi as G.K. Chesterton shared the view that "the indefensible acts of violence" of fascism must be judged from a different point of view than that of normal morality and concluded by

---

[10] "The merit of nationalism has been that of affirming with admirable theoretic clarity, the necessity of the counterrevolution . . . and the merit of fascism has been that of having brought about such a life-saving revolution" (Giuliano, *L'Esperienza Politica dell'Italia*, p. 306). In 1932, in his talks with Ludwig, Mussolini said: "We need to speak of permanent revolution because it exerts a mystical influence upon the masses. It is stimulating, too, for persons of higher intelligence. When we talk of permanent revolution, we imply that the times are exceptional, and we give the man in the street a feeling that he is participating in an extraordinary movement" (E. Ludwig, *Talks with Mussolini* [Boston: Little, Brown and Co., 1933], p. 103).

stating that "it is just as easy and in one sense quite as just to call Michael Collins a murderer as to call Mussolini a murderer."[11] To put on the same "revolutionary" level Michael Collins, who never had been supported by the police and the bench and the army of England, Scotland, and Ireland, and Mussolini, who had been backed by those same forces in Italy, required a rather exceptional effort of good will. On the basis of the fact that fascism was not "terrorism" but "revolution" it was easy to discover that all Fascist acts of violence were legitimate: "We have here, in fact," writes an English propaganda agent, "a revolution in many ways as fundamental as the French and Russian Revolutions. . . . Unfortunately excesses are the inevitable accompaniments of every great revolution. Every fair-minded person will make allowances for them."[12]

The Christian mystics resolve all the logical inconsistencies of their thinking in an act of supernatural love in which all contradictions disappear. Mussolini resolved all contradictions in the magic word "revolution." Those who believe in the "revolution" must live in danger, challenge life, dare or die. Action for the victory of "revolution" does not need to be justified either by logical rules or by moral principles. To youth, Mussolini offered the idea that he and his party alone were working for the "revolution" while all other parties were betraying the "revolution." To this youth he was the leader, "il Duce," the "Savior," the "messenger of God," the "man of destiny." He worked up a large section of the youth of Italy into a state of frenzied excitement.

The future historian who will try to call back to life in his pages the men and the events of Italy's "Fascist revolution," and who will know more than we do because a further century of research shall have been added to our records, will most likely conclude his narrative of the Fascist origins and early development by such a simple statement as: Mussolini was not the creator of the Fascist movement, but he was really and truly the creator of the Fascist myth and of Fascist mysticism.

[11] G.K. Chesterton, *The Resurrection of Rome* (New York: Dodd, Mead & Co., 1930), pp. 210 ff.

[12] J.S. Barnes, *The Universal Aspects of Fascism* (London: Williams and Norgate, 1928), pp. 14–15.

22

The
Populist Party
and the Vatican

During 1919 and 1920, the Populists were compactly anti-Fascist and anti-Socialist. It could not have been otherwise, given the antireligious attitude of both the Fascists and the Socialists. In addition, there was lively competition between Socialists and Populists in trade union activities—a competition which, as we already know, often assumed forms of extreme violence. This competition was well received by the conservative clerical faction of the Populist party insofar as it prevented the Socialists from gaining undisputed monopoly over working-class organizations. But the sentiments of the conservative clericals reversed when the Populist trade unions demanded higher wages, went on strike, and showed such disrespect for the rights of property as the Socialists also could be proud of. In addition, the Populist rank and file would have been willing to cooperate with the right-wing Socialists as soon as the latter had prevailed over the Maximalists and extremists. The conservative clericals worried about this danger. They endured Don Sturzo and his democracy as one endures an inoculation of rabies or tetanus in small doses to prevent rabies and tetanus in more frightening forms.

Until the summer of 1920, Pope Benedict XV, his secretary of state Cardinal Gasparri, and the bishops ignored the activities of the Populist party. The official theory was that the Populist party was autonomous from the ecclesiastical authorities and that the latter left it full liberty and responsibility. The first symptoms of ill-humor in the high clergy showed themselves in the summer of 1920—that is, between the military revolt of Ancona and the occupation of the factories, when it seemed that Italy was really on the brink of social revolution. On August 6, 1920, Cardinal Boggiani, archbishop of Genoa, issued a pastoral letter to the clergy of his diocese, in which he forbade the associations recognized as Catholic by the ecclesiastical authorities to affiliate themselves with the Populist party. This party had nothing to do with the Catholic Action, he said. Its deputies not only had no mandate from the Catholics, but "had shown that they did not possess the necessary qualifications to obtain legitimately and to carry out successfully such a mandate."[1]

The discontent aroused by this letter was so strong among the Populists of Genoa that Pope Benedict XV, although approving of Boggiani's way of thinking, recalled him to Rome, in a letter which for the moment remained confidential, and gave him a less imprudent successor.

Soon it became clear that Cardinal Boggiani was not alone. In September 1920, during the weeks of the occupation of the factories, the municipal elections began to take place all over Italy. These elections, unlike the political ones, were not carried out by the method of proportional representation. The list which received the most votes gained four-fifths of the seats; the list which received the second highest number of votes received one-fifth of the seats; the other lists got nothing. "National blocks" or "anti-Bolshevist leagues" arose everywhere with the intent of opposing the Socialist candidates. These coalitions everywhere asked the Populists to become their partners. Don Sturzo and the national executive of the Populist party, faithful to the will of the rank and file, decided that the party should nowhere ally with any other parties.

Not only were the protests from the "anti-Bolshevist leagues" loud, but on September 24, 1920, several newspapers of Rome announced that Cardinal Pompilj, bishop of Velletri, had issued a letter to inform his "block" that Benedict XV "did not approve of the electoral tactics of the Populist party." The next day, the Rome mouthpiece of the Populist party, the *Corriere Italiano*, asserted that the letter was forged. But on September 28, another prelate, Cardinal Pignatelli, bishop of Albano, took the field; in an interview given to the newspaper *La Tribuna*, while he denied that there existed a circular from the Vatican on the subject of the elections, he blamed the tactics of the Populist party, announced that Cardinal Pompilj

---

[1] *I due anni dell'episcopato genovese del Card. Pio Boggiani: Atti pastorali* (Acquapendente: Stabilimento Tip. Lemurio, 1922), p. 137. Cf. *Corriere della sera*, August 8, 1920.

was of the same opinion, and added: "I do not believe that it is far from the truth to assert that this is also the thought of the Vatican, opposed to that of the directors of the Populist party."[2] Thus, even if the letter of Cardinal Pompilj might have been a fake, his thought had not been at all faked. Immediately afterwards, the *Settimana Sociale,* official mouthpiece of the "Unione Popolare," which depended officially on the Holy See, entered the fray. According to this paper, electoral isolation should be the rule every time alliances were harmful or useless; but to such a rule "prudent, as well as worthy exceptions" should be made when alliances with other parties were "the only means of preventing the triumph of ideas contrary to religious principles and social order." On September 27–28, 1920, the *Osservatore Romano* interpreted the words of its brother as a "warning to the Catholics that they should concern themselves seriously, before it was too late, with situations which, on account of complex moral and religious reasons, could not be dealt with from merely political and electoral standpoints." The paper ended by inviting the national directorate of the Populist party "to an unimpassioned and free examination of several local conditions." They should remember that "in comparison with higher interests, religious and civil, political interests and party interests, especially in a moment of exceptional gravity, ought not to sacrifice themselves, but coordinate themselves with those higher interests."

From this moment on, the conservative clericals could maintain that if they rebelled against the Populist party, they were obeying "higher religious and civil interests," according to the advice given by the Vatican. In the large cities, in which, for thirty years, the clericals had allied themselves with the Conservatives in the municipal elections, the rebellions and threats of rebellion were so great that Don Sturzo and the directorate of the party did not dare to buck the tempest, and they announced that they were willing to permit "anti-Bolshevist" alliances wherever the necessity was evident. In Rome, no alliance was allowed, and the party presented its own list. In Turin, Don Sturzo permitted the local branch of the party to participate in the "anti-Bolshevist" alliance. In Ferrara, Modena, Venice, Padua, Brescia, he closed his eyes and let the Populists enter "anti-Bolshevist" blocks.[3] In Milan, Don Sturzo advised the Populists to abstain, but the conservative clericals did not obey. The Catholic newspaper *Italia,*

---

[2] *Tribuna,* September 28, 1920.
[3] Interview of Don Sturzo with the *Giornale d'Italia,* November 3, 1920; Vercesi, *Il movimento cattolico in Italia,* p. 167.

November 3, 1920, and a deputy enrolled in the Populist party, Nava, summoned the Catholics to vote for the "anti-Bolshevist" list. On November 5, 1920, the paper *La Perseveranza* announced that "a very high ecclesiastic figure" (in whom everyone recognized Cardinal Ferrari, archbishop of Milan) invited "whoever had at heart the real good of the city" to vote for the anti-Socialist coalition.[4] In the smaller cities and in the countryside, the Conservatives and the high clergy made no headway. The rank and file remained compact behind Don Sturzo.

When the Fascists, at the end of 1920, began to destroy the Socialist organizations, the conservative elements of the Populist party sided with the Fascists with all their hearts.[5] In the rank and file there was a beginning of confusion. Where the Socialists had established their own monopoly and had shown themselves to be overbearing with the Populists, the latter considered the Fascist offensive against the Socialists as a liberation. But hardly did the Fascists set out to smash the Populist organizations, than the mass of the party, although without associating with the Socialists, became thoroughly opposed to the Fascists. Don Sturzo, now as always, sided with the rank and file.

And behold, in his maiden parliamentary speech of June 21, 1921, to the great astonishment of everybody who knew of his past antireligious record, Mussolini offered the alliance of the Fascists not only to the Socialists, but also to the Populists. Nay more, he asserted the necessity of solving the Roman question:

> There is one problem which is much more important than all others which are but contingent. That is the historic problem of the relations between Italy and the Vatican. . . . I assert that the Latin and imperial tradition of Rome is represented today by Catholicism. . . . I think and I affirm that the only universal idea which exists today in Rome is that which radiates from the Vatican. . . . I think that if the Vatican will definitely renounce its dreams of temporal power—and I believe that it is already on that path—lay Italy must furnish the Vatican with material help and facili-

---

[4] M. Vaussard, "La crise du Parti Populaire Italien," in the *Revue Bleu*, June 18, 1921, pp. 382–83; Vercesi, *Il movimento cattolico in Italia*, pp. 167–83.

[5] U. Questa, *Mussolini e la Chiesa* (Roma: Casa Edit. Pinciana, 1936), p. 63–64: "Those groups which might be termed old Catholics, whether enrolled or not in the Populist party . . . , followed with sympathetic attention and even with unconcealed pleasure, the Fascist action." This author was enrolled in the Fascist party.

ties for the schools, the churches, the hospitals, and with any other support that a secular power has at its disposal. The development of Catholicism in the world is both an interest and a source of pride for us Italians.

This invitation fell on deaf ears. The moral conscience of the "thin people" organized by the Populist party had been offended by the cruelty of the civil war. Even had he been another man, and had he given in to the urging of Mussolini, Don Sturzo would have been followed by no more than a scanty minority of his party. On the other hand, the tenderness of Mussolini for the Vatican was so unexpected that no one trusted it. In August 1921, Benedict XV publicly condemned "the cruel expeditions, perpetrated by men of evil intentions" in Istria against the clergy of Slavonic language: "Priests, guilty of no other crime than that of belonging to the same nationality (Slav) and speaking the tongue of the worshippers . . . are victims of bloody atrocities and insults of every kind." The pope deplored also that "the above-mentioned crimes were committed without punishment."[6]

Instead of agreeing to the entente with the Fascists, several groups of the Populist party, in the summer of 1921, began to discuss publicly whether it was not advisable to ally with the Socialists for the formation of a cabinet which would disarm the Fascists and put an end to civil war. On September 13, 1921, the weekly *Il Popolo Nuovo*, the official organ of the directorate of the Populist party and controlled by Don Sturzo, announced the terms that the Socialists should accept to make an alliance possible. They were to respect "the liberty of Christian conscience," to

[6] Giunta answered the letter of Benedict XV and charged the Slav priests with "being the most fierce propagandists against Italy." "In Trieste itself, and right in the Church of Sant'Antonio where sermons in Slavic tongue are allowed, the Fascists have had to interfere because Italy was being insulted. In certain localities the Communists depend on the priest, who, being Slav, agrees with them in sabotaging Italy. The Fascists in Venezia Giulia have friendly relations with the Italian priests and are in perfect harmony with the Populist party itself. I will say furthermore, that the Populist party of Trieste voted for the national list, that is to say, for the Fascists. In Istria, the Fascists asked for the cooperation of the Populists. This was fully conceded, nay more, it was ordered by Don Sturzo, but it failed to materialize as a result of erroneous standpoints of the directors of the Populist party in Istria. During the electoral struggle, the Fascists, of course, fought with all means in their power. To the treachery of the Slav propagandists they sometimes opposed violence. It was a question of saving the Fatherland of Nazario Sauro [an Italian war hero who was sentenced to death by the Austrian military courts during the War of 1914–18] from the shame of electing as representatives the stranglers of the martyr. In the name of Sauro, the Fascists fought for Istria against the Slavs as the Crusaders fought for Palestine against the heathen in the name of Christ" (*Popolo d'Italia*, August 26, 1921).

specify a reasonable program of immediate financial and economic reforms, and to grant to the Populist organizations rights equal to those of the Socialists. The *Tribuna,* on September 14, 1921, commenting upon this statement, said: "For the first time, the Populists have presented to the Socialists a definite basis for an understanding and common action."

The problem was discussed in the national congress of the party, which took place at Venice on October 20–23, 1921. The conservative clericals, feeling themselves to be a slender minority, did not dare propose that the party should ally itself with the Fascists and with the conservative non-Catholic groups; they confined themselves to demanding that this alliance not be forbidden. The democrats, who held the enormous majority in the congress, agreed not to exclude absolutely an alliance toward the right; but the declaration voted by the congress offered the alliance to the Socialists, provided that the latter "put aside the apocalyptic illusion of the dictatorship of the proletariat," accepted a "policy based on realities," and "assumed the responsibilities of government effectively and efficiently."[7]

If this offer had been accepted by the Socialists, a solid government, supported by a powerful majority of Parliament, would have been born a year before the "March on Rome." Perhaps it would have reestablished public peace in Italy and saved parliamentary institutions from disaster. But the Maximalists were doped by the formulae of Marxism, and the right-wingers were undecided and fearful of assuming the responsibilities of government. As a consequence, when they advocated an alliance between the Populist party and the conservative non-Catholic parties reinforced by the Fascists, the conservative clericals had the advantage of advocating a possible policy. The Populists, paralyzed by the blindness of the Maximalists and the indecision of the right-wingers, had no chance for a positive action.

To the assistance of the conservative clericals came the *Osservatore Romano* in an article of January 1, 1922. The official newspaper of the Vatican lamented the days when "Catholic action is less felt by politicians, by organizers and writers." Then the *Cittadino* of Brescia came in, attacking the Populist party and the economic organizations depending upon it insofar as they gave the first place not to Catholic action, but to "least sound politics." The *Avvenire d'Italia* of Bologna came in third. For a year it had been advocating the alliance between the Populist party and the

---

[7] Vercesi, *Il movimento cattolico in Italia,* p. 210.

Fascists. It, too, denounced the danger that "big organizations" (that is to say, the unions depending on the Populist party), might forfeit "that unifying force which is to be found only in Catholic Action." Then the *Unità Cattolica* of Florence began to demand with fervid zeal that the Catholics return to their "glorious traditions." The conservative clericals did not dare to charge the Populists with being democratic. They threw out against them the insinuation that they were not sufficiently Catholic. They hoped to bewilder the rank and file.

The campaign of the conservative clerical newspapers in January 1922 was certainly willed by the Vatican. Proof of this fact is the article of the *Osservatore Romano.* Articles on matters of that kind are never published in that newspaper unless they have first been sanctioned by the secretary of state.

To understand this attitude of the Vatican, one has to know that the Holy See was going through serious financial difficulties. Already at the time of Pius IX, Peter's Pence hardly covered all the needs of the Vatican. Leo XIII earned for himself the reputation of a miser by reducing expenditure with inflexible will. In order to increase his resources, he engaged in real estate speculations in Rome; that is, he endeavored to make money by profiting from the fact that the city was developing as the capital of Italy —this while he was protesting that Rome should not be the capital of Italy. The tragic crisis in real estate which came in 1887 devoured a lot of his savings. Pius X had to live from day to day. To meet the most essential expenses, he sold all the valuables which were offered him by the devout. Under Benedict XV, during the war, the Catholics of France and Belgium had to cut drastically their contributions to Peter's Pence, not only because they were impoverished by the war, but above all because they were discontent with the policies of Benedict XV and Cardinal Gasparri. The French religious corporations which had invested huge capitals in Russia had lost everything as a result of the Bolshevist revolution; not only were they unable to contribute any longer to the upkeep of the Holy See, but they needed to be helped by the latter. At the end of the war, even the Austrian bonds fell to zero, while in 1915 Cardinal Gasparri had alienated a part of the Italian securities which the Holy See possessed in order to buy Austrian securities.[8] The frightful economic crisis which Austria and Germany had

---

[8] We owe this information to a reliable source—that is, to a person who had an important position in the bank of Rome, whose directors advised the Holy See to carry out this operation.

to undergo from 1919 on left the Vatican without the contributions of the German Catholics, while the French and Belgians continued to strike. The Vatican in the postwar period lived for the most part on the contributions from North and South America, but this income did not cover all expenses. Benedict XV was sometimes driven to beg from his visitors: from the wife of a great Piedmontese industrialist he asked a million lire.[9] To increase the worries of the Vatican, in September 1920 Giolitti had Parliament pass a law which required owners of public or private securities to register them under their own names so that they would not escape dead duties or personal levies. This system existed in England. But the Vatican and the religious corporations were terrified. If they had to register their securities under the name of some possessors, they would have had to entrust their capital to persons who usually were old people; as a consequence, very high death duties would have to be paid very often and within a few years would have devoured the entire capital.[10] As if all these troubles were not enough, the Bank of Rome, to which the Vatican and many Catholic institutions had entrusted a good part of their money, had been so poorly managed that it was on the brink of bankruptcy.

Under all these circumstances, the Vatican was eager (and the conservative clericals insisted) that the Populist party should ally itself with the Conservative and filo-Fascist groups who were willing to pay for its alliance by repealing the personal registration of securities and rescuing the Bank of Rome. The rank and file of the Populist party knew nothing about these affairs, and they refused to ally with the Fascists. This is why the Populist party was in disgrace with Cardinal Gasparri.

The journalistic campaign of January 1922 was not carried on against Benedict XV's will. He must have felt the financial worries no less than his secretary of state. Furthermore, an alliance of the Italian Catholics with the Socialists was too much of a leap in the dark. Leo XIII had encouraged the Christian Democratic movement with the encyclical *Rerum Novarum* (1891), and then with the encyclical *Graves de Communi* (1902) he had put a brake on it. But it is idle to speculate about what Benedict XV would have done if he had lived. The fact is that he died on January 22, 1922, and was succeeded by Cardinal Achille

---

[9] C. Loiseau, *Politique romaine et sentiment français* (Paris: Grasset, 1923), pp. 38–39.
[10] L. Einaudi, *La guerra e il sistema tributario italiano* (Bari: Laterza, 1927), p. 368; G.E. Curatolo, *La questione romana da Cavour a Mussolini* (Roma: Libreria del Littorio, 1928), p. 176.

Ratti, archbishop of Milan, who took the name of Pius XI.

Achille Ratti's father had been a foreman in a silk factory in Lombardy. Achille Ratti, as a young man, had lived as a preceptor in noble families in Bologna and in Milan. As a pope, he conferred the title of count upon his brother who had gotten rich during the war,[11] and he pompously celebrated in the Vatican the marriage of his niece, as if she had been a princess of imperial blood. Pius X, who also came of humble parentage, had never allowed his relatives to abandon the social station to which they had been born.

Pius XI came from that section of the clergy which had always longed for the conciliation between state and Church in Italy in order to oppose the rising tide of socialism with the compact resistance of all the conservative elements, be they Catholic or "Liberal." In the summer of 1920, when the armies of Bolshevist Russia arrived under the walls of Warsaw, Monsignor Ratti was in that city as apostolic visitor. All the other diplomats ran away. He remained at his post. This contact with authentic bolshevism seems to have left on his spirit an indelible impression. Of all that which was happening in Italy in 1919 and 1920, he read in Poland what the conservative newspapers of Milan were saying and denounced the "bloody tyranny of Italian bolshevism." Monsignor Ratti was persuaded that in Italy affairs were going as in Russia and in the sections of Poland which were infested with the Bolshevist contagion. Benedict XV made the best possible gift to the Milanese conservatives when he recalled Ratti from Poland and appointed him archbishop of Milan (June 13, 1921). It is likely that Achille Ratti, after his return from Poland and before his appointment as archbishop of Milan was officially announced, had come in contact with Mussolini and disarmed his belligerent anticlericalism. If this really was the case, the address made by Mussolini on June 21, 1921, in the Chamber was the outcome of those first exchanges of views. Be that as it may, the cardinals were well aware of what they were doing in February 1922 when they chose Achille Ratti to be pope. As Pius X had been chosen at the death of Leo XIII, so Pius XI was chosen at the death of Benedict XV; in both

---

[11] The well-known French journalist, Pertinax, in 1929 heard the rumor in Rome that the brother of Pius XI was one of those businessmen in Lombardy who had subsidized the Fascists before the March on Rome ("Why the Pope chose to sign the Concordat," in the *New York Times*, March 31, 1929). This information did not appear in his book, *Le partage de Rome* (Paris: Grasset, 1929). We do not know whether this disappearance was due to the fact that Pertinax became convinced that the rumor was unfounded, or whether it was advised not to throw an indiscreet light on a significant precedent.

cases, the cardinals wanted a pope who strengthened the conservative elements in Church and society.

The new pope found barely 600,000 lire in the coffers of the Holy See —that is to say, hardly enough to pay the everyday expenses for no more than one week; in addition, there was the prospect of the registration of securities and the impending failure of the Bank of Rome. To restore the finances of the Vatican, it was necessary to bring about the solution of the Roman question.

In taking over office, Pius XI repeated the oath to "assert and defend the inviolable rights of the Church and of the Holy See," but he blessed the crowd which was waiting in St. Peter's Square. This change in ceremony gave evidence for the fact that a new situation had been created.

The "esprit nouveau" was not slow in showing itself. In June 1922, Marquis Cornaggia, a conservative clerical of Milan and a personal friend of the new pope, founded an "Italian Constitutional Union" *(Unione costituzionale italiana)*. The new association, like the Populist party, avoided declaring itself Catholic but "asserted that religion should be the basis of public and private morality." In addition, Marquis Cornaggia announced that his organization proposed to open its ranks to those Catholics who would break away from the Populist party if it went so far as to ally itself with the Socialists. Questioned as to whether or not his initiative had the approval of the new pope, he answered (or rather, did not answer):

> I am in no position to answer this question. I have not seen the pope for a long time, and I do not believe that he has as yet expressed any opinion on the matter to which you refer. But I can say to you that Pius XI has been informed of our thoughts and our aims, and that in a recent occasion he sent . . . a telegram which contained encouraging, and if you wish, significant expressions. For our part, we have never approached the Vatican.[12]

The *Idea Nazionale*, on June 29, 1922, commented upon these statements in the following terms: "If, to these clear statements, we add a fact known to all—that is the links of devoted friendship between Marquis Cornaggia and Pius XI—we may conclude, without giving us the credit of

[12] Letter of Marquis Cornaggia to the *Corriere della sera*, June 13, 1922, and an interview with the *Popolo d'Italia*, June 27, 1922.

revealing a secret, that the pope accompanies with his consent the work which has been started."

The *Osservatore romano*, always ready to reject, on behalf of the Vatican, every responsibility for the work of the Populist party, did not deny in any way the pope's "consent" to the initiative of Marquis Cornaggia.

Depite the publicity given him by Fascists, Nationalists, and "Liberals," Marquis Cornaggia failed miserably. The rank and file remained loyal to the Populist party. His attempt, however, was significant. An outsider who was following with the curiosity of an historian and with the sympathy of a democrat the movement of the Populist party wrote in June 1922:

> The conservative clericals and the Nationalists would like the new pope, Pius XI, to return to the policy of Pius X. If he forced Don Sturzo to abandon the secretaryship of the Populist party, and subjected to the control of the bishops the electoral and political activities of the organizations affiliated with the Populist party, and if he condemned the most radical Populists, Pius XI would become a great pope for all the Italian Conservatives. But it seems very unlikely that Pius XI will try today, against the Populist party, a new edition of the ruthless surgical operation performed by Pius X between 1904 and 1906 against Christian democracy. At the time of Pius X, a mass of more than a million trade unionists, for the most part small landowners, tenant farmers and metayers, had not yet appeared on the scene. Today, a shift of the Populist party toward the Fascists, Nationalists and large estate owners, would result in the disbanding of these multitudes. The Socialists would reap what the Populist party had sown. Fascist outrages have intensified in the Socialist party that evolution toward the right-wingers and toward cooperation with the Populists, which a few months ago was barely noticeable. The more the Socialists drew near to the idea of cooperation with the Populist party, the more the cleavage in the Populist party between the elements of the right and those of the left intensified. Marquis Cornaggia, who was the most authoritative personage in the clerical-conservative movement at the time of Pius X, promotes today the rise of a Catholic organization of the right. Pius XI seems to approve of this attempt. Already he is being called "the pope of the Lombard Conservatives."[13]

[13] G. Salvemini, *Il Partito Popolare e la Questione Romana* (Florence: La Voce, 1922), pp. 45–48.

The symptoms of the "esprit nouveau" soon became more clear. Cardinal Boggiani again published his letter of August 1920 against the Populist party and took pains to point out that it "had been neither blamed nor condemned by Him who alone would have had, and *would have* the right to do it." In proof of this statement, he published the approving note which Benedict XV had sent him. Cardinal Boggiani spoke of "Him who alone would have had and *would have* the right" to condemn. He was thus pointing out not only Benedict XV ("would have had"), but also the living pope ("would have"). He would not have made this statement had he not been so authorized by Pius XI. To dispel any least doubt, the *Osservatore romano* of July 30, 1922, announced that "if Cardinal Boggiani's words were dated several years back, they still retained the same strength which inspired them at the time. His just rebukes and wise warnings have been, in the last few years, fully confirmed by men and circumstances. . . . This book is a true handbook of doctrine and discipline, useful to the Catholics, especially *in these times of oversights and errors.*"

23

The General Strike of August 1-3, 1922

On February 2, 1922, Bonomi's cabinet resigned. Its vacillating attitude had disgusted both Fascists and anti-Fascists. Giolitti could not succeed him because he had armed the Fascists and nobody trusted him. Nitti would have provoked a Fascist armed revolt supported by army chiefs. A Nationalist-Conservative-Fascist cabinet might have counted on the loyalty of no more than one hundred deputies. On the other hand, the fact that the Socialists and Communists would vote against any cabinet made the parliamentary situation hopeless.

It might have seemed impossible to discover a prime minister more incapable than Bonomi. One was found in Facta, a fifth-rate politician whose intelligence was no greater than that of a hen. He was regarded as a stopgap waiting for something to turn out that might bring about some improvement in an otherwise desperate deadlock.

Decidedly, three diseases existed in the Italian body politic: parliamentary paralysis, civil war, and military sedition. Either Parliament must recover its power and put an end to civil war and military sedition, or it would be stripped of all powers or altogether wiped out.

For this situation the heaviest responsibility rested with the Socialist deputies. They had separated from the Communists at the beginning of 1921. By so doing, not only the right-wingers but also the Maximalists had implicitly rejected all plans or hopes for social revolution. They now ought to have felt it their duty to secure a government which could at least appear

357

not worthy of contempt. Such a government only would have been possible if they had consented to form a coalition with the Populists and the Democrats. The right-wingers were in favor of this policy. But the majority of Socialists were Marxists of the strict observance. They could not think of cooperating with any other social class but their revolutionary proletariat. They called themselves Maximalists and revolutionists, but all they knew how to do was to wash their mouths with a revolution which never came. They made reforms impossible without knowing how to bring about a revolution. Overcome by the blind obstinacy of these intellectual proletarians, the right wing lost a whole year without making any attempt at breaking the deadlock in the House. Men like Turati and his followers were disinterested and well-meaning people. But they did not dare to act against the will of the majority in the party. They were afraid of being charged with personal ambition if they became members of a cabinet, or even supported it, without being permitted to do so by a majority in the party. They were waiting patiently for their comrades to change their minds. They did not realize that the brains of Marxians of the strict observance are like eggs in boiling water: the more they boil, the harder they become.

As was natural, the civil war went on unabated. Between May 31 and June 2, 1922, 10,000 Fascists from neighboring provinces concentrated in Bologna and demanded the dismissal of the prefect, accusing him of being the accomplice of the "Bolshevists." It is plain that the prefect would have prevented this concentration if he had been able to count on the army, but General Sani was absent during the whole crisis, just as he was during the "March on Ravenna" eight months earlier.

On July 19, Facta also had to resign. For a fortnight negotiations for a new cabinet went on between the different groups and between their leaders and the king. In the course of those days an important new development occurred: the majority of Socialist deputies, rebelling against the Maximalists, who controlled the central executive of the party, declared themselves ready to support a new cabinet on condition that it restored public peace. On July 29, the right-wing leader, Signor Turati, with the consent of his colleagues, had an interview with the king to discuss the political situation.

But the restoration of public peace could not be attained without disbanding the Fascist organization. This meant challenging the military "Black Hand" which was already too deeply compromised in the Fascist adventure. In censuring the postwar Chambers for their incapacity to form a stable ministry, one must distinguish the cause which paralyzed the Chamber from November 1919 to July 1922 from that which made itself felt in July 1922. Up to July 1922, the cause of the paralysis lay within the Chamber itself; all stable coalition was made impossible by the intransigent attitude of the Socialist deputies and by the mistrust which all parties felt towards the Populists. In the July of 1922, these internal troubles were on the point of disappearing. But now an external cause paralyzed the Chamber: the Black Hand, having little strength in the Chamber but a formidable armed organization outside, laid its veto upon the parliamentary coalition of the left which the new attitude of the Socialist deputies was making possible. "The Chamber," said Turati, in an interview with the newspaper *Epoca* on August 1, 1922, "is in the clutch of fear, physical fear."

Had the Socialists taken their decision in July 1921, they would probably have saved the country from the evils of military-Fascist anarchy and free institutions from destruction. In July 1922, it was too late. But a year earlier, immediately after the ill-omened elections of May 1921, what Socialist could have taken this step without arousing the revolt of all his fellows? The more one reflects on the events of these sad years, the more unpardonable appear the politicians who, at the end of 1920 and the beginning of 1921, armed the Fascists as instruments of chastisement and electioneering pressure.

While the parliamentary groups were stopped dead by this obstruction and the king was unable to find a prime minister who, backed by the majority in the Chamber, would stand firm against the Fascists outside, a Genoese paper, *Il Lavoro*, on July 30 announced that a general strike was called for August 1.

This crazy step was taken by an "Alliance of Labor," which had been formed in the previous December by the representatives of the Railwaymen's National Union, the General Confederation of Labor, the Federation of Seamen, the Italian Syndicalist Union, and other lesser organizations.

In the central executive of the Railwaymen's Union, the Anarchists had a great deal of influence, although the great mass of members were anything but Anarchists. The Confederation of Labor was led by, and mainly composed of, right-wing Socialists, but there was an active and noisy minority of Communists and Maximalists. The Italian Syndicalist Union consisted of Anarchists and Revolutionary Syndicalists. The Seamen's Federation and the other lesser organizations were made up of members belonging to various parties. The initiative in forming the Alliance of Labor had emanated from the central executive of the Railwaymen's Union. The aim of the Anarchists, who preponderated in it, was to form a coalition of the economic organizations of the working classes, rejecting all contact with Parliament. The leaders of the Confederation of Labor had joined the Alliance under pressure from their Communist and Maximalist members, in the belief that it would never achieve anything and hoping to curb the extremists. For the first six months of 1922, the Alliance of Labor had confined its activities to vague talk of a general strike. In July 1922, the discussion grew heated. Those most eager for the strike were the Anarchists; the leaders of the Confederation of Labor were against it. After a month of wrangling, the motion for a strike was carried by a slight majority against the vote of the Confederation of Labor.

It is probable that, besides the extremists who hoped for a genuine revolution as the outcome of the strike, there were *agents provocateurs* among those who prompted it.[1] But it must also be remembered that the working classes throughout the country were infuriated by the prospect that the new cabinet would be in league with the Fascists or, at any rate, impotent to disarm them.

The final impetus was given by the disorders at Ravenna of July 26–29. Here, on July 25, a small local strike of wagon drivers degenerated into a riot in which a Fascist lost his life.[2] A conflict with the police ensued, in which seven strikers were killed. The affair might have stopped here. But on July 26, three thousand Fascists from nearby provinces, fully armed with guns, bombs, and machine guns, fell on the city. The Republican, Socialist, and Communist leaders were ordered to leave the city within twenty-four

[1] This is the opinion of Don Luigi Sturzo, *Italy and Fascism* (London: Faber and Gwyer, 1926), p. 107. Don Sturzo, as general secretary of the Populist party, was in a position to obtain reliable information. His opinion finds support in the fact that four weeks before the strike was proclaimed, the author of the present book was asked by one of his friends, who was on the Central Executive of Railwaymen, to advise him as to how to vote in connection with the proposed strike. He had noticed that the most zealous advocates of the strike were men suspected of being spies of the railway management. He thought that the management wanted the strike to lure the union into a disastrous battle and then dismiss the most active of the leaders. On the advice of voting against the strike, he did so. When the strike was called, he obeyed the order. He was dismissed, while many of those who had advocated the strike were retained.

[2] Our source is the *Corriere della sera*. It must be born in mind that the correspondents of the paper were favorable to Fascism and tended to make their adversaries responsible for the first acts of provocation. We can vouch for neither the accuracy nor the completeness of the particulars. We merely attempt to give some idea of the facts as they appeared, not to anti-Fascists, but to those who favored Fascism, even if not approving of its extremes.

hours. On the 27th, the Fascists destroyed the *Casa del Popolo* and attempted to invade the Chamber of Labor, the town hall, and the chief premises of the cooperative for the whole district. The following day, they destroyed the offices of a newspaper and a cooperative branch, burned down a club, and with an incendiary bomb set fire to the chief premises of the cooperative. Only the ground floor and one wing of this fine palace where Byron had once lived, were left; the damage amounted to one and one-half million lire, representing twenty-five years of steady and able work. "The conflagration of the great building," writes Italo Balbo, leader of the Fascist bands in the heroic exploit, "projected against the dark sky in the night lurid flashes of light. We must give above all a feeling of terror to our opponents." Socialist organizer and M.P. Baldini had remained at his post in the building up until the last moment:

> When I saw Baldini come out of the burning building with his hands in his hair and the mark of desperation on his face, I understood the whole of his tragedy. In that moment with the palace of the Ravenna cooperatives it was the dream and the labor of his whole life that was disappearing into smoke. There was all or most of the strength of the Socialists in that region. It was a mastodontic organization directed with methods essentially honest. But it was a political, not an economic institution.

On July 29, Balbo started from Ravenna at the head of a long column of trucks filled with Fascists, for a raid in the province to last up to the dawn of the next day:

> We passed through Rimini, St. Arcangelo, Cesena, Savignano, Bertinoro, through all the centers and villages between the province of Forli and Ravenna, destroying and burning all the houses of "reds," headquarters of Socialist and Communist organizations. It was a terrible night. Our passing was marked by high columns of fire and smoke. The plains of Romagna up to the hills were submitted to the exasperated reprisals of the Fascists. . . . Numberless episodes. Encounters with the Bolshevist rabble in open resistance, none. The leaders had all fled. Leagues, clubs and cooperatives were almost deserted by the Socialists.[3]

[3] I. Balbo, *Diario 1922* (Milano: Mondadori, 1932), pp. 103, 109–10.

Balbo omits to mention the acts of violence to persons, as he often does throughout his diary, but the picture is eloquent enough and needs no comment.

Under the influence of these happenings, the Alliance of Labor proclaimed the general strike.[4] As Ravenna was the chief stronghold of the right-wing Socialists, these were weakened in their opposition to the strike. Many of those who, at the last moment, were swept into voting for the strike not only meant to protest against the senseless Fascist destruction, but hoped that a large display of anti-Fascist forces, proving that the Fascists were not masters of the country, would bring about the formation of a cabinet of the left. To drag in these nonrevolutionary elements, the Alliance of Labor, in calling the strike proclaimed that it was necessary to "crush the attack made by the reactionary forces on the organs of the state."

The news took the right-wing Socialist deputies by surprise in the midst of negotiations for the new cabinet. The strike undid all their efforts toward parliamentary cooperation. Prevent it they could not, because the extremists who had proclaimed it were not under their control, and the leaders of the Confederation of Labor, having made the initial mistake of joining the Alliance, were pledged to abide by the decision of the majority. Had they disavowed the strike, they would have been held responsible for its failure, at a moment when the Fascists would take advantage of the failure to launch a new offensive. Had they kept silent, they would have been accused of awaiting results before making up their minds. In this embarrassment they made the worst possible choice: that of supporting those elements whose intention in striking was to protest against the danger of a Fascist cabinet but not to carry out a revolutionary movement. When interviewed on the afternoon of July 30, Turati declared that the impending strike aimed at defending the constitution against anticonstitutional strikes: "It would be a strike in defence of legality (*sciopero legalitario*)," he said. "The proletariat will stand by the state to defend it from the Fascists."[5]

But a general strike, if intended simply as an anti-Fascist demonstration, would have had to be called for a definite period (not more than twenty-four

---

[4] Signor Villari (*Awakening of Italy*, p. 153) makes this strike spring up like a mushroom in the night and then pronounces: "Of the many strikes which had occurred during the last three years none was more absolutely unjustified than this."

[5] *Corriere della sera*, August 1, 1922.

hours) and would have needed the cooperation of the Populist organizations. These had not been consulted, and they declared against the strike. Moreover, no time limit was set, since the Anarchists and other extremists who promoted it deluded themselves with the hope that they could carry through a revolution, after eighteen months of irresistible Fascist pressure!

To this incoherent challenge, the leaders of the Fascist party replied with an able move. They proclaimed that the Fascists would wait forty-eight hours for the state to assert its authority: "At the end of this period the Fascists will assume complete liberty of action, and substitute themselves for the state, which will once more have given proof of its impotence" (*Popolo d'Italia*, August 1, 1922).

If the general strike had not been general, its failure would have been visible by the end of the second day: the Fascists, taking the field on the third day, would have claimed all the glory of the victory. If, on the other hand, the strike had been general, the first forty-eight hours would scarcely have sufficed for the government to put the machinery of repression into motion: the Fascists, arriving on the scene just as the machinery had begun to work, would again have taken to themselves all credit for the repression. Whatever the turn of events, the Fascists would present themselves as the sole saviors of the country.

The first result of the proclamation of the strike was that the king broke off all negotiations for a settlement of the cabinet crisis and retained Facta as prime minister, so as to have some sort of government to restore order.

From the beginning, the general strike was a fiasco. The railwaymen, whose representatives in the Alliance of Labor had most strongly advocated the strike, answered the call partially and irresolutely. Of 229,000 men, only 60,000 came out.[6] The other groups responded in the same incoherent way. It was the last ill-timed move of the pugilist who is about to receive the knock-out blow. On the night of the second day, the Alliance of Labor called off the strike for noon of the following day, August 3.[7]

---

[6] Amministrazione delle Ferrovie dello Stato, *Relazione per l'Anno 1922–23* (Roma, 1924), p. 124.

[7] This general strike of August 1–3, 1922, is constantly invoked by Fascist propaganda as a proof that Italy was threatened by bolshevism even on the eve of the "March on Rome." For instance, Signor Villari writes in *The Times*, August 27, 1927: "It is very misleading to state that bolshevism was at an end a year before the Fascist March on Rome. As late as August 1, 1922, the political general strike proclaimed by the various allied subversive parties would, but for the Fascist reaction, have suspended the whole life of the country, as the authors of the general strike in Great Britain in May, 1926, attempted to do." The English general strike of May 1926, involved five million workers and lasted nine days. What is "very misleading" is to put the two strikes on the same footing.

On August 5, the Fascist press bureau issued "the first approximate list" of the towns in which the Fascists, in reprisals, had occupied town halls or wrecked Chambers of Labor, cooperatives, etc: Alessandria, Ancona, Antignano, Ardenza, Campicaneto, Falconara, Figline Valdarno, Florence, Fornovo, Gallarate, Gravina, Intra, Leghorn, Milan, Muggia, Noceto, Novara, Novi Ligure, Oderzo, Pavia, Pegazzano, Pistoia, Ponte a Signa, Rimini, Ronco, Rebocco, Sampierdarena, San Secondo, San Jacopo. Savona, Scandiano, Schio, Spezia, Tabiano, Torre, Torino, Vigevano, Voghera. These reprisals continued until August 17.

The occupation of the town hall of Milan and the outsting of the Maximalist mayor and councilors made a tremendous impression all over Italy. Nobody would have ever thought possible such an outrage in the city which had always been regarded as the citadel of the Socialist movement in Italy. The workers of Milan this time did not react in any way. They were thoroughly disheartened.

While this storm of violence raged throughout the country, Facta concentrated all his efforts on negotiating with the Fascists to prevent them from occupying Rome. Having secured their promise to respect the capital, he left them a free hand in the rest of Italy. He was the most convenient of all possible prime ministers for the Fascists, until such time as they should decide to occupy the capital as well. The House, which had refused to accept Facta's policy on July 19, gave him a vote of confidence on August 10 and went into recess.

In August 1922, the organization of the Fascist army, according to the Gandolfo plan, appeared insufficient, and a new plan with greater centralization and the creation of a military directorate was decided upon by the Fascist national executive. To form this directorate were called De Vecchi, Italo Balbo, and General De Bono. The new plan was prepared by the two former in Torre Pellice and was ready by September 15.[8]

Nobody thought that the new cabinet would survive the recess. August and September were months of intensive negotiations behind the scenes.

On September 20, eight senators belonging to the Populist party published a letter to Don Sturzo, in which they deplored that "the Populist party, born with the aim of promoting harmony between the social classes, had never known how to rid itself of certain internal conflicts and certain external deviations." They continued:

[8] Balbo, *Diario*, pp. 140 ff. The plan was made public by Mussolini's paper on October 15, 1922.

We know that certain people wrongly charge the Populist deputies with craving for an alliance, or an understanding with parties incompatible with the principles, which, for us, are fundamental. . . . All the same, it is not out of place to reaffirm that certain alliances would run counter to the most sacred and basic principles of social life, and therefore cannot be agreed with, still less solicited (*Corriere d'Italia*, September 20, 1922).

One of the eight signatories, Count Santucci, was president of the Bank of Rome; he and another of the signatories, Count Grosoli, would have had to answer to justice had the Bank of Rome failed; two others, Montresor and Crispolti, were known to all as trusted men of Pius XI and Cardinal Gasparri. The eight senators did not dare to say explicitly that the only alliance compatible with "the most sacred and basic principles of social life" was with the Fascist party. They confined themselves to rejecting the alliance with the Socialists. The rest would follow by itself.

The danger of a parliamentary coalition between Populists, Democrats, and right-wing Socialists became greater after the Socialist National Congress was held at Rome on October 1–3. In this congress, the right-wingers represented 29,119 votes, and the Maximalists 31,106. The first had gained 15,000 supporters, and the latter had seen 67,000 of their "war Socialists" vanish into thin air. The right-wingers broke away and formed a new party which took the name of "Unitary Socialist party"—an odd name in a country with three Socialist parties, without counting the Reformists who were led by Bonomi and who still pretended to be Socialist. As a result of this split, the General Confederation of Labor dissolved its connection with all Socialist parties. But it went on being rent by disputes between right-wingers, Maximalists, and Communists.

Now there was in the Chamber a group of seventy right-wing Socialists prepared to cooperate with other parties. The way was clear for a stable resettlement of the parliamentary groups: a coalition majority consisting of 107 Populists, 167 Democrats and 70 right-wing Socialists (total 334); a right opposition consisting of 35 Fascists, 10 Nationalists, and 13 Conservatives; and an extreme left opposition consisting of 50 Maximalists and 14 Communists. No definite agreement between the newborn right-wing Socialist party, the Populists, and the Democrats has as yet been arrived at. But such a resettlement was a matter of a few months—possibly even of a few weeks. Conversing with the Belgian Socialist leader Vandervelde in

August 1922, the king anticipated this solution of the crisis and was pleased with it.

Among the most anxious for this parliamentary resettlement were the Communists and the Maximalists. After the new cabinet had pacified the country, they would accuse the right-wing Socialists of having betrayed the proletariat by allying with the bourgeois parties to obtain office. In the summer of 1922, the longing for peace after three years of war and four of disorder, abhorrence of the cruelties of the civil war, anxiety aroused by the military anarchy, worry over the economic and financial situation of the country (which, though no longer desperate, seemed still to be so), weariness of the futile maneuverings of the parliamentary groups, contempt for the ineptitude of a prime minister like Facta—all these feelings resulted in a widespread mood of shame and discouragement. To escape from a moral situation which had grown intolerable, the country would have accepted any fresh government on condition of its restoring public peace.

Such a solution disconcerted the plans and hopes of many people besides Pius XI, Cardinal Gasparri, and their conservative clericals. The bankers also were eager to secure the repeal of the 1920 law which had obliged the owners of all public and private securities to register them in their own names. Many industrial firms during the war had supplied all kinds of material and products to the government. They were anxious to see disbanded a parliamentary committee which was investigating transactions and discovering scandalous grafts and robberies. The insurance companies looked with fear to the approaching year 1923, in which, according to a law enacted in 1912, they had to turn all their business to the National Institute of Insurances to be managed as a government monopoly. To all these groups the thought of a government in which Socialists, no matter how moderate, had a share, was very disheartening.[9]

---

[9] These three groups of capitalists were among the very first to be rewarded by the new Fascist government. Hardly had the new cabinet been created than, on October 31, the General Confederation of Industrialists declared that the industrial class would support the efforts of the government to enforce "the right of property," "the right to work," discipline, to develop industrial initiative, to foster "national sentiment above Parliamentary currents" and "to strengthen the classes which were preparing the economic rebirth of the nation" (*Corriere della sera.* October 31, 1922). In the session of the Chamber of November 17, 1922, the right-wing Socialist leader, Turati, remarked: "No one can fail to see the strange parallel which exists between the declarations of the last congress of the industrial organizations and the measures taken in the meetings of the ministers." An industrial deputy, Tofani, interrupted: "It cannot help being thus." Turati: "This is an authoritative confirmation."

Army chiefs and Fascists openly worked now hand in hand. Anyone going through the Fascist papers would find hundreds of names of army officers who, in 1922, openly enrolled amongst the Fascists, shared in their public ceremonies, and sent telegrams of support to Mussolini. For the three months of July, August, and September 1922, the *Popolo d'Italia* mentions the following generals: Zirano (July 5), Bertolini (July 8), Moriani (July 30), Campomazza (July 23), Ceccherini (July 25), Zampieri (July 26), Gandolfi (July 30) Fiori (August 1), Pastore (September 8), De Merzhiach (September 14), Milanesi and Oro (September 9).

Between September 30 and October 4, 7,000 Fascists from Lombardy and Venetia concentrated on Bozen and Trent to protest against the civil governor of the province. No one intervened to prevent their transit on the railways.

At 2:00 P.M. on October 4, the commandant of the Seventh Division of Trento assumed plenary powers for the maintenance of order. The result was to increase the disorder. At 4:30 P.M., a colloquy took place between the Fascists and the governor in the presence of General Ghersi, commanding the Verona army corps, the general in command of the Acqui Brigade, and "other officers of various ranks." The Fascists demanded that the governor should resign and leave the district and were not satisfied by his answers (*Popolo d'Italia*, October 5, 1922). The following night, the Fascists besieged the governor's residence:

> The troops were disposed in such a way that the slightest move on the Fascists' part would have so intermingled soldiers and Fascists, that the soldiers would have been unable to use their arms. In this situation the Fascist leaders contented themselves with a solemn display of strength, a spectacle which lasted till three o'clock in the morning (*Popolo d'Italia*, October 6).

In the afternoon of October 5, the Fascists raised the siege of the palace: "General Ghersi had assured them that the governor would leave immediately" (*Popolo d'Italia*, October 8).[10]

A Populist-Democratic-Socialist coalition in the Chamber could only be

---

[10] Balbo, in his *Diary* (pp. 163–34), writes: "I receive a letter from De Bono and De Vecchi asking me why I did not notify them of this expedition. I did not know anything about it myself. I learned it from the newspapers. . . . De Bono is furious. 'In this way,' he says, 'we cannot make either war or a revolution.' "

forestalled by an antiparliamentary *coup d'état.* On this point the testimony of Signor Villari, the Fascist propaganda agent, is decisive:

> Within the Socialist party the problem of accepting the idea of collaborating with a bourgeois government was hotly debated. The leaders of the collaborationist group worked hard to convince their comrades, and at one moment it seemed as though it had a good chance of being adopted. Among several of the other parties there was a regular competition to secure the support of the collaborationist Socialists for the formation of the future cabinet, *as it was believed that a combination with the moderate reds would secure it a long term of office.* . . . The Fascists, Nationalists, and the right generally were rigidly opposed to this experiment. . . . *Revolutionary socialism was no longer a serious danger;* the Communists might commit occasional outrages and acts of terrorism, but they had lost the support of a large proportion of the laboring classes. *But collaboration represented a much more real and insidious danger* (*Awakening of Italy,* pp. 150–68).

Another striking piece of evidence on this point comes from a highly placed Fascist personage, Professor Volpe, a personal friend of Mussolini and the official historian of Fascism. Volpe wrote in 1932:

> We must acknowledge that during the second half of 1921, and much more during 1922, conditions in Italy, or some of them, had begun to show improvement. There were encouraging signs of economic recovery. The people of Italy were back at work. Infatuation for Russia and its bolshevism was disappearing. . . . The Italians were finding themselves again. . . . All this can and must be acknowledged. . . . But while many even among the Fascist sympathizers thought that the time had come for fascism to disarm . . . fascism to the contrary pushed forward the mobilization of its forces. The main target was now the government, or, we may say, the parliamentary regime (*Storia del movimento fascista,* pp. 73–75).

In conclusion, the March on Rome was planned not because parliamentary paralysis had become intolerable, but because parliamentary paralysis might come to an end in a coalition of democratic groups.

Balbo's *Diary* throws a great deal of light on this point.

On October 16, a secret "war council" was held in Milan, to which Mussolini called two retired generals, Ceccherini and Fara, besides De Bono. He explained that "in the revolutionary action he thought it was useful to have generals in their army uniforms at the head of the insurgent groups" (Balbo, *Diario*, p. 177). Ceccherini and Fara had been among those generals who, in September 1919, had joined D'Annunzio at Fiume. In the "war council" Mussolini stated that fascism would be in the necessity "of initiating an insurrectional movement any moment" because "it could not allow a parliamentary solution which is against the spirit and the interests of fascism." To his question whether the military forces of fascism were ready and sufficient for the task, General De Bono and De Vecchi answered that in their opinion they were not ready and that some further delay was necessary. Balbo thought that there was no time to be lost:

> I am worrying about the development in the political situa-
> tion during these last days. I think it is dangerous to wait.
> The maneuvers of the parties in parliament are very decided.
> Fascism is under the menace of remaining a prisoner of the
> intrigues against it through the trap of a general election. I
> think that if we do not try now a *coup d'état*, the spring will
> be too late. In the mild climate of Rome, Democrats and
> Socialists will reach an accord. It will not be difficult for the
> new cabinet to enforce more energetic measures of police
> and to enlist the army against us. Now we have the advan-
> tage of the surprise. Nobody believes in the seriousness of
> our insurrectional intentions. But within six months, the
> difficulties will be ten times more. Better try today a definite
> action, even if our preparation is not complete, than tomor-
> row when together with ours the preparation of our oppo-
> nents will also be complete" (Balbo, *Diario*, p. 179).

No final decision was taken. But a quadrumvirate to lead insurrection was appointed, formed by De Bono, De Vecchi, Balbo, and the general secretary of the party, Michele Bianchi. Two days later, the quadrumvirs met in Bordighera to work their plans in detail with the assistance of Colonel Sacco, formerly of the general staff of the army. While this meeting was held, "in the utmost secrecy," the old queen mother, Margherita, who was passing the summer in her villa in Bordighera, knew about the presence of those gentlemen and invited them to luncheon, at the end of which she "expressed her best wishes for the realization of our plans which could not aim but at the salvation and the glory of Italy" (Balbo, *Diario*, p. 185).

The Vatican was not informed of these preparations. It worked on its own account to make impossible an accord between Populist deputies and Socialist right-wingers. On October 2, 1922, Cardinal Gasparri entered the campaign in person. In a circular directed to the Italian bishops, he "protested energetically" against the "absolutely false and calumnious insinuations" which represented the Populist party as "an emanation from the Holy See or the exponent of the Catholics in the country and in Parliament." The Holy See intended to remain "faithful to its principle of not allowing itself to be drawn into political competitions." It "had always remained, and intended to have no connections with the Populist party just as with any other political party." To be sure, it "reserved for itself the right to assume toward the Populist party, as toward any other party, an attitude of reproof and of blame whenever it came in contrast with the religious or moral principles of Christianity." Nor did the Holy See deny the bishops and the priests the right to have, as private citizens, their political preferences. But "in so far as they were bishops and priests, they must hold themselves entirely aloof from the struggles of the parties, and above political competition." It was not easy to draw a dividing line between the private citizen and the bishop or priest. In doubtful cases they were to abstain.[11]

The Populist party had repeated for four years, in all tones and in all circumstances, that it was not an emanation from the Holy See. Cardinal Gasparri, therefore, was telling an unadulterated truth. But the harsh and cutting form that he gave to this truth was equivalent not only to a refusal of responsibility, but to a condemnation. He condemned as an "absolutely false and calumnious insinuation" every rumor about a link between the Vatican and the Populist party, as if the latter were a criminal association. The Vatican was ready to condemn the Populist party as soon as it behaved badly. But if it were to behave well, the Vatican would ignore it, from the moment it had nothing to do with it. Even the moment which Cardinal Gasparri chose to issue his circular was significant. He summoned the clergy to break loose from the Populist party if the latter did not pay due attention to what the religious authorities wanted, just when a coalition between the Populists, the Democrats and the right-wing Socialists appeared possible.

[11] *Giornale d'Italia*, Rome, October 20, 1922.

On the same day he sent out this circular on the Populist party, Cardinal Gasparri sent to the bishops another circular on the "Catholic Action." By means of the Catholic Action, he explained, the laity cooperated in the religious mission which rightfully belongs to the Church. The Catholic Action, "because of the necessary connection of all things, had to descend even into the economic-social field, touching also political questions." But in so doing, it always kept in view "supernatural interests" and worked "for the moral and religious elevation of the people." As a consequence, Catholic Action was a religious and not a political organization. Being a religious organization, it was "entirely dependent on the ecclesiastic authority." It was not entitled to issue "directions of theoretic nature." It could only "carry out work in practical fields." On the basis of these principles, the pope would reorganize Catholic Action and ask the bishops to give their opinions on its new constitution.[12]

The logical connection between the two documents, dated the same day, is obvious. Pius XI returned to the policy of Pius X and put the organizations of the Catholic laity again under the control of ecclesiastic authorities. The Populist party was placed in a dilemma: either to submit to the control of the ecclesiastic authorities as a branch of Catholic Action, or face the competition of the Catholic Action as the only organization in whose ranks the Catholics could act with the approval of the Holy See.

[12] *Pio XI e l'Azione cattolica* (Roma: Via dei Cestari, 21, 1929), pp. 332–33.

24

The
March on Rome

As early as September 29, the central executive of the Fascist party knew that, in the event of a Fascist uprising, "the army would observe an attitude of neutrality."[1] Mussolini himself, in a speech of October 30, 1923, revealed that in October 1922, he knew "that at the opportune moment the government machine guns would not fire on the revolutionists." The American ambassador at Rome, Child, an ardent pro-Fascist, was informed that "the army secretly favored the movement."[2] By the word "army" one has to mean the heads of the army.

On October 14, it was announced from unofficial sources that the government had entrusted General Badoglio with the task of getting ready to crush fascism and that Badoglio had said: "At the first shot, fascism will crumble down." The news caused commotion in Fascist headquarters. Mussolini, in a passionate article on the *Popolo d'Italia*, professed not to believe it to be true: "The national army will never fight against the Blackshirts, for the plain reason that the Blackshirts will never fight against the national army"; "General Badoglio will refuse to become the executioner of Italian fascism." Commenting upon this event, Balbo wrote in his *Diary:*

---

[1] This information was given by Mussolini's private secretary in an interview with the *Popolo d'Italia*, October 27, 1923.
[2] R.W. Child, *A Diplomat Looks at Europe* (New York: Duffield and Co., 1925), p. 171.

It is strange how little the generals know the mentality of their soldiers. We have already the most documented evidence that the greatest part of the army is with us. Just now has been brought to me from Ferrara the last report from our men of confidence at the War Office. It gives interesting information about mixed batallions of carabineers, policemen, royal guards and custom-guards to be formed and used against us. I will wait for further information about their eventual location. If the government counts on such forces to attack fascism, this means that they have no confidence in the regular army. As for us, enemies of this kind leave us altogether unscared.

The next day the newspapers announced that Badoglio had stated that there was no truth in the news circulated the previous day. Balbo wrote in his diary: "I am most glad."[3]

According to Balbo's *Diary*, at the "war council" of October 16, De Bono and De Vecchi thought that the Fascist troops were not ready and postponed any decision, whereas Balbo maintained that the insurrection would face more serious obstacles if postponed to the next spring. This seems to show that the spring of 1923 was considered as the date in which the Fascist forces could be ready. According to the same source, the final decision to mobilize the Blackshirts immediately and to send them against Rome was taken in Naples during the night between October 24 and 25, at a meeting presided over by Mussolini. The aim of the "mobilization" was to be to force the Facta cabinet to resign. Then the Fascists would "seize power through a cabinet which had at least six Fascist ministers in the most important ministries."[4] During that same night, General Baistrocchi came to tell De Bono and Balbo that "the army in southern Italy was following with great sympathy the Fascist movement."[5] On the following day, while still in Naples, Balbo received, from a messenger who had been sent by the "man of confidence" at the War Office, "a copy of the instructions issued a few hours before by the minister under the utmost secrecy."

They are not secret for us. . . . It appears that the formation of the mixed battalions is still on high sea. Orders to this

[3] Balbo, *Diario 1922*, pp. 174–76.
[4] Balbo, *Diario 1922*, p. 196.
[5] Balbo, *Diario 1922*, p. 198.

> effect have been given to the commanders of army corps. We know how long these things drag under the regime of military bureaucracy. We do not need to worry. The army does not worry us. It is more ours than Soleri's.[6]

After the decision for immediate action had been taken at Naples, Mussolini left there, crossed Rome without stopping, did not go to Perugia (which was to be the headquarters of the sedition), and made for Milan— that is, for a city which was 400 miles distant from Perugia and Rome. In Milan he remained until the night of October 29. Lussu has humorously pointed out that Milan "was a curious position for directing a battle": "even according to modern ideas of strategy, four hundred miles from the main fighting force is a great deal; but on the other hand, Milan had the advantage of being conveniently near the Swiss frontier."[7] Had he foreseen the sudden and overwhelming victory of October 28, Mussolini would have stayed in Perugia, so as not to have to share with others the glory of the "battle" and of "victory." He had no faith in the adventure. He betook himself to Milan within two hours from the Swiss frontier, ready to fly if things turned out badly.

During the month of October, Mussolini carried on secret negotiations with Giolitti on the one hand and with Nitti on the other. He demanded six places in the cabinet for the Fascists and a new general election.[8] This was not the plan of the army chiefs and of the Nationalists. They wanted a fully conservative-reactionary-militaristic government. Their candidate for the premiership was not Mussolini, but Salandra. They wished to use Mussolini and the Fascists with the purposes of reserving for themselves the fruits of victory. On August 22, the *Giornale d'Italia* of Rome had published a letter signed "a group of officers of the army" in which Mussolini was challenged to speak frankly his intentions about the monarchy. He had answered in his newspaper reassuring them that the monarchy was not in danger of attack by fascism, and later, in a speech of September 20, in Udine, had reiterated that same assurance and made a monarchical profession of faith, casting aside the republicanism professed by fascism at its beginning.[9] In spite of this turn to the right, the army chiefs and the

---

[6] Balbo, *Diario 1922*, pp. 199–200. Soleri was the war minister. He was not popular among the brass hats because of his speech of March 4, 1919, in the Chamber (see Chapter 11).
[7] E. Lussu, *The Road to Exile* (New York: Covici Friede, 1936), p. 51.
[8] Rossi, *The Rise of Italian Fascism*, pp. 271 ff.
[9] Balbo, *Diario 1922*, p. 154–55.

Nationalists stuck to their choice of Salandra as the future prime minister. Mussolini was unwilling to play second fiddle in a Nationalist cabinet, which would have resolved itself into a military dictatorship and would have afforded less opportunity for a new change in his favor. He spoke of the imminent "March on Rome," as he had done other times, because he did not wish to remain out of the game if the "March on Rome" actually took place. But he kept two other irons in his fire, Giolitti and Nitti. The first was the candidate of the right-wing Socialists. The second was the candidate of the Populists and Cardinal Gasparri. However things turned out, Mussolini was sure of obtaining a niche in the new cabinet. But he preferred a Democratic cabinet and counted on the following national election to reach the premiership.

On the evening of October 27, the "mobilization" was officially announced, and during the night, Fascist groups began to converge upon Rome from the neighboring districts of central Italy. De Bono was meant to direct the movement from Perugia, but Balbo's *Diary* shows that he never directed anything. Four other retired generals, Fara, Maggiotto, Ceccherini, and Tiby, commanded the Fascist groups which were "marching on Rome." A fifth general, Zamboni, was in command of the "reserves" at Foligno in the neighborhood of Perugia. There he was joined by another general, Novelli.[10] Other officers—some pensioned, others in service but on official leave—were commanding the Fascist groups which were to seize the railway stations and the telegraph and telephone centers in many of the most important cities in northern and central Italy.

The king, who was at his summer place of San Rossore, near Pisa, hastened to Rome on the evening of October 27. He is said to have been indignant against the Fascists and to have said in the Piedmontese dialect: "Rather than give in, I will go right away with my wife and my boy." Italians revert to their local dialect in moments of anger.

On the night of October 27, the cabinet decided to declare martial law; while awaiting the king's signature to the proclamation, they notified the prefects of the provinces to hand over their powers to the military authorities. They were sure that the king would sign the decree of martial law.

During the night, all over Italy, when in obedience to the decree of

[10] In Ludwig's *Talks with Mussolini* (Boston, 1933), pp. 91–2, to the question: "What do you think of generals who break their oath of allegiance to an established government, in order to set up a new one, like the four who participated in your March on Rome?" Mussolini's answer is: "In certain historical crises that must happen."

martial law the civil authorities surrendered their powers to the military authorities, the latter everywhere confined the troops to barracks and allowed the Fascists to take possession of the railway stations, telegraph and telephone offices, stores of weapons and ammunition, newspaper premises. Wherever the Fascists advanced, the army chiefs tactfully retired.[11] Here and there, was some army chief who did not belong to the conspiracy and did not withdraw before the Fascist uprising. Where and when this happened, it was the Fascists who retired or were wiped out.

The well-known English writer Israel Zangwill was staying in Florence during the last days of October 1922. In his eyes, the events of those days resembled comic opera more than real revolution. Curzio Malaparte, one of the Fascist leaders in Tuscany, describes the episode in his little book *Coup d'État: The Technique of Revolution* (New York: E.P. Dutton & Co., 1932). He endeavored to persuade Zangwill that he was witnessing a revolution, and to convince him Malaparte drove Zangwill to the gas works, the telephone exchange, the telegraph office, the bridges, and the railway stations. All these "strategical positions" were in the hands of Blackshirts. The result of this demonstration was disastrous for Malaparte's thesis. Zangwill observed that the Fascists had seized all these positions without striking a blow, while the police had taken refuge in the prefecture behind rows of carabineers, royal guards, and armored cars. Not only that, "the troops of the garrison, the infantry and cavalry regiments were under orders to remain in barracks; for the time being the authorities were observing a benevolent neutrality."

Malaparte called Zangwill's attention to the fact that the prefect of Florence could not communicate with the other authorities because the Fascists held all the telephone and telegraph offices. He neglected to tell him that in Florence the military headquarters is only 200 yards away from the prefecture and that in five minutes the prefect could have sent orders to the commanding officer to clear out the Fascists from their "strategical positions." Even without knowing this significant detail, Zangwill might well have wondered why the prefect made no use of the police, concentrated in the prefecture, to expel the Fascists from the telephone and telegraph offices and from the central railway station—all of them within a quarter of a mile of the prefecture.

The attitude of General Gonzaga, the commanding officer of the garri-

---

[11] About this fact, Rossi (*The Rise of Italian Fascism*, pp. 300–04), has collected striking evidence from many cities.

son of Florence, as described by Malaparte, was, if anything, still more ambiguous than that of the prefect. After confining all troops to barracks, and thus enabling the Fascists to seize the "strategical points" without striking a blow, he learned from the newspapers that the king was negotiating with Mussolini and likely to invite him to become prime minister. At the moment, the news was fictitious. But General Gonzaga telegraphed the ministry of war in Rome for confirmation: apparently the military authorities still had at their disposal the wireless service which the Fascists had forgotten to commandeer. The ministry of war refused to answer directly, replying that the name of the king must not be brought into party quarrels and that the news was probably premature. The general's next step was to go to the Fascist headquarters in Florence and ask if the news was correct. He was assured that it was. This "good news" put an end to his conscientious scruples and lifted a great responsibility from his shoulders—that of dislodging the Fascists from those "strategical points."

A typical case occurred at Padua. General Boriani, the commander of the garrison of that town, was away on leave (or apparently so) on the night of October 27. General Emo Capodilista, who was in temporary command and did not belong to the military set who were in collusion with the Fascists, was preparing to take the necessary steps to dislodge the latter when General Boriani hastily ended his leave, took over the command again in the middle of the night, and confined the troops to barracks.[12]

A Fascist who with his comrades occupied the railway station of Cancello, south of Rome, says in an account of his adventures: "The rumor reached us that the carabineers were proposing to break our lines. We were posted with a one day's ration of bread and corned beef. But it was a false alarm. They never appeared. Instead of that a quartermaster came, singing the praises of Mussolini, and offered us a truckload of all sorts of good things."[13]

On the morning of October 28, four groups of Fascists were available for an actual "march on Rome." About 4,000 were at Santa Marinella near Civitavecchia, some 30 miles west of Rome; about 2,000 at Orte, some 30 miles north of Rome; about 8,000 at Tivoli, 15 miles east of Rome; and a group whose number is given by no source at Valmontone about 20 miles south of Rome. They had no means of transport at their disposal, and all

[12] Report given by an eyewitness to the author of the present book.
[13] P.N.F., *Pagine eroiche della rivoluzione fascista* (Milan: Casa Editrice Imperia, 1925), p. 319.

the rails towards Rome might have been torn out at a moment's notice by the regular army with the willing help of the railway men. Between these four groups scattered to the west, east, north, and south of Rome there was no direct liaison. As for their armament, we can trust the *Popolo d'Italia* (November 1, 1922), when it tells us that "one of the features of this powerful postwar army is its quaint uniforms. Its chief weapons are bludgeons and revolvers, but there are also numerous guns with scanty supplies of cartridges." Two other eyewitnesses, the Belgian member of Parliament Louis Pierard and the American journalist C. Beals, described them as "men armed in the most fantastic manner, with revolvers, sporting-rifles, cudgels, machine guns and hoes"; "armed with guns and table legs."[14]

The men at Foligno, who were meant to act as "reserves," numbered 3,000, but no more than 300 of them possessed arms. Their number rose to 5,000 by the evening of October 28, and only during the night between the 28th and 29th did they take hold of two armament stores and so manage to arm themselves. Anyhow, from Foligno, about 75 miles distant from Rome, they would have been of no use on October 28.

The forces of the regular army, concentrated in Rome, amounted to 12,000 men. They might easily have dispersed those mobs one by one. A pitched battle would have been unnecessary. It would have been enough to leave them without victuals and water in the desert which surrounds Rome, cutting them off from their bases. After twenty-four hours of this treatment, a few judiciously administered shots and a fair amount of kicks would have sufficed to send them home in a chastened mood.

In Rome, the decree proclaiming martial law was posted at 10:00 A.M. on October 28. As soon as the news was known, the Fascists of Rome were seized with panic. They feared that the army chiefs, recalled to their oath of allegiance by a peremptory order from the king, would set going the machinery of repression. From 10:00 A.M. to noon, not a Fascist was to be seen in the streets of Rome. A Fascist deputy, Acerbo, fled, dressed in his black shirt, to the Chamber of Deputies and, trembling in all his limbs, asked whether he could be sure of not being put under arrest as long as he remained there.

Meanwhile, Prime Minister Facta took the decree to the king for the

---

[14] L. Pierard, *Le Fascisme* (Bruxelles: L'Eglantine, 1923), p. 7; Beals, *Rome or Death*, p. 290. Analogous reports from the Spanish journalist Rafael Sanchez Mazas, cited in L. Vicentini, *Il Governo Fascista giudicato fuori d'Italia* (Milano: Barion, 1924), p. 43; and Rossi, *The Rise of Italian Fascism*, p. 315, n. 2.

signature. He had been forestalled. Admiral Thaon de Revel had "advised" the king to yield to the "revolution." General Diaz, one of the army chiefs, also arrived at the palace. He was in Florence on the afternoon of October 27, at the moment when the headquarters of the Fascist party ordered the "mobilization" of the Blackshirts. He had accepted a demonstration of enthusiasm from the Fascists, had given an interview to the Florence daily *La Nazione* in which he had expressed his complete faith in the Fascist movement, and had rushed off by car to Rome to "inform" the king that the army would not fight against the Fascists.[15] General Cittadini, aide de camp to the king, was himself a partisan of the Fascist movement and supported Thaon de Revel, and Diaz. Federzoni also came to the palace and, on behalf of the Nationalists, gave the same information. The news arrived that the king's cousin, the Duke of Aosta, was at Bevagna, near Perugia, ready to have himself proclaimed king as soon as the actual ruler should abdicate or be deposed by the Fascists.

The king was scared by all this "advice," "information," and "news." Facta was still more scared than the king. Moreover, it seems that in his imbecile vanity, he imagined that if he helped the king and the Fascists to find a compromise, he would be asked to form a new ministry with the cooperation of the Fascists. Therefore he did not advise the proclamation of martial law. "Sir," he said to the sovereign, "think it over." The king thought it over and refused to sign.[16] With his weak character, it was easier not to sign. He acted exactly like the generals commanding provincial garrisons: he left the way open to the Fascists.[17]

Now they had obtained the revocation of martial law, Thaon de Revel, Diaz, and Cittadini suggested that the king summon the man on whom they could count, Salandra. The latter was in Rome, waiting for the high destiny which was in store for him.

The king's advisers soon discovered that they had made a big mistake.

[15] "Not for nothing was General Diaz—how reminiscent of Mexican politics is the name —in Florence on the night of the 27th" (Beals, *Rome or Death*, p. 286).

[16] C. Sforza, *Makers of modern Europe* (London: Elkins, Mathews and Mariot, 1930), p. 315–16.

[17] We owe our information regarding the behavior of the king and Facta to Giovanni Amendola, who was one of the cabinet ministers in October 1922; to a friend of Taddei who was home secretary in October 1922; and to Alberto Cianca, who was in Rome as chief editor of the daily paper *Il Mondo* and was in hourly touch with Amendola. Don Sturzo's version (*Italy and Fascism*, p. 119) and Sforza's version agree with that given by our sources. Don Sturzo was at that time in Rome and had immediate knowledge of what was happening. Sforza was in Paris, but afterwards he discussed this matter with Giolitti, who in his turn doubtless was informed by trusted friends he had in Rome.

The revocation of the martial law was a boomerang. As soon as it was made known, at 12:15 P.M., the news sent a thrill of triumph through the Fascists all over Italy. They poured into the streets, stormed the trains, and "marched on Rome." It was a mad scramble to reach there first. It was impossible to stem the tide. Even carabineers left their barracks, fraternized with the Fascists, and accompanied them on their "march on Rome." It was a case of unexpected mass suggestion. By refusing to sign the decree of martial law, the king not only had disarmed the existing cabinet, but had lost his own freedom to choose the new prime minister. Until 12:15 P.M. of October 28, Salandra, holding the decree of martial law in his hands, could have negotiated with the Fascists. After 12:15 P.M., Mussolini was the master of the boat. The king was no longer a king but a prisoner of war with the title of king.

Of the two "quadrumvirs" who were in Rome, De Vecchi was working on behalf of Salandra, while the secretary general of the party, Michele Bianchi, with unflinching stubbornness supported Mussolini. On the evening of October 28, he realized that with no martial law in Rome or in Italy, with thousands of Fascists pouring toward Rome from all sides, Mussolini could easily snap his fingers at the Nationalists, and he persuaded the other quadrumvirs that Salandra should be shelved and Mussolini should get the premiership.

In Milan, Mussolini was slower to grasp how overwhelming had been his victory. Since the king had entrusted Salandra with the premiership, Mussolini thought that the only thing to do was to negotiate with Salandra by telephone about the number of seats in the cabinet which should be given to his party. It was Finzi, one of the friends who was around him in the offices of the *Popolo d'Italia*, who seized the receiver out of Mussolini's hand, declared to Salandra that he must make way for Mussolini, and cut short negotiations. For twenty-four hours, Salandra endeavored in vain to get together the new cabinet. In the afternoon of October 29, he acknowledged his failure. The Nationalists were furious, but they too had to give way. The king had no alternative but to send for Mussolini.

All political movements are in need of leaders. And leadership finally falls on those who keep themselves more in the limelight. Mussolini had always kept himself in the limelight. He had become the "articulate voice of fascism." So, when the hour of victory came, the mantle of the Fascist pontificate fell upon his shoulders because he had been the prophet who had spoken with tongues. At the invitation of the king, he left Milan on the evening of the 29th and "marched on Rome" in a sleeping car.

Meanwhile, after the revocation of the decree of martial law, during the afternoon of October 28, the whole of October 29, and the following night, thousands of Fascists had "marched on Rome" and joined those who had already "marched" during the night of the 27th and on the morning of the 28th. A few of them, like the Duce, "marched" in sleeping cars; the majority "marched" in the trains they took by storm, others in lorries, on horseback, or even on foot. Wherever they passed, there was a prodigious slaughter of poultry and draining of wine casks. Any peasant indiscreet enough to claim rights of ownership over his fowls or his wine ran the risk of being given short shift as a "Communist" and an "enemy of his country."

The more people that gathered in the four meeting places, the more the situation of those hungry, thirsty, and disordered crowds became both ridiculous and tragic. Pelting rainstorms confounded the situation even more. The countryside around Rome had already seen such scenes in times of old. One of them is described by Tacitus, the Latin historian; it was the "march on Rome" of Vitellius: *sexaginta millia armatorum sequebantur, disciplina corrupta.* ("Sixty thousand armed men followed him, who had cast aside all discipline.")

On the evening of October 29, the leader in charge of the 13,000 men who had gathered to the north of Rome, no longer knowing what to do with all that crowd, turbulent, hungry, thirsty, watersoaked, sent to the leader of the crowd, who had taken refuge at Tivoli, a message that "in view of the impossibility of remaining in Monterotondo" he would leave for Rome on the following morning and asking him to do likewise.

On the morning of October 30, Mussolini arrived in Rome and assumed the post of prime minister. It was impossible for him to order those 40,000 men who had "marched on Rome" to return home without entering Rome. Therefore, the military and railway authorities dedicated the whole day of October 30, that night, and the morning of the 31st to disciplining as best they could that anarchy. The hordes who were nearest to Rome were put up and fed as well as circumstances allowed. Those further away were brought on railways. Thus it was possible to classify them according to carriages and give them a superficial order before they arrived in Rome. At the same time, with the help of the Nationalists, the military authorities distributed in Rome among spur-of-the-moment recruits some thousand blue shirts—the uniform which the Nationalists used to distinguish themselves from the Fascists. To these men in blue shirts the army entrusted horses on October 31. In this way a cavalry was improvised, whose job was to put down eventual lawless outbursts on the part of the Fascists when they entered Rome. When everything had been staged for a monster demonstration at last, on the afternoon of October 31, this demonstration took place. Fifty thousand men paraded in the streets of Rome to celebrate their victory after a "march on Rome" which had never happened. An old Roman prelate who had been at the Vatican with Pope Pius IX on September 20, 1870, when the Italian troops took the city, losing only twenty men, commented on the defence of Rome in 1922 by the royal government with a remark not unworthy of Tacitus: "We, in our day, put up a better defense."[18] Neither the "mass suggestion" of October 28, the failure of Salandra, the putting forward of Mussolini for the premiership, nor the demonstration of 50,000 daredevils in the streets of Rome had been foreseen. The "march on Rome" was a "comedy of errors." "Luck and the passing mood rule the world," says La Rochefoucauld.

In Fascist historiography, this opera bouffe is termed a "revolution." Was it a revolution?

The French "revolution," at the end of the eighteenth century, began with a *coup de main*, the storming of the Bastille on July 14, 1789, which was made possible by a mutiny among the troops in Paris, the dissentions which paralyzed the nobility and the clergy, the administrative muddle, and the futility of the king. This *coup de main* set in motion four contemporary "revolutions" which helped each other: (1) the peasantry set fire to the feudal castles and expelled or murdered the tax collectors; (2) the populace of the towns attacked the octroi barriers and the food shops; (3) the middle classes refused to obey the administrative personnel; and (4) a considerable section of the regular army refused to take part in the suppression of disorder. During the "spontaneous anarchy" which, after the main crisis of the summer of 1789, lasted for several years, numerous *coups de main*, or *coups d'état*, took place. The outcome of all these events was, after 1799, the emergence of a middle-class-controlled society.

In 1917 Russia was the scene of a "revolution." Millions of men rose in revolt against military discipline, killed their officers, returned armed to their villages, and seized possession of the land, expelling or killing the former owners. Other groups invaded the big cities and paralyzed by their

---

[18] V. Ojetti, *Cose viste* (Milano: Treves, 1923), 1:265.

numbers the action of the old political and administrative authorities. All the interests, habits, ideologies, and superstitions composing the old society crashed to the ground. In the midst of the social chaos there still floated, in the autumn of 1917, bits of wreckage of the old structure. In October 1917, the Bolshevists, taking advantage of the conditions created by the preceding revolution, seized power through a *coup de main*, wiped out all the remnants of the old regime, and then they went on building up a new military, administrative, and social structure partly on the pattern of their own Marxian or would-be Marxian ideology and partly under the pressure of unpredictable needs.

One must distinguish between *coup de main* and "revolution." The "revolutions" in France of July 1830 and February 1848 were strictly speaking *coups de main* which succeeded because of the weakness of the military and civil authorities, either afraid to count on the army or incapable of acting with the necessary energy and intelligence. In September 1870, the French did not even need a *coup de main* to put an end to the Second Empire; military defeat brought with it the collapse of the government, which abdicated without striking a blow. The Paris "commune" rose out of a *coup de main* which was meant to be the beginning of a social revolution, but it remained an isolated attempt, and Thiers was able to muster sufficient troops to crush it. The German republican revolution and the disintegration of the Austro-Hungarian monarchy of autumn 1918 were phenomena comparable with the governmental collapse which in 1870 produced the third French Republic. These changes of regime differ from the French and Russian revolutions in being "political" and not "social" revolutions. They only resulted in some changes in the men at the head of the central and local government, whereas social revolution entails the economic and political expropriation, or even the actual physical destruction, of the former ruling classes. Anyhow, "revolution," either "social" or "political," always results from the uprising of extragovernmental forces against the regular forces of a government.

If this is "revolution," can one ever seriously think that the "march on Rome" was a "revolution?"

The "march on Rome" no doubt possesses certain of the elements of a *coup de main* or "political revolution," in that a group of men who were not in power, taking advantage of the weakness of the king and the stupidity of the prime minister, seized the government. But in a revolution, the army chiefs remain loyal to the regular government, and the army is beaten by the revolutionists. In the case of the "march on Rome," men who were not in power seized the government with the connivance of army chiefs. Thus the "march on Rome" should rather be termed as a military *coup d'état*. During the summer and the autumn of 1922, the Fascists spoke of an impending *coup d'état* and not of a revolution.[19]

Yet a military *coup d'état* is made by men who are in the highest posts in the government. Typical instances are the *coups d'état* of Brumaire 1799 and December 2, 1851 in France. Napoleon Bonaparte and Louis Napoleon openly took the responsibility of abolishing Parliament. In Italy in 1922, the king was the first victim of the uprising. What really took place was a "military sedition" interwoven with a "dynastic intrigue" and camouflaged as a "popular revolution" aimed at compelling the king either to abdicate or to make a *coup d'état* against Parliament. The king, finding himself caught between an imbecile prime minister and a military sedition masked by a bogus popular insurrection, rather than abdicate in favor of his cousin, yielded to the "advice" (i.e., the pressure) of the military clique and carried out, though to his own personal distaste, the antiparliamentary *coup d'état* by depriving the civil government of the indispensable means of legal repression and by summoning Mussolini to the premiership.

To term the "march on Rome" a "revolution" is to whitewash the chiefs of the army and the king himself of any disloyalty to the constitution and to surround Mussolini's head with the halo of a "revolutionary conqueror" who, to seize power, had to face heaven knows how many pitched battles and dangerous ordeals.

AUTHOR'S NOTES TO CHAPTER 24

How many were the Fascists who, on the morning of October 28, were available for an attack upon the city of Rome?

A Fascist newspaper of Rome, *La Patria*, in giving on October 31, 1922, a flamboyant description of the epic days which had elapsed, affirmed that the "Fascists who were camping outside the gates of Rome during the night of October 29 numbered approximately 70,000" (reproduced by the *Popolo d'Italia*, November 1, 1922). The number 70,000 is found again in the book of Sir Percival Phillips, the English journalist: according to him, the Fascists numbered nearly 120,000, or, more precisely 117,000, "of whom 70,000

---

[19] Rossi, *The Rise of Italian Fascism*, pp. 255, 293.

were Blackshirts of the first line troops."[20] Sir Percival's words are worthy of being fully given:

> It was a march of simple peasants, some of whom saw a large city for the first time, and of working men from the mills and factories, intermingled with other elements of society, all demanding liberty. Nearly 120,000 armed men, all loyal, all pledged to put self aside and think only of their country, gathered at the gates of Rome. They came like the legions of old, in cohorts, in companies commanded by centurions, in "manipoli," or sections, bearing names made famous by their exploits in action. By next morning they (the Fascists) were moving on the first three points of concentration, under the direction of General Fara. The Supreme Council of three (General De Bono, Signor de Vecchi, and Signor Balbo) remained at their general headquarters at Perugia. Blackshirts from Umbria, Romagna, and Tuscany concentrated first at Foligno, and then moved to Monterotondo, twenty miles north of Rome. More from the Abruzzi came down from their mountain homes and gathered near Tivoli, about the same distance from Rome on the northeast of the capital, under Signor Bottai. Fascist units from Genoa, Milan, Bologna, and the northwest generally moved down the seacoast to Santa Marinella, a little port near Civitavecchia, where Signor Pollastrini was in command. Thus Rome was surrounded on three sides by an army of nearly 120,000 men, perfectly organized and disciplined and ready to fight. I am asked to emphasize the fact that this converging movement was one of small units, not of large military hordes. Squadre and manipoli simply met at their usual rendezvous and made their way direct to the mobilization center. They traveled by train, motorcar, and lorry. They were equipped with carbines, revolvers, and trench-helmets.[21]

In 1924, Villari, the Fascist propaganda agent in English-speaking countries, gave the figure as 70,000 for the troops in the front line, and put the rear guard at 20,000 (*Awakening of Italy*, p. 74). Two years later, in the *Manchester Guardian*, March 27, 1926, he raised the total to 200,000. Sir Ernest Benn, an English publisher and self-styled student of politics and

---

[20] *The Red Dragon and the Black Shirts*, pp. 14, 15, 54–57.
[21] *The Red Dragon and the Black Shirts*, pp. 14, 54–55.

economics, judged 200,000 not enough and raised the figure to 300,000 (*Star*, April 6, 1926). None of these gentlemen ever asked himself how many trains and trucks would have been required to transport in one night 70,000 men, much less 200,000 or 300,000.

Mussolini's own organ, the *Popolo d'Italia*, on November 3, 1922—a date too early for the Fascist legend to have been invented—stated that between October 31 and November 1, the railways had evacuated 45,000 Fascists from Rome. In a speech on March 24, 1924, Mussolini said that he had had at his command 52,000. By June 17, he increased the number to 60,000, although in a letter written on October 28, 1924, he reduced it again to 50,000. Probably then, his "troops" on October 30 numbered between 50,000 and 60,000.

But the Fascists who entered Rome on October 30 were not those who, on the morning of October 28, might have been called upon to face the regular army. The big rush of Blackshirts to Rome took place only during the afternoon of October 28 and the next two days.

The figures that we have given have been drawn from the statements which De Bono, Balbo, and the other leaders of the "March on Rome" made without realizing that they were destroying the Fascist saga. (See Rossi, *The Rise of Italian Fascism*, p. 315).

25

The
Matteotti Murder

At the time of the March on Rome, the Chamber of Deputies was made up of the following groups: (1) Fascists, 35 seats; (2) Nationalists, 10; (3) Conservatives, 43; (4) Populists, 107; (5) Democrats of different brands, 167; (6) Republicans, 7; (7) right-wing Socialists, 71; (8) Maximalist Socialists, 50; (9) Communists, 11; (10) Slavs and Germans, 8; (11) unaffiliated, 16. The first three groups were favorable to Mussolini but could not muster more than 88 votes. Groups 6 to 10 and most of the deputies of group 11 were against Mussolini, and together they commanded about 160 votes. The fate of Mussolini's cabinet depended on the 107 deputies of the Populist party and on the 167 Democrats. If the Populist party had decided to stand against Mussolini, a large proportion of the Democrats would have joined the opposition, and Mussolini's cabinet would have been outvoted. Then Mussolini would have had either to resign, to disband the Chamber and call for a national election, or to do away altogether with the Chamber. In the latter case, the king would have had to make another *coup d'état.* Everyone, beginning with the king, would have had to assume openly and directly his own responsibilities.

In the Populist party, a minority was in league with Mussolini. The majority were hostile to him but did not dare face his wrath. In the vote of confidence, only two of them were courageous enough to vote against Mussolini. Four or five absented themselves from the hall. The others behaved just like a herd of cattle. Most of the Democrats did the same.

There were 306 votes in favor of Mussolini and 116 against him. One hundred thirteen deputies were absent from the voting, most of them for fear. Thus the Chamber of Deputies committed suicide.

Many hoped that the Fascists, now that they had gained control of the government, would put an end to their lawlessness. They were soon disappointed. In his book *Un anno di dominazione fascista*, Rome, 1924, Giacomo Matteotti enumerated more than 2,000 murders, more or less serious woundings, clubbings, castor-oil purges, looting of private houses and headquarters of associations, and burning down of newspaper printing presses and premises, all of which took place from November 1922 to October 1923.

During the night of December 17–18, a Fascist was killed in Turin in a quarrel arising from private and nonpolitical motives. The local Fascist leader, a certain Brandimarte, assumed that it was a political crime deserving reprisals. The Blackshirts were left free for a whole day, with no interference from the police, to use their revolvers at will and to burn down private houses and the premises of trade unions, cooperative societies, and political organizations. Brandimarte publicly declared: "Out of a list of three hundred revolutionists, twenty-four were selected and entrusted to the best squads for punishment." The bodies of only fourteen of the victims were found. Brandimarte stated: "The river Po will deliver the remaining bodies, if it chooses, unless they are found in ditches and ravines around Turin, except two who escaped." Two days after the Turin massacre, on December 22, a royal decree granted a general amnesty to those guilty of "political" crimes, even murder—on condition, however, that such crimes had been committed "for a national purpose either direct or indirect." "National" meant "Fascist." The amnesty made it plain that the Fascists could count on the full support of the government after the deed was done.

A few days later, the Royal Guard was disbanded and by a royal decree of January 14, 1923, the Fascist "squadrons" which had carried on civil war during the two preceding years were gathered together into an official "Voluntary Militia for National Safety." The task of the militia was that of "protecting the inevitable further developments of the Fascist revolution" and of "upholding at all costs the regime which came into being with the March on Rome" (Mussolini's proclamation of January 12–13, 1923). The cost of its maintenance was to be charged to the state budget, but in order to become a militiaman, membership in the Fascist party was necessary, and the militiaman had to take an oath of allegiance to Mussolini. The leaders of the local Fascist "squadrons" were made officers of the militia. Those responsible for the most cruel murders of the two preceding years now appeared clad in the insignia of consuls (colonels) or generals of the militia. Brandimarte obtained the rank of colonel.

The decree was unconstitutional since Article 5 of the Constitution of the Realm outlawed any armed forces bound by an oath of allegiance to anyone but the king himself, "who commands all land and naval armed forces of the kingdom." The decree took away from the king one of the fundamental prerogatives of the crown.

The creation of the militia marks a turning point in the history of fascism. In 1924 a Fascist commentator wrote:

> The substantial purposes of the Fascist movement are to be carried out, necessarily, in the midst of the indifference or initial hostility of the masses. Hence the necessity for the master to possess also a force of his own, different from any other, and independent of any other authority, and aimed solely at attaining the purposes of the master. Such is and must remain for the Fascist government, the Voluntary Militia of the Blackshirts. It is, therefore, one of the fundamental bases of the Fascist government.[1]

More cogently, Mussolini wrote in 1927:

> The creation of the militia was the fundamental and irrevocable event which put the government on a level totally different from that of its predecessors. When the militia was created, the death sentence of the old democratic system was sealed. From that time on, the old free state was waiting to be buried.[2]

Professor Volpe, the official historian of fascism, wrote in 1928 that the establishment of the militia "meant, at least implicitly: Here we are and here, until the accomplishment of our work, we shall remain, whether the other parties like it or not."[3]

A week after the creation of the militia, there was in the city of La Spezia

---

[1] Pellizzi, *Problemi e realtà del Fascismo*, p. 121.
[2] In the preface to the book *Il Gran Consiglio nei primi cinque anni dell' Era Fascista* (Roma: Libreria del Littorio, 1927), p. xi.
[3] Volpe, *Lo sviluppo storico del Fascismo*, p. 22.

a repetition of the massacre at Turin. On the night of January 21, a Fascist was murdered by Fascist comrades. As usual, the responsibility was laid at the door of the "Bolshevists." The next day reprisals set in. Fourteen dead and about one hundred more or less seriously wounded appeased the Fascist wrath. The police were conspicuous by their absence. Nobody was ever arrested or tried. When, on February 10, this matter was mentioned in the Chamber, Mussolini silenced all discussion by declaring:

> In matters of domestic policy there is no call for discussion. All that happens happens by my will and precise order, for which I assume full responsibility. The difference between the Democratic and the Fascist state consists just in this: that the Fascist state not only defends itself but attacks its enemies.

From November 1, 1922, to March 31, 1923, the Fascists, as far as one can gather from available sources, killed no less than 118 persons.

It would be unfair to affirm that all these acts of violence were ordered by Mussolini. But the fact remains that those responsible for these crimes were never punished. Signs of hostility towards the Fascist regime were manifesting themselves throughout the country. Terror was indispensable to stem the opposition. Mussolini, therefore, avoided repressing them, even when at heart he believed that the acts of violence were excessive or unnecessary. In many cases, he himself commanded them. In June 1924, the Undersecretary of the Interior Aldo Finzi and the chief of Mussolini's press bureau, Cesare Rossi, revealed that several acts of violence, and especially those against journalists and deputies of the opposition, had been ordered by Mussolini in person.

In February 1923, the Fascist party and the Nationalist party were fused into a single organism. As we have already seen, during the two preceding years the Nationalists had everywhere filtered into the Fascist ranks, and, since they were the only ones who knew what they wanted, they had powerfully contributed to make of the Fascist movement an instrument of capitalist and military reaction. But the Nationalist leaders did not officially adhere to the Fascist party and kept their own organization. This state of things often led to friction between the followers of the two parties: the "aristocratic" Nationalists looked down upon the "democratic" Fascists; in their turn, the Fascists accused the Nationalists of being parasites who lived by their sacrifices. To put an end to these frictions, the leaders of the two parties, in February 1923, decided that their followers should merge into a single party.

This event had a great influence on the intellectual orientation of the Fascist party. After the seizure of the government, the purely negative mysticism of "revolution" (violence), was no longer sufficient. Neither Mussolini nor the other leaders of the Fascist party had the preparation, the habits, or the time to construct by themselves a new doctrine, whereas the Nationalists had been for fifteen years and more advocating a "strong government" and the abolition of democracy and parliamentarism—precisely the doctrines of which Mussolini and his followers were in need. The Fascist party lacked a brain, and the Nationalist leaders gave it that brain. In return, the latter found in the Fascist party the body which they had never been capable of creating by themselves. After the fusion of the two parties, all the Nationalist leaders became prominent personages in the Fascist party. They injected the Nationalist doctrines into the arteries of Fascism. The "philosophers," the "jurists," and the "historians" of the Fascist regime were almost all former Nationalists.

Mussolini defined the spirit of his regime in a speech of March 7, 1923:

> One may perhaps ask: "Why so many armed men?" I declare that I wish to govern, if possible, with the consent of the great part of the citizens. But while waiting for this consent to be formed, to grow and to become strong, I keep at my disposal as many forces as possible. Because it may happen, by chance, that the force may bring consent; but at any rate, if consent should be lacking, the force will remain.

Consent, at that moment, meant the consent of a majority in the Chamber.

In April 1923, the deputies of the Populist party split up: sixteen openly went over to fascism; and ninety-one, under pressure from the rank and file, passed over to the opposition. Consequently, Mussolini had to face an opposition which consisted of half the Chamber. Moreover, among deputies who voted for him, there were at least one hundred fifty who had rushed onto the bandwagon after the Fascist victory but who were in favor of the "Fascist experiment" and not of "fascism." They were ready to go over to the anti-Fascist camp as soon as the experiment failed.

Since he did not have a sure majority in the existing Chamber, Mussolini had to get rid of it and form a new one with a clear majority in his favor.

A new election under the existing electoral system, however, was not to be trusted. The electorate might again return an anti-Fascist majority. Hence the need of a new electoral system aimed at securing a Fascist majority. Such a system could not be enacted by royal decree. This would have meant making another *coup d'état* and exposing the Crown too much. A bill had to be passed by the Chamber. Thus, in order to get rid of his opponents, Mussolini had to ask those very opponents to pass a bill which would prevent their own reelection.

The bill was introduced in the Chamber on April 17, 1923. As we know, according to the system in force in 1923, the country was divided into large districts; in each district, each party obtained a number of seats proportionate to the number of votes given to its own list. The new plan preserved the division of the country in large districts, but it prescribed that in each district each party should nominate no more than two-thirds of the deputies allotted to the district. The votes obtained in all districts by any one party were added together to form the "national total" of any one party. The party which received the highest national total would receive two-thirds of the seats (356 out of 535) in all the districts, even in those in which it had not obtained the plurality. That party, therefore, would control two-thirds of the votes in the Chamber. The other parties would share, in each district, the remaining one-third of the seats, in proportion to the number of votes they had obtained there. A system of "disproportionate representation" would thus take the place of proportional representation.

When the bill came up in July for discussion in the Chamber, the Socialist and the Communist groups, and those Democrats who were led by Amendola, took an immediate stand against it. The final issue depended on the attitude of the Populist deputies. If these had voted against it, the conflict between the cabinet and the Chamber would have opened the way for the king's intervention. Had the king sided with the Chamber against the cabinet, Mussolini would have had either to resign or to undertake a *coup d'état* not only against the Chamber but also against the king.

Among the Populist deputies, the more conservative or less courageous were willing to give in, but Don Sturzo was an uncompromising opponent of the bill, and he had the support of the rank and file of the party and of the majority of deputies. The bill was bound to meet with a strong opposition and even defeat.

There was only one solution for Mussolini: force the Chamber to swallow the bill. The Fascist militia was in readiness. The House (Montecitorio) was put under the custody of the Fascist militia instead of the regulars, as had been the custom in the "old era." The regulars had been under the orders of the speaker to guarantee the freedom of the deputies. The Fascist militiamen were under orders from the prime minister to intimidate the deputies. The Fascist press published savage attacks against the opposition deputies. Most of these were shadowed. One of them, Signor Misuri, on May 29, 1923, had been nearly cudgeled to death; his assailants, though known to everybody, remained "persons unknown" to the police. At the same time, Fascist newspapers and Fascist orators in public meetings announced in truculent language that if the Populist party did not yield on the electoral bill, Italy would witness the most violent outburst of anticlericalism ever recorded in its history. Don Sturzo, they argued, was a priest. As such, he was under the discipline of his ecclesiastical superiors. These latter were responsible for the policy of the Populist party. Therefore, the Fascist party should include in its hostility not only Don Sturzo and his political party, but also the whole ecclesiastical hierarchy to which Don Sturzo belonged.

On July 10, 1923, the bill came up for discussion before the Chamber. The lobbies were filled with Blackshirts who displayed ropes prepared to hang—as they shouted—those deputies who dared to cast a dissenting vote. The deputies knew very well, because of what had happened to Signor Misuri on May 29, that it was not a mere matter of simple verbal manifestations. Don Sturzo writes:

> The political atmosphere was sultry and oppressive. Blackshirts were concentrated in Rome. On every hand wild rumors circulated of violent outrages and personal vendettas; the armed forces of fascism paraded in growing strength; even the galleries of the Chamber and its corridors and lobbies being thronged with them.[4]

In spite of all this, the opposition revealed an unsuspected energy. And behold, on July 11, Don Sturzo resigned from the secretariat of his party with the following declaration:

[4] Luigi Sturzo, *Italy and Fascism* (London: Faber and Gwyer, 1926), pp. 137–38. Signor Villari (*Awakening of Italy*, p. 247) throws a discreet veil over the methods by which the electoral reform was forced through the Chamber. Alluding to the Populists, he writes: "The party was no longer as compact as it had been, and the government continued to enjoy the support of the Vatican, which was, of course, a most valuable asset."

> I can no longer be a pretext, insidiously utilized, for misconceptions as to the relations between the Populist party and the Church, dragging this latter into political quarrels which the party must meet on its own responsibility in complete independence. I therefore think it my duty to prevent without delay the attack against the Church from going further than ambushing and threats (*Il Popolo*, July 11–12, 1923).

The Liberal newspaper, *La Stampa*, was more explicit than Don Sturzo:

> In the Vatican it was feared that Fascist hostility would spread to the clergy in general. High Fascist circles had warned the Vatican that it was impossible to safeguard any longer the person of Don Sturzo or the clergy in general in the different regions of Italy. The Vatican was alarmed by this state of things, and since Don Sturzo had previously offered to withdraw, should his person create difficulties for the Vatican, the latter let Don Sturzo know that the time had come for his resignation, which was first made known to the Vatican.

Il Popolo, the Populist paper edited by a friend of Don Sturzo, reproduced in its issue of July 12–13, 1923, these words of *La Stampa* without any correction either from Don Sturzo or from the Vatican. Therefore, we must consider that they give a fair statement of the case.

But this was not the whole truth. The whole truth is that in January 1923, Mussolini and Cardinal Gasparri, the pope's secretary of state, had had a secret interview in the house of one of the directors of the Bank of Rome. They had agreed to solve the Roman question, and Mussolini had pledged himself to save the bank at the expense of Italian taxpayers.[5] He had kept his word. Bankruptcy had been avoided. It was up to the pope

---

[5] The fact that there had been this interview between Gasparri and Mussolini became known from a letter to the newspaper *Il Popolo di Roma*, August 22–23, 1929, written by Count Santucci, who in 1923 was the chairman of the Bank of Rome. According to this letter, Gasparri and Mussolini had only agreed that it was time to solve the Roman question. But in August 1929, Mussolini and Pius XI were involved in a sharp conflict concerning the interpretation of the Lateran agreements, and Mussolini instructed the newspaper which published Santucci's letter to add a note saying, "We have also evidence that in the interview between Cardinal Gasparri and Mussolini, the question of the salvage of the Bank of Rome was discussed." The official press agency, Stefani, the next day communicated to all papers the text of Santucci's letter with the note appended. Since it was known that dispatches of the Stefani were first submitted to the approval of the government, it was evident that Mussolini had published that note in order to remind Pope Pius XI of their deal. Cardinal Gasparri did not dare to issue a contradiction.

to return the favor. Don Sturzo was told that he had to resign from the secretariat of the Populist party. There was nothing left for him to do but to obey.

After the shepherd had been smitten, the sheep had to scatter. On July 13, the offices of many Catholic organizations all over Italy were attacked and looted. This was another warning to such Populist deputies as had not yet understood the advisability of surrender.

On the same day, the king was brought to the fore. The newspapers published the text of a decree which authorized the prefects of provinces to "admonish" the editors of newspapers who put into circulation "false or malicious" news. Any editor who was "admonished" twice during a year would lose the right to edit a paper. The decree openly violated the constitution on a field which had always been closed to royal decrees. Neither the cabinet nor the king had ever enacted such provisions without the previous approval of Parliament. The king had not yet signed the decree. Mussolini, by giving out the news that it had been signed, created the impression that the king was openly siding with him and was ready to back him even on unconstitutional ground. The king kept silent. The Chamber was thus warned that they should either yield or face another *coup d'état*, since Mussolini had the king in his pocket.

After the Chamber had discussed the bill for four days, on July 15, Mussolini made an unexpectedly mild speech, in which he gave hopes that, as soon as the bill was passed, all lawlessness would cease throughout the country. With an unfortunate lack of political acumen, the leader of the anti-Fascist Democrats, Amendola, allowed himself to be taken in by this promise and, sacrificing his anti-Facist sentiments to his desire for public peace, declared that he would abstain from voting against the bill. This gave the signal of "every man for himself" for all those who either were in a hurry to earn the good graces of Mussolini or had no desire to taste the Fascist bludgeon.

The bill was passed with 235 votes in its favor. Only 100 Socialist, Communist, and Democrat deputies and 39 of the Populist deputies were plucky enough to vote against it. The rest were either absent or abstained from voting.

That same day, the king signed the decree against the press. Since the Chamber had renounced its honor and independence, he felt less guilty about destroying another piece of the old Constitution of the Realm. The decree, however, was not published in the official gazette; it remained in

Mussolini's drawer ready to be published and applied whenever Mussolini should wish. This also was an innovation in Italian constitutional (or, rather, unconstitutional) practice. Never before had any king been presented by any prime minister with a decree to be published and enacted, not soon after the king had signed it, but at a future time when the prime minister thought it advisable.

Even with the new electoral system, a general election might produce some unpleasant surprise. It was necessary to make sure that a Fascist majority was returned. It was still necessary to hitch force and consent to the same cart.

The Reverend Giovanni Minzoni, rector of the parish church in Argenta (Ferrara), was a fearless leader of the Catholic boys organization of the district and opposed with all his might Fascist propaganda among the boys. On August 23, three men from Ferrara fell upon Argenta and silenced Don Minzoni forever by breaking his skull with billy clubs.

On November 29, the Blackshirts took by assault the residence of former premier Nitti; his house was ransacked and his furniture destroyed. On December 26, Amendola was attacked on one of the main streets of Rome and beaten into unconsciousness.

Neither Don Minzoni, Signor Nitti, nor Amendola were Socialist or Communist. Fascist rage was not less merciless and ruthless against those men who represented lawabiding groups. Needless to mention, none of the perpetrators of these outrages was ever punished. The *Osservatore Romano*, official organ of the Vatican, ignored the assassination of Don Minzoni: the *entente cordiale* between Pius XI and Mussolini was yielding its fruits.

In January 1924, the king again came to the fore. By a royal decree of January 24, he placed under the surveillance of the prefects those associations which "derived in whole or in part their financial means from contributions of laborers." The prefects were authorized to disband the directors of such associations, to substitute for them extraordinary commissioners, and, if necessary, to order the liquidation of the societies' assets. There were in Italy thousands of societies for mutual relief, especially for old age pensions, established by the workers, usually in trade groups, and supported by the contributions from the members. There were also thousands of institutions for educational and recreative purposes, and about 20,000 cooperative societies. Finally there were the Socialist and Populist trade unions, which still kept a high membership notwithstanding the violent pressure which the Fascists had applied against them for the last three years. As a result of the new decree, the workers had to choose: either they would submit to Fascist control, or they would have the funds of their organizations—fruit of half a century of work, thrift, and trials—thrown to the winds. This decree was no less unconstitutional than the one on the press of July 15, 1923, had been. The king, after taking that first step, had forfeited all sense of honor.

On January 28, 1924, addressing a national assembly of Fascist leaders, Mussolini announced his ultimatum to the nation: the country must give a full vote of confidence to his government, a Fascist plebiscite; the Fascist list must win, "cost what it might"; "whoever dares to lift his hand against the Fascist militia, will be riddled with lead."

The leaders of the anti-Fascist parties were too frightened to attempt a coalition of their candidates so as to obtain a majority of the votes. Not even the strong feeling that this was their last desperate fight could overcome their fear of Fascist violence. Each group accordingly presented its own separate list. Mussolini, on the contrary, admitted to his list only 256 of the militant Fascists; the remaining 100 places he distributed among those politicians of the "old era" who had not been niggardly in their support of fascism, or were willing to be converted at a price. This was again a clever political maneuver. By including in his list such names as those of the two former premiers, Salandra and Orlando, and several others who still had a strong grip over their constituencies, particularly in southern Italy, Mussolini prevented them from being listed in the opposition ranks and secured for his own list the votes of large sections that would otherwise have gone to the anti-Fascists.

During the election campaign, in different parts of Italy, hundreds of anti-Fascist canvassers were put under arrest by the police, and twenty-five of them were sped out of this vale of tears. Opposition parties were unable to hold meetings or even to put up posters. Amendola was prevented from delivering his election address in Naples; he had to deliver it in a private house before a small group of friends. Signor Forni, a dissident Fascist who dared to come out as a candidate in the district of Pavia, was attacked in the railway station of Milan and beaten almost to death by the same gang that on the following June 10 was to assassinate Giacomo Matteotti. This bit of work had been ordered by Signor Giunta, undersecretary in Mussolini's cabinet: Mussolini wrote in the *Popolo d'Italia* an article entitled "He who betrays, perishes," which approved the feat. A candidate in the district of Reggio Emilia, Antonio Piccinini, was murdered. In many constituencies, especially in southern Italy, it was impossible for the anti-Fascist parties even to nominate their candidates; the Fascist party nominated all candidates for both majority and minority. Many municipal administrations controlled by Fascist mayors refused to issue ballot papers to anti-Fascist voters.

It was during this electioneering campaign that the neo-Hegelian philosopher, Signor Gentile, then minister of public education, speaking in Palermo on March 24, 1924, referred to the bludgeon as an instrument of intellectual and moral education in a eulogy that deserves a conspicuous place in the history of modern philosophy:

> It is idle to distinguish moral from material energy. Every energy is moral energy, because it always aims at modifying the human will, and whatever argument may be used—whether the sermon or the cudgel—it can only be efficacious if it succeeds in stimulating a man's inner conscience and persuading him to consent. Which of the two arguments, the cudgel or the sermon, should be employed, is not a matter of abstract discussion.[5]

On election day, April 6, especially in the rural areas, the halls in which voting was to take place were guarded by armed Fascists who forbade the anti-Fascist electors to cast their votes. In many places the voters were brought to the polls in lorries under the supervision of Fascists, received the voting papers from the Fascists, and had to put them in the ballot boxes without entering the polling booths. Several persons who tried to go to the polls were wounded or killed outright. In a great number of precincts, the opposition parties were not allowed to send representatives to supervise the polling. The Fascists, free to do as they pleased, filled the ballot boxes with fake votes, so that in many districts, their list received the votes of every voter on the register, even of those who were dead or abroad. Where the opposition parties were not allowed to nominate their candidates, the Fascist candidates were returned for both government and opposition seats.

Despite all this, 2,300,000 citizens had the courage to vote for the non-Communist opposition candidates. The Communists received 265,000 votes. The Fascist candidates totalled 4,613,000 votes. Of these latter, the bulk (2,700,000), came from southern Italy; in southern districts

---

[5] G. Gentile, *Che cosa è il Fascismo* (Firenze: Vallecchi, 1925), pp. 50–51.

government officials always "cooked" the election returns according to the wishes of the party in power, even in the pre-Fascist era. In northern Italy, the Fascist list obtained only 1,800,000 votes against 1,285,000 votes for the anti-Fascist lists, exclusive of the Communists who polled 185,000 votes. In several of the larger northern cities, the Fascists received fewer votes than the sum total of the non-Fascist lists.

In the new Chamber there was, against a majority of 374, a scattered minority of 159. With such a Chamber, with a Senate in which the old Conservative and the new Fascist members stood behind the cabinet, and with the militia at his back, Mussolini was fully master of the situation.

Yet a parliamentary opposition did still exist, and as long as it continued to exist, it was to be expected that it would carry on its normal function of discussing the policies of the government. Moreover, the majority in the Chamber knew that it did not represent the majority in the country, and the minority denied its right to hold power.

On May 30, 1924, right-wing Socialist deputy Giacomo Matteotti denounced the violence and fraud used during the last elections. He recited at length instances of threats and acts of violence and of general tampering with ballots and returns. In conclusion, he moved that the elections should be declared void and without effect, and that new elections should be held under conditions that would allow the voters freedom to express their preference.

There was a highly dramatic tension in the Chamber. Matteotti's speech was interrupted at almost every sentence by the cries, denials, insulting remarks, and threats of the Fascist majority, but the fearless deputy, calm and unmoved, continued his indictment of Fascist violence to the end. Then he turned toward his colleagues and said in the same calm, firm voice, "And now get ready for my funeral." He knew well that by his act of courage he had forfeited his life.

On the afternoon of June 10, 1924, in a street of Rome, in broad daylight, Matteotti was attacked by five men and dragged by force into a car. Two months later, his burial place was discovered under some bushes forty miles outside Rome.

The judicial investigation disclosed the following facts: (1) that the leader of the gang which kidnapped and murdered Matteotti was a certain Dumini, a man employed by the chief of Mussolini's press bureau, Cesare Rossi; (2) that the automobile used in the abduction had been procured by a certain Filippelli, chief editor of one of the Fascist daily papers in Rome;

(3) that Dumini acted under a commission given him by Giovanni Marinelli, general treasurer of the Fascist party, and by Cesare Rossi, head of Mussolini's press bureau. It seems that Dumini's plan had been to kidnap Matteotti, take him to some secluded spot of the countryside around Rome, kill him, and leave the corpse there. But Matteotti, within the motorcar, began to fight his kidnappers and made an outcry. One of his assailants then pierced his chest with a dagger and thus silenced him.

As soon as the disappearance of Matteotti was known, though there was as yet no evidence that he had been murdered, the Italian people surmised that he was dead and why and by whom the crime had been committed. A wave of horror and disgust swept over the country.

On the afternoon of June 12, in the Chamber, a right-wing Socialist deputy asked a question about the disappearance of the deputy. Mussolini already knew that Matteotti had been killed, because Dumini had come back to Rome during the preceding night, and Filippelli, Marinelli, and Rossi had been informed of the feat. It is absurd to think that none of them had informed Mussolini before the latter went to the Chamber to face the storm. Mussolini stated that "Matteotti had unexpectedly disappeared, in circumstances of time and place not yet ascertained, but such as to arouse suspicion of a crime. This crime, if it had been committed, could not but arouse the indignation and emotion of Parliament." A Socialist deputy exclaimed, "Then Matteotti is dead." A Republican deputy cried, "Let the prime minister speak." There was a silence. Then the Republican deputy shouted, "He is an accomplice." He was with difficulty saved from the rage of the Fascists.

For several days the sidewalk where Matteotti had been overcome and dragged away was strewn with palm branches and flowers; a crowd of men, women, and children thronged there, knelt, and murmured prayers. The Fascists did not dare to molest them. The newspapers regained courage and filled their columns with comments upon the murder and with discussion of the clues that came to light from day to day. The Fascist leaders were stunned as if by an irreparable disaster; the rank and file of their followers deserted them; the Blackshirts disappeared from the streets. It was one of those spontaneous reactions of the moral conscience of a whole people which no regime can prevent or try to suppress by force. Mussolini himself, all his courage and daring gone, waited hopelessly for the coming catastrophe. There were several days of tense expectation.

Nothing happened. The Maximalist and Communist deputies, who for years had been talking revolution, did not dare to call a general strike. The right-wing Socialist, Democrat, and Populist deputies were averse to any revolutionary solution of the crisis. The only thing opposition deputies of all groups did was to decide to abstain from attending the sittings of the Chamber as a protest against the government. They drew up a well-written manifesto in which they demanded light on the crime and a return to a constitutional regime.

In an article in the *Mondo*, July 2, 1924, Guglielmo Ferrero described the situation in the following terms:

> There is a point on which the Opposition and the Majority will never speak the same language: whether the present Chamber is legitimate or not. For the Opposition to accept the electoral procedure of April 6 as lawful, would be to commit suicide: it would be to grant the Majority the right to destroy the Opposition by fire and sword. For the Majority to acknowledge the election as unlawful would be to commit suicide: it would confess that it had usurped its power. Opposition and Majority will never be able to meet: this insoluble question will always rise up between them. Giacomo Matteotti officially gave notice to the Chamber that the Opposition regarded it as illegitimate; and a few days later a hand from out of the darkness stabbed him. Today, Opposition and Majority form two distinct Chambers which disown and exclude each other. It is a delusion to expect that these two Chambers can be gathered into one assembly as the legitimate expression of the national will. Between them there is not only a dead body, but a question of legitimacy. This question cannot be solved by either of them, but only by the nation. The small Fascist minority, after forcing itself on the country, wishes to be accepted as the legitimate representative of the majority. But under a representative regime such as exists in Italy, and of which the Royal House is sworn guarantee, the Fascist minority can have no rights, except that of competing on equal terms with the other parties.

The opposition deputies hoped that their absence from the Chamber would paralyze Parliament and that the king would be forced to ask for Mussolini's resignation. The king had already, in January and in July 1923 and in January 1924, signed three unconstitutional decrees showing how little troubled he was by his sworn guarantee. The opponents did not realize that words were useless when action was needed. Events proved that it was their absence and their refusals to engage immediately in a parliamentary battle, while the resentment of the country was at its highest pitch, that really saved Mussolini.

After the first moment of depression, Mussolini, encouraged by the inertia of the opposition, rushed to repair the damage. The first indication that he had already weathered the storm appeared on July 10, 1924, when he took out of his drawer and published the royal decree of July 15, 1923, on the press, adding to it another royal decree in which power was given the prefects of the provinces to "confiscate at their discretion" all papers which published "false or malicious news." Thus once more the king gave notice that he was backing Mussolini. This ought to have opened the eyes of the parliamentary opposition, which still believed the king capable of taking the initiative in dismissing Mussolini. But their dreams were not at all dispelled, and they went on waiting for Mussolini's dismissal.

In fact, anti-Fascist feeling was still running high in the country. Notwithstanding the decrees against the freedom of the press, the Matteotti murder was featured on the front page of the opposition press during the whole summer and autumn of 1924. During the second half of 1924, the anti-Fascist newspapers in all Italy had a total circulation of 4 million copies as against only 400,000 of the Fascist press. The anti-Fascist *Stampa* of Turin had a circulation of 400,000 copies as against only 30,000 of the Fascist *Gazzetta del Popolo*. The *Corriere della sera* of Milan reached the round figure of half a million copies, while Mussolini's newspaper *Popolo d'Italia* could barely sell 40,000 copies. In Rome, the two Fascist dailies *Idea Nazionale* and *Impero* did well when they could sell 10,000 copies each, while the humorous anti-Fascist *Becco Giallo* ("Yellow Beak") in August 1924 was printing and selling more than 350,000 copies of each issue. The patients in the General Hospital of Milan bought daily 290 anti-Fascist and 62 Fascist newspapers. If these facts mean anything, they mean that most Italians were anything but Fascist.

During the summer, the leader of the anti-Fascist Democrats, Amendola, came into possession of two memoranda written one by Filippelli and the other by Cesare Rossi, both of whom were implicated in the murder and were detained in jail. Fearing to be made scapegoats, the two men had written those memoranda and had entrusted them to friends to be used, if necessary, in their defense. The friends had passed them over to Amendola.

Filippelli affirmed that both Cesare Rossi, the chief of Mussolini's press bureau, and Marinelli, the general treasurer of the Fascist party, had told him that the order for Matteotti's murder had been given personally by Mussolini. Cesare Rossi kept silent on this point, but he charged Mussolini with being personally accountable for many acts of violence committed by the Fascists from the March on Rome on.

Furthermore, Finzi, who was assistant secretary at the Home Office at the time of the murder, had confided to several persons that the order to suppress Matteotti had been given by Mussolini himself.

To be sure, Filippelli's and Rossi's memoranda and the Finzi statements were not definite evidence of Mussolini's guilt, but they afforded more than sufficient reason for a motion in Parliament asking the appointment of a parliamentary "committee of investigation," independent of the investigation made by the judiciary. The anti-Fascist parliamentary opposition had in hand sufficient weapons and ammunition to engage in battle. But they should have gone to the Chamber. It was clear by this time that their withdrawal from the session of Parliament had been a mistake and had worked to the advantage of Mussolini. To persist in the same tactics would be sheer folly. Nevertheless, they did persist in the same tactics. And in December 1924, at the opening of the Chamber, they decided to continue in their abstention. Only the Communist deputies returned to the Chamber, but they declared that the Matteotti murder was a "bourgeois" affair in which they were not interested, and that they would not attack the government on that account.

The Democrat, Populist, and right-wing Socialist deputies were confident that the pending judicial investigation would reveal Mussolini's responsibility in the murder and hence would give the king no other choice but to dismiss him. The eventual rebellion of the Blackshirts could be easily overcome by the regular army, and the crisis would be solved in a constitutional way. Everything seemed simple and clear. They did not realize that the problems created by the murder of Matteotti could not be solved by mere judicial procedure as if it were a common criminal case. The judges in charge of the case were in no hurry. They were marking time and waiting for the political forces to find a way out of the impasse. They carried on the inquiry in a leisurely way and, during six months, questioned hundreds of supposed witnesses who had nothing to say, while they carefully avoided questioning and confronting the executors of the crime with the originators of it, lest Mussolini's name should be brought directly into the affair.

While abstaining from the sessions of the Chamber, the opposition tried to drag in the king. Amendola, about the middle of November, put into the king's hands the memoranda of Rossi and Filippelli. He thought that the king, once in possession of such evidence, could not refuse to act. The king gave no sign of life.

After the Chamber adjourned for the Christmas recess, Amendola published on December 28 the memorandum written by Cesare Rossi, keeping Filippelli's memorandum for later use. This publication made an enormous impression, because Rossi had been one of the most intimate assistants of Mussolini and because it gave evidence that many acts of violence had been ordered directly by Mussolini. Amendola and his friends sat still, waiting to see what the king would do. The king did not lift a finger.

Mussolini, on the contrary, lost no time. He knew that he had the king in the hollow of his hand. In August, September, and October, he had made several tours in northern and central Italy, delivering everywhere inflammatory speeches against the opposition. The squads had resumed their "punitive expeditions" with ruthless efficiency. On October 22, 1924, the official organ of the Vatican, the *Osservatore Romano*, stated that in the district of Piacenza alone, during the preceding four months, thirty-six priests had been attacked and beaten and that one of them had been wounded to death. The priests were members of the Populist party. This was only one of the parties which formed the opposition, and Piacenza was only one of the ninety districts into which Italy was divided. This will give an idea of the situation prevailing in the country during those months.

On December 30, 1924, to prevent all comments on the Rossi memorandum and (still more) the publication of that of Filippelli, which accused him directly, Mussolini unearthed a law more than sixty years old which gave to the prefects the power to take control of "all branches of public service" in case of emergency. The press was regarded as a branch of the public service, and so the prefects were authorized to take "such measures as they might judge necessary" to prevent the papers from publishing any obnoxious news. From that time on, the anti-Fascist press was overwhelmed by a flood of confiscations as soon as they tried to give any news which the prefects regarded as obnoxious. By this fresh *coup d'état* against the press, "the problem of the press was solved in January 1925," as Mussolini stated in a speech of October 10, 1928. At the same time, the Blackshirts were carrying on spectacular "punitive expeditions," especially in central Italy.

Now that the press was silenced and the country terrorized, Mussolini came before the Chamber on January 3, 1925. He disclaimed any participation in the murder of Matteotti but assumed political responsibility for the atmosphere of violence under which the country had been living for the last four years:

> It is said that fascism is a horde of barbarians encamped in a nation, a movement of bandits and robbers, the moral question is brought on the stage. . . . Well, here before this assembly, before the whole Italian people, I declare that I take upon myself, I alone, the political, moral, and historical responsibility of all that has happened. . . . If fascism has been an association for crime, I am the head and the responsible chief of this association for crime. If all the acts of violence have been the result of the historical, political, and moral atmosphere, I am the one responsible for all this because I, by my propaganda, have created this historical, political and moral atmosphere.

Then he challenged the opposition to dare to put him under impeachment, and concluded, "Be sure that within forty-eight hours after this speech, the situation will be clear."

There was no opposition group in the Chamber who could immediately meet the challenge. To make doubly sure that none of them would come forward during the forty-eight hours, the speaker adjourned the session immediately after the challenging speech and did not assign a date for the Chamber to convene again. The members of the opposition could have asked for Mussolini's impeachment only outside the Chamber—that is to say, by a revolutionary act which would have given the Blackshirts a good pretext for massacring them. The gagged press would not even have been able to announce to the world the happy event.

Only five days later, the opposition deputies issued a "manifesto" written in elegant literary style and filled with fine moral sentiments but containing no explicit indictment of Mussolini. It had value only as a document of final defeat, and the government was glad to allow its publication.

Signor Rocco, minister of justice in Mussolini's cabinet from January 1925 to July 1932, has written: "The memorable speech of January 3, 1925, ushered in an era in the Revolution. All remnants of collaboration with other parties were eliminated. The debris of the old political world disappeared, and fascism alone dominated the state."[6] Mussolini in person asserted in 1927 that the democratic regime in Italy, after having been killed in January 1923 by the creation of the militia, was definitely buried on January 3, 1925.[7]

From the political standpoint, the murder of Matteotti marks the decisive turning point in the evolution of fascism. Mussolini seized power in 1922 thanks to the support of the bankers, great industrialists, and big landowners, with the connivance of the military chiefs and the acquiescence of the king. But these persons had no desire for a dictatorship like that which arose from the Matteotti murder. Parliament had to be emasculated, the press gagged, popular suffrage "disciplined," but the external form of the constitution was to be preserved. The Conservatives had been denouncing for many years what they called the "parliamentary" system and wanted it to be superseded by a "constitutional" system. The king had to "govern" and not merely to "reign." They had no idea of establishing a dictatorship that would strip the Crown of all its attributes and rights. Their ideal monarchy was the Prussian monarchy as it had been under Bismarck.

In 1923 and 1924, it was the extreme Fascist left wing that clamored for radical constitutional reforms and threatened to proclaim a republic if the king opposed resistance. Mussolini, absorbed by the daily task of government, let the intellectuals make and unmake their abstract theories, using or discarding them according to practical needs. His main program during those years was to remain in power: "I came here in order to stay as long as possible."

As a result, the Fascist regime during the first two years of its existence was characterized by the most absurd contradiction between word and fact, theories and practice, law and government. It was a period of local anarchy on the one hand and of centralized abuse of power on the other. Fascist squads went out to perform acts of violence, but those acts of violence were condemned by the law. The anti-Fascists were in actual fact deprived of personal and political rights, but Italy was still a country in which, according to the existing constitution, citizens without distinction of party were supposed to enjoy personal rights and political liberties. A single political party, the Fascist party, claimed to represent the whole nation. Parliament

[6] A. Rocco, *La trasformazione dello Stato*, in the volume *Lo Stato Mussoliniano e le Realizzazioni del Fascismo nella Nazione* (Rome: 1930), p. 10.

[7] In the preface to the volume *Il Gran Consiglio nei primi cinque anni dell'era fascista*.

was delivered into the hands of a Fascist majority by methods which the old constitution had not contemplated, and the members of the opposition were prevented by violence from exercising their lawful task of discussing and criticizing the acts of the government. But political parties still existed within the law, and a parliamentary minority was still expected to function. The press was gagged, but the law guaranteeing freedom of the press had not been directly abolished. Editors and publishers of anti-Fascist newspapers were beaten and their premises were looted and burned, but anti-Fascist newspapers were still allowed to appear. In short, the forms of a democratic state were still standing, while democracy was being crucified.

The open break with even the forms of the old democratic regime came with the crisis subsequent to the Matteotti murder. During this crisis, it was no longer possible for Mussolini on the one hand, as the *duce* of fascism, to authorize the crimes of the squads and on the other hand, as prime minister, to disavow them. He could no longer promise that justice would be done and at the same time use the machinery of government to procure impunity for the executors of the crime. To overcome the crisis, to save himself from being submerged, Mussolini had to block all the constitutional channels by which opposition could pass into lawful action. He had to destroy completely the freedom of the press and to suppress by any means every manifestation of dissent in the country. By assuming publicly, in his speech of January 3, 1925, the responsibility for "the historical atmosphere" that had brought about Fascist lawlessness and violence, he put an end to the ambiguous policy of his regime. The empty forms of the democratic constitution were now frankly cast aside.

The king also was forced to come to the fore. As long as Fascist violence was officially disavowed by his prime minister, the king, like Pontius Pilate, could wash his hands. But when Mussolini officially took the moral and political responsibility for all Fascist deeds, the king was forced to assume his share of responsibility. The oath taken at his inauguration mentioned explicitly his obligation to observe and uphold the constitution of the kingdom inherited by his father. On July 31, 1925, however, he signed an amnesty which allowed the Fascist, guilty for the Matteotti murder, to escape punishment. He thus became an accomplice in the overthrow of the constitution.

Mussolini's victory set the seal on his supreme and absolute control not only over his opponents, but over his own party. Whatever other minor Fascist leaders had said and done to save fascism in the hour of danger, it was Mussolini who, by assuming the whole responsibility for Fascist deeds and by openly challenging the opposition to a final duel, had brought the crisis to an end. From that moment on, there was nothing that he could not dare to do. His victory intensified in the rank and file of his party the faith in the myth of the "invincible *duce*" and the conviction that blind obedience to him was essential to the existence of fascism. The party became more and more a military organization in which the first duty was the old military slogan, "Obey first and do not try to understand." By successfully overcoming the crisis, Mussolini realized not only the helplessness of his opponents, but the measure of his own power.

26

The Constitution of the Totalitarian State

THE ONE-PARTY STATE

After the *coup d'état* of January 1925, the country was kept under the regime of terror until the end of 1926. In 1925 and 1926 the Chamber, disencumbered of all opposition, and the Senate, in which a mere handful of men dared to criticize the new legislation, discarded the ancient free constitution of Italy and gave juridical form to the dictatorial regime.

The rights granted to citizens under a free constitution fall under three main categories: (1) personal rights—that is to say, the right of habeas corpus, freedom of thought, of worship, of education, of work, etc., and the right to be judged according to due process of law; (2) political liberties— that is to say, freedom of speech, of the press, and of association, and the right to participate in peaceable assemblies; and (3) the right of self-government and political representation—that is, the right of the majority of the citizens to change the men in power in the local and central governments by means of elections.

When the liberal movement originated in the eighteenth century, it aimed at establishing the rights of the lower-class majority against the privileges of the clergy and the nobility. After the political privileges of these minorities were abolished, a new peril arose: parties in power might suppress the liberties of minorities. Then the definition of liberty became more complex. The liberal doctrine came to imply not only the principle that the right to rule is vested in the majority, but also the principle that

409

the right to disagree with the majority is vested in the minority. The rights of the men in power were limited by the rights of the men in opposition. Political liberty is fundamentally the right of the citizens to disagree with the party in power. From this right to disagree with the party in power spring all the other rights of the citizen under a free constitution: freedom of speech, freedom of the press and of association, the right to participate in assemblies, and the right of representation. Personal rights, political liberties, and parliamentary institutions are meant to protect minorities against possible oppression by the party in power. The best test of the standards of a free constitution is the provisions that it makes for minorities.

Under a dictatorship, one party alone—the party in power—is allowed to exist. One man controls the central machinery of government. Men who enjoy the confidence of the supreme master control every subordinate department of national life. Actual or potential opponents of the men in power are placed beyond the pale of the law.

The constitution of the Italian dictatorship affords a perfect example of what a one-party state is bound to be. The Fascist party is the only party that is allowed to exist. All other parties are unlawful.

The Fascist party is not a private organization, but a public institution recognized by law. The constitution of the party is published by royal decree, and its text is law. The emblems of the Fascist party are part of the coat-of-arms of the state, framing those of the dynasty. Whoever commits an act of disrespect against the emblems of the party is punished by imprisonment of from one to three years, and up to twenty-four years if the crime is committed in foreign territory.

The Fascist party organization is a rigidly centralized system. Mussolini is its *duce*—that is, its supreme head. He appoints the secretary general of the party. The secretary general lays before the *duce* the members of the national directorate and of the provincial secretaries. In their turn, the provincial secretaries, subject to the approval of the secretary general, appoint their own staffs and the secretaries of the local branches. The local secretaries appoint their staff subject to the approval of the provincial secretary.

Each Fascist owes unquestioning obedience to his superior. The new recruit takes the following oath: "I swear to obey without discussion the orders of my *duce* and to serve the cause of the Fascist Revolution with all my power, if need be, with my blood." This oath is binding for life. Disobedience is punished by expulsion from the party. This implies that the unsubmissive heretic is ousted from every public office. He becomes an outcast. No Fascist for any reason whatsoever should be in contact with those who have been expelled. Whosoever acts against this duty must be denounced to the police authorities.

Mussolini, like the prime ministers of free regimes, combines the position of prime minister with that of leader of the party which controls the government. Mussolini is at the same time the head of the govenment and the *duce* of fascism. But in free regimes, the party is a private organization and party leadership is a kind of private arrangement within the party itself and not a public office like the premiership. In the Fascist dictatorship, the party is a public institution. Mussolini is primarily *duce* of fascism and then is the head of the government. As head of the government he carries out his will as the *duce* of fascism. This situation is the logical outcome of the fact that Mussolini is supposed to have seized power by armed force, and his right to power is derived from the fact that he is the chief of his own armed forces.

According to an act of December 1925, "whoever offends by words the person of the head of the government is liable to imprisonment up to thirty months." The authors of the penal code which was enacted in 1931 thought that thirty months were not sufficient and raised the minimum to five years.

The executive power in the central government no longer depends on the legislative power. Parliament is stripped of any actual authority. Each deputy, as a member of the Fascist party, is subject to party discipline, and if the secretary general of the party were to expel or suspend him from party membership, he would be *ipso facto* expelled or suspended from his office of deputy. If he criticized some action of the *duce* of fascism and head of the government, he would become liable for "offending" his person. Thus, the head of the government is not responsible in any way to Parliament. It is Parliament that is responsible to him. "Whenever reasons of urgent and absolute necessity require it," the government may modify any existing law in any field of administration and enact new laws by royal decree without the previous consent of Parliament. Thus placed at the mercy of the executive and stripped of every power, the Chamber of Deputies is reduced to an office for the registration of bills and decrees and a phonograph for chanting the praises and benefits of the dictator.

Elective local government is abolished. Local bodies are run by officials appointed by the central government.

All associations whose activities may be regarded as hostile to the party in power are unlawful. Anyone reorganizing, under new names, associations which the police has ruled to be unlawful becomes an outcast. All associations, even charitable institutions, athletic clubs, bowling clubs, etc., must be run by men who stand well with the party in power and are designated by the leaders of that party.

Any kind of antigovernment manifestation or activity is severely punished. Any meeting in a private house is unlawful and subject to severe penalties, whatever the number of those attending it, if obnoxious political discussions are held in it.

All means of education and information must aim at creating a standardized mind according to patterns drawn up by the dominant party. Editors of daily papers and reviews must be men in the confidence of the party in power. Books distasteful to the party in power are confiscated. The clergy of all churches must either keep silent on matters distasteful to the party in power or join in singing its praises. Teachers must swear an oath of allegiance to the party in power and pledge themselves to use the functions of teaching for the purpose of forming citizens devoted to the existing regime. Public officials and judges are dismissed from their posts, and barristers, solicitors, physicians, chemists, and engineers are not allowed to carry on their professions if they set themselves in opposition to the party in power.

Political crimes are tried, not by regular judges, but by a special tribunal which is composed of a general and five officers of the Fascist militia, who as Fascists have sworn to obey the orders of the *duce* without discussion.

The police are empowered to put under surveillance, or intern on penal islands and in remote villages, those who have been tried and sentenced after they have served their terms, and even those "who have manifested the deliberate intention of committing acts subversive of the social, economic or national order, or capable of prejudicing national interest." The person is seized and, often without examination, taken handcuffed to the place of internment. The internment may be for a period of up to five years. When the first five years are over, a fresh period of five years may begin, and so on indefinitely, at the discretion of the police.

Letters are opened by the police. Anyone found outside his own town without an identity card may be "stopped" by the police—that is, kept under arrest at the discretion of the police. Employers may not employ workers without cards. Hotels may not receive guests who fail to show their cards. The police have only to withdraw a man's identity card to bring him to starvation.

Any attempt to leave the country without a regular passport, or any assistance to any person so doing, is punishable by up to five years' imprisonment. Anyone caught attempting to cross the frontier by any other than the few authorized routes may be shot dead by the frontier guards. It is a summary death penalty dealt out by the guards, who are at once accusers, judges, and executioners.

In short, not only political liberties but also personal rights are discarded. This is not due to caprice, bad will, or chance. The institutions which spring from the liberal doctrine are indivisible. A political regime which grants the citizen the right to elect the men who are to represent him before the government must be based on the principle of competing parties—that is, on the right of the opposition parties to step into the shoes of the party in power when the latter has lost the confidence of the majority of the electorate. The right to change the party in power would be stultified if it were not coupled with the right vested in the opposition to criticize the party in power. This means that the opposition parties must enjoy freedom of speech, of the press, and of association and the right to assemble. In their turn, these political liberties would be reduced to a sham if the party in power were entitled to violate or suppress altogether the rights of the citizens whenever they tried to make use of them in order to oppose the party in power. Thus, representative institutions, political liberties, and personal rights form a chain whose links are inseparably bound together.

If, on the other hand, one accepts the principle of the one-party state or the "totalitarian" state, one has not only to suppress or reduce to a sham representative institutions, but also to suppress political liberties and personal rights. In fact, if the citizen were granted the right of opposition with all its appurtenances—that is to say, freedom of speech, of the press, of association, and the right to assemble—but could not change the party in power by lawful means, those rights would burst out into the violence of revolution. When political liberties are suppressed, personal rights also must be suppressed or strictly curtailed. How could one suppress freedom of speech if freedom of thought remained unhampered? How could one suppress the freedom of the press if freedom of teaching remained untouched? How could one prevent the formation of any opposition movement if the police were not empowered to supervise even the private lives of all those who were suspected of being opponents? What more efficient method of suppressing opposition, when it arises, than to send opponents to jail or reduce them to starvation?

The institutions of the one-party state are as indivisible as those of the plural-party state. One has to accept or reject the whole of either. Either freedom or dictatorship, or as the French say, *"C'est à prendre ou à laisser."*

CORPORATIVE INSTITUTIONS

The institutions of the Fascist dictatorship are no novelty in history. France, under Napoleon I and again under Napoleon III, lived under institutions of the same type as those of Fascist Italy. In establishing their totalitarian systems, however, the dictators of former times had to think only of those currents of opposition that might develop among the upper and middle classes of society. The working classes in town and country were politically inert and could be safely disregarded in matters of governmental policy:

> The authorities knew precisely where to apply police surveillance: at the office of such and such a newspaper, in the environs of such and such a music-hall transformed into a club, in the neighborhood of the home of such and such a citizen who was suspected and watched. Economic developments had not yet given rise to the enormous groups of human beings who are massed together in big factories today. The social consequences of industrial progress imposed new necessities and new tactics upon dictatorships. What use is it to abolish the right of assembly, to shackle the press, to prohibit manifestations in the streets, if one tolerates the development of revolutionary centers within the factories? What use is it to prevent the workmen from engaging in any kind of political activity outside of the works if one allows such activity to arise within the works, on the innumerable occasions when the workmen come together apart from their work, as they go in and out of the shop? There was every necessity that the new government should adopt an attitude of strict surveillance towards the groups of workmen.[1]

[1] L.R. Franck, *L'Economie Corporative Fasciste*, pp. 50–51.

This is why, in dictatorships nowadays, there is a set of institutions which has no precedent in the dictatorships of former times: the so-called corporative institutions.

Italy is divided into provinces. In each province, for each group of employers, employees, or professional classes, a single organization enjoys legal recognition. The law admits the existence of *de facto* organizations outside the legal ones, but no one has yet dared to form any such *de facto* organization. Such an attempt would be regarded as a subversion of the "national" order and would be severely penalized.

Nobody may join the official Fascist organization of his trade if the secretary does not admit him, and the secretary may expel any members who, in his opinion, are "undesirable." But everybody must contribute annual dues to the organization for his trade whether he belongs to it or not.

The Fascist organizations are grouped into nine national confederations: four for the employers, four for the employees, and one for the professional classes.

The presidents of the national confederations are appointed by Mussolini. The secretaries of the provincial organizations are designated by the presidents of the confederations after consulting the highest authorities in the Fascist party. The secretaries of the provincial organizations designate the officials of the local groups. All officials can be removed by the government if they fail to manifest a sufficient degree of "undoubted national (that is, Fascist) loyalty."

Thus, the officials are not "elected" by the members but are "appointed" from above. They are accountable, not to the membership of their organizations, but to the leaders of the party in power.

In this there would seem to be no difference between the associations of the employers, on the one hand, and the unions of employees or the organizations of the professional classes on the other. All have their officials appointed from above. But the conditions actually obtaining in the different classes are not identical.

Among the employers there is a sharp division between the big industrialists, landowners, and bankers, on the one hand, and the small men on the other. When an official is to be appointed in an association of employers, the big businessmen—few in number—foregather at their business or social meetings, choose their man of confidence, ring up some of the leaders of the party in power, and give the name of the chosen man. The chosen man is appointed. For instance, the president of the Confederation of Industrial Employers today is Count Volpi, who may be called the Italian Rockefeller. It cannot be doubted that he represents perfectly Italian big business.

The small industrial employer, the small shopkeeper, and the small farmer do not take part in this game. They have no voice in the appointment of the officials of their associations. The directors of their associations are the agents of big business, not representatives of the small men.

As regards the workers, there is no difference among them of more powerful and less powerful, big and small. All are small, all are powerless. They are too numerous. They are not allowed to meet and discuss their business. They cannot ring up the leaders of the party in power and lay their own nominees before them. The directors of their organizations do not represent anybody. They are the men of confidence of the party in power which controls their unions. This holds good for the professional classes also.

In the Fascist corporative state, big business is an active factor and runs the associations of employers. The classes of the small employers and of the employees and the professional classes are passive elements, subject to whatever their officials think of it.

When one has formed a clear idea of those legal organizations and their officials, one grasps what is meant by the statement that all contracts concerning wages, hours of work, etc., are drawn up by the organizations of employers and employees and that these contracts are binding on all the employers and workers, whether they are members of the organization or not. Those contracts are drawn up by men in the confidence of the big employers and by officials who have been appointed from above to control the unions of the employees. The members of the unions have no say in such matters. If any member was not satisfied and ventured to grumble, the secretary of his union would turn him out of the union, and so all the members who remain within the union become satisfied and contented.

Strikes are forbidden and punished by a severe and progressive scale of penalties, the maximum being seven years' imprisonment.

Lockouts are forbidden as well as strikes. Thus, the Fascists claim that capital is put on the same level as labor. But where strikes cannot take place, lockouts become unnecessary. Moreover, the law, while forcing workmen to labor under threat of imprisonment, cannot force an employer to give work if he declares that he can no longer maintain the old wages. The stoppage of work is then not a lockout, but a closing down induced by a "justified motive."

When the representatives of the employers and the officials who run the workers' unions do not agree, their dispute must be decided by the labor court, both regarding contracts in course of execution or those in process of formation. The court consists of a judge and two experts, and all experts must be university graduates. In this way the workers are automatically excluded from the court.

The Fascists justify the abolition of the right to strike by the following theorem: The state is no longer the state—i.e., is no longer sovereign—if it is not able to deal out justice in conflicts between social classes and categories, forbidding them to exercise private justice, just as this is forbidden to individuals and families. But in labor disputes, who is the "state?" In the "corporative state," we find on the bottom rung the men of confidence of the big employers and the officials appointed from above to run the unions of the employees; on the upper rung we find the judges and experts of the labor courts. On neither of these two rungs have the working people any real representation. Therefore the "state" turns out to be the employing class.

Let us take an instance to show how the system works in actual practice. In March 1927, the representatives of the rice cultivators and the officials who run the unions of the rice weeders signed a contract to the effect that the wages should be cut by 10 percent. Fifteen days before the beginning of the harvest, the employers announced that they could not pay the wages agreed upon, because, after the signing of the contract, the price of rice had sunk 25 percent, and they asked for a further wage cut of 20 percent. The officials who run the unions offered a second reduction of 2.5 percent. This was judged insufficient by the employers. When the question was brought before the Court of Labor, the latter authorized only the cut of 2.5 percent to which the officials had kindly consented, and it made the workers give back to the employers what they had already received in excess. The daily papers announced that the Court of Labor had defeated the employers. They took care not to explain that in actual fact, that year, wages had been cut by 12.5 percent.

In 1928, the government decided that a fresh cut of 7.5 percent should take place. During 1929, the price of rice went up 20 percent, and the growers offered the workers an increase of 1.5 percent. The officials of the union accepted with gratitude. But in 1930, the price fell again and the officials generously accepted a further reduction of 17.5 percent.

In 1931, the employers requested another cut of 35 percent. The officials hastened to offer a cut of 20 percent. The Court of Labor granted a cut of 21 percent. In 1933 and 1934, wages were again reduced. Thus the wages of 200,000 workers, mostly women, were cut from 1927 to 1934 by from 55 to 61 percent, according to the different categories of rice weeders.

Above the organizations of employers and employees we find in Italy the twenty-two so-called corporations. From these corporations the Fascist dictatorship has drawn its denomination of "corporative state."

What are these corporations? They are bodies, each one of which deals with a given category of industry, agriculture, or commerce. For instance, one deals with textiles, another with the production and sale of wheat, another with the steel industry, and so on.

The members forming these corporations fall into four classes: (1) cabinet ministers and high officials, appointed by Mussolini; (2) experts, appointed by Mussolini; (3) members of the Fascist party, appointed by the secretary general of the party, who is in his turn appointed by Mussolini; and (4) so-called representatives of the employers and employees, designated by the presidents of the confederations, who are appointed by Mussolini and who are not obliged to render account of their acts to the members of the organizations. The employers, of course, are represented by big businessmen, while the employees are represented by union bureaucrats who are not accountable to their members.

Mussolini is the president of all these councils and designates their vice-presidents. He is entitled to change the composition of the councils whenever he thinks fit and to rid himself of councilors who have become "indiscreet." If the opinions of the councils do not coincide with Mussolini's opinion, he is empowered to reject them, and he can even prevent those opinions from being published in the press. The councils are convoked at Mussolini's pleasure. If he never convoked them, nobody could object, and things would go on just the same.

The twenty-two corporations were inaugurated on November 10, 1934, and first began to function in January 1935. Until now, all they have done is to give advisory opinions on technicalities; as, for example, what names are to be given to the different types of cheese, so that one may not be confused with another; whether it is impossible to use silk produced in Italy instead of cotton imported from abroad, etc.

In many countries today there are, side by side with the ministers of labor, advisory councils partly appointed by the government. They can exercise a remarkable influence on the policies of the governments since their advice is published by the press, is publicly discussed, and cannot be ignored by the ministers. If one were to say that there are today in Italy "advisory councils" on economic questions, that the members of such councils are all in the hollow of Mussolini's hand, and that such councils are powerless if Mussolini does not agree with them, everybody would at once understand that such institutions are the most futile bureaucratic bodies that the world has ever known.

Mussolini pompously announces that in "the corporative state labor is no longer the object of the economic system, but is subject," because in the corporative state "the direction of production is not imposed from above, by an organ or a body external to the productive activity; it is imposed by the economic groups themselves, for each economic group expresses itself through the corporations. The corporation is the instrument through which production organically disciplines itself." Noble sentiments and fine words if one does not look at the actual working of Fascist corporative institutions. If one looks at them, one can reach only one conclusion: labor has in the Fascist corporative state no more active part than have the animals in a society for the protection of animals.

TOTALITARIAN ELECTIONS

In 1929 and 1934, the organizations of employers, employees, and professional classes formed the basis upon which the Corporative Chamber of Deputies rested. The Italian Parliament in the pre-Fascist regime consisted of two houses: the Senate and the Chamber of Deputies. The Senate consisted of members chosen by the prime minister and appointed by the king. It would be the ideal chamber for a dictatorial regime rendering an elective chamber superfluous. Therefore it was retained in the Fascist constitution. An "elective" chamber also was retained. If Italy did not from time to time go through the motions of having national "elections" or, as Mussolini scornfully called them, "pulp-paper revels," the other civilized countries which still remained infatuated with the ridiculous procedure of election would have thought that the Fascist dictatorship was not founded on popular consent. But the Fascist "elective" chamber was a chamber "without an opposition." The "chamber without an opposition" was "elected" by a procedure which rendered it impossible for the voters to "elect" opponents of the government.

When a new chamber was to be formed, the provincial and national officials of each confederation met in Rome and drew up a list of their own nominees. The procedure of nomination was as follows: The president of each confederation (who received his appointment from Mussolini), in accord with the national leaders of the Fascist party (who were likewise appointed by Mussolini), prepared the list of nominees and read it out to the meeting of the officials of his confederation. The officials approved it *en bloc* by acclamation, and a list of the nominees of the confederation was drawn up.

The confederations were allotted 800 nominees. Two hundred more candidates were nominated by bodies of a cultural or charitable nature designated by the government. The method of nomination was the same for these privileged bodies as for the confederations. The president of the body, who had been appointed by the secretary general of the Fascist party —who in his turn had been appointed by Mussolini, announced the names and the meeting accepted them by acclamation. Authority came from above.

The names of the 1,000 nominees were then "presented" to the Grand Council of Fascism, a body of about thirty high Fascist personages chosen by Mussolini. The Grand Council drew up the list of the 400 future representatives. But it was not restricted to the 1,000 nominees. It could also choose persons who were not on the list. Such unlimited discretion made the "presentation" of the preliminary list a mere farce.

After the Grand Council had "designated" the 400 representatives, the names went to the electorate for "ratification." For this purpose the whole country formed a single electoral unit. The voter was asked to declare whether he approved or not of the whole list of 400 names.

In other words, the task of nominating the candidates did not belong to political parties, but to the presidents of the confederations and other privileged bodies, who directly or indirectly were appointed by Mussolini. The right to "elect" the deputies belonged not to the electorate but to the Grand Council of Fascism, whose members were likewise appointed by Mussolini. And the electorate was left with the sole task of saying "yes" or "no."

When it was called upon to say "yes" or "no," there were no opposition press, no opposition party organization, no possibility of campaigning against the official list, and no opposition candidates. Whoever refused to go to the polls revealed himself an opponent of Mussolini and became an outlaw.

On entering the polling station, the voter received two ballot papers, a tricolor one with the word "yes" and a white one with the word "no." The tricolor ballot was printed on paper so thin and transparent that even when folded it could easily be distinguished from the white one. The voter, however, was allowed to retire into an enclosed space and there, in the most absolute secrecy, to put one of the two ballot papers—the one which he did not wish to utilize—into a box. When he left the enclosed space, he had to hand over the other ballot paper, the good one, to the recording officer.

In the "plebiscite" of March 1929, the government was in a position to announce that 89 percent of all registered voters had cast their votes and that there had been over 8.5 million "yes," as against a mere 136,000 "no," votes. Either those "no" votes were magnanimously presented by the government to a nonexistent opposition in order to avoid the absurdity of complete unanimity, or else they show that in March 1929 there were to be found in Italy 136,000 courageous but insane men ready to defy the Blackshirts for the satisfaction of dropping a perfectly useless "no" into a ballot box.

The results of the plebiscite of March 1934 were even more flattering to the dictatorship than those of four years before. Out of 10,433,536 registered voters, 10,041,997 (that is, 96.25 percent) went to the polls; the "yes" ballots were 10,025,513 (that is, 99.84 percent of the voters). Hitler is less "efficient" in his plebiscites than Mussolini: he received only 92.8 percent in November 1933, 89.09 percent in August 1934, and 98.79 percent in March 1936.

In 1934, in the entire province of Aquila, the plebiscite gave only eight votes against the regime. A few days later, in the town of Pratola Peligna alone, there was a rising of the people, in which seven were killed, thirty were wounded, and about two hundred arrested. Clearly all these persons, minus eight, had voted "yes" on the day of the plebiscite, and in the rest of the province no one had voted "no."

Satisfaction was unanimous even among the Germans of South Tyrol and the Slovenes and Croats of Istria. In South Tyrol there were 51,952 registered voters; of these, 48,543 went to the polls, and only 516 voted "no." The provinces of Fiume, Gorizia, Pola, and Trieste, containing

500,000 Slovenes and Croats, had 240,599 registered voters, of whom 230,954 went to the polls and no more than 418 voted "no." Yet in the spring of 1931 the Fascist press had stated that on account of anti-Italian feeling more than 100 crimes, including 15 homicides and 30 armed attacks, had been committed in less than 4 months in the region inhabited by Slavs. Eighteen schools and factories had been burned. There had been 8 crimes of terrorism and 4 of espionage. The Special Tribunal for the Defense of the State, between February 1927 and July 1932, sentenced 106 Slavs to a total of 1,124 years in prison, and 5 to death. The plebiscite of March 1934 shows that the more arrests, death penalties, prison sentences, and internments on penal islands multiply among the Slavs, the more they grow enthusiastic about Mussolini.

In speaking of Fascist "elections," Mussolini's propaganda agents stated that in Italy voting was no longer done in territorial but in occupational constituencies. They took great pains to explain that man's major interest is not residence but occupation, and that the citizen should vote for his own representatives within his own class and not according to the chance of his residence. This political doctrine would have been worth discussing if in Fascist Italy the representatives really had been elected by the members of each confederation. As a matter of fact, the nomination was made by the presidents of the confederations and other privileged bodies, and the choice was made by the members of the Grand Council of Fascism. All these gentlemen were Mussolini's appointees. Their operations had nothing to do either with territorial or with occupational constituencies. When the moment came for the voter to answer "yes" or "no," he gave his answer not in an occupational but in a national (i.e., a huge territorial) constituency, and he had to answer "yes" if he did not wish to find himself in jail.

As far as the 400 representatives were concerned, they represented no one and nothing. No bond united them to any electorate. Those who were constrained to say "yes" enjoyed no means for either approving or disapproving them. The so-called representatives were under the military discipline of the Fascist party, and both in the House and outside had to obey Mussolini's orders.

Not even such a "chamber without an opposition" was to Mussolini's liking. On November 14, 1933, he stated:

> The Chamber of Deputies has never pleased me. . . . Even the name of the Chamber of Deputies is an anachronism.

It is not an indigenous institution in Italy, and is foreign to our traditions and to our Fascist philosophy. It presupposes a world which we have left behind, a plurality of parties and political competition. On the day when we did away with the plurality of parties the Chamber lost its reason for existence.

According to Mussolini's statement of March 25, 1936, the Chamber was to be replaced by the general assembly of all the twenty-two corporations, which were to be called the "Chamber of Fasces and Corporations." This reform was enacted in 1938. From that time on, the members of the "Chamber of Fasces and Corporations" were without further ado appointed by Mussolini and remained in office as long as Mussolini kept them there, and the "plebiscite" was abolished.

27

Church and State

The relations between the Vatican and the Italian government were put on a new basis by the Lateran agreements of February 1929. These agreements consisted of three documents: a Treaty of Conciliation, a financial convention, and a Treaty of Concordat.

The Treaty of Conciliation concerned the position of the pope as head of the international organization of the Catholic Church. The Italian government explicitly recognized the pope not only as the owner of the Vatican but also as an independent sovereign over the area on which the Vatican stands. Thus, a Liliputian state was formed in the heart of Rome, officially called "Vatican City" and independent from any Italian sovereignty. In its turn, the Holy See recognized as legitimate the Kingdom of Italy with Rome as its capital.

This meant that the pope recognized the existence of an Italy which had already existed for fifty-nine years without his permission; and Italy recognized the pope as sovereign over a small area on which, for fifty-nine years, he had been allowed to live as a sovereign. The change was in formulae; the realities remained unchanged. The only important actual innovation was that the pope was now enabled to issue postage stamps and postal cards. In return, the Italian government would no longer be branded by Catholic preachers outside Italy as the pope's jailer. No sensible Italian could object to such a settlement of the Roman question. Pacification is preferable to hostility, even if in actual fact hostility has already subsided.

424

By the financial convention, the pope received 90 million (pre-Roosevelt) dollars, which, if not squandered, should have given him a yearly income of $4.5 million. The Law of Guarantees in 1871 had granted him an annuity of $600,000. This was the sum which had been placed on the balance of the old pontifical state as the contribution of the pope's subjects toward the maintenance of the central services of the Catholic Church. The Catholics of all other countries defrayed the rest. In 1919, it was estimated that the Vatican needed an income which would correspond to a capital of about $30 million. From 1929 on, the pope would have no financial worries. He received a capital which gave him an income three times greater than that which in 1919 had been considered necessary to meet his annual expenses. The Italian people paid $4.5 million a year on its daily bread to defray the expenses incurred by the central services of the international organization of the Catholic Church. It would seem only just that the Catholic Church, based on the religious faith of 300 million people living in all parts of the world, be maintained by the gratuitous contributions of all the faithful, and not by the compulsory tribute of one people alone.

The Treaty of Concordat, the third element in the Lateran agreements, concerned the relations between Church and state in Italy. To understand this treaty, one has to remember that in Italy under the pre-Fascist regime, all religious denominations enjoyed the same treatment; the Catholic clergy had no privileges of any kind, and there was a system of almost complete separation of the Church from the state. By the Treaty of Concordat, in 1929, separation was supplanted by a system which was termed one of "cooperation" between the two powers. This new system arose, not through an act of legislation enacted by the Italian government, but as a result of an international treaty between the head of the Catholic Church and the Italian government. From now on the Italian Catholics were under the protectorate of a foreign power, the Holy See, and this foreign power was entitled to represent them before the Italian government. This is the basic significance of any Catholic concordat whatsoever: a dual sovereignty is being created over the Catholics of the country the government of which signs a concordat: that of the secular government and that of the pope. If President Roosevelt should sign a treaty with Stalin which granted a particular juridical status to the Communists in the United States and gave Stalin the right to watch over that juridical status and to protect the American Communists before the American government, President Roosevelt would sign a "concordat" with Stalin analogous to those which the Holy See endeavors to get from every government in the world.

As a result of the Concordat of February 1929, the 60,000 ecclesiastics living in Italy become a privileged caste. They are exempt from military service. In Italy, military service is not voluntary: each young man, when he is twenty years of age, must serve eighteen months in the army or the navy. This is the heaviest form of taxation on all citizens. Any youth becoming a priest or monk, however, is exempt from military service. Moreover, the members of the clergy are immune from income tax on what they earn in the exercise of their priestly ministry. If you are a doctor, a lawyer, a teacher, or a shopkeeper, you pay income tax on your earnings, no matter how small they are; if you are a priest, you do not pay it. Finally, an ecclesiastic who commits a crime is not subject to the same treatment as other unfortunate mortals: he "is treated with the respect due his clerical status," and in case he is convicted, he is to serve his sentence in quarters separate from those intended for laymen.

The clergy forms a body which is under the jurisdiction of the Holy See and of the bishops. Unfrocked priests or those who have incurred censure cannot be employed or retained in a teaching post. A man who has been shut up in a seminary from the age of ten to his twenty-first year, and who became a priest without knowing anything of the world, will remain under the thumb of his bishop during his whole life. Should he change his mind and relinquish priesthood, his bishop will prevent him from earning his living in the only field which would usually be open to him—teaching. He will consequently see himself forced to stay in the clergy even if he has lost his faith. Thus, the sovereignty of the Vatican does not affect only the territory of Vatican City; it spreads from this territory and is felt all over Italy by all those Italians who become members of the clergy.

The Holy See and the bishops exercise sovereignty over Italian schools. The Concordat enacts that the teaching of Christian doctrine, "according to the form handed down by Catholic tradition," must be "the foundation and capstone of public education in elementary and secondary schools." To form an idea of the meaning of this provision, one needs but to read an article which was published in the review *Civiltà Cattolica* in 1929 (June 1). This review is edited in Rome by the Jesuit fathers under the personal control of the pope. The review maintained that nothing contrary to Catholic doctrine was to be taught in secondary schools. Therefore, it would be well to free the professors of history from the task of teaching their students about the religion and history of the Hebrews, the origins of Christianity, the organization of the Church, and other risky subjects. These matters should be entrusted to the teacher of religion, who is designated by the diocesan bishop. Only the Catholic philosophy, as systematized once and for all by St. Thomas Aquinas, should be taught. Unfortunately, it is not to be expected that all the instructors in philosophy will alter the spirit and doctrine with which they are imbued. So the best solution would be to abolish altogether such a dangerous subject as philosophy. Should it prove impossible to reach such a radical solution, a working arrangement might be found in the expectation that the mentality of the teachers should alter in accord with the new regulation. The teacher of religion will teach Catholic doctrine, exposing all adverse doctrines; the professor of philosophy will avoid any topic "which might harm or disturb the religious and moral consciousness of the pupils." Thus, any clash between the teaching of religion and the teaching of philosophy and history will be avoided.

The concordat recognizes the sovereignty of the Holy See over matrimony among Italian Catholics. Until 1929, whoever wished to give his family juridical status in Italy had to have a civil marriage before the municipality. Nobody was forbidden to have a religious marriage besides. The Catholics went before the parish priest, the Jews to the synagogue, the Protestants to the ministers, and those who had no religion went only before the local mayor. When civil marriage à la française was introduced into Italy, in 1865, taking the place of the old system, under which the Church had matrimony exclusively in its hands, the Catholic clergy stirred up a great furor; they disparaged civil marriage as concubinage and tried to prevent people from performing it. The results of this struggle were bad. Many a man married a woman before the parish priest and, to the good pleasure of the priest, did not go before the local mayor to marry. After some years, they found that their wives were no longer so pleasant and decided that some other girl might be more convenient; then they went to marry before the local mayor; this second marriage was the valid one in the eyes of the law, while the first marriage, although valid in the eyes of the Church, had no legal value. At last the clergy found out that it was better to yield in its struggle against civil marriage. The Holy See instructed all parish priests not to marry persons if they were not assured that they would also marry before the municipality. Thus it became the common law to marry first before the municipality and afterwards before the parish priest. During the current century, nobody discussed the subject any longer. The Church had given in, even on this ground. Unexpectedly, in the Lateran agreements, matrimony between Catholics was again recognized by the Italian government as a sacrament. Catholics who wish to marry are to go only to the parish priest and marry before him, while Jews and Protestants are to go before their rabbis or ministers. In the United States, the couple about to marry has first to get a license from the municipality, whether they are married according to religious rites or by a justice of the peace. In Italy the parish priest, minister, or rabbi performs the ceremony, and all that is left to the town clerk is the task of filing the record of the case. The unbeliever goes only to the municipality. But in actual fact, if he goes to the town hall before performing the religious ceremony, he is singled out as a black sheep and gets into trouble.

The concordat enacts in addition "that cases having to do with the nullification of marriage are reserved to the jurisdiction of ecclesiastical tribunals and courts." If a treaty of this type existed between the Holy See and the United States, all those American Catholics who wished to have their marriages annulled would have to go, not before a United States court, but before the episcopal court of their diocese and, in the last resort, to the court of Vatican City. These ecclesiastical courts would judge the case, and the sole task of the American courts would be to take the sentence pronounced and file it.

Paragraph 1070 of the Code of Canon Law, according to which the papal courts judge cases, enacts that marriage between a nonbaptized person and a person who has been baptized in the Catholic Church is null and void. Consequently, the Holy See may annul a marriage which was lawfully celebrated before an Italian municipality, if either the wife or the husband were not baptized and as soon as one of them becomes baptized and sees fit to marry another baptized person. In 1853, for instance, a Jewess of Cento, a town in the states of the Church, eloped from her husband with her lover, received baptism, and asked to be allowed to marry the lover. The archbishop of Bologna declared the first marriage null and void and married the woman and her lover. Even in this case, the secular court would confine itself to filing the annulment of the former marriage and the celebration of the new one. Paragraph 1072 of the Code of Canon Law enacts that the marriage of a priest is null. As a result, the secular authority is not authorized to marry an unfrocked priest; if such a marriage takes place, the ecclesiastical court may annul it and so permit the wife to marry another man. Paragraph 1014 of the Code of Canon Law admits secret marriage which is not published and the records of which are kept in a special registry in the bishop's archives. Thus, marriages may be performed in Italy of which the secular authority is not aware, but which are legally valid and render other marriages unlawful.

The Lateran agreements contain several other provisions, the form of which is so vague and equivocal as to mean everything and nothing. One of the provisions, for instance, enacts that "sentences and decisions pronounced by ecclesiastical authorities, which have to do with ecclesiastical or religious persons, in spiritual or disciplinary matters, will have full juridical efficacy immediately in Italy, even so far as the civil effects are concerned." This might mean that the courts of the Holy See and the episcopal tribunals may condemn an ecclesiastic guilty of heresy or of indiscipline to confinement in a cloister, where he must do penance. If the priest refuses to obey the sentence, the Holy See communicates the fact to the secular authorities, and the police are to force the rebel to do penance. Another proviso states that the government shall "grant to ecclesiastics protection where it shall be necessary, for the carrying out of their spiritual ministry." These words may simply mean that the government pledges itself to protect the Catholic worship against whoever wanted to impede it. They may also mean that the police are obliged to carry out a sentence pronounced by the Inquisition against a heretic or by an episcopal court against a lady who wears her skirts and sleeves too short. Another provision enacts that the government is pledged to "prevent, in Rome, anything which might clash with the sacred character of the Holy City." This vague formula may mean, for instance, that no Protestant temple shall be open to public worship in the city of Rome, just as when the city was under papal rule. It may also mean that no street in Rome shall be named for any famous heretic. Or again, it may mean that no religious or scientific congress which is not authorized by the Holy See shall be held in Rome. On June 2, 1930, D'Annunzio's tragedy, *La Figlia di Iorio*, was given in the open air in one of the squares of Rome. Contrary to many other of D'Annunzio's works, this one does not present a case of sexual perversity, but only a case of passion unbridled by any moral law. The official newspaper of the Vatican, the *Osservatore Romano*, on June 2–3, 1930, protested against this performance: "We ask whether the performance of a work forbidden by ecclesiastical authority, staged in the open, in one of the public squares of Rome, corresponds to the respect due to the character of the Holy City." The interpretation and enactment of these and many other vague provisions depended on the pressure which the Vatican was able to bring to bear, case by case, upon the Italian government. Pius XI declared that the Lateran agreements were but the "beginnings of new developments." Nobody could foresee what these new developments might be.

Two facts, however, were certain. The first was that from 1929 on, the Italian government was not allowed to change, on its own initiative, its domestic legislation on matters in which the Holy See claimed an interest. If the party in power should change and Parliament wished to introduce divorce, for instance, into Italian legislation, it would have to bear in mind that a bilateral treaty between Italy and the Holy See obliged the Italian government to consider matrimony between Catholics as an indissoluble sacrament. Consequently, if the Italian government wished to introduce divorce, it had to grant it only to those citizens whose marriages had not been celebrated before a parish priest. To grant divorce indiscriminately to all Italians, Parliament would first have to denounce the concordat.

What did Mussolini obtain in return for so many concessions? First of all the international propaganda machine of the Catholic clergy was put at Mussolini's service. Cardinals, archbishops, bishops, priests, monks, nuns, and journalists all over the world waxed enthusiastic about Mussolini.

Moreover, Article 24 of the Treaty of Conciliation created a new juridical situation, the importance and seriousness of which were revealed in following years. That article runs as follows:

> With regard to the sovereignty pertaining to it in the field of international relations, the Holy See declares that it wishes to remain and will remain extraneous to all temporal disputes between nations, and to international congresses convoked for the settlement of such disputes, unless the contending parties make a joint appeal to its mission of peace; nevertheless, it reserves the right in every case to exercise its moral and spiritual power. In consequence of this declaration, the state of the Vatican will always and in every case be considered neutral and inviolable territory.

G. La Piana ("The political heritage of Pius XII," in *Foreign Affairs*, April 1940) has pointed out that by this article the Holy See promised not to mix uninvited in the temporal quarrels among states, and in return obtained a guarantee of the neutrality and inviolability of Vatican City.

This means that the Holy See is no longer free to be or not be neutral in international quarrels. It has pledged itself to the Italian government to remain neutral; it cannot break away from its policy of neutrality without the consent of the Italian government—that is to say, unless the Italian government decides that the Holy See, by intervening in an international dispute, would foster the Italian interests. La Piana remarks:

> Mussolini uses Article 24 only to deter the Holy See from expressing any opinion unfavourable to his regime. If at any time, however, he wants the moral support of the Vatican and Catholic opinion, he not only forgets Article 24, but invites the Holy See to violate it by taking sides in an international conflict.

Thus, in 1936, after the Ethiopian campaign had ended in an Italian victory, Pius XI bestowed his benediction upon "the triumphal joy of a great and good people"—that is, of the Italian people whose armies and poison gas had crushed the Ethiopians. During the Spanish civil war, the pope praised the Italian "volunteers" (organized and equipped by the Italian regular army) who were fighting in Spain. When the pope complained that he was a "prisoner" in the Vatican, he could not only freely criticize the Italian government, but even invoke its downfall. If he did so today, the Italian government would be entitled to declare null and void the treaty of conciliation and violate the independence of Vatican City.

In 1929 the treaty of concordat aroused deep discontent even among the Fascists. This unrest was increased by the indiscretion which the members of the clergy displayed as soon as they got wind of their victory.

In March 1929, a swimming pool was opened in Bologna for the pupils of the municipal schools. The archbishop of Bologna felt it his duty "to call the attention of the spiritual shepherds" to the moral peril that might lurk in this pool and aroused the parents of the boys "not to permit any risk of losing the most charming quality of youth, modesty." The next morning, the people of Bologna found that, during the night, unknown hands had dressed the naked Neptune which adorns the main square of the city in a pair of drawers. In the streets of Genoa, in May 1929, zealous youths were posted who stopped women and marked with charcoal the point to which their skirts should come on their legs. In August 1929, in a village near Bologna, the parish priest, armed with a knotty club, entered the theater which was filled with people, leaped upon the stage, and ordered the actors to stop playing. The police had to remove the priest before the performance could continue.

In order to temper the discontent of his followers, Mussolini was obliged to assume towards the Church an attitude of aggressiveness which was certainly not in his first intentions. In his speech of May 13, 1929, he stated that he had confiscated more Catholic journals within the last three months than during the seven preceding years. "It was the one way," he explained, "to bring them back to the correct tone." In carrying out those provisos of the concordat whose vague wording allowed a large as well as a restrictive interpretation of the Holy See's claims, the Fascist government adopted the policy of conforming itself only to the most restrictive interpretation. The discourses of the Fascist politicians and the writings of the journalists and publicists who are in the service of the Fascist regime, were all inspired by the concept of reducing to minimum importance the concessions made by Mussolini to the pope, and to quibble even over those parts of the concordat which were the least subject to controversy, in order to prove that the pope had, in reality, obtained nothing.

The pope reacted with recriminations, protests and menaces. For the time being, that controversy was patched up. In 1931 another serious clash broke out, and this quarrel also calmed down. But the underground discontent never subsided.

According to the Lateran agreements, the concordat is "the necessary complement of the Treaty of Conciliation." Pius XI gave this formula its authentic interpretation when he stated that "treaty and concordat shall stand together and fall together." This means that if any Italian government ceased to carry out the concordat according to the interpretation given it by the Holy See, the latter should be entitled to declare that the Treaty of Conciliation has also been annulled and will cease recognizing the legitimacy of the Italian state. In 1929 the pope consented to renounce his sovereignty over his ancient territory in central Italy on condition that the whole of Italy should be subjected to his spiritual authority. The day Italy throws off the concordat, the Vatican will again claim its sovereignty over the lost territory and will again set in motion against Italy its international machine of propaganda.

At his death in 1903, Pope Leo XIII left a political testament for the College of Cardinals and his successors. In this document he urged that only one way lay open to the Holy See in order that it should preserve its independence with regard to the Italian government: it must never come to terms with the Italian government. The day that the Holy See relinquished its uncompromising attitude, it must irretrievably fall under the influence of the Italian government and make itself subservient to the interests of Italy. This would be a danger to Catholic unity. The Lateran agreements of 1929 did nothing to dispel that suspicion and that danger. By the agreements of 1929, Pius XI placed himself and his successors under suspicion. Before 1929, no one suspected a snare in the fact that the majority of the cardinals and the officials of the Vatican were Italians. Now Catholics outside Italy grumble against the excessive preponderance of Italians among the cardinals and in the Vatican, and some even demand that the tradition shall be broken according to which the pope, since the sixteenth century, has always been an Italian. Many Catholics outside Italy no longer understand why the Holy See kept them in hot water for more than half a century over the Roman question, just to let them know, one fine day, that this question could have been solved simply by signing a scrap of paper by which the pope's sovereignty over a paltry hundred acres of land was recognized. Peter's Pence decreased in all countries as soon as the faithful learned that the pope was no longer either a poor man or a prisoner. The Belgian Catholics sent the pope only 300,000 francs in 1929; while in 1928 they had sent him twice that.

When the Italians regain the right to use their good judgment again, they will act wisely if they do not challenge the pope's sovereignty over the Vatican. It was a political mistake not to recognize that sovereignty explicitely in 1871. This mistake was rectified in 1929. It would be a mistake to raise the issue again. But all the other concessions contained in the Lateran agreements will last only so long as the Fascist regime lasts. The first act of those who succeed the Fascist dictatorship will be to declare null and void the Treaty of Concordat and all the other provisos of the Treaty of Conciliation which are not the necessary upshot of the pope's sovereignty over Vatican City.

Index